THE
MANDATE OF
VICTORY

THE
MANDATE OF
VICTORY

MARK L. PROPHET
ELIZABETH CLARE PROPHET

SUMMIT UNIVERSITY ☙ PRESS®
Gardiner, Montana

THE MANDATE OF VICTORY
by Mark L. Prophet and Elizabeth Clare Prophet
Copyright © 2017 Summit Publications, Inc. All rights reserved.

This book is a compilation of Mighty Victory's dictations from August 14, 1960 to July 7, 1996. They were previously published as *Pearls of Wisdom*.

For information, contact
Summit University, 63 Summit Way, Gardiner, MT 59030 USA
Tel: 1-800-245-5445 or +1 406-848-9500
www.SummitUniversity.org

Library of Congress Control Number: 2017942402
ISBN: 978-1-60988-280-8 (softbound)
ISBN: 978-1-60988-281-5 (eBook)

SUMMIT UNIVERSITY 🔥 PRESS®
Summit University Press® is an imprint of The Summit Lighthouse®.

The Summit Lighthouse, Summit University, Summit University Press, 🔥, The Summit Lighthouse Library, Church Universal and Triumphant, Keepers of the Flame, Keepers of the Flame Fraternity logo and *Pearls of Wisdom* are trademarks registered in the U.S. Patent and Trademark Office and in other countries. All rights reserved.

20 19 18 17   1 2 3 4

CONTENTS

PROLOGUE

There's something special about the people on this planet: we like to strive. We like to drive ourselves to greater accomplishments. We like to win. And yet, the number of plans conceived but never executed and projects started but aborted could fill a good-size ocean to overflowing. Why?

Well, these things just happen, we say, world wise and perhaps a bit world weary. Success is random. You can't win them all. You win some, you lose some. My fault or somebody else's fault, same difference. Statistically speaking, you can only expect to succeed fifty percent of the time so failing the other fifty percent is normal, isn't it?

That's indeed one way of looking at it. But this veiled "failure consciousness" is not heaven's way. Heaven—the higher dimension, right beyond our plane of sight—is filled with beings who *did* succeed. They completed their life plans and attained the ultimate prize: their immortality, in the form of their ascension in the light. Jesus Christ is the great example of an overcomer who attained his ascension, but there are many others, including the prophet Elijah, Gautama Buddha, Mother Mary, Kuan Yin and Confucius.

Liberated from the wheel of birth and rebirth, these blessed souls from

East and West are free to roam the vast cosmos and keep expanding their spiritual awareness into the farthest, highest reaches of space and time and consciousness. Amazing things await these successful ones. Some go on nightly exploits with the archangels, rescuing souls from the depths of misery and despair. Some help create new worlds which will one day, in the far future, be populated by brand-new civilizations. Some ensoul entire stars or planets or solar systems. Some become teachers of mankind, helping seekers of light make spiritual progress from lifetime to lifetime until they, too, can attain their ultimate freedom. And then there's Mighty Victory—a cosmic being in a class all by himself.

Don't speak to Mighty Victory about such simple things as rah-rah cheerleading and winning and success. I suspect these are human trifles to him, trinkets he has long since left behind. No, he has set his sight on an entirely different kind of overcoming. Eons ago this vast being set himself the task of becoming the living embodiment of the flaming fire of victory. And it paid off. "All that I have attempted to do," he says, "has been victorious! There is not such a thing as the memory of a single limitation in my consciousness, or world of activity, and has not been for a tremendously long period!"[1] Elsewhere he adds: "I have known only victory for thousands of centuries."[2]

Only know victory? That's humanly impossible, we say—and so it is. The human mind and emotions by themselves are not capable of this kind of superhuman positive attitude. But simply acknowledging that fact of life is not good enough for Mighty Victory. Enough, he says, with the human mind and emotions. To become a spiritual overcomer you need a completely new mindset. What you need is the Victory Consciousness!

Mighty Victory himself is the best qualified coach to teach us what this Victory Consciousness is—and how to put it into action in our daily lives. And he's willing to help us out. Witnessing how people like you and me struggle with the statistics of success and wanting to lend a helping hand, Victory stepped forward to teach us how to do what he himself has done. In forty messages delivered through the messengers Mark L. Prophet and Elizabeth Clare Prophet in a span of almost forty years, he presents the secret formulas for a full and final victory for the lightbearers and freedom fighters on this planet. This book—*The Mandate of Victory*—contains all forty messages.

But don't expect a basic seven-step self-help program or eight practical pillars or nine secret handshakes or anything like that. The Victory Consciousness doesn't work that way. Rather, it's a state of being that simply transcends the human mental and emotional modalities. You can't learn how this works by following a cookie-cutter process—one size fits all. Rather, you absorb this higher state of being by osmosis—straight from the very heart and soul of this great cosmic being.

Does that mean there are no processes or techniques you can apply to attain the Victory Consciousness? Not exactly. There's a central technique you'll find woven through the messages, or dictations, in this book: *Affirm, Affirm, Affirm.* Affirm out loud the timeless, priceless statements that Mighty Victory gives you to completely transform your consciousness, almost as in the twinkling of an eye. And then press on!

Mighty Victory's messages in this book contain numerous affirmations. Here's my absolute favorite, straight from the master:

I AM a majestic sense of Victory!

Jump out of bed in the morning, throw the windows wide open, drink in the fresh morning air and proclaim in the fullness of your divine inheritance, "I AM a majestic sense of Victory!" Immediately the winds of victory will billow your sails and your day will unfold with an upward thrust you never thought possible. Try it, feel that majestic feeling rush into your being, and you'll quickly prove this for yourself.

As you begin to pursue your own victory goals in earnest, you'll love to shout this mantra to the universe and immediately feel the return current from Mighty Victory's heart:

Cycles of Victory Appear!
Cycles of Victory Appear!
Cycles of Victory Appear!

Spirals of Victory Descend!
Spirals of Victory Descend!
Spirals of Victory Descend!

I AM an electrode of Victory in action here!
I AM an electrode of Victory in action here!
I AM an electrode of Victory in action here!

At the inevitable moments when the seas get rough, when you are in a pickle or run into nefarious opposition to your goals, swiftly make this call:

Beloved Mighty I AM Presence and beloved Mighty Victory,
Help me! Help me! Help me!
Get me out of this condition right away, right now!

Then you top it off with this command to the universal divine presence, the eternal nameless one of love and light whom many people call the Almighty or Almighty God:

O God, give me your Victory,
give me your Victory, give me your Victory!

Once you get the hang of this new state of being called the Victory Consciousness, you'll even want to drop the howdies and hellos and instead salute your friends and loved ones with this powerful fiat that proclaims the path of victorious overcoming for everyone you meet:

Always Victory!

THE VICTORY GOAL

If you tried the fiats above, you'll have already felt in your bones that the Victory Consciousness far transcends the goals and outcomes we commonly associate with success. Worldly success, that is. The energy charge of the Victory Consciousness is completely different. It belongs to an altogether different type of feeling and knowing, since it is based on associating with a higher state of being.

This means that as you start working with Mighty Victory, you'll have some sorting out to do. You'll have to decide which of your goals are worthy of cooperating on with a cosmic being. Which are the keepers? Which are lesser human goals that need to go? Wealth, fame, control, good grades in school, being thought well of by your friends, material security, winning the lottery—these will quickly fall by the wayside. Instead, you'll find yourself gravitating to a larger, more transcendent goal: realizing and actualizing the divine potential safely tucked away in your soul for a time such as this when you feel yourself waking up to a higher calling.

Once you lock into that higher goal, you begin to see your lesser goals for what they are: stepping stones to the greater goal. And some of the ones you thought important decrease in prominence. Others come more clearly into focus as essential steps to attaining your ultimate goal: self-transcending your human limitations and becoming a God-free being. In truth, that's the only real goal worthy of Mighty Victory's attention and assistance.

As you read the dictations in this book, you'll also find that Victory often speaks about broader issues than just our personal strivings. Like other ascended masters, he will regularly direct your attention to society at large—the social, cultural, economic and political scene within which we pursue our own personal path.

We can't live in ivory towers, the masters emphatically tell us. Rather, the society and community we live in are in great need of spiritual attention, direction and healing light. The ascended hosts will not interfere with mankind's free will unless asked to, so only we who are in embodiment have the authority to call them into action and ask them to direct their spiritual energy into situations that need their help.

Therefore, as you learn to invoke the Victory Consciousness for yourself, you'll also experience the excitement of learning to direct that same flaming consciousness into the world at large, where our brothers and sisters are in great need of spiritual assistance. In fact, performing this kind of world service has such a beneficial effect on our own karmic load that it will hasten us to the fulfillment of our own overarching goal!

HOW TO USE THIS BOOK

Though you're free, of course, to work with Victory's material any way you want, below are three different ways that will help you benefit the most from the wisdom and guidance in this book. They range from the least involved to the most involved, making this a true do-it-yourself experience.

Level 1 – Read

As a Level 1 reader you do just that: you read the book. Front to back, back to front, start in the middle, it doesn't really matter—though I suggest you follow the "beginning to end" approach to see if you can detect the spiral unfolded by Mighty Victory himself in the course of these forty releases.

As you read and study, you may want to try a delightful experiment: formulate a question in your mind—a real, meaningful question, of course, not something frivolous. Center in your heart, ask Mighty Victory to enlighten you, and then randomly open the book. A paragraph or sentence may jump out at you that gives you a new perspective on the question or problem you are struggling with.

Level 2 – Affirm

As explained earlier, in this book Mighty Victory gives us a number of ready-made fiats and affirmations. I recommend that as you come across them, you write them down in a journal or notebook so you have them ready in one place for when you need them.

But in addition, many of the master's statements can be turned into customized affirmations. There's an ancient formula for doing this the right way.

First, you compose your own affirmations. The best way is to turn them into "I AM" statements. The secret behind the power of I AM statements is the power of the name of God. In the Jewish and Christian tradition, God self-revealed his name as "I AM" or "I AM THAT I AM."[3] In India we find the same concept: AUM TAT SAT AUM. "Thou Art That.

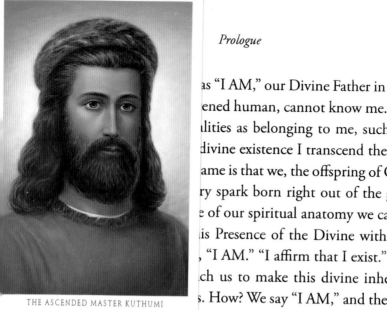

THE ASCENDED MASTER KUTHUMI

as "I AM," our Divine Father in essence told ...ened human, cannot know me. You cannot ...lities as belonging to me, such as Love or ...divine existence I transcend them all."

...ame is that we, the offspring of God, started ...ry spark born right out of the great divine ...e of our spiritual anatomy we call the I AM ...is Presence of the Divine with us, we can ..., "I AM." "I affirm that I exist."

...ch us to make this divine inheritance the ...s. How? We say "I AM," and then we follow this with a positive statement of being that immediately draws the divine light into it.

For instance, in chapter 14, Mighty Victory says, "Will you please remove from your mind and consciousness tonight that you are a deficient person and enter instead into the consciousness that you are an efficient, God-free being determined to embark upon the course of your own cosmic victory?" Right away you can turn this into an affirmation:

> *I AM the removal from my mind and consciousness of the notion that I am a deficient person and I enter instead into the consciousness that I AM an efficient, God-free being determined to embark upon the course of my own cosmic victory!*

Secondly, when you get to the point of wanting to be more specific in your affirmations, such as affirming a detailed goal for yourself, it's good to expand the formula. For instance, you may have a need for $2,000 for a promo campaign for your small massage business that serves the people in your neighborhood.

When we work with needs such as this, we do not want to impose our human will on our divine plan. To prevent this human-need intrusion we insert a filter: we pass our perceived needs through our I AM Presence and then through the stepped-down level of consciousness that is called the Christ, or Krishna, consciousness, which mediates between our I AM

Presence and our human self. Here's the safe formula: "In the name of my Mighty I AM Presence and Holy Christ Self, I AM…." For instance, you might affirm:

> *In the name of my Mighty I AM Presence and Holy Christ Self, I AM the manifestation of $2,000 which I need to promote my business, drawn forth from the limitless abundance of God and made manifest in my hands and use today. I accept it done right here and now in accordance with the will of God for my lifestream.*

By passing our affirmation through this filter of the divine consciousness and accepting with equanimity whatever God will bring us, we ensure that the energy we draw forth from the divine realm will remain free from the karma-making desires of the lower human self. Try this formula for yourself and experience its powerful results.

Level 3 – Plan Your Victory Spiral

Goal accomplishment follows a little-known spiral that you can use to better guide your projects and plans. The ascended masters teach that every project follows a clear pathway as it descends into the physical. The better you understand this process, the more successful you can be in the completion of your plans and projects.

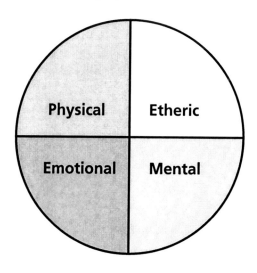

a. Etheric Stage

Any plan or project begins with an idea, a blueprint, the conceptualization. This is its etheric stage. If you chart the entire process on a clock, this etheric stage takes place in the etheric quadrant, or Fire quadrant. Here you catch the spark, see the vision or the matrix, are inspired and become enthusiastic about the project.

A very important step at this early stage is to make sure that your plan is spiritually sound; it should be devoid of selfishness or harm to others, and it should resonate with what you know in your soul to be the highest divine blueprint or aspiration that you can muster.

b. Mental Stage

The next stage takes your project into the mental plane, or Air quadrant. It's now time to work out the specs and do the detailed planning. You determine the size, the color, the quantity, the location, the people involved, the people who will benefit from it, the time frame, the budget and where the seed money is going to come from. Describe this vividly, with as much detail as you can wrap your mind around.

c. Emotional Stage

Now we're crossing over into the second half of the clock and enter the realm of the feelings and emotions—the Water quadrant. Nothing will become reality unless it is imbued with feeling.

The secret to the Victory Consciousness in this quadrant is knowing there are two distinct kinds of feelings: human feelings and the divine feeling. Human feelings are tainted with concerns and worries and emotional ups and downs based on our mood. The divine feeling, on the contrary, is a powerful, steady radiance of complete faith and wholeness and unstoppable purpose. It comes down to you from your own I AM Presence and from the higher reaches of the heaven-world. Love, gratitude, deep bubbling joy—these are some of the transcendent feelings that will inexorably pull the divine light down into your victory matrix.

As you read Mighty Victory's words, you'll find yourself being imbued with this divine radiance that pours forth from the master's words. At first this may take some getting used to, since in this world of duality we are not exposed to such a steady stream of positive feelings. Just let it come. Let it wash over you and permeate you with its glorious intensity. Before you know it, it'll become such a real part of your life that you feel the Victory Consciousness forming itself in you right where you are.

d. Physical Stage

Finally, in the physical, or Earth, quadrant, your plan spirals into physical manifestation. Your project starts—the right way, with the divine wind in your sails. Victory!

At this stage, it's very important to protect and claim and affirm the victory so that there's no last-minute hitch or holdup, no slip between cup and lip.

HOW TO USE THIS PROCESS

To plan your own victory spiral, it's best to do it in two steps. First, map out your goal, great or small, according to the steps above. Then, as you read this book, find and create victory affirmations that fit each of the four quadrants.

- For the etheric quadrant, look for affirmations that draw the perfect plan down from heaven.
- For the mental quadrant, find affirmations that help you perfectly design and visualize the details of your plan.
- For the emotional quadrant, create affirmations and fiats that fill you to overflowing with the sense of divine radiance.
- Finally, for the physical quadrant, give affirmations that simply, unequivocally, help you protect and draw down your goal.

As you go through the stages of your plan, give these affirmations daily and claim your victory spiral every step of the way.

A DIVINE SELF-HELP BOOK

Summing it up: in the ultimate analysis, this is a self-help book after all—but one unlike any others in the marketplace. It's a divine self-help book, designed to deeply connect you to your spiritual source and imbue you with the Victory Consciousness. Whatever you do with it—read it, give the affirmations, plan your victory spirals—it offers you a unique, individual path to self-transcendence that will make you wonder how you could have ever lived without it.

As with all of the teachings of the ascended masters, don't just take my word for it. Prove these ancient formulas for yourself. Try it! What do you have to lose other than a boring statistic that says you can't win them all? Shake it off. Have faith. With Mighty Victory's help you *can* win all the way!

Always Victory!

Carla Groenewegen
Director, Summit University

A PRIMER
ABOUT MIGHTY VICTORY AND
THE ASCENDED HOSTS

Who is this majestic being called Mighty Victory? We don't know much about him for he is an ancient, ancient soul. The few things we *do* know may surprise you, since they open a window onto a realm of spiritual existence that is not commonly known or understood—and hotly contested by today's science and orthodox religion.

A Cosmic Being

Mighty Victory is what is known as an ascended being. The ascension is a technical term for those who have completed their rounds of birth and rebirth in a material world such as our own planet. Different religious and spiritual traditions use different names for this state of being beyond the common human condition. The term "ascension" comes from the Christian tradition, in honor of Jesus Christ's public demonstration of this process of balancing one's karma, fulfilling one's mission or dharma and ascending into the heaven-world.

Many have accomplished this feat of the ascension and are now known to us as ascended masters or ascended lady masters. For instance, the ascended master El Morya was previously embodied, among other life-times, as Thomas Becket, Sir Thomas More, and India's Mogul Emperor Akbar the Great. His friend and brother Kuthumi once lived as Saint Francis. Kuan Yin is an ascended being from the East whose previous lives are lost in legend. The well-known ascended master Saint Germain was incarnated as Saint Joseph, Roger Bacon, Christopher Columbus and Francis Bacon.

Becoming an ascended master is only the first step in our spiritual journey after the cycle of human embodiment. The vast cosmos opens up for the ascended ones, who may pursue a number of avenues of service to life. In the course of this journey they continue to develop their consciousness to the point of being able to encompass vast reaches of space or embody an entire aspect of the divine consciousness. We call such advanced spiritual beings "cosmic beings."

Mighty Victory is one of these cosmic beings. Long ago he devoted himself to ensouling the consciousness of victory. His devotion to the flame of victory for more than a hundred thousand years has given him the authority over that flame throughout vast reaches of cosmos.

The Tall Master from Venus

Most of these powerful cosmic beings serve at high levels in the cosmic hierarchy. They do not ordinarily come into contact with unascended beings who are still evolving in the schoolroom planets in the universe. However, on occasion they may determine their assistance is needed and press closer to human evolutions such as ours to accomplish a specific goal. This is what happened with Mighty Victory.

In the 1930s, when he first became known to the people of Earth, Mighty Victory was referred to as the Tall Master from Venus.

The ascended masters explain that Venus, considered to be Earth's sister star, was once home to a physical evolution such as ours. Like on Earth, some of its inhabitants, known as the fallen Venusians, gave in to lower manifestations and were ultimately removed to other planets, whereas many others were able to transcend their physical limitations and have ascended into the light. Venus' physical environment has gone dormant and life there exists now solely in the etheric realm.

Earth, too, has a lively etheric realm. It is the highest vibrating sheath of the four planes of Matter, which range from the physical (where we live in physical bodies) through the astral, or emotional, plane (the domain of our feelings) through the mental plane (the domain of thought and mind) to the etheric plane (the realm of pure ideation). Ancient alchemists called these the planes or kingdoms of Earth, Water, Air and Fire, respectively. The etheric realm is where we find the etheric retreats and cities of light where ascended and cosmic beings abide when they are working with the physical evolutions of a planet.

The first account we have of Mighty Victory is in the book *Unveiled Mysteries* by Godfré Ray King (pen name of Guy Ballard), published in 1934. He is described there as at least six feet six inches tall. He has brilliant, piercing, violet-blue eyes and his hair is a glorious pure gold.[1]

In one of his dictations through the messenger Guy Ballard, the master explained how he came to be known as Victory: "I was given the name of 'Victory' by the ascended masters who have made the ascension from your Earth, because all that I have attempted to do has been victorious! There is not such a thing as the memory of a single limitation in my consciousness, or world of activity, and has not been for a tremendously long period!"[2]

Victory's Twin Flame

Like your soul and my soul, Mighty Victory is blessed with a counterpart of the opposite gender. We call these pairs of twin souls "twin flames," since they came forth from the same fiery divine spark at the origin of their existence.

Mighty Victory's twin flame has a lovely name: Justina. On January 1, 1978, Justina dictated for the first time, in this case through the messenger Elizabeth Clare Prophet. In this landmark address she said:

> Now I step forth, for Almighty God has weighed these several systems of worlds and the evolutions therein, and Almighty God

has pronounced that certain evolutions of lightbearers do now contain within themselves enough consciousness of the victory of the feminine ray that I might stand forth and be, with my Beloved, the focal point for the Father-Mother God in total awareness of the victory of evolutions in these systems.

Beloved ones, the one whom you call Mighty Victory is indeed androgynous, as I am, as is Alpha, as is Omega. But as we come forth together, descending into lower and lower dimensions of awareness, we bring a greater complement of the spectrum of cosmic polarity as a polarity of manifestation to those of lesser evolution. Therefore, though one may be sufficient in the whole, always twin flames are required for the transmutation of a cosmos.[3]

Since Mighty Victory and his twin flame are One, we can claim the sense of victory from Justina as well as from the master himself, or invoke it from both of these masterful beings at the same time.

Legions of Victory Angels

In addition to twelve masters assisting him in his cosmic work, Mighty Victory has under his command "numberless numbers" of legions of victory angels. These fierce angels, clad in the golden fire of illumination, come forth in answer to the distress calls of mankind. They flood us with their Victory Consciousness, if we are ready to accept it.

Mighty Victory once said in a dictation:

Do you know, beloved, that it is very difficult to fail in the presence of millions of legions of Victory? Yet I must tell you, it is still possible to fail in their presence. It takes more than proximity! It does take *appropriation*—to *appropriate* the *spirit* of Victory, to *appropriate* the *flame* of Victory, the *joy* of Victory, the *mood* of Victory, the *momentum* of Victory![4]

Elsewhere he explains how his angels have tremendous determination but are also very practical and hands-on as they assist mankind:

Do you know that the legions of Victory relish a good fight? Do you know that they are the first to leap into the fray or into the icy waters or into the fire, with their hoops of fire of flaming victory?

So they come. Whatever aspect of mortal consciousness must be brought low, the legions of Victory have a means, a method and even a tool; it is as though they had packs on their backs. You should see these legions of Victory as they enter the fray. Perhaps a wrench, perhaps a sword, perhaps a rolling pin, perhaps a purple fiery heart—nothing is too small or too great. If it works, it is used by the legions of Victory.[5]

Sense of Humor

Mighty Victory's messages range from down-to-earth to ethereal and elevated. As our souls traverse this spectrum of concepts and emotions while reading his words, he sometimes treats us to a wonderful dose of ascended master humor that shatters our human preconception of what an ascended being should be sounding like. For instance, speaking about Saint Francis (now the ascended master Kuthumi), he says in chapter 14:

He became the divine poverello, as he was called, because he said: "I will give myself unto thee. I will give myself unto God." And what has really transpired? Well, God already had him, but the devil seemed to have a hold of one foot; and somehow or other he was disturbed somewhat if that one foot was pulled upon. Well, I want you to understand that it doesn't matter if they have you by *both* feet if you understand that God is inside of you and he that is in you is greater by far than he that is in the world.[6]

This injection of unexpected bits of humor echoes something told us by other ascended masters: "Don't take yourself too seriously!"

By this admonishment they mean, don't pay too much attention to your human personality with all of its quirks and idiosyncracies. Make a valiant effort to weed out the undesirable aspects of yourself but don't be concerned about trying to perfect your human self. It's a waste of time. Just laugh at the nonsense and rise above it. Focus on blending with your divine nature and little by little, step by step, the human will lose its grip on you and your real self will shine through.

Yellow Topaz

Mighty Victory makes use of the yellow topaz to anchor and focus the consciousness of victory, which he describes poetically as "the crystal fire of golden consciousness."[7] Since this precious stone carries the vibration of victory, wearing it on one's person is a powerful aid to assimilating the Victory Consciousness!

1

A COSMIC SENSE OF VICTORY

I AM a being of cosmic victory who has never at any moment known any state less than absolute victory and perfection. And I charge into your world this afternoon the beneficence of my radiance and my victory in the cosmic light.

I think, perhaps, it would be well if the children of earth tried to firmly anchor in their own mundane consciousness a radiant sunbeam of our light and our God feeling concerning victory. Mankind, somehow or other because of the pull of human creation and misqualification, has continually turned in vacillation from the idea of their own cosmic victory.

Oh, they can well conceive of the victory of others, but it seems so difficult for them to conceive of their own victory. At times the human consciousness is so immersed in the mundane affairs of life that it can look to the great ascended beings with reverence, as though they were on a pedestal, and say, "These ascended beings have merited this great honor. Perhaps in another day I, too, shall be like them."

Mankind has somehow failed to acknowledge or to realize that to this purpose and for this cause were they born, and that all came equally into this world to attain their cosmic victory. God would never have intended one of his sons or daughters to attain absolute cosmic victory and divine perfection and then intend a lesser state for myriad others wherein they would function in limitation and even in unhappiness.

I AM Victory! I AM Victory! I AM Victory! Are these words mere words or do they embody a thought about eternal life? If they embody a thought about eternal life, then I ask you, children of the light, to think of the words *appropriation* and *application* and apply in God's holy name, I AM, a feeling of God-victory to your own lifestream. This is the only way in all creation any part of life will be free.

This afternoon here in Harlem I AM producing and sustaining a cosmic action of the light. This cosmic action of the light is a blazing shaft of pure ascended master light substance, blazed from our planetary home to yours and carrying with it in this connection all of the beauty and transcendent glory of our home, Venus.

O Hesper, thou radiant sphere, thou dawning diadem in the eternal solar galaxy, how honored art thou to be graced by the magnificent Lady Venus, the beloved Sanat Kumara and the Holy Kumaras, as well as others who have offered up to life the precious offering of their lifestreams and all their radiant energies! How paeans of praise are continually offered up from thee, O thou radiant star!

I ask in God's name I AM, beloved Helios and Vesta, that Earth receive her victory swiftly, so that she may take her place in this great solar system and system of worlds to hold, as God intended, such beauty and reverence in pure manifestation over all of the apparent vicissitudes of life.

KARMA IS FOR A PURPOSE

Children of the planet Earth, when you pick up your daily newspaper and place your attention upon all the discordant happenings [recorded] there, it does not seem as though victory were manifesting upon this planet. Would it not be well, therefore, especially for those of you who feel the compulsion to keep yourselves well informed, to use the violet fire of freedom upon each of these happenings? And would it not be well for you to also see the other side, the radiant side of light concerning those happenings, and realize that the action of karma is for a purpose?

Very puzzling to mankind has been the idea of accidents, sickness and despair. These are states opposed to victory and I cannot cognize these opposing manifestations. But mankind seems to have exceeded me in that particular respect, as they have almost become perfectionists in misqualifying energy. And I smile somewhat as I realize that by so doing they have caused all of their misery.

I am hopeful that through the spirit of cosmic victory they will come to understand that each one must shed the cocoon of ignorance and that no one, even if they would, could accept for another the pathway of their victory. If I could accept the pathway of victory for another I would take on the karma of very individual upon this planet, but the cosmic law would not allow it.

I am not alone. I tell you that Sanat Kumara, in his long sojourn upon the planet Earth, has pleaded countless times with Alpha and Omega to set aside the cosmic law so that he might take upon himself the karma of the entire planet. But the great councils were adamant and refused [to allow it].* And therefore to the present day, as was originally designed, each individual must walk through the doorway of cosmic initiation, taking his initiations in the world of form into the arms of light, as was so beautifully epitomized in the story told by beloved Jesus of the prodigal son who returned to his father's house after he became tired of eating the husks of life.

IGNORANCE OF THE LAW IS NO EXCUSE

Your cosmic victory is imminent, but it must be invoked with the same fiery intensity with which you call forth your trials in ignorance. Ignorance of the Law is no excuse before the great cosmic law of justice. And I shall not attempt to salve your feelings today with the idea that you can escape from the cosmic law and the justice thereof.

I would far rather see you hang your head in despair and then [decide to] do something about it than I would have you continue on in ignorance

*Bracketed material in this book denotes words unspoken yet implicit in the dictation, added for clarity in the written word.

of the great cosmic law of life. Every cosmic being, every ascended master desires one specific manifestation for each one of you and that is your cosmic victory, the light of your own ascension, your cosmic purity, your cosmic overcoming of all weakness.

It is not shameful for mankind to have weaknesses, but it is shameful to continue in them, because only by freeing themselves in cosmic victory and the baptism of cosmic victory can they enter in to our realm of light, love and harmony eternal.

If beloved Morya and others of the ascended hosts knew of any other way in which you could escape the action of the great cosmic law of karma, I am sure they would have directed you to it long ago. Only through the use of the violet transmuting flame of freedom and divine love, only through persistence, through Gethsemane and through taking the hand of your own God Presence can you come to a sense of overcoming victory.

Remember, beloved hearts, you who have not yet manifested your cosmic victory in expression here walked away from the light in times past, and now it is your sacred duty and responsibility to return to that light with almost the same ferocious intent as that which stirred your hearts to walk away. The allure of the senses, the pleasures of the eye and the mundane consciousness took control then and directed you away from your cosmic victory. Who else but you, if I may speak frankly, can direct your way back again to your own God Presence?

Do you think that the Father has not continually extended out arms of love? Do you think that all of us of the ascended host have not continually extended out arms of love? We have indeed done so and continue to do so. But it is the responsibility of your individual lifestream, not mine, that you walk back into the heart of God.

Victory is a reality. Victory is truth. Victory is perfection. Victory is God in manifestation. You are God in manifestation. You are perfection in your Higher Self, but it is up to you to draw down and draw forth from your heart flame this beauty and this perfection.

PALLAS ATHENA'S LOOM

I like to think often of the beauty of Pallas Athena in some of her embodiments in Greece. She was quite lovely and very persistent. Often beloved Pallas Athena would sit for hours and hours at her lovely loom and weave magnificent paintings in threads of many colors.

Her loom was her pride and joy. And she spent hours conceiving of glorious ideas and then outpicturing them carefully and painstakingly as the shuttle wove in and out to produce these magnificent pictures of light. If it were possible for you to free yourselves from mundane thoughts long enough to enter into my mind and heart, you could perceive today some of these lovely pictures that Pallas Athena actually produced from her own God flame.

Beloved ones, patience is a virtue that you must learn to practice yourself. You must have patience with yourself. You must not despise yourself because you have made mistakes. Beloved Pallas Athena made mistakes many times and pricked her finger and then painstakingly drew back the thread. And as she drew back the thread, she selected the proper place in which to replace it and then it was a beautiful picture again, you see. This is the plan of life, to try and try and try again until you attain your victory.

HOW THE ASCENDED MASTERS OVERCAME THEIR TRIALS

I tell you, if I were to go to the akashic records and draw forth some of the experiences of the ascended hosts, you would find that many were at times in dire circumstances, in diverse mental states in which they suffered many problems of a limiting nature. They refused in God's name to submit to these problems. And they determined, with all of the God-determination of their hearts, that they would have their victory, that they would attain reunion with their God Presence and that they would overcome whatever was the apparent cause of their trouble or discord. And I tell you, they did it without the benefit of the radiation that we pour out to you today.

In those days the great God flames were not flickering as they are now upon the altars of earth. There were ages then of despair and shadow and pain when hordes of armies moved across various parts of the world, when modern anesthetics and modern surgical techniques were not available, when mankind had not the means to alleviate pain that they presently have.

And I tell you that those conditions were primitive and disturbing and physically discomforting far beyond what mankind endures today. You will find some of these primitive conditions in parts of Africa and India even at the present time, and I must tell you that here in New York State, if you would actually look around, quite primitive conditions exist in a few places.

Be that as it may, it is not our intention to distract you or to turn your attention upon the limiting pages of history but to draw you away, as it were, from all limiting concepts and conditions to make you aware of the great cosmic approach that is manifest upon our planet, Venus, and which can and shall be manifest upon Earth when mankind prove themselves ready and worthy of it.

This organization, The Summit Lighthouse, is intended as a forum of the ascended masters and much more. It is intended as a means, as it were, to convey to mankind our radiance, our love, our strength and our light until mankind is able to do for themselves that which we presently do for you. Therefore many of you are going through initiations and training in preparation for just that very thing.

Do you think, beloved students who have served the light for so long, that Saint Germain would draw you forth and bring you thus far on the pathway and then decide to let go of your hand?

I am sure that you have decided not to let go of Saint Germain's hand. And therefore, inasmuch as it is unthinkable that he would let go of yours, I pray to the heart of God—and notice that I, as a cosmic being say, "I pray"—that you shall sense that your hand is in Saint Germain's hand and in that of the ascended hosts.

And having placed your hand there, [know that] your victory is assured, because to be anchored here upon earth and to hold the hand of the God of Freedom is not only a privilege, it is an honor unparalleled for all mankind. There is not a cosmic being on any planet who would not joyously take the hand of Saint Germain and pay him tribute for all that he has meant to this beloved earth and this system of worlds, as well as to the universe.

To be a God of Freedom to a planet such as the earth is a high honor. And I hope you understand that Saint Germain is willing to share that [honor] with each one of you. He is willing to take the crown from his own head and place it upon yours whenever you are willing to master your energy and attain your own cosmic victory and become the chohan of the seventh ray. Yes, he would even give it up before the two thousand years are up if one of you would actually attain to a standard where you could take over and do it as faithfully as he is able to do.

Did you ever stop to think, therefore, how magnificent his love is or the love of any ascended being? They serve, like the little boy with his finger in the dike, only until someone else is ready and willing to take their place to hold back the riptides of human confusion and to be a healing Cosmic Christ to life here.

God did not bring you to this work that you should merely stumble and fall by the wayside. God brought you here to attain your cosmic victory. Beloved Mother Mary, whose ascension day anniversary occurs on the morrow, holds the immaculate concept for each one of you.

I ask you in God's name, What kind of a concept do you hold for yourself? Do you think that you have the right to hold a lesser concept than that of divine victory? Do you think that your own past mistakes in some way form an invincible fabric, an eternal fabric that cannot be altered or changed? Do you think that life itself is unkind to you?

I tell you, man has been unkind to life and life has forgiven him for it. But life expects and demands certain reverence, certain adoration from the flames with which God has endowed and empowered mankind.

What is this adoration?

It is the adoration of victory, the song of victory. Some of you have recently read the Song of Ruth and you have understood something of Ruth and Boaz.[1] I tell you, your union with your God Presence is the greatest union in all creation. It is the only way that you can attain your victory and it is your reason for being.

YOUR GOD PRESENCE CANNOT FAIL

Beloved ones, at times I am grateful for the quality of pliability in mankind and then at times I regret it. I am grateful when I see individuals who are pliable enough to accept the idea that God can change conditions. And I regret that pliability when I see that they feel somehow or other that they themselves must take command because the Presence doesn't seem able to carry out what they want.

Now this may sound very foolish to you but it is the human way of looking at things. Individuals are actually saying "God cannot do it and therefore I will" when they act in a human way. Because the Presence, if it be acknowledged as the only power that can act, cannot fail. And although you do not realize it, when you therefore fail to manifest your God perfection you are saying to God that you are greater than the light.

Nevertheless, I tell you, ignorance is not a lawful excuse. And I must this day, because of the solemnity of the moment, take this occasion to adjure each one of you to call to God in the remaining days of your life with a diligence you have not hitherto carried out and to determine that no human quality or condition or characterization or picturization or thought shall hinder you from manifesting the victory that life wants to give you.

Do you think that this messenger is standing here today pouring out his energy because it is his desire to impress you in some way with his human consciousness? If so, I would almost say, Fie upon you! For I tell you, God is speaking to afford you a greater opportunity to accept the serious responsibility that you have for the hallowed offering [of the Holy Spirit] that the Maha Chohan spoke of, so that you may enter in to life.

Is this not a strange condition that I, a cosmic being, should come down here and charge my electrical energies and my forcefield around this place to individuals who have not attained their victory and offer them my feelings of God-victory?

It may seem strange to the outer but it is not strange to the inner. For within your heart each one of you, even a doubting individual, cannot help but sense that I am a cosmic being of divine splendor and reality and that I am pouring out my energy for the sake of the faith and the faithful, for the sake of the immaculate concept of Mother Mary, for the sake of the cosmic protection of beloved Michael the Archangel, for the sake of protecting this work, for the sake of causing its expansion among men until the leaven of righteousness leavens the whole human loaf and it becomes the bread of heaven, the bread of angels.

Beloved hearts, I plead with you to accept your victory and to let nothing sidetrack you from attaining it. You have thought at different times that you wanted a certain condition or a certain thing to happen, but when you want your ascension more than you want anything else, you will begin a different form of attack upon the problems of life and you will overcome as the ascended ones have done.

I CALL FORTH PINK GLOBES OF COSMIC VICTORY

Thou infinite cosmic light, I, Victory, speak to thee directly.

By the power of invocation present in the high priests of Atlantis and Lemuria and by the power of invocation from the planet Venus, I draw forth from the heart of God the feeling of God-victory.

I call forth nine magnificent pink globes three feet in diameter, with magnificent white wings of cosmic light substance, and I call them forth from Venus to Earth. And as I call forth these beauteous globes with all their radiant pink qualities of light, I charge them with my own feeling of cosmic victory.

I command these nine globes in God's name to wing their way to this earth, to this forcefield, to this city. And when they strike this forcefield, which shall be in a matter of seconds, I ask that they shatter their ascended master light substance one hundred fifty miles in every direction and centralize their focus here to give everyone a feeling of their cosmic God-victory, which I am in cosmic manifestation, eternally sustaining, all powerfully acting and ever expanding.

Now, come forth in God's name and blaze thy victory here! Blaze thy victory here! Blaze thy victory here! I AM Victory and nothing, no, nothing can stand before the cosmic blazing light of eternal victory from the heart of Almighty God!

Children of earth, the solemn hour has come when the golden age shall respond to the very fingers and hands of God as he blazes forth his victory, which nothing shall deter and nothing shall stop. The victory of Golgotha, the victory of Gethsemane shall be transcended as beloved Jesus said it would [when he spoke the words,] "And greater works than these shall ye do."[2]

Take now, then, this charge and accept it and go forth commissioned in the name of Almighty God to so live and so direct your world and your affairs that nothing but victory shall ever manifest there again. You can have this feeling and you can retain this feeling if you will. But *you* must make up your mind. That I cannot do for you.

I thank you and I bless you as a brother of light and glory eternal. Good afternoon, my sweet heart-friends, until we meet in realms of light eternal, where I hope to clasp the hand and heart of each one of you and keep you sealed in the warmth and beauty of my own victory, which I joyously declare I AM.

August 14, 1960
Harlem, New York City
MLP

2

THE DIVINE MANTLE

According as his divine power hath given unto us all things...
ye might be partakers of the divine nature...
II Peter 1

I AM come.

I AM Victory.

I AM a manifestation of that God-free perfection which it is the right of every child of earth to manifest.

I AM the victory from the spheres of Venus' perfection brought to this beloved planet tonight in order to seal and seal and seal the hearts of mankind in the divine mantle, in the name of their perfection, the perfection of their God Presence, and the eternal flame of the sacred fire.

I am well aware of the desire on the part of the students to retain a youthful appearance in their physical forms. I am well aware of the desire of the students to manifest the divine immortality. I am well aware of the yearning of your hearts to express your God-victory. I am aware of the feeling that you have, seeking from God his gifts and graces which will give you the buoyancy of the angels, a feeling of lightness and happiness and compassion and understanding.

I want you to know, ladies and gentlemen, that this victory, this power, is now pulsating through the atmosphere of this room. The pulsations may not be sensed by all of you. The light rays which I am blazing through this room may not seem tangible to some of you. But as surely as there is illumination here from the electrical devices present in this room and the flame of these candles upon the altar, our radiance is pouring forth through your four lower bodies and blessing and hallowing you with our radiation of Cosmic Christ victory.

I am not intending tonight to spend a great deal of time in giving you instruction. For I want to tell you tonight that the instruction given you by Paul the Venetian, who spoke to you before I did,[1] is so magnificent that any number of the angelic beings from the cosmos stood around in loving adoration and wonder as they saw the vibratory action from beloved Paul's aura. You see, we are like you in one way. We appreciate a job well done.

Ladies and gentlemen, learn to appreciate the Christ in one another as it expresses in the various ordered services which transpire here in the world of mortal form as well as that which occurs above—as Above, so below. You are truly gods in the becoming,[2] and therefore, what is true of you is true of all mankind upon earth. For the victory I bring you tonight is intended by God the Father to be the victory for all who will accept it upon this earth.

And we have no bars, we have no gates, we have no prisons to separate man from their victory. For when they desire their victory more than they desire the manifestation of materialism and human ideas, they will have it. And no power in heaven and earth can keep them from it. For the law of God can never be broken. The fiats of God cannot be altered.

They remain today, as in ages past, accurate, inviolate, correct, and decipherable by the soul who truly desires to know the truth that they may be free[3]—the individual who feels the need to shake off the fetters and the lethargy of the human consciousness and enter into the feeling of our victory, of God's victory, of the victory of their Presence, of the victory of life, of the victory that surrounds them always, of the victory that is present in every atom of creation, of the victory of the sacred fire, the victory of the sacred host, the victory of your own Christ Self, the victory that has been brought forth by the ascended masters, the victory that causes the worlds to turn in space accurately, the victory from the Great Central Sun, the victory of Alpha and Omega brought to everyone, the victory of life.

O blessed and beloved ones, will you not sense what it means to have your God-freedom? Will you not sense what it means to no longer be fettered, as it were, and bound in the human, material flesh form?

Realize, however, that you are in this form in order to achieve your victory. And at the moment that victory is fully achieved, no one can keep you from your ascension or no thing can keep you from it, for the Law will act and your mortal form will take on the appearance of the Christ. Even the garments you wear will drop as they are changed by the light and you will arise as did the Christ until the great radiance of God receives you out of the sight of mortal consciousness and mortal mind.[4] And in its place you enter into our abode, the realm of your victory from whence you too, as the Christ, shall come at will to bless, to hallow, to heal mankind, and to inspire future evolutions of this earth as well as other systems of worlds.

You know not what you shall be. But when the Christ-victory of your life shall appear, you shall be like that Christ-victory; for you shall then see it as it is.[5] And it is now before you if you will but recognize it. And I pray you, ladies and gentlemen, recognize it within if you do not recognize it without, and accept it.

Let there be a pressure of acceptance in your feelings as I speak, that you may have the benefit of my radiance and that my feeling of God-victory may penetrate your auras, penetrate your consciousness, and alter and change your inner feelings so that you will feel that that which could not be done yesterday can be done today and that that which you thought could not be done a moment ago can be done tomorrow.

Get this feeling of victory and hold it and pray that it be anchored within your consciousness. And then I think that this meeting shall be well worth your while, for we will then have accomplished for this little group a specific service.

And those who shall read these words in print and shall desire to apply this law shall receive the selfsame benefit and blessing as you received tonight. For that is the beauty of the expanding light of God, the light of victory which never, never, never fails.

Ladies and gentlemen, the salutation of the lovely Lady Venus be to you tonight, the salutation of beloved Sanat Kumara, the salutation of the Lords of the Flame from Venus, the salutation of the entire Great White Brotherhood.[6]

And the *peace* and Christ-victory of God be anchored in your world tonight as never before until you yourselves are breathing, living, tangible expressions of that victory before the eyes of all mankind as well as before us who are your friends, your co-workers, your companions in light, and those who love you and love the earth and its evolutions free in the holy name of God.

I thank each one of you for your time, your attention, your devotion, and your love.

Adore your Presence. *Adore* your Presence.[7] Adore your mighty God Self, the I AM of you. And be, then, as we are—receivers of all the benefits of that Presence and the full power of your victory made manifest forevermore.

I thank you. Good night.

September 3, 1961
Woodstock, Ontario, Canada
MLP

3

BREATHE IN THE SPIRIT OF COSMIC VICTORY!

Beloved Great Divine Director and friends of freedom, I salute you in the name of Victory. In the name of God, I salute you this day.

Did you know, blessed ones of Boston, that God's name is Victory and that I am his namesake? Does this not give you the pressure to realize that it is the intention and purpose of eternity that each one of you have the breath of freedom, and the breath of freedom that you shall have shall embody within it the qualities and the characteristics of victory?

With each breath you draw, if you so qualify it, ladies and gentlemen, you can accept victory into your world. You say, when you call forth your breath from the atmosphere, that it is a simple process that goes on automatically. True, but ladies and gentlemen, if you call forth victory in that breath and say to your own God Presence, *"Mighty God Presence and beloved Victory, flood your sense of cosmic victory into my being as I accept these elements,"* you will realize that you are imbibing it from the fountain of life, which is the fountain of victory.

Every ascended being has breathed the atmosphere of earth and has utilized its atoms of energy. The atoms of oxygen and hydrogen that enter your nostrils were breathed by them and by myself in times past. Therefore, if you would extract from those atoms the great quality of God-victory, you must do so by conscious God-design and intent.

I do not propose, ladies and gentlemen, that you police each breath you draw in and that you stand and say, "Now I am breathing in victory." But I do propose that you consciously qualify your breath with victory at various times during the day when you think of it and extract from it a life-giving essence which, like a transfusion of new blood or a reception of the atoms of energy manifest in vitamins, will infuse you with a great power of cosmic victory. Therefore this impetus will move you forward to overcome some of the vicissitudes of life that presently distress you.

WHAT IS TRUE COMPASSION?

Ladies and gentlemen, I am so aware of the momentum of victory that it is somewhat difficult for me to behold the sea of troubles that I understand surrounds mankind. Now, if you were to enter into my state of divine consciousness, you too would be somewhat unaware of the sea of troubles surrounding mankind. Mankind, then, might tend to look upon you as one without compassion.

Ladies and gentlemen, is it compassionate to perpetuate an earth that is suffering and in pain and misery? Is it compassionate to perpetuate life when that life is in great distress? Is it not kinder to elevate life into a sense of its God-intended victory and its God-intended freedom?

Individuals have often gone astray because of a sense of human sympathy, and the ties they have contracted in life have caused them to feel great sorrow for the members of their family, their friends and their loved ones. I would like to point out that all of you have a great heavenly Father and this heavenly Father has the greatest compassion that you could ever conceive of. By his Great Law he moves the universe in a pathway of love, yet he is apparently oblivious to those who are in great distress simply because they have accepted a human momentum and the pressure of that momentum.

It is true that they are presently in ignorance but, ladies and gentlemen, they were not always this way, for there was a time in Atlantis and in Lemuria and in ages past when the same lifestreams who now seem so ignorant were quite learned. They had the same opportunities you now have to sit in the temples of wisdom and they sat at the feet of many of the same beings who today are ascended masters. And they heard through their lips a service of great light, yet they went out into the world of form and rendered disobedience unto the Great Law.

The reason they are not manifesting victory is [because of their karma returning] to their own doorstep, and it is up to them as individuals to realize this and to realize that no power of the ascended hosts or the angelic hosts can change those conditions.

Blessed ones, when you behold a beautiful flower breathing forth its essence of God-victory into space, you realize that it is not a weed. A weed today can but produce after its kind, but how many of you know that all of the weeds upon earth were beautiful flowers at one time?

God-victory [can be demonstrated] by individuals who hold to a conscious design and accept God's great light into their world in the same way as the great currents of light flow through the nerves and the cells of the body until the body, glowing with the manifest perfection you call good health, manifests spiritually as God-victory.

Can you understand, blessed ones, that victory is a manifestation of the perfect plan for each lifestream, which in itself is victory because it is the image of God? I AM in the image of God. I AM in the image of God. I AM in the image of God, and you were created in that same image of God-victory if you will accept it.

WE SEE THE EARTH AS A HOME OF LOVE

Today upon the rolling planet Venus there is a great cosmic manifestation of light. And a pulsating light ray from the beloved Lady Venus and Sanat Kumara is shining down upon the earth and anchoring itself right over this forcefield to transmit from that planet the vibrations of the dignitaries of the Great White Brotherhood who are assembled there.

They are assembled there to greet the Earth, the sister planet and home of love, for as such do we see the Earth. We see the Earth as a home of love contemporary with our own world. The fact that the world does not hold the immaculate concept for itself does not interfere with our concept of victory for the Earth.

We do not subject ourselves to human discord or inflict it upon our consciousness. We absolutely refuse to accept it. We will not have in our world, we will not accept upon our planet, we will not accept in our octave the discordant vibrations of disunity, disharmony and confusion that the Earth insists on manifesting.

We accept instead God-victory because it is the natural outpouring of heaven. And we are so happy and delighted to see individuals here who will accept the pressure, momentum and joy of God that manifests in your midst today and that tangibly manifests in my consciousness in all ways and in all directions.

My body today has taken on a spherical form. And like a great luminous pool, I am radiating out pulsations of victory around the world from the center of this sphere, to give mankind a sense of victory over every human condition and every situation that at times causes individuals to feel as if they might go down to defeat.

Blessed ones, you will never go down to defeat if you accept the pressure of your own I AM Presence. The light of God never fails! The light of God never fails! The light of God never fails! I AM that light of victory and you are too, blessed ones, if you will only accept it and be free.

COME INTO A SENSE OF YOUR COSMIC VICTORY

Individuals do not realize how mighty the armies of heaven are in contrast to the earth. They look at the great preparations for war. They look at the power of the spies; they look at the power of the outer world in the monetary marts of the world and they say, "This is overwhelming." Let them come for a moment to our octave and see the power of heaven in demonstration. By contrast, their finite and puny consciousness is like a penny candle to the sun.

O blessed and beloved ones, come then to a sense of your cosmic victory and realize that its manifestation is a vestment of true glory not to be compared with the physical garments that you wear. Our sense of cosmic victory is so glorious, I tell you, that even the lilies are not arrayed in its glory.[1]

O ladies and gentlemen, do not let the temporary vicissitudes of the outer world and its disturbing vibratory actions rob you of your God-peace or of your opportunity for service or spiritual progress in the Great White Brotherhood. This is an august body. It is the actual governing body for the entire planet Earth.

Beloved Virgo honors, respects and accepts the great emissaries of the Great White Brotherhood with an eternal garland of beauty the world around. Where it is spring the spirit of Amaryllis trips forth and brings a sense of divine radiance to welcome the emissaries of the Great White Brotherhood and to honor the Lord Maha Chohan, the [representative of the] Holy Spirit.

MY LIGHTNING OF COSMIC VICTORY

O blessed ones, preceding my talk to you today the Great Divine Director gave you so many wonderful thoughts that I said to myself, "He has stolen much of my thunder." And yet because I still have lightning left, I give you the lightning of cosmic victory!

Will you accept my lightning, blessed ones, and realize that it is a tangible gift and not merely the utterance of this messenger? Will you accept it and realize that it is a gift from Mighty Victory that comes from the planet Venus?

Will you accept that I have the power and capacity to create a form exactly as depicted in the pictures of me?[2] Will you also accept that I have the power and capacity to take on a spherical form and be a great radiant point of concentrated God-victory?

Do you realize, blessed ones, that when you reach our state of consciousness you are less concerned with form than with the quality and manifestation of the thoughts, feelings, heart, being, existence and consciousness of your own identity?

I am, you see, a part of God. I am all of God in one sense and I am a part of God in another, because I, too, was given the gift of individual life and this is the beauty of heaven. Every one of you are facets of God, the facets of the divine jewel—the sacred jewel in the heart of the lotus of creation that is intended to be the sacred chalice into which the Spirit was poured as the divine essence and flame.

Upon our planet is taught the law of the flame. We hope that individuals receiving the Keepers of the Flame instruction through The Summit Lighthouse will realize that they have been given a priceless jewel that they are required to polish. It is up to them to externalize the beauty crystallized within their own nature, which at times is covered over with human effluvia and distress.

They must scrape off these barnacles so that they may be able to sail across the great sea of human confusion into the calm of Christ-peace and God-victory. And when they come to our home of light they will realize that it is worth every effort and much more. If it required a million years to achieve, it would be worth it; and if it required ten million years to achieve, it would still be worth it! The fact that you can receive your eternal freedom in less than one lifetime is breathtaking. It is phenomenal. It is outstanding. You do not realize, unless you think of it, what a transcendent opportunity is yours. I know, for I read the cosmic record of the great pain and length of suffering that occurred in some systems of worlds in order to achieve what you, blessed people of earth, are able to achieve far more easily because of our gifts.

YOU ARE DESTINED TO BE GODS OVER YOUR OWN UNIVERSE!

O blessed ones, do not think that the outer conditions of the mind have any power. They have no power except that which you give them and when instead you give us dominion over your world, you will achieve a sense of our pulsating God-victory. And you will know that freedom in God's name is the destiny of every child who first utters a tender cry as he comes forth [from the womb] and is placed in his mother's arms.

You, blessed ones, are destined by the Cosmic Mother of all life to be

Gods over your own universe, to be God's victor over all your affairs, to join the universal chorus on an equal basis when you come together with the other sons of heaven. The Father did not intend to have a race of slaves or serfs. Instead he intended to create beings equal in stature to the highest outpourings of the great God flame of life as it pulsates forth from the heart of Alpha and Omega in the Great Central Sun.

The solar altars, the altars of Venus, are all dedicated to the name of God, I AM, to Eternal Being, to the great unfailing light of God. The distress call of the Great White Brotherhood upon this planet is

> *The light of God never fails!*
> *The light of God never fails!*
> *The light of God never fails!*

Spoken three times it is a fiat of greeting in our world. To us it has a different meaning. It calls us to a great spirit of concord and rejoicing. When we hear it given [on earth] we come to assist you and to give you our momentum of peace, our momentum of victory, our momentum of love to remove from you the discordant elements of your nature, to say to the waves of human selfishness, "Peace, be still!" and to restore divine harmony wherever it exists not and to give in its place God-victory and the peace of the Cosmic Christ.

I thank you.

December, 1961
Boston, Massachusetts
MLP

4

YOUR LAUREL WREATH OF VICTORY

May the victory and peace of the morning enter into your heart, beloved people of planet Earth, and may you know and feel with all of your heart [the truth of] the words, "I AM a son of God." May you sense the power of your own victory, which gives to everyone upon earth the sense of the fullness of their victory.

I would like to remind you, blessed people of this planet, that as a rosebud is enfolded within a shield of green before opening, so mankind are enfolded in the greenness of their ignorance and they do not know or perceive the fullness of that which shall be. For that which shall be is their own victory pushing up to manifest through their body, their mind and their entire being.

The spirit of victory is the Spirit of God, for God *is* Victory. And Christ's victory, which in a sense is commemorated each year by the renewal of life [at springtime], perpetually made manifest by the rising of the crocus and the daffodil and the flowers from their beds of slumber, is the manifest token to mankind of the beauty of their own divinity. The mighty onrush of perfection and power [of their divinity] is the heritage and inheritance of all life upon this planet.

I AM Victory. And for a tremendous length of time as reckoned by mankind, I have never known anything else but the absolute Spirit of Victory. I do not know the meaning of defeat. I do not know the meaning of anything less than absolute perfection. And I desire this morning to convey to you the idea of your own victory, the idea of your own perfection as a state into which you will enter.

I ask the builders of form this morning to construct, as a spiritual symbol of that victory, a laurel wreath composed of the delicate green that now surrounds the people of this area in manifest nature and I ask that this wreath of victory rest upon the brow of every sincere chela in this place and throughout planet Earth.

I ask you to envision for a moment what will take place when your specific laurel wreath of victory, now placed upon you, is changed by divine Christ-illumination into the golden substance of your victory. You will then wear your own golden crown of Christ-victory because by the power of illumination you will have drawn forth from the Godhead the necessary power that is required to exercise dominion over your four lower bodies and lifestream until you walk as a Christed one into the realm of absolute perfection.

Entering into that Christ perfection, illumination and love, you as a disciple will be crowned not only with the laurel wreath of attainment but also with a crown that will be turned into a golden crown of victorious achievement in the golden age. This is my gift to you in memory of this precious spring, in memory of the springtide, in memory of the power that elevates and lifts man from a mere idea into the perfection of the Creator.

YOU ARE AN IDEA OF DIVINE PERFECTION

Beloved ones, you must first recognize that in his mind the Creator conceived of each one as an idea of divine perfection. And this idea, rushing forth into time and dimension, was designed by God to assemble all the facets of its own pristine purity and to cause that power to manifest its own divinity. It did not do so because of its misuse of free will, and so the victory God intended for man did not manifest.

But it shall do so in the golden age of life's perfection when the fulfillment of the prophecy that the lion shall lie down with the lamb comes to pass. Then mankind will perceive the taming of the lion part of their nature. And the assertion of the power of the "Lamb of God, which taketh away the sins of the world,"[1] will harmonize with the fierceness drawn forth by mankind and charged into the atmosphere of the world. All of this shall be transmuted and changed into "the peace of God, which passeth all understanding."[2]

I would like to call to your mind the power of victory that beloved Jesus exercised from the ship when he commanded, "Peace, be still,"[3] and immediately all was calm. This was the power he manifested by having a momentum of cosmic victory. Because beloved Jesus communed with his own mighty I AM Presence and was completely and wholly identified with the Father, the I AM Presence of each one, he was able to draw forth a great sea of quiescence around him, which poured forth and calmed the raging seas of outer manifestation.

So individuals who love God enough to recognize that he intends them to have their victory will procure from him the power to still the raging turmoil around them not only by divine demand but also by the power of divine command. It is the will of God that man should attain his Christ-victory; and having attained it, that he cause the devils of human fear to tremble because he is able to maintain absolute God-control over all the elements in his world.

A SENSE OF UNIVERSAL VICTORY

I pause now, beloved ones, for I am determined to call forth my legions of cosmic victory and ask them to bless all of you here this morning with a sense of the victory of the ascended Jesus Christ, with a sense of my own victory and, above all, with a sense of the universal victory outpouring from the Great Central Sun. For from the heart of Alpha and Omega this day, the sustaining vibratory action of their victory made manifest pours forth unto all universes without end.

Blessed ones, do you realize the meaning of that victory? Then accept the gift, the precious gift of the angels of victory who shall now bless you.

[30-second pause]

Blessed and beloved ones, I want to speak to you now concerning the perfect plan of God for every lifestream. Individuals are prone to imitate the human discord that they perceive around them, and this very action of their mind, the mimicry of human ideas and visualizations, has caused all their difficulties. When they lost the power to see into the octave of spiritual perfection and thus become identified with their own inner divinity, at that precise moment they were only able to perceive the outer in action.

Do you see? And perceiving only the outer, they were unable to hold the image of Christ-victory that otherwise would have manifested more easily in their worlds.

REALIZE THE GIANT STATURE OF A SON OF GOD

Some of you are aware of the scriptural passage that records that "There were giants in those days . . . when the sons of God came in unto the daughters of men."[4] Blessed ones, these are things you ought to ponder and [you ought] to realize the stature of your own being, the giant stature of a son of God.

Instead you have gazed into your mirror and perceived human imperfection for so long that you have become habituated, as it were, to recognize imperfection. I ask you, ladies and gentlemen, from this day forward to perceive yourself in your Christ image when you gaze into your mirror. Call to your mirror and know that within that mirror itself is the power to reflect your own spiritual identity.

The miraculous electronic particles that compose the glass are pulsating within the glass. And if, when you gaze into the glass each day, you call to the God within those particles and demand that they manifest their victory and atomic power to radiate forth the true Christ image of yourself, you can in truth manifest the perfection that the individual known as Coué tried to bring forth.

He told mankind that they should say "Each day, in every way, I am getting better and better."[5] He did not know the full power of the I AM and yet he said "Each day, in every way, I AM getting better and better."

Now, beloved ones, if you are going to exercise Christ-dominion over yourselves and over the earth, you must take hold of your energy and you must say to this energy, "You are wholly God. You are divine. You are radiant. You are light." And you must call forth the magnificent Christ light of victory from the atoms that compose your body.

You must set your mind free from all mankind's decadent thoughts and call for the transmuting light of God to pour forth through the atoms that compose your brain and your being. You must also call forth the power of victory to flow through the stream of your thoughts—all the thoughts you have ever thought throughout all your embodiments.

You must ask for your etheric body to be purified and have that body shaken loose—and I mean shaken loose as one would shake the grates of a furnace—until all of the ash of that transmuted substance is shaken out and is no longer a part of your world. And then wherever it [the ash] goes, call for its transmutation by the power of the violet fire until the action of Cosmic Christ victory it asserts will make your mind the Mercurian diamond-shining mind of God.

When you have this diamond-shining mind of God it will, like a great cosmic mirror, reflect the perfection of God. Then you will not see limitation, death, discord or any other condition manifesting upon this planet or any planet in any other solar system, for you can by the power of your invocation call forth the perfection of the universe.

Man does not realize or understand in his finite mind the power of a light year or what a light year is. Blessed ones, a light year is the eternal perfection of God. And mankind, because of these vast distances, conceives of scientific notions that are completely unrealistic from our standpoint; for we are able to say "I am here" and "I am there," and instantly it is so.

It is like the centurion who came to the Christ and the Christ spoke to him and said, "Verily I have not found so great faith, no, not in Israel." For this centurion had previously said to the Christ, "I am a man of authority, having men [soldiers] under me; and I say to this man 'Go' and he goeth and to this man 'Come' and he cometh."[6]

This is the power that mankind must learn to exercise over life, the power to call forth his victory and to say to all conditions of the outer *Go* and they will go and to say to the conditions of the inner light of God's perfection *Come* and they will come. And by exercising your divine authority you will no longer be a puppet or a marionette; instead you will be a son of God, manifesting the same Christ-victory the people of the planet Venus manifest and I am manifesting today.

I WISH YOU COULD GAZE UPON MY FACE

Oh, I wish you could gaze upon my face. How I wish that you in this room had the scales taken from your eyes as did Paul on the road to Damascus, so that you could see the victory in my face. For I am shining before you today like the sun in its strength, and my eyes are like luminous orbs of cosmic fire. I am only admiring the perfection of God therein, and you can do the same within your own being.

Blessed and beloved ones, God exalted in man is the manifestation of the perfect man and you can exalt God in yourself and have perfect humility. I assure you, ladies and gentlemen, it is only in human thoughts and ideas that individuals have ego, and the power of the human ego is given to vanity and the power of vain expression. But in our octave there is naught but the absolute perfection of God made manifest as eternal springtime.

We are not idle beings. We are not beings who float on a luminescent cloud and play harps. Blessed and beloved ones, we are doing the work of the eternal Father. We have immortality. We have eternal life. Many things manifesting in your world are manifesting Above as below.

Life here is not so different [from life on earth] as you might think. The supreme difference, blessed and beloved ones, is that we know the power of eternal victory and we refuse to accept the power of imperfection. Oh, we recognize, even in our octave, that there is a progressive movement toward the ultimate. But there is no ultimate in the universe itself, for the whole Godhead moves on in a great cosmic realm of infinite perfection, transcending itself moment by moment, and there is no stopping the wheels of the Father's progress.

"In my Father's house are many mansions" is a true statement,[7] and the words of the Christ live on today in the manifestation of his victory over death. His victory lives on today and is the full perfection of God made manifest through his mission of cosmic teacher to mankind.

Blessed and beloved ones, how I love you! I love you with the infinite power of your own God Presence, your own I AM. I love you with the power of the great cosmic beings, with the power of the Spirit of the Great White Brotherhood, your beloved El Morya, your magnificent Saint Germain, your beloved Jesus, beloved Maitreya and all the ascended host.

We all love you and we are determined, O Earth, that this year shall be a year of great blessing and infinite unfoldment for the mankind of Earth who will recognize their opportunities and hold on to them.

O blessed and beloved people of Earth, the celestial planet Venus, turning in its glorious orb, sends its blessing to the Earth, and the flame of the seven Holy Kumaras is sent earthward like a giant star. May it spread out now in your midst and blaze unto Earth the power of the secret love star, the love of God, the love of God in manifestation, the purity and holiness of the sacred fire and all that raises, transmutes, changes, elevates, ennobles and blesses man with the fullness of his divine stature, the nobility of his soul, the shining raiment of his garment that strips from him fear, doubt and sinful conditions and raises him into a state of sinlessness, fearlessness, purity, exaltation, resurrection and dominion over all the elements that were given into his hands by the first fiat of God, by the power of the first Magna Charta, the spoken Word that became flesh.

I thank you for your rapt attention upon your own mighty I AM Presence, your divinity within. And I love you, I love you, I love you. I take my leave of you now but I remain very close to you when you whisper my name. If you desire to attain your victory with all of your heart, when you are faced with perilous problems call to your God Self first and then to me and say: *Mighty Victory, I am calling to you. Give me your feeling of victory!*

I shall be there, behind the sunbeams of your attention. I shall be wherever you are, for I will come, swifter than lightning, on the rays of cosmic radiance from the heart of God.

I thank you and I bid you good afternoon.

March 25, 1962
The Theosophical Hall
Washington, D.C.
MLP

5

BELIEVE IN YOUR OWN VICTORY

I AM the fullness of God-victory outpoured upon the waiting hearts of men that they may diligently perceive in every breath of life their infinite capacity to have and to hold joy in the completeness of their being. I urge you all now to open the doors of your consciousness to hear from far-off spheres of light all that God intends you to hear of your own Christ-victory and perfection, which is poured out upon you without limit today and forever.

Beloved ones, as I descend into the atmosphere of this planet, I carry with me a torch—a torch that is alive with the flames and energies of Almighty God. I come at the behest of the ascended masters and in response to invocations from the waiting hearts of men. I come with the fullness of the consciousness of Christ-victory, which overcomes the world and all the manifestations of the world that are less than the perfection of Almighty God. And I come to sustain and hold aloft the flag of eternal Cosmic Christ purity.

Beloved ones of the light, I am enveloping this room in the consciousness of victory—victory and perfection [that we are] pouring out upon mankind whether or not they are aware of it. I will sustain my feeling of cosmic victory in the radiance of the life flame within mankind. And all of the joy of the angels is poured out upon them today to initiate into their feeling world a sense of the cosmic victory that overcometh the world.

Precious and beloved of the light, it is the divine intent that every man and every woman be a full and complete manifestation of the eternal law. Do you know what that means? Do you have a cosmic sense of the fullness of the statement I just made to you this night?

If you do have a sense of it, I urge you, then, to realize that it is the crying need of the hour. Its hour has come. And at this moment I am determined to see mankind, propelled by the power of God within them, awaken from the lethargy of the ages and enter in to an era of Cosmic Christ peace and freedom [that is a gift] from the heart of God. They may then in diligence work at the loom of life and weave tapestries of immortal loveliness thereupon, as the beauty externalized upon our planetary home, Venus.

O Venus, thou radiant and shining orb of perfection, how the hearts of all the Lords of the Flame love thee! How we adore the fullness of all thou art, the magnificence of thy mighty being offered upon the altar of Almighty God with the full understanding of your great capacity to ray out from within the solar luminosity a flame of light. [This flame of light is] to be poured out as a cup of life from which all may drink, in the unity of universal perfection that is the understanding of the life flame and the life plan of God.

INVOCATION TO HELIOS AND VESTA

Now, an invocation is issuing forth from the solar altars upon Venus to mighty Helios and Vesta: O Helios and Vesta, hear now the call of the sons of the flame and of the Lords of the Flame from the planet Venus. Give our brothers upon Earth their freedom to enter in to an understanding of the infinite capacity of the solar radiance to set them free from every discordant manifestation, known or unknown, within the folds of their being. May they know their eternal freedom and may they walk in the destiny of Almighty God and in the transcendence of life's perfection poured out upon them without limit until the Earth is free.

I call now for the eternal perfection of the spheres, for the radiance of the angelic host who long ago sang the song of joy to the shepherds of men: "Glory to God in the highest, and on earth peace, good will toward men."[1] May that resounding cry now enter into the tone of every bell upon planet Earth. May it cause the peals of those bells to repeal the dictates of human selfishness and set free by the power of the Holy Spirit the life flame within mankind so that they may shape and mold this earth in accordance with the divine plan fulfilled.

I COME TO FLOOD THE EARTH WITH COSMIC UNITY

I AM Mighty Victory. I have come this night to flood the earth with the sense of cosmic unity and perfection that long ago graced the Christ as he manifested in his tiny infant form, the infant Messiah, the light of the Christ. May his light expand in every heart and may the joy of mankind know no bounds. May the tenderness of the love of God spread out in the hearts of men as it did in the hill country of Judea until the hearts of all men shall sing a new song, the song of the risen Christ, the song of the rising energies of perfection within them.

May the resurgence of the Christ energies flood forth and exalt man's understanding of the purposes of the sacred fire upon the heart-altar of Almighty God in the center of his being. May he know the meaning of the mysteries of God—the mystery within the ark of his being.

May the great cosmic cross of white fire of Lord Gautama [and Jesus] blaze between all brothers of the sacred truth of God until Mother Mary's spirit and spirit of cosmic unity touch every son of heaven anew and each son of heaven is exalted to where he can recognize and perceive the virtue of God flooding forth from the hearts of his brothers. Then, in that cosmic sense of victory, he will gather up the trailing garments of his fallen brethren and exalt within them the perfection of Almighty God.

He will not desire to crucify them on a cross of imperfection but will desire to raise the fallen and bestow the cup of salvation upon all on earth, not looking with a disrespectful eye to perceive the faults and the ignorance of men but desiring to perceive them with the unifying eye that is the

All-Seeing Eye of God. [He will see] the perfection of the divine plan and perceive the love flame within their own heart and will extend that love flame as a cup of cold water to every son of heaven to multiply the victory of Almighty God without limit upon this planet.

I BRING YOU THE CONSCIOUSNESS OF THE DAYSTAR

By the flame of the Holy Spirit, by the flame of the Holy Spirit, *by the flame of the Holy Spirit* and the victory of life eternal, I AM come. I AM come to bring the consciousness of the Daystar rising within thee, the transcendence that caused us to rejoice with the morning stars that sang together for joy and to behold the eternal unifying light.

That light is spread out across the firmament and brings from the realm and aureole of the dawn the shining perfection and rainbow light of God from the east unto the west, covering the world around with such love and such a mantle of love as shall know no bounds. This mantle of love and light and perfection is destined to smother within mankind the influences that corrupt the youth of the world and [is destined] to cause mankind to awaken at last to their eternal destiny.

Within the archives of planet Earth are stories of many a ceaseless struggle. From them man can learn of the unnecessary struggle of human beings to pursue a vain human end, for the end thereof is merely the terminus called death. Beloved ones, you are engaged in the immortal struggle of the ages, which ought to be no struggle. It ought to be a sense of absolute Christ-victory.

You are engaged in service to the light. Therefore invest yourselves now with the full feeling of mounting victory, which floods forth into your waiting hearts. Let this flame of Cosmic Christ victory raise in you all that is of God and transmute on the instant all that is not the purity, the perfection, the love, the compassion, the understanding and the infinite strength and capacity to be a living son of immortal life.

I AM Victory! I AM *your* victory! And when you desire a charge of my flame, call to me in the holy name of God and say to me:

Beloved Mighty Victory, come now into the forcefield of my heart through the open door and let your flame of cosmic victory flood through my body, brain and being.

Make me the completeness of God that you are. Give me your joy and your perfection, for I, too, am a son of light and a son of perfection.

BELIEVE IN THE UNIVERSAL CHRIST

Children of the light, be at peace. Let not thy heart be troubled, neither let it be afraid.[2] Ye believe in God. Ye believe in the goodness of the universe. Believe, then, in the universal Christ, the light within your being. And, I tell you, that light shall expand within the very firmament of God, within the heart of the earth and out, out, out into the borders of infinity.

You will know the ageless friendship of the ascended masters and cosmic beings. You will have us for your friends, in due time tangibly manifest, who will clasp your hands and hearts unto your own Christ-victory. This is no empty promise that we offer you. It is the power of God unto salvation to all who believe and are impelled to act accordingly.

I come not with a spirit of condemnation but with a sense of the God-victory that I bequeath to you all and to all mankind. It is your eternal, immortal, invincible, life-giving inheritance. Take it and be free. Carry it and hold high the torch of life. I think that in the annals of eternity, in the chronicles of heaven, your names will be written as those who believed in the crowning wreath of Christ-victory, for from the beginning it was known of God that mankind should achieve and become the fullness of all that he intended them to be.

Blessed be his name and blessed are ye who are his flames. I thank you and bid you good evening.

November 24, 1962
Long Island, New York
MLP

6

I AM THY VICTORY!

From spheres afar and yet so near, I AM come this night to the earth in the living consciousness of God-victory. Hail, O earth! Hail, O people of the world! Hail, beloved friends of the heart of God! Hail, O glorious golden wreath of cosmic victory; descend now to earth I pray, and be a crown upon the head of all who love the presence of immortality, all who revere the sacred flame, the solar breath, the inner radiance of the name of God.

O divine love, thou crowning radiance! O divine compassion, which extends itself through the rolling spheres and cosmic avenues, through the years and through eternal realms of spatial greatness! O vastness of the spirit of truth, expanding and expanding and expanding throughout space, how glorious is thy presence, how charged is the universe with the pervading intelligence and love of God!

I AM come this night to stir the mankind of earth, to stir them to a greater understanding of the purpose of coming into embodiment and form. Behold, I say unto thee, the hour is at hand and now is, when men ought to roll away the stone from [the tomb of] their crystallized consciousness and human concepts to emerge as the victorious all-living Christ, who speaks to others and says: "All Hail! All Hail, beloved ones!"[1]

because he is expressing the attainment of victory—victory over the condition called death.

I tell you, beloved ones, it is chronicled in the human heart that mankind has cringed before the death brought upon them by the mortality of their limited concepts; they cringe in fear, and nothing on earth is more destructive than the concepts of death and finality that man has come to accept in his world.

Therefore, the empty tomb on Easter morning, beloved ones, spoke to the world of eternal hope, which God created in the beginning as part of the triune beauty of life. The triune power of God is ensouled, beloved ones, by Faith, Hope and Charity, great beings who express the victory of God even as I do. Hope was therefore renewed in the hearts of a waiting world on that priceless morning, when the sun arose and caused its roseate colors to pour forth love and hope.

Several years ago the words "The world is waiting for the sunrise" were made popular [in song] on this planet; but, beloved ones, that song was written far too late, for the sunrise the world awaited blossomed on that Easter Day.

IMMORTALITY IS A GIFT FROM GOD

Some of you may smile and say, "Why is Mighty Victory speaking to us tonight of Easter at the beginning of the New Year?" Well, beloved ones, it is a timely and a timeless subject. It is a subject that brings a sense of buoyancy to your bodies, a sense of uplift. Like cork, which cannot sink beneath the waves of human thought, it buoys you up and strengthens you with renewed hope, for you realize that the precious and priceless consciousness within you, which beats your heart and sustains your life, is immortal.

You realize that God, who cannot lie, who cannot err, created mankind and made them in his own image. "In the image of God, created he him; male and female created he them,"[2] and he endowed them with the image and completeness of himself. He endowed mankind with the image of immortality, and that image can never be lost. Thus, beloved ones, immortality is a gift of God unto you who have this great understanding.

It is true, beloved ones, that a condition known as the second death came about because mankind had served beneath the spiritual sun year after year, lifetime after lifetime, and ignored the promptings of the spirit of holiness, purity and truth. Then the great cosmic law spoke, and when it spoke, with one mighty stroke it decreed that at the end of that embodiment the life's energies of those disobedient ones should run out.

The Law further decreed that whatsoever was left of their individualized consciousness should be returned to the Great Central Sun for repolarization and that the overlay of etheric and unhappy memories imposed upon that lifestream should be vaporized, as wax is melted by the flame of a candle.

This was the great mercy of the great cosmic law, especially in the case of world tyrants, men who had caused bloodshed and untold suffering to continents and who were unable to pay back that karma. The great cosmic law decreed that those individuals should pass through the change called the second death as an act of cosmic mercy, to wipe out for all time the imponderable karma that rested upon their heads.

And, therefore, in a sense, by passing through the change called the second death those individuals lost their immortality. But, beloved ones, I would like to remind you that the life's essence within them, the part of them that is God, returned to the Great Central Sun, was repolarized and issued forth again.

And therefore, in one great sense, life for them, too, was immortal. But it was stripped of its memory processes and its identity, and they had to begin all over again. Do you see the great mercy of the cosmic law, beloved ones? Yet, I am certain that none of you would like to begin all over again, enter the world of form and build up your memory body.

THE BLESSING OF REEMBODIMENT

I would like to remind you, beloved ones, that the youth of the world come into embodiment today endowed with great reason and understanding. At a very early age they master the principles of body mechanics and are able to walk without tottering. Some are able to speak many languages, seemingly without learning them; for they pick them up very quickly, beloved ones, and master them to the extent of appearing like geniuses, and they are noted by mankind as such.

What is this process, beloved ones? It is the reembodying of the personality of the soul who returns to the scene of earthly life and takes up its abode among mankind. And as it begins the process, it reintegrates itself with the knowledge of the past and, therefore, much of what it learned before is retained still, for it issues forth from the halls of memory deep within the psyche of the individual.

Therefore in the memory body nothing is lost of that which has been given to individuals. For the learning that has accrued to them through experience in past embodiments to assist their lifestream is released when it is desirable to further their spiritual progress. And so we find that men are not born idiots or without sensation or without understanding. They quickly master the world and the understanding of the world and they adapt themselves quite readily to the environmental conditions that surround them.

Well, beloved ones, this is a blessing. It is a blessing, for it is a part of the victory flame. If you stop to think of it, it is the part of man's victory that assists him to climb the stairway leading to his spiritual attainment, to the glory of God in the highest.

JOY IN HEAVEN OVER ONE
WHO RETURNS TO THE FOLD

Beloved ones, I would like to remind you of one of the statements of the Christ, that there is a great joy in heaven over everyone who repents and returns to the fold.[3] Beloved ones, do you not see that the eternal, creating, loving, All-Father supreme, the mighty I AM Presence in the Great Central Sun, is concerned about you as an individual and is concerned about every part and facet of his creation?

Do you not see how the victory flame within life sustains the learning processes whereby men are able to master their environment as well as the energy passing through their form? Victory is attained by seizing the hand of your mighty I AM Presence and commanding those conditions that are not a part of your victory be permanently eliminated from your world. Your victory is won in the acceptance of your real identity and the willingness to be molded by the spiritual God flame that surrounds you with the pressure of its victorious acceptance of life.

What do you think the difference is between the ascended masters and yourselves, beloved ones, insofar as the mighty I AM Presence is concerned? It is merely a matter of the outer conditions acting [in your world]. Ascended beings do not have outer conditions acting, for they have mastered those conditions and they have become the victory of their mighty I AM Presence.

Beloved ones, you have but to lay aside the so-called sin and the weight that does beset you, those conditions of unhappiness that are densifying, stultifying and distressing. Permit, then, the great powers of the continents of the air, the glorious radiance of the Christ, the blessed and potent wind of the Holy Spirit to descend through your physical form and to buoy you up until you reach the solar fires. And when you reach the solar fires, you will find that human conditions will drip from you as wax.

You remember, beloved ones, the myth of old, about an individual [called Icarus] who passed into the air with wings that were attached to him, and when these wings melted he dropped to earth and was destroyed. Well, beloved ones, symbolically Icarus represents human aspirations without the Spirit of Victory, without Christed accomplishment—those who sought to take heaven by storm but had not readied themselves or prepared themselves through the necessary solar initiations to bear the pressure of the solar heat of the divine radiance.

Beloved ones, you have heard it said that there is more than one heaven; you have heard it said that there are gradations of consciousness. This is true, beloved ones. If you were exalted into higher states of consciousness, it would be enough to melt and dissolve your physical form as if you were dropped into a bucket of molten steel.

Of course, you do not want this to happen, and therefore the great love of God, the victorious power of God tempers the wind to the shorn lamb of man's identity and causes him to adjust to the spiritual state in which he is. Some would find it desperately uncomfortable to sit in your midst as I am pouring out my flame of cosmic victory. They would be made unhappy by the stepped-up radiation and the power that we are outpouring tonight through the mighty star of victory, which is shining over this city in which I speak.

Beloved ones, man's four lower bodies must adjust themselves to the solar radiance and as they do, man will be able to outpicture the level of consciousness to which he is adjusted. Do you see, beloved ones, how Victory takes you by the hand and leads you up the cosmic stairway step by step?

YOU ARE ALL VICTORY'S CHILDREN!

You will recall, beloved ones, in an address given to you during this class, how the powers of heaven were concerned about the prayers of a single child. I would like to tell you that the prayers of one child are of great value to those on high. This does not mean that heaven turns a deaf ear to the prayers of adults, for in one very real sense you are all children. You are all *my* children; you are Victory's children.

You are Victory's children because, as I speak to you, I am completely immersed in the sense that I AM God, that the I AM in me is God. Therefore you are my children and I am your brother of light bringing you the flame of your own cosmic victory, causing that flame to rise within your heart, to pulsate above your forehead, to extend itself as a tangible unfed flame reaching into the golden heavens of illumination and drawing down therefrom the secret wisdom of God that will enable you to control the atoms of your body by the divine intelligence that gave them birth and design and form.

Beloved ones, I tell you, in the outer world you would never be able to perform the service to cause each electron, each cell, each molecule, each organ of your body to function according to its God design, until you were able to raise that body in the victory of the resurrection, the victory of the transfiguration or the victory of the ascension.

It is necessary for mankind to receive a very special wisdom, and this wisdom must be released to their Holy Christ Self. When it is released to their Holy Christ Self, that wisdom takes hold of the four lower bodies of man and produces its perfection automatically. But man must understand that he must have his heart purified by the radiance of the Goddess of Purity and the purity of his own mighty I AM Presence before this great law will act out its great pageantry of completion within his life.

This pageantry of the fulfillment of the divine plan is a glorious and wonderful experience whereby his own mighty I AM Presence, active as the Father principle of all life places his loving arms around man's head and neck and crowns him with a wreath of victory. Then he places a golden chain upon his neck and declares to him, "Thou art my beloved son. This day have I begotten thee."[4]

Beloved ones, when this occurred to me, I recall hearing the mighty peals of thunder accompanying the voice of God. For I tell you, a strange occurrence takes place when a son of God is brought to the state of the fullness and completion of his Victory and there is, as it were, a rumbling that seems to divide apart the universe itself.

It is similar to the rending in twain of the veil in the temple during the crucifixion of the Christ, and opening up of the earth and the thunder and lightning that accompanied that event. For in a spiritual sense, a great outpouring of the voice of God, the fiat of creation occurs, and great power moves through the universe whenever and wherever a son of God is given this benediction: "Thou art my beloved Son in whom I AM well pleased."[5]

Well, beloved ones, when those words were spoken of me, I knew that my Victory was won. And the *Spirit* of that victory seized my being with a force and power that has not diminished in thousands and thousands of years.

I BRING YOU LOVE FROM VENUS

I am come tonight, therefore, from our planet, Venus, to bring you the greetings of the seven Holy Kumaras and the beloved Lady Master Venus, who salutes you by blazing the pink star-radiance of her love through this forcefield and through the individual forcefields of each one, so that you may have the power of her love as a beautiful pathway, a stairway, a ray of light, a radiant path beaming through the heavens, blessing you with the fullness of her love.

Feel that love now as it pours out to you. Accept it as the gift of the twin sister planet, beloved Hesper, beloved Venus, radiating to Terra, to Virgo, to Earth, in the holy name of God. (Ladies and gentlemen, will you please be seated.)

Man in his emotional body, man in his mental body has yet to master the victorious principles of eternal stillness and peace. Those of you familiar with the principles of aerodynamics prior to the jet age are aware of how the pitch of a propeller could be altered. You are aware that with the changing of the pitch, the tone of the propeller was also changed.

Well, beloved ones, this aerodynamic principle is important in explaining the mechanics of the ascension. For when men make their ascension in the light, an alteration occurs within the forcefield and magnetic circuit of completion surrounding the auric shell of their physical form. And this alteration causes the atomic, spiritual and electronic radiation of their forms to be stepped up as though someone controlled a lever and had begun to move that lever from the left to the right.

As the lever moves toward the right, the pitch is gradually increased, the tempo is increased and the acceleration of spiritual energies is increased. It is like the atomic accelerator, like the chair, beloved ones, in which so many sat and were raised to the glory of their ascension, according to the great cosmic law as revealed in the sacred writings of Saint Germain.

Beloved ones, this condition has not ceased. It has *not* ceased, for tonight in the state of California two individuals, a man and a woman, are being transported by the Brotherhood to the Royal Teton Retreat. And this night, at the hour of twelve your time, these souls will rise in the ascension in the light to become ascended masters.

They walked the earth in your day. They poured out their devotion to their Christ-intelligence. They communed with the ascended masters. They sent the shaft of their attention to me upon Venus. They poured out their love to God unceasingly and they merited, according to the great

Karmic Board, their ascension in the light.

And I am here tonight to tell you of it, to give you a renewed sense of hope. This is truth, and although truth may be stranger than fiction to the consciousness of mankind, it is as true as the fact that I am standing here. And I am standing here!

Beloved ones, I know that you will recognize, as I intensify my light energy, that an ascended being, that a spiritual cosmic being can speak to you and can step up the radiation of mankind to assist them in the attainment of their own Christ-victory.

INVOCATION FOR PEACE AND JOY

O thou crystal clear radiance of Sanat Kumara, thou Lord of the Solar Flame upon the planet Venus, blaze thy radiance through these walls, through the body temples of these precious lifestreams emanating from the Father of all. Let them feel the stepped-up radiance of the solar flame within their four lower bodies.

Melt and dissolve within them the accumulation of discord that has caused their very bones to feel a sense of human decay. Blaze through their minds the energies of the sacred fire to give them sharpness, clarity and the mounting beauty of the inner level concepts and to see the clarity of the face of God.

Blaze through their memories and quicken in them the sense of the angelic wonder that accompanied the first fiat of creation in the beginning, in the genesis of the known creation and in the genesis of the unknown creation, as recorded in the history of this earth. Pour out upon them the oil of peace and let them feel the great solar quiet within the music of the spheres. [60-second pause]

Gently, gently, gently, bring these souls into the peaceful sense of joy that surrounds the heart of a living Christ. Let them feel as content and safe and happy, O God, as though they were wafted to earth like a falling leaf, safely nestled against the heart of Mother Earth. O beloved Virgo, receive them in tempore. *

---

*in tempore: at the right moment

They belong to the sky and their bodies and their minds and their beings are of the sky and the kingdom of the air, the kingdom of light, the kingdom of peace. They belong not to the clay. They belong not to a state of reduced energy. They belong to the quantum of the eternal light itself and they are one with the deathless solar flame and solar radiance.

Wrap them now in golden flame.

Wrap them now in golden flame.

Wrap them now in golden flame, in thy power of victory.

KEEP YOUR HEART AND MIND STAYED UPON VICTORY

In the holy name of God, I AM, I, Victory, say unto you that the peace of God, which passeth all understanding shall keep your heart and mind stayed upon victory. And as you keep your heart and mind stayed upon victory, it shall magnetize that accomplishment to you individually and to all who make the necessary application.

We deal in a Reality that transcends all human wisdom and knowledge. We deal in a Reality that we scarcely dare to reveal, for mankind in their present frightening emotional state, in their present frightening mental state hasten to utilize the energies of the universe for destruction. The present rate of fallout and of misuse of atomic energy is appalling to the Lords of Flame on Venus and yet it feels as though it has been brought to the attention of the leaders of the world. For the moment they seem to recognize the need to keep the peace.[6]

As I look forward to the days of the coming year, I am counting, as is the Brotherhood, upon the vigilance and the diligence of the students of this activity and allied movements to maintain constant intercessory prayer for and on behalf of their brothers here upon this planet, that peace upon earth may become a reality, that religious peace occur within the religions of the world, that political peace occur within the family of nations, that the disintegration within the human psyche be nullified and that man become an integrated being—body, soul and mind in perfect balance.

BALANCE THE THREEFOLD FLAME

Beloved ones, if you will take the *V* of my name, Victory, you will notice that it has three points, two upper points and a lower point. You will recognize the need, then, to have a balanced action of the threefold flame to attain your victory.

As I gaze upon you now, I must speak the truth and I cannot conceal from you the great truth of your being. For I see some of you expressing a condition of great power. Others are expressing great mental faculties, for the intelligence is very vast in its development. Others are expressing intense feelings of love. But in many I see a lack of balance.

Beloved ones, it is necessary to call for the threefold flame to be balanced for you to attain your victory. How would the letter *V* look if one side were a foot higher above the other? You must have balance in all that you do, and as the new year looms before you, let it be flooded with the hope of your resurrection and your ascension.

You need not look toward the grave nor toward fear. You need not be disheartened. You need not express the fear of being overcome by outer conditions. You can seize the hand of your mighty I AM Presence and alter all outer conditions to some degree or another. And if you are still not satisfied with those conditions, you may again petition the powers of heaven and tell them that you wish to attain your victory.

PERSIST IN INVOKING HEAVEN

I would remind you of the parable of the unjust judge revealed by beloved Jesus during his Palestinian mission. He told the tale of a woman who day after day consulted a judge who would not grant her request. By and by, the judge said, "I will grant this woman's request, lest by her continual coming she weary me."[7]

Therefore, beloved ones, it is possible for you to persist and persist and *persist* in invoking the presence of an ascended being, until that being, in divine compassion for himself as much as for you will usher in the victory of God that you desire to have and ought to have because you have persisted in seeking it.

Do you realize that many of the ascended masters walked among you and many of them even knew some of you when they were embodied in an era in which you also lived? Well, beloved ones, don't you think that they are plugging for you right now? Don't you think that they would desire to see you make your ascension? Don't you think that their hearts are stirred somewhat?

Do you think that now that they have attained their Victory they sit there, according to the ideas of visionary people, and play harps with great delight, floating upon pink clouds of divine radiance while their brothers and sisters toil and labor under the delusion of mass maya?

Well, I tell you, beloved ones, they do not. They are vitally concerned about each one of you and about this blessed planet and they are rendering an incomparable service. Your beloved Jesus continues to serve this planet and is indeed a potent force in its redemption and the redemption of its people. Your beloved Saint Germain continues to shower forth his own conscious victory to the mankind of earth. Your beloved El Morya lavishes his attention upon mankind by daily outpourings of devotion to the will of God for each lifestream upon this earth.

Beloved ones, some of this lavish attention is not merited by any individual's conscious act, but the great cosmic law, through the mercy of God, has permitted these blessed masters to continue to pursue mankind as the hound of heaven. Your victory is at hand. It is even at the door.

Where is the door, beloved ones?

The door is your conscious attention upon your God Presence I AM at the door. You have heard the words, "Behold, I stand at the door and knock. If any man hear my voice and open the door I will come in to him and will sup with him and he with me."[8] Beloved ones, the living Christ, the Christ of your being, desires to commune with you that he may give you the fullness of the seamless garment he wears, the garment of Christed victory, and he wants to bestow it upon you this year.

Well, beloved ones, I wish that you would not look back upon past years and say, "Well, God didn't give me my victory in any of those other years. Why is he going to give it to me now?"

Beloved ones, remember that God didn't give us our victory either until the appointed hour was come. The fullness of time must come for each one and you must wait for it in patience not in impatience, not in fear and trembling, beloved ones, fearing that God will not give it to you.

Have fear and trembling only where the great law of God is concerned, that you might understand that you ought to hold a holy awe for the law of God, for it is the source of your victory. The I AM law of life is the source of your victory. You cannot attain your victory if you are living according to human concepts.

In the name of heaven, dear people, do you think that the eternal powers in heaven are mocked?

The eternal powers in the heavens are not mocked. The wisdom of God is inviolate. The wisdom of God is perfection. The city is indeed foursquare. The pillars of light cannot be moved by vain human reasoning. Mankind must accept the gift God has offered. They cannot reject the chief cornerstone of their being and then expect to build a temple of holiness and purity to God.

To attain their victory, they must desire it. They must believe in it. They must serve in conscious waking attention, knowing with certainty that the Law will be fulfilled in them as it was fulfilled in all who have preceded them in the journey back to the heart of God. You will recall, beloved ones, the statement, "Then shall two be in the field; the one shall be taken and the other left. Two women shall be grinding at the mill; the one shall be taken and the other left."9

Well, beloved ones, men do not all attain heaven at a given instant. Men do not all ascend together. Would to God they could. Would to God they would. Would to God that our service to this beautiful planet could end in a flash. We would like that.

But we know that man, according to his state of evolution and development, requires admonishment, requires teaching, requires some service and struggle, because through that service he is able to understand the beauty of God. He could never understand the beauty of God, he could never understand the love of God if he were just endowed with it.

Remember, beloved ones, the story of beloved Gautama, the Lord of the World, when he was yet embodied as Siddhartha Gautama. Remember how his father kept the truth from him of the conditions in the world. He was not permitted to see that the condition of death existed. He was not permitted to know that sickness existed. He was shielded by his father and kept within the confines of the palace walls. Well, beloved ones, the day came when he found out the truth about the conditions in the world.

So you see how the Great Law functions. You see how the Father, in his great power and wisdom, gives to each man the understanding of eternal reality and eventually all come to understand thereby the truth of their being.

DO NOT BE CRITICAL OF OTHERS

You must not have fear concerning others, concerning the mankind of earth. You must permit only diligence to function in your world, for diligence will bring you your victory. Do you realize, beloved ones, that when you in your own feeling world have doubts about whether a lifestream will make his ascension, when you gaze upon a precious lifestream who came forth from the heart of God and you say to yourself, "The way this individual is living, he will not attain his victory," you are helping to hold back that individual and by so doing you are holding yourself back from attaining your own ascension in the light.

Inasmuch as I feel a mounting pressure on the part of the students here and the general student body throughout the world for a greater impartation of the sacred teaching, I feel compelled to speak to you tonight in a most forthright manner concerning this law.

Beloved ones, in each embodiment many individuals lose the opportunity to win their eternal freedom simply because they are critical of other lifestreams. And as the Law acts and returns to them whatsoever they send out, they are unable to hold the vision of the purity of their own being because they are so concerned with the idea that someone else will not attain his victory.

Beloved ones, would it not be a most generous, a most glorious, a most wonderful thing if every individual in this movement and throughout the world would hold the thought that the entire world could ascend together? By the magnetization of such a thought, beloved ones, you would be giving your lifestream a tremendous push towards your victory and it would not harm the world at all. Do you see, beloved ones, how the great law of love acts?

Love is a buoyant, joyful, radiant, wonderful blessing from the heart of God. Love never faileth. Though tongues may cease, love never faileth. Beloved ones, the love of God is the victory of God. And you will win your victory by that love. Would it not then be the better part of valor for you to lay aside the weapons of human ingenuity—the weapons and defenses that protect your changing personality from the persecutions and ideas of men?

I AM THY VICTORY!

If you would just conscript your energies and then place them upon the solar altar of your being and say:

Beloved God, you are my victory.
Beloved God, you made me victorious.
Beloved God, I am born of your flame.
Beloved God, I am a part of your name.
Beloved God, you have taken Moses through the Red Sea.
Beloved God, you have parted the waters of affliction.
Beloved God, you have endowed Noah with the wisdom to
　　construct the ark of safety.
Beloved God, you raised the Christ from Bethany's Hill.
Beloved God, you have life and our eternal life forever.
You are my destiny.
I live in you, I move in you,
I have my being in you and I am complete now.
No one can take from me my victory or my sense of victory.

For I am both now and forever the completeness of thy Victory
  made manifest upon earth.
I AM thy Victory. I AM thy Victory. I AM thy Victory.

If you would chant this each night as you pass into sleep and mean
it with all of your heart, [Master sings:] *I AM thy Victory. I AM thy Victory.*
I AM thy Victory. I AM thy Victory. I AM thy Victory, beloved ones, what
do you think this would do for your four lower bodies? How can a body
that is actually rippling with the rhythms of the words *I AM* (which is
God) *thy Victory* (which is God) manifest a condition less than perfection?
How can your mind express a condition less than perfection if your mind
is charged with the idea *I AM thy Victory*?

Precious ones of the light, your victory is a tangible reality! It is no
figment of human imagination. It is as concrete and solid and practical as
life itself, for it *is* life and you *are* life. O beloved ones, human delusion
and illusion is so stubborn that it seems to require some force of tremendous power to move men to accept the pressure of reality!

Reality in our sphere, beloved ones, stands ever before us. In your
octave it seems so different, for you have come to accept the density of
your human form, and you say to yourself, "Well, here I am. I have so
much avoirdupois."* Or, "Here I am. I am either limited or unlimited in
my wisdom." And many among mankind feel that they have a great deal
more wisdom than they have. Yet many among mankind do not give
themselves nearly enough credit for the wisdom God gave to them. Many
are almost like Solomon of old; they have great discriminating intelligence
but they do not use it. They do not use it. They do *not* use it.

Well, beloved ones, I am here tonight to charge into your worlds the
use of that divine energy and all the radiance that the ascended masters
have poured out in all the addresses throughout this class, previous classes
and former ascended master instruction and through the power of light
that gave you birth.

I think, beloved ones, when you start to use even one-tenth or one
one-hundredth of the instruction we have released to you that you will see

---

avoirdupois: weight or heaviness of a person; a system of measurement which uses pounds and
ounces as units

such a change taking place in your world that you will not know yourselves at the same time next year when you pass though the cusp of the year.

Beloved ones, the time is at hand and now is "when the dead shall hear the voice of the Son of God and they that hear shall live."[10] Beloved ones, do you realize that the fulfillment of this prophecy is imminent? Do you realize that those who are dead are those who are conscious of death as a requirement of nature and the Law? They do not realize that man in his divine sense is far more immortal than these priceless flowers.

I accept this star of victory[11] tonight and I AM charging it with a consciousness of victory from our planet. I AM charging it with the Christ illumination of the seven Holy Kumaras and I AM charging it with the power of the Brotherhood of the Royal Teton.

I GIVE YOU A SOLEMN WARNING

I shall end my address now. But I speak a very solemn warning: Beloved ones, these conclaves are for the purpose of the perfection of men. All who come here ought to remember that God is, and that God is their victory.

All who come here ought to realize that that victory is the very substance through which they move. All who come here ought to be grateful for our words. None should strain to be about their human business. None should desire to have our words end, for our words are vitality from the heart of God. They are charged words, charged with the radiance of God. And the longer we sustain that action, the greater the blessing bestowed upon your four lower bodies.

Well, let the Law act. Victory shall continue to be with those who love him. God is love. And those who would live must also be love. God is light and those who live must love light. They must love light in themselves and in those graduates of the earthly school, the ascended masters.

They may think, through human vanity, that they do not need the ascended masters. Let them remember that mankind themselves have created a hierarchy upon earth after the pattern in heaven. Let them remember that kings of old and high priests of old were ordained by man and God in order to govern and control the movements of peoples, tribes and kingdoms, to maintain order in that which otherwise would have been chaos and to sustain the flame of victory among mankind.

There is more reality, dear people, in this than is dreamed of as you merely observe the passing of these words. Let your minds be alert to discern the meaning of that which I say, for the opportunity of the hour is given and now passes your way.

Will you drink my flame of victory?

Will you quaff the elixir of life? Or will you pass that cup to another without drinking?

The choice is yours. For free will has always been both the bane and the beauty of man's existence. Yet without it, the law of love could not have fulfilled itself or have given to man the great glory that he achieves through his conscious realization that he is a part of God. He must attain the understanding and conscious intelligence of the All of God by his free will, through no force but through the freedom flame, through the victory flame, through the resurrection flame, through the purity flame and through the ascension flame.

O pearls of great price, arise and take your beautiful ampoule of light that surrounds your physical form, this beautiful sphere, iridescent and shining. [Audience stands.] Think of yourself now as having a round, beautiful sun-like body, not a starry body with two hands extended and two legs extended, but a spherical body of pure light, a disc of light that did descend from heaven's height.

Think of yourself now as abiding in this beautiful disc of light, this solar radiance, and feel that disc of light ascending toward the Great Central Sun, as a shining, golden, radiant solar disc going back to the heart of God to be recharged with the golden radiance of the Great Central Sun, with the golden radiance of victory, with the pink flame of love.

Know that as you enter into the heart of Alpha and Omega in the Great Central Sun, you will be given the comfort of your spiritual Father-Mother God and you will recognize that you have achieved and attained to a state of heavenly consciousness, eternal bliss and the pearl of great price.

In the name of cosmic victory, in the name of the victory of God in all, I humbly thank you, one and all, for this opportunity to speak to your hearts.

Thank you and good evening.

December 31, 1962
The Dodge House
Washington, D.C.
MLP

7

SCULPTING THE IMAGE OF YOUR VICTORY

I AM come this day with the buoyancy of your eternal victory. Beloved ones, we bridge the gap between your world and ours but there is no space between your hearts and ours. For we hold with God the sense of all life consecrated to one idea, the idea of immortal perfection manifesting within the beating heart, thence from the divine idea within, carried out into the world of form until it is a constructive effort in four dimensions.

Beloved ones, I call your attention to the laurel wreath I wear, the laurel wreath of your victory and mine. I call to your attention that men of old were given this emblem as a badge of valor signifying that they were men of renown. I would like to call to your attention that God, who is no respecter of persons, expects every individual to manifest the laurel wreath of his own individualized victory.

Therefore, I come today dedicated to the idea of conveying to you the import of the little things that you can do to assist you day by day in building a momentum of victory. You, perhaps, imagine that when you touch your toes to the floor upon arising that it is an insignificant act. Let me tell you, beloved ones, that the manner in which you do this can determine the buoyancy of your feelings throughout the day.

If you do it with alacrity, with a sense of buoyancy, with a sense of gratitude for the previous night's rest, with a sense of what you desire to achieve on that specific day, you are tying into the energies of Mother Earth and of your mighty God Self. And because of the dual pole of your existence, the fact that you are anchored here between the world of form and the great ideational world of the divine idea, you will then manifest the dual polarity, the flame above transcendently meeting the pulsating flame below, blending the matrix of consciousness in the ascending son of God.

This, then, is manifest in your beating heart. The sense of victory pulsates and rises as the sun in the heavens sheds forth its first light, blazes forth across the sky unto the perfect zenith at noon and then sets in the west. So, with the touch of the feet upon the floor, the human consciousness seeks an ascending spiral of achievement, not the mere achievement of ephemeral goals but of eternal goals crystallized in form and vivified with the warmth and power of the Holy Spirit in action.

Now, beloved ones, the little acts that seem so insignificant are the acts for which you are accountable. And I tell you, ladies and gentlemen, when directed into the chalice of the cosmic sense, these minute acts make the difference in the balance scales in favor of one who becomes an ascended being and against those who yet remain in their sins, as it were, their inequities, their lack of achievement.

BECOME A CO-WORKER WITH THE MOST HIGH GOD

Inasmuch as I realize full well that you desire to overcome all outer conditions, I call to your attention that it is the power of your Presence that is able to give you your freedom. But you, as the individual monad, must respond to the voice of your Presence and rise to achieve that which cannot be done by the divine idea alone.

For the divine idea requires the response of your will and your willingness to accept that precious idea into the matrix of your own consciousness and being. Then, with a gestation period for the accomplishment of the form, the Manchild will come forth, or the living Christ in you, who himself is your victory. And in essence, then, you will be the victory of God.

Do you understand, beloved ones, that God created you and conceived you in his own immortal perfection? And when you manifest the perfection that is God, you are fulfilling the divine idea and bringing to fruition the divine plan, which makes you, in a very real sense, a partner or co-worker with the Most High God.

Through mutuality of understanding, through co-serving, man identifies with his own victory. It is this victory that has manifested in the heart of every ascended being and it is this victory that must manifest in you too ere you join the ranks of the ascended hosts of light.

Now I realize full well, ladies and gentlemen, that some among you cannot yet conceive of yourselves as ascended beings. For you have thought of yourselves as mortal for so long that it seems difficult for you to fit yourselves into the pattern of heaven.

I think, however, you would not object to it once you became accustomed to it, for you would find that much that is unpleasant in life would be sloughed off as you ascended into our radiance. You would find that much of what you love in life would be intensified, glorified, vivified, resurrected and ascended into a full-orbed realm of existence.

HOW TO SCULPT YOUR OWN WORK OF ART

I would like to point out to the students this morning the importance of accepting the dawn of the first tracings of your divinity and victory. Beloved ones, when a sculptor sets about to create a statue or work of art from his mental image, and the pure [uncut] marble stands before him, you must remember that the first chippings of the stone yield little else but an image that in itself is practically nothing.

The first chippings of the stone do not seem to produce any reality whatsoever, and it is only the final finishing strokes of the work of art that reflect the true embellishment of the divine idea. Therefore, bear in mind, as the sculpting goes on and the hammer and chisel are actively guided by the divine will, that until almost the final stroke, the statue has manifested naught but what appears to the consciousness as a ludicrous image or a caricature not at all like the divine. Yet I would point out that it is steadfastly approaching the divine.

Beloved ones, when you consider this factor from a higher standpoint, you will have revealed to you a very great law, and I would expound still further on that law to assist you to your victory. Beloved ones, the most crude image, a work that has just commenced, is of course distinguishable from one that has been under the influence of the chisel for some time. But when you consider that the final strokes are quickly accomplished, you will realize that no one is altogether free from mars of imperfection. And therefore, do you see, it is but a matter of the finishing strokes being applied to a lifestream.

If you consider this more fully, you will recognize that those who are almost perfect require few strokes of the chisel to bring them to a manifest perfection, whereas those who are farther from perfection may not resemble that which is almost perfect. Do you see, then, beloved ones, the comparison I am drawing for you?

It does not, then, behoove any individual to gaze upon the caricature of another with criticism or condemnation, for this is ever the action of the human that hinders the one so doing far more than the one discussed or criticized. I would call this to your attention because these are the things that hinder you from expressing your victory, and these are the negative qualities you must shun and shed if you would escape into the higher octaves.

Now, ladies and gentlemen, I would like to call to your attention that you yourself often hold in your hand the chisel of your attention, struck by the hammer of power, guided by your spiritualized will to produce in your own being those refinements of character for which you long and for which you strive.

I would like to point out to you, however, that at times a certain action takes place whereby a stroke of the chisel brings about a condition that was not in the mind of the designer. Thus it is necessary to start again to create a different form from the original pattern, which ultimately must be made true to the original design. This means, beloved ones, that some backtracking is necessary for individuals who have made a few wrong strokes in the development and refinement of their character.

Patience, then, is needed by every chela in attaining his victory, and all chelas must be particularly patient with each other if they would receive patience for themselves from the great mercy of life. Frequently individuals wonder why they are not making proper progress although they have made intense application.

Well, let me tell you, beloved ones, sometimes it is not so much what you have not done as what you *do* that brings about your downfall. For the little things that seem so insignificant are actually a hindrance to your victory. And by shedding these conditions, the full momentum of your lifestream given to you in the beginning from the heart of God will be able to make its mark and quickly perform a work of God perfection in your world to show forth your victory and make you worthy of wearing the laurel wreath of spiritual achievement.

BE ALERT TO IMPLEMENT YOUR VICTORY!

On behalf of the great ascended host, I desire to express our gratitude to the students for the mighty tides of love and light that have been sent out constantly for and on behalf of mankind, enabling us to propel the evolutions of this planet still closer to the heart of God and to the grand design of the Great White Brotherhood, kept so wondrously for this planet by the Great Silent Watcher.

Ladies and gentlemen, I implore you now to cast off the weights that so easily beset you and to recognize the need to be watchful, to be wakeful, to be alert for the causes that will propel you toward your victory. Yearning is not enough; you must implement your yearning with right action, and this right action must be under the guidance of the Holy Spirit.

The Holy Spirit, beloved ones, is never fooled by the outer action of the human mind or by the feelings of mankind. The Holy Spirit is itself a direct descent of the essence of God's consciousness and therefore must be recognized for what it is, the blessed vehicle of the divine expression, a messenger from the very heart flame of the eternal One, an ambassador of goodwill who will help each individual to flood himself with the essential ideas forthcoming from the mind of God at the center of victory.

THE GOLDEN LAUREL WREATH OF VICTORY

I would like to point out to you that in the great flame of God's victory there is a golden laurel wreath of cosmic victory that is never given to any individual; it is given solely to their divine God Presence. This golden laurel wreath of victory is given to the individualized God Presence of each one when a complete merging of the mighty manifestation of God in man with the mighty Presence of life has occurred, so that man has ascended into his perfection.

When this is accomplished, the great crown of victory and the golden laurel wreath of cosmic achievement is given to the God Presence. For I tell you, your God Presence plays a tremendous part in your own achievement, and it is this God Presence that deserves the full blessing for all the manifestations of power magnetized into your world.

I tell you, ladies and gentlemen, it is not your human self who brings you your freedom. It is that marvelous protector of the sheep, the Good Shepherd of your Divine Self, who has yearned over you and exalted you and lifted you up out of imperfection and out of unholy vibrations time and time again, and will continue to do so until you shed the last vestiges of human creation and stand forth as a son of God born of pure flame.

[You shall be] worthy, then, through the divine union with your God Presence, of participating in the receipt of the golden laurel wreath of your cosmic achievement from the heart of God in the Great Central Sun. You will have become the golden man in manifestation for the eternal golden age of living perfection. [You will have attained] the ascended consciousness of those entrusted with the secrets of the universe, to whom God can impart the innermost secrets of his heart.

This, then, is the goal. Who, then, is worthy to receive it?

I say unto you, the life above that has magnetized and drawn you to the great power of the ascending flame is able. You, then, ought to pay allegiance to that God Self and the sense of cosmic victory so that you may receive from the heart of your Presence the impetus of God-victory in your world and make it a part of your daily ritual of living.

To develop a sense of victory and to retain it is indeed a marvelous empowerment for every lifestream, for a sense of victory will actually infuse itself into your bones until you recognize that victory is manifest physically, mentally, emotionally and spiritually by your God-control of every outer circumstance, whereby the soul of God in you, the soul of victory, controls the outer form in absolute purity of meaning, essence and being.

Ladies and gentlemen, in the name of your eternal victory from out the Great Central Sun, I salute you and bid you good afternoon.

November 10, 1963
The Dodge House
Washington, D.C.
MLP

A DISPENSATION OF THE FLAME OF VICTORY

Hail, O mankind of earth! I AM come from Venus, our lovely star, to speak to you of your victory, and as I am speaking to you, it has been arranged by the entire Great White Brotherhood that my voice should be heard in the Grand Teton Retreat simultaneously with this transmission here at Beacon's Head. You will appreciate, then, that solemn moments and joyous moments conspire to bring about meetings of the Brotherhood all over the planet on behalf of victory for the earth and her evolutions.

I am certain that mankind has been diligent, or at least they have felt that they were diligent, in many matters pertaining to the kingdom of God, but, beloved ones, I would like to call your attention to the fact that human judgment is always relative to human experience. And I think, then, that you will acknowledge (and if you will not acknowledge it, I am certain that your higher mental body will) that the power of light and the wisdom of light exceed the domain of human reason.

And therefore, we want to tell you now—not by reason of discouragement but to bring about encouragement of greater effort—that the services rendered by mankind of earth, including the spiritual people of ages past, have been insufficient to meet the demands of life itself in the onward rush toward perfection.

Thus, the forces of evil and human discord have actually grown up in the garden of God, as weeds grow up in gardens unattended or relatively so. And therefore this precious earth, which ought to be Victory's garden, which ought to be like my garden, is not, you see, a garden of victory.

In many cases it is a garden of hopelessness, for man continues to follow the same old patterns of imperfection without regard to the wondrous outpouring of love and light that has descended from on high to this planetary body in the person of the countless avatars and blessed ones who have given their all.

Tonight I am particularly conscious of the magnificent service of your Mother Mary. I am particularly conscious of the service of Saint Teresa of Avila and I am particularly conscious of the service of Jeanne d'Arc. You see then, precious ones, that mankind has been served, in many cases, by the feminine ray, although masculine leaders are often more popular, perhaps because they have a bit more dash and verve.

KEEP THE VISION OF YOUR PERFECTION

I think mankind today is coming into greater awareness of the reasonableness of reembodiment and many understand in a wider way that life is an onrush toward perfection. You see, precious ones, there is something very hopeless about the concept of having only one life wherein individuals feel that they have made mistakes and that those mistakes were very great.

When they feel that they have made mistakes and they feel the onrush of age in the human sense of the time-space continuum, they sometimes enter into the concept that life has passed them by. And they feel then (which is actually playing into the sinister hands of the evil strategists) that there is no need for them to change their ways. Indeed, they do not feel capable of doing so.

Precious ones, you must not believe this lie. Among yourselves you have a saying "You are only as young as you feel." Well, I would call to your attention that your victory lies in resurrecting a spiritual vision of perfection from the mind of God and letting that vision flow through your flesh form, through your mind, through your feeling world to assert its God-control, which will give you your victory here and now as has always happened in every other system of worlds similar to your own.

I think that many of you are aware of the fact that in the vast cosmos, the earth is but a pinpoint of light. Therefore you have no illusions about this planet being the hub of the universe and you recognize accurately that the Great Central Sun is the center of all that goes on in the cosmos. Then, precious ones, recognize the power of the perfection of the mind of God and call forth that perfection by [amplifying and] re-amplifying the power of light in your own consciousness.

THE POWER OF INTENSIFICATION

I would call to your attention that you can place a candle upon an altar, light it and see that it gives forth the light of one candle. You can then place another candle beside it to have two candles, and the power of three is easily added.

Suppose, precious ones, you were to place a series of candles within the space of one square foot so that the entire area was taken up by the flames of these candles. Do you see, then, how one square foot of space could manifest a much greater light when completely filled with light than when it simply contained the flame of one candle?

Therefore the power of intensification must be understood. You can actually add to the power and victory of your light by a concentrated effort of faith. I could cite several examples of individuals who felt that they were relatively insecure in their worlds by reason of their limitations, who quite suddenly became aware of the tremendous opportunity of the mind of God.

They then threw off the yoke of human limitation and recognized the power of cosmic victory. This amounted to the lighting of many candle flames within the perimeter of their identity, as opposed to the dying out of the embers of the flame that they had imagined they had and that they had presumed was going out because the oil and saturation of tallow in the wick was coming to an end.

Precious ones, you are connected to God and his limitless light energy. You need never feel that you are limited by reason of human concepts, for they do indeed become a weight that holds you down, like the power of gravity itself, in a situation that resembles the grave.

You call it a rut, but I tell you, it is worse than a rut; it is a living grave. For it is the placing of life's opportunities into a shroud of insecurity, into a shroud of degradation and into the grave itself, and thus mankind do not permit themselves the full range of divine expression that they otherwise would have in an embodiment.

ONE WITH GOD IS A MAJORITY

You have heard it said and you have mentally accepted the concept that one with God is a majority. But, precious ones, have you put it into practice or is it merely a matter of accepting that which sounds wholly reasonable? Let me tell you, precious ones, there is a vast difference between just accepting that which is wholly reasonable and actually practicing it by going out to do the will of God to become an overcomer.

I take the example of your own precious Saint Germain in his embodiment as Christopher Columbus. You recognize, of course, that at the court of Queen Isabella there were many opponents of the support she gave him. And tonight I am particularly interested in calling your attention to the fact that an individual here in this room is one who you would never believe was actually in physical embodiment.

This individual, in feminine form, is the reembodiment of Queen Isabella. She herself has no idea or awareness of the fact and is wholly innocent of the position and authority she then held. She is here tonight because Saint Germain has never forgotten to express his gratitude to her lifestream for the assistance she gave him in the discovery of this great land of America.

I shall not reveal her, lest she herself be lifted up with human pride and tempted by the powers of darkness. I therefore ask that none of you speculate as to who she is, for this is not nearly so important as is your understanding of how the gratitude of Saint Germain, your own Saint

Germain, has flowed back to this lifestream. He has seen to it that she was propelled into this activity to receive the violet-flame instruction and a mighty assistance of light toward her ascension.[1]

BUILD A MOMENTUM OF GOOD KARMA

Thus, do you see, precious ones, that every single act and right thought is recorded in the records of akasha? Do you see that life itself provides an impetus to victory for all? Is it not wise, then, to build a momentum of good karma before God and man?

Is it ever wise to spew out your untransmuted human venom upon an individual, simply because you cannot contain it within yourself? Is it ever wise to be an individual filled with vitriolic hatred toward any part of life?

I think not, for these things hinder your victory and cause you to be gravity bound for a much greater period of time. The power of light that assists you to your ascension is the Christ light of your higher mental body, transferred down to the domain of the physical body so that all of the dross and gross senses can be purified by the power of light.

And as the substance leaves your body as smoke at the top of your head, the power of transmutation's flame actually creates a condition of relative loss of weight. For example, an individual weighing one hundred pounds might find that if the substances of hate and hate creation and human selfishness were removed from his bones he might lose as much as ten pounds in one day. Do you see, then, that these conditions actually hold down the body to the earth. They are dense substances that need purification in order to give you your freedom and your victory.

Now, I hope that none of you will be so foolish as to rush to a scale to weigh yourselves to see whether your density has increased or decreased simply because of my statement! But I hope you will realize that in the eyes of God a good karmic record, a mark for victory, can be recorded in the higher octaves. Then in a given moment, a number of pounds, up to a hundred or even a hundred and fifty, can drop from you until you weigh perhaps as little as one or two pounds.

Then, when the mighty power of the Holy Spirit comes along by the power of light to stand over you like a mighty magnet, as it did over beloved Jesus, your body in its relatively weightless condition will rise up into the cloud of light that is waiting to receive you. Do you see, precious ones?

And then in that cloud of light you can be completely renewed with even the white hair on your head restored to its proper color. In fact, precious ones, if necessary, the very teeth in your mouth will grow in at that very moment and every condition in your body will be restored to absolute perfection—a perfection that you do not even dream of.

RESOLVE TO HAVE YOUR VICTORY

You will recall that after his ascension beloved Jesus did appear to Saint Paul by the wayside and did say unto him, "It is hard for thee to kick against the pricks."[2] You see, precious ones, after his ascension beloved Jesus had the power to appear to mankind and he still has the power to materialize his form.

In the higher octaves of light, however, it is so much more comfortable to move about sans the physical body, or flesh body of form, such as you now wear. Therefore, your electronic body of light is the comfortable body that mankind desires to wear. Would it not be, I ask you, a wonderful gift to you right now if your physical forms were without weight and you did not feel the pressure of bones and substance within that flesh form that sometimes causes you to feel a bit uncomfortable?

Perhaps when you are in our radiation your body takes on more of the qualities of light, provided you are properly attuned. But then I am sure that you are not content to sit as you now are in a state of inertia and let us do it for you. You want your own victory! [Audience rises.] I am certain you do and therefore I say to you, there is no reason under heaven why you cannot have it! It is up to you, strictly up to you, precious ones.

Countless numbers of individuals have ascended in the past year and I think that the forthcoming year shall also see a number of ascensions. Therefore there is no reason for you to put off the resolution that will give you your victory; you might as well make up your mind now rather than later. What better time is there than right now? Why defer it, precious ones?

Do you realize when you summon the power of light to your cause and say to the light, "I wish to make my ascension. I wish to have my freedom as soon as possible," that you actually set in motion a great cosmic law that will assist you to your victory? Well then, precious ones, do you see how important it is that you do not further delay making this resolution? (Won't you please be seated.)

A DISPENSATION OF THE FLAME OF VICTORY

I come here tonight to give you a great momentum of my victory. Therefore, in an almost unprecedented action, I have asked the seven Holy Kumaras to release their tremendous flame of victory into this room so that their momentum will become available for you to draw upon and to have and to hold for twenty-four hours, so that you might have the pressure of their light and love to reinforce your resolution.

Well, precious ones, how would you like to know the truth of what has happened? It almost took an act of Congress, as you would say, to get this through. Yet, because of the yearning of the powers of light to see more people have their freedom, we have been able to get this concession from the Lords of Flame from the planet Venus.

Therefore they are now sending down mighty streams of light to the planetary body. [The light] has not yet reached the periphery of the outer atmosphere of the earth but I will tell you when it does, so that you may attune with it and feel the great surge of their God flames.

Precious ones, I call to your attention that I think beloved Jesus, beloved Saint Germain and beloved Master Morya provided you with a greater measure of perfection than you dreamed of when you elected to come to this class. And I think that you must also recognize that [this dispensation] is not something we are bestowing only upon you; it is something we wish to make available to all on this planetary body on the occasion of their reading my words or listening to them for the first time.

Do you see, precious ones? We have asked the Lords of Karma to place a charge within the lifestream of every individual upon this planet, which can be activated or reactivated as the case may be, at the specific moment they read this instruction or hear it for the first time. They may then enter into the selfsame attitude of comprehension you do, and the same opportunity may be given to all to be assisted by the momentum of the seven Holy Kumaras and the Lords of Blue Flame from Venus.

Now, precious ones, the beloved Lords of Blue Flame have contacted the outer atmosphere of the earth and they are beginning their descent into this area. I call to your attention that they come with great light, almost meteoric in its flashing forth.

The [Cosmic] Christ, Lord Maitreya, and beloved Jesus have both lowered their eyes at this moment. They have raised their hands in holy prayer and adoration to God for this glorious outpouring of love and light. Now, precious ones, the Lords of Blue Flame, the seven Holy Kumaras and a certain cosmic being, who was not at first revealed, are within one hundred feet of this building and coming on. [pause]

They are here! [Audience stands.] And as the light of ten thousand suns, they blaze forth their tremendous radiance and assistance to this planet for the commemoration of the victory of your beloved Jesus, and of every ascension that has ever been made by the power of light!

I add my flame of victory to it and I pray that all of you will recognize this wondrous and marvelous outpouring of light for all that it can and shall mean to your lifestream if you will accept it! It is a penetrating substance. It flashes forth through your very bones. It has the coolness of running water and the electrifying vigor of the elixir that Saint Germain administered to David Lloyd.[3] It is a tremendous assistance of light! It is a tremendous power to your whole lifestream!

Drink deeply, then, of the draught of the sacred fire, the gift of these beloved beings. Know that every child of light in the universe desires to send his momentum of cosmic victory through your being so that you can be a representative of God upon earth and stop the action of human karma and karma making.

Precious ones, I say to you now and always, accept your victory, love your victory, feel your victory, be your victory, know your victory, and declare it by saying:

*I AM my victory fulfilled right now
by the power of the three-times-three and
by the power of the sacred fire,
worlds without end.*

In the name of God Victory, who I AM, I thank you and I bid you good evening.

April 18, 1965
Beacon's Head
Vienna, Virginia
MLP

9

VICTORY IS TO THE FREE

I AM come! Victory is my name and I AM charged with victory, not only with my victory but also with the victory of life, the victory of Almighty God.

I see, then, this planet as a jewel of immortal perfection, a diadem of magnificence, and I feel the great flame of life, which pulsated in the mind of God as he conceived this holy sphere charged with beauty and purity and light essence and iridescence and all that is perfection and cosmic charm.

Why should I look and gaze upon the thrusts men have made into the pool of vanity? Why should I submit to the vicissitudes and wrong ideas of men? I shall not and I do not expect that you should either.

O precious ones of the light, yours is a spiritual search whereby the great victory beam of your mind penetrates the miasma of mortal consciousness and sees, through the pall of human misery, the pure plan of the future projected on the screen of life. Yours is [the resolve] not to submit, not to recline in a consciousness of mortal ideas but to gaze upward to the mighty strength from on high.

You have heard the cry that went forth of old, "I will lift up mine eyes unto the hills, from whence cometh my help. My strength cometh from the Lord, which made heaven and earth."[1] Well, charming ones, let me tell you that if you are to be flowers in the garden of my heart, it must be because you are willing to shine with the light of the sun and to be an immortal being even while you are yet cast in the pall of mortal shroud.

You see, gracious ones, the unfailing light of God does not depend for its sustenance upon mankind and human effort. It moves effortlessly through the universe and accomplishes the pure purposes of life. You, O beloved ones, are surrounded, it is true, with all manner of mortal thoughts and arrows of hostility, but these have no power over the immortal soul or over the original divine plan.

Therefore thy strength, as my strength, is in the great God flame. You cannot permit yourself to go down in this struggle but must always release yourself, as your beloved Saint Germain has said, from the sense of struggle to hold inviolate in the mind of Christ, the pure mind of God, the awareness and the realization that truth is stronger than fiction.

I COME TO GLORIFY THE PERSON OF LIGHT THAT YOU ARE

You have a saying here that "Truth is stranger than fiction." Well, I tell you, truth is stronger than fiction. And I repeat it for you that you may let it sink down into the channels of your heart and feel the buoyancy that I AM.

I AM the full buoyancy of God. I AM the full radiation of his victory. I AM the full consciousness of cosmic achievement. I hold, then, the purity of light in my being. And as I come to you tonight it is not in any way to glorify my person but to glorify the person of light that you are.

For the reality of God is just as real, precious ones, in an individual who is not deemed worthy of notice by ordinary mankind as it is when the mind of God flashes forth to behold one whom the world acclaims. You see, precious ones, Almighty God considers every son of his heart equal, willing and able to fulfill the destiny of the beloved Son.

In his heart and mind, God has no limitation concerning anybody, no matter who they may be or what they may have done. For human error and human dust do not have power over the mortal mind when that mortal mind can be dashed to the ground as a broken vessel and the pure flame of the soul can reach up and be the mind of Christ in healing action.

The mind of Christ in healing action must be invoked. Mankind must be willing to invoke it and take the consequences thereof. When individuals are unwilling to invoke the mind of God because they wish to hide in the shadowed pools of their own lowliness of spirit, it is a great pity, for mankind will only find release from mortal suffering as they shed the consciousness of the mundane and cognize the pure flame of the Spirit.

HOLD THE LIGHT INVIOLATE IN YOUR BEING

And now, precious ones, a more than ordinary action of light is about to take place in this room. At first I projected into the room a ray of light from on high and from the Holy Kumaras upon Venus, but now I have descended and I am here, in the very center of this room, radiating my love and my light to those students who are able to feel and to know that I AM the power of God unto salvation to those who can hold the blazing victory of light inviolate in their being.

O precious ones, some do not understand even the meaning of words. When I say *inviolate,* I mean that no power in heaven or earth shall have any power whatsoever over that lifestream but only the power of their victory.

You see, other ideas take possession of the mind and then victory must take a back seat and the individual must wait until it can manifest. But when those other ideas take a back seat and victory comes to the fore, then there is a special action whereby the individual is given an accelerated activity to speed up his spiritual power and victory. (Won't you please be seated.)

MANKIND FEARS THE FUTURE

Now, then, let us examine the world situation. At the present moment, when millions of minds are focused upon the idea of world conflict and disorder, when millions of minds are determined that fear and shadow and domination are about to descend upon them and they seek only for the protection of their own little corner of madness, then, you see, you have a holocaust of division.

Then the souls of men, rather than working in unison, function individually in complete dissipation of the cosmic power of Mother Earth, for man does loot the wondrous spiritual treasures vouchsafed to him. Think you, precious ones, that when an individual prays unto God for the destruction of another individual that that prayer brings about victory to any part of life?

You see, however, that the brothers of the shadow, through their wrong thought creations, project human discord into the minds of men through the miasma of fear. They cause individuals to fear the future when that future is securely held within their individualized God-victory.

You see, no individual upon the planet can substitute for another insofar as his karmic responsibility goes. When an individual performs a wrong act, it must fall as the hammer of justice before the feet of that one and in some cases such a one must be brought to his knees that later he may be raised.

This is the law of being, for whatever men send out into the universe, whether it be in ignorance or in understanding, the Law is impartial in the return of those currents. And mankind will one day feel and know the very lash that they employ.

Those who employ the beatitudes of love and the purity of Christ's concepts and illumination cannot help but feel, reap and be the fullness of that which they have sent out. Therefore the path Godward, the meteoric rise in splendor, is accomplished by a sense of victory.

When men forget the delusions that have caused them only pain and suffering and feel that every atom of their being is a reflection of Almighty Victory, it shall bring about a change in the consciousness of that one. This is an irrevocable law.

PLACE YOUR FAITH AND TRUST IN GOD

Somehow or other, individuals have come to divide the world's thought —and I refer here to the world's religious thought—into classifications, whereby individuals on the Path who search for life do classify and thereby subjugate themselves to these classifications.

If, for some reason, they find a specific religious quality to be an anathema to their parents or friends, they may not deign to take notice thereof. They may decide that they will pursue another path or perhaps pursue no path at all. This, then, effectively restrains them from being the beneficiaries of Almighty God's intent.

But when an individual is willing to cast out of his day-to-day consciousness the towering thoughts of his own magnificence as an excellent judge and simply place his faith and trust and his hand in the hand of Almighty God as a child would do, then a beautiful flow of spiritual magnetism occurs in his world.

And it happens almost on the instant, so that the sense of victory that I seek to convey tonight can come about as if by magic, as individuals begin to feel and know that they are the victory of life and not a reflection of human thought and consciousness. Feeling must be subdued by light, for feeling is often seething emotion, like a bubbling pot that somehow or other does not accomplish the purpose for which it was set to bubble.

Therefore I say to all of you, be still and be at peace. Be still and know that I AM God. Be still and know that thou art God. Be still and know that thou art God Victory. Still the human ideas and even the human ideals that are not rooted in the purity of divine concepts. Admit into the great forcefield of your being the pulsations of my victory.

I GIVE YOU A JEWEL OF LIGHT

Now tonight, as I stand here before you vested with the spiritual power of the seven Holy Kumaras, I am anxious to bestow a portion of my momentum upon those who can recognize in their heart the meaning of what I am saying.

Be still, then, as I seek to penetrate thy consciousness with a ray of victory to impart to you a magnificent jewel that I hope you will always wear in your heart as a token of remembrance. Then, precious ones, whenever you feel inclined to human decrepitude, whenever you feel inclined to let the mind go down into the valleys of negation, you can gaze with inward eyes upon the brilliant diamond-shaped jewel I have placed within the hearts of all who accept my love tonight.

And seeing that jewel embodying a ray of imprisoned victorious splendor flashing therein, you may recall this night that I spake unto you and urged you to accept a ray of my victory now and forever.

CHOOSE A QUALITY TO EMBODY

Victory is the quality I embody. It is the quality you can embody, and no desecration occurs therein. For the beauty of God is that whenever an individual desires to embody a specific divine quality and to amplify that quality—not to parade it before his fellowmen but to bless and heal them with that quality—that individual can gather an accumulation thereof.

Then, just as money is deposited in the bank and the balance continues to rise, so individuals will find this specific divine quality becoming more and more evident in their world. You see, then, a thought of goodness, a thought of service, a thought of victory, a thought of purity can accomplish its purpose.

And one by one, individuals can take a thought and expand it in their world until the full meaning thereof is released to them from the heart of God—he who embodies all sacred qualities and is the fullness of them all.

Let me tell you that in my own case I chose and elected to embody the quality of victory; and because the quality of victory flooded my being, by the power of that single quality of love and light from the heart of God I succeeded in winning my Victory, my ascension and my freedom. Therefore I did not need to externalize any other quality, for in my search for victory I found them all.

I discovered their reality and used and employed them all in obtaining my Victory. Therefore, to me the mighty flag of cosmic victory is the most beautiful, the most wonderful, the greatest quality of all life, for it means your freedom.

Your beloved Saint Germain chose to take another quality. He expressed the flame of freedom and expanded that flame even as I expanded the flame of victory. Your beloved Paolo Veronese, the beloved Paul the Venetian, chose to expand the flame of liberty and the pure love of liberty.

Every individual can choose a flame. And the beauty of it, precious ones, is that it does not make any difference whether you choose a flame for yourself that we have already honored or another. For the power of expandability in the consciousness of God is such that all his sons and daughters may elect and choose for themselves a quality they desire to have help them on the pathway to their victory.

Therefore I do not care, precious ones, if you choose and elect to take another quality than that of pure victory, for each one will assist you to find the victory you seek. And I know that just as you have a saying that "Every cloud has a silver lining," so behind the appearance of something less than victory, a little bit of victory is lurking.

For, you see, there is no such thing as non-victory, for victory is life and life is God and God is victory! Therefore you cannot make a non-God. You cannot make a non-victory. You can never extinguish my flame in the universe or in yourself.

"HEAR, O ISRAEL, THE LORD THY GOD IS ONE LORD"

Whether you accept my flame, whether you accept the pulsation of that flame, whether you realize it, whether you feel it expanding out into the atmosphere, whether or not you are aware of the angels of victory I bring with me, it does not make one bit of difference—not one tiny bit of difference. For the time will come when every part of life everywhere in the universe will be compelled by the mighty advancement of life itself to accept the flame of victory that I AM, to acknowledge the flame of victory that I AM, to be the flame of victory that I AM.

Thus we will merge our flames as one in the heart of God. "Hear, O Israel, the Lord thy God is one Lord."[2] Hear, O ye who can, all that is real:

the Lord thy God is One. Hear, O mankind of earth, let those who will, beat the drums of dissonance and discord. Let them choose and elect the offbeat rhythm that they may break up the patterns of purity.

They shall rue the day they chose ill and pay the full penalty and the last farthing thereof. Not one soul who has set his hand to the plow, who has forgotten and forsaken the ways of the world and the ways of non-victory to choose to pursue the path of victory will ever rue the day. For the light of God that never fails is the fullness of the victory of every individual who can feel, know and be that which I AM both now and forever.

OUR WORDS ARE A RELEASE OF SACRED FIRE

You see, O mankind of earth, the words I am speaking to you are more than mere words. They are a release of the sacred fire essence from on high, from our planet, Venus, and they are charged with the holy love of the beloved Lady Venus and the beloved Sanat Kumara.

O precious ones, as I am speaking to you, the blazing light of Sanat Kumara is drawing very near. I feel the beloved Ancient of Days as he chooses to utter the power of the sacred name of God, I AM, from on high to blaze a pathway from the stars to this focus to see the magnificent accomplishment [taking place] here tonight in the temple of the unfed flame.

Now, a recalcitrant condition, which would not yield to the power of light and would not yield to the power of the calls of the individuals who have long pursued their victory, must drop away from them now as they grasp the flame of victory I am releasing here tonight. It is the fullness of the light of God that never fails.

Therefore the hand of beloved Sanat Kumara bears a blazing torch, carrying the very fire of the star of his being upon his forehead. I am also causing the great flame of victory upon my forehead to rise to three times its normal height. [I do this] that men may feel the ultra-release into their world of that flame of victory so that they may choose thereby to magnify it tonight in a world that so solemnly needs more of the sense of victory and less of the sense of defeat.

O precious ones, it is so strange that mankind must continually be enthralled by the senses and think that the living, blazing realities of God are mere figments of the imagination. Why, I tell you, precious ones, we could burst out laughing and laugh forever if it were not such a serious matter. For it is a serious matter for individuals who do not understand that the great pall of ignorance clouding their minds must be dissipated by the light of transcendent truth.

DO NOT DOUBT MY REALITY

Therefore I say to you all tonight: With joy and happiness cast aside and discard your human reason that tells you I do not exist. Some individuals have doubts about the reality of my being, for they come from other religious activities and are not familiar with my name. They are not familiar with my reality.

I do not hold this against them but I assure them that if they would call upon me for the next seven days and recognize that there is a very strong possibility that I am real, I will make every attempt to cross the valley they have created in their consciousness and bridge this chasm of shadow by the release of a specific accomplishment for which they have longed for some time.

I will do this as a token of regeneration. I will do this in order to assist their faith to mount up as with eagle wings. I will do this in order to produce greater harmony in the world by enlarging the borders of the kingdom of God. This is our will. This is the will of God. This is the will of the Great White Brotherhood.

This is the mighty challenge of life. This is the purification of the world of man, for man has made his world a very muddied one indeed. And the impure colors that are worn today by many among mankind must yield to the beautiful pastels and radiance of the rainbow rays.

The power of victory in life must become more evident physically that the purity of light and the example set before the youth and children of the world may be manifest not only here but elsewhere upon the planetary body. Then shall the great scientific accomplishments of our beloved planet, Venus, be made known unto the Earth and man shall understand how he can perform great surgery and services of light by spiritual light rays.

Man shall understand that he no longer need employ the old techniques that will be aborted by the onrush of new and victorious accomplishments in every field of human endeavor, specifically in the realm of Spirit. For he must learn that Spirit can conquer dust and flood forth the ascension light to free mankind now and forever.

THE RECORD OF JESUS' ASCENSION

I call to your attention tonight an image of Bethany's hill as a summoning of regeneration in thought and feeling. I have asked the angel of record responsible for the recording of the ascension of your beloved Jesus to bring that record into this forcefield tonight to see that his ascension energies are released into the atmosphere here so that you may experience some action in the inner realm that will assist you to attain your own ascension.[3]

Therefore, as they are getting ready to play this record through our cosmic recording mechanism, I would like you to pass through the great drama and ritual of Jesus' ascension in the light. Will you stand, therefore, in the awareness that by uprightness of heart mankind is able to assimilate uprightness of spirit. [Audience stands.]

God is upright. And when men ascend, they do so because they have cast off the old and filthy garments of mortal thought and have changed them, by the power of the sacred fire, into the great victory of life. Life flows through their atoms, and therefore their flesh form feels the mighty light rays of God remove the old, tired, fatigued state of consciousness from their being, causing the roseate hue of the dawn of spiritual victory to flow through the blood and change it into golden liquid light.

Then the mighty fire of the heart, breaking forth from the chalice thereof, surges up with the golden light of victory. This beautiful golden light pours through the hands and the light rays are directed downward toward earth to release the hold of gravity. The beautiful Christ consciousness rises upward from the ground, first a half an inch, then an inch, then a foot, then three feet, then seven feet, then twelve feet and then on and on and on until the great cloud of spiritual light, the substance from on high, the sacred fire jewel from the heart of God, the chariot of fire that raised Elijah descends and bears that victorious Christed one out of physical sight.

When this occurred to your beloved Jesus, he said, "Lo, I am with you alway, even unto the end of the age."[4] And so the angels descended and said: "This same Jesus, which is taken up from you into heaven, shall so come in like manner as ye have seen him go into heaven,"[5] and the victory of light produced this perfection. He has descended many times since and has manifested his beautiful luminous presence unto mankind in many parts of the world, and the prophecy has been fulfilled and will be again and again and again.

And one day, as each of you wins the victory of your ascension as he did, you will know, as he did, the bond of spiritual brotherhood.

You will understand the healing touch of his hand.
You will understand the power of light's band.
You will understand the power that thrust through
And is your victory—the victory of you and you!
Each one must attain the reality of life.
Each one must put an end to mortal strife.
Each one must purify himself
And be the essence, the life, the love of victory.

YOUR VICTORY IS MY VICTORY

Your victory, then, is my victory. When each one of you attains the victory of life, you become as I am. And I am as you are in reality now. For, precious ones, perhaps you think that you are less than perfect now. Nay. I say the image of Almighty God, which he held of thee as thou camest forth from the pure white-fire essence, the white-fire core of life, is still the same today, yesterday and forever.

It is the changeless garment that you need never change. It is the changeless radiance that you would not change or part with. It is the great reality and truth of life that ends for every lifestream all struggle and sense thereof. It is the blessing of life, when men begin to experience a new birth in higher octaves and go on to become illustrious in the mind of God.

That which is here on earth is but a beginning, a tender beginning. All that is here of pain, suffering and sorrow is but an ending of mortality flashing forth, that on the morrow the beauty and purity of the new page, the new beginning, may be made known. Then, as you begin to live in the consciousness of the throne of power and victory over yourself, you will know the meaning of the words we caused to be put upon the temples of old, the ancient inscription "Man, know thyself."

I say to thee tonight through the power of Serapis, who has flashed forth his consciousness and stands beside me upon this platform, that the power of the ascension action for three individuals in this room shall occur within the next ten years. I do not choose to have it hovering over you as a point of speculation; therefore, I have increased the range that you may not know what I mean.

But the ascension currents are spiraling up from the temple of the unfed flame and you may bask in this radiance and set yourselves free as I am free. You shall be free, as all shall be free and as we shall be together in our great victory that is to come:

The victory that cannot be denied,
The victory that cannot be decried,
The victory that shall be, is now and is to come.
Man, know thyself.
Man, know that we are one.
Man, know that God is manifestation,
That manifestation when correctly understood
And accepted is God,
That God is Victory,
That the simultaneous action of freedom
Is instituted here, as it is elsewhere,
That many souls now in captivity may go free,

That the light of God and its strength
May become the light of men.
Wait not long and thou shalt see,
For victory is to the strong
As victory is to the free.

I thank you and I bid you adieu.

June 13, 1965
Los Angeles, California
MLP

10

BECOME THE MASTER OF YOURSELF

Hast thou seen the Pleiades?
Hast thou seen the bands of Orion?
Hast thou beheld creation's fire?
Then thou hast seen Victory! Mighty is the fire of creation touched by the hand of God, and every earth peals forth her note of beauty in the orchestration of our Father, your God and my God.

I AM Victory and victory belongs unto you! I AM the servant of mankind in the name of God. I desire to serve you [by assisting you] to obtain the priceless heritage that God has reserved for those who love him enough to win their fight against the forces of opposition. These forces would tear from them their wings of light, which God gave to all that all may rise.

Be still and know your I AM Presence! Be still and know the great Source, for the Cosmic Clock shall not become unwound. The great life-power of universal law will continue the creative round. And those who drop out of the holy place reserved for them by God—the place of sacred uniqueness that is the uni-tie between man and all creation—will be but wandering stars, to whom is reserved the mists of darkness forever.[1]

The light of God does not fail. And if men choose to deny the possibility of their own freedom and victory, it is man who walks into the dark. And I declare it: They shall not take God with them, for the LORD dwelleth in the light, and the secret place of the Most High God is the place of light. And the soul of man is intended to be a palace of light twinkling with myriad magnificent stars of consciousness.

THE MAGNIFICENT REALITIES OF LIFE

You recall in the enigma of Revelation, the Book of Revelation of John the Beloved, how the angelic beings are often compared to mighty stars.[2] Let me tell you of the star that is the focus of your Divine Presence within you. Let me tell you of your mighty threefold flame, which to some of you may appear as but a remote place upon the map of being.

O precious ones, when the realities of life, the mighty realities become interpreted by the soul as it ascends to the fount of divine wisdom and obtains the sacred keys, the revelations you will receive about yourself— and I say this to you all—are so magnificent as to compel you to turn your gaze forward, for no longer will you desire to look at former things.

Former things shall have passed away and all things will be ever-new joy, as the face of victory is turned to you and you become aware of the mighty purposes of creation within the fount of light in thy mind, the fount of illumination that by the transforming power of the Holy Spirit makes of the finite mind the mind of God and makes of the mortal mind the mind of Christ.

GOD CELEBRATES THE INDEPENDENCE OF MAN

Do you realize, precious ones, on this day throughout the land when men are shooting off their rockets and exploding various devices to celebrate the Fourth of July, the independence of the nation America, that God himself is also engaged in the practice of celebrating the independence of man from all forms of self-created tyranny?

For it was an act of God in the early days of this nation America that interceded on the part of the roughshod men and women of the thirteen sovereign states and caused them to have the stamina, the courage and the will to victory. You must understand, precious ones, that the power of God entered in to the hearts of these men to formulate their rising courage in the face of an entrenched tyranny and a mighty temporal power.

You must understand that there was a uni-tie between the hearts of the individuals who dwelt in the different states of that blessed union. You must understand that today, with the passing of time and the remoteness of historical events in the mind of present-day man, much of the glory and the power, much of the struggle and the winning has been bypassed.

Thus the youth today, and I am sorry to say, even some of the more mature have unfortunately lost sight of the struggles that were necessary in the winning of victory for the nation America. You must understand, then, that the spiritual struggle, which is of such cosmic worth, must go on, that high resolves must become not crystallized mental thought but vitalized cosmic action.

You must recognize that great cosmic beings and mighty masters of wisdom came down to the planet and in some cases spoke directly through the voices of the men of the time and reinforced their courage by directly moving their lips to speak the words of God and of liberty.

YOU ARE SPARKS OF FREEDOM

Similarly, in this day and age and in all ages, there is always a point of contact between the higher octaves and the planet itself, else the Light would go out, else Darkness would come, else the vanities of men would so smother the flame that there would be no oxygen to supply it and to assure it a continued existence.

The flame today needs to be fanned by many sons of freedom and liberty. You are sparks of freedom who are intended by God to function not only in the sociopolitical domain but also in the spiritual domain. [In the spiritual domain] especially, you can help to quicken the sons of earth who have lost their way. You can show them the pathway that leads to the mansions of light, which are above, ever above.

You must understand the pull of senseless activities, which in this present age are causing mankind to be discouraged and are multiplying the terrors of the dark. You must understand how these things are generated, as the Old Man of the Hills told you,[3] by a reaction from the powers of darkness who lash out against the spiritual forces of light, who would regenerate mankind and bring in the golden age.

The forces and powers of shadow, who function behind the flesh forms of individuals by tricking their minds and emotions, have created a commercial Gargantua today that threatens to engulf the entire planet in an opposing and contradictory force to the socialist and communist countries of the world to directly bring about the destruction of world society.

They do not care, my beloved brothers and sisters, whether or not they destroy the earth. They do not care whether or not they create chaos. They do not care whether or not the Spirit of Christ is fashioned in this day or the great carpenter of Nazareth is able to build and reconstruct a new world. Nay, they would prefer a shambles, which would mean the utter destruction of all planetary life.

They would rejoice in the destruction of mankind. For I want you to remember that if they were able to destroy the life that you now have upon this planet and to cause mankind to abide in other realms outside the body in the naked state of their souls, so to speak, a gnashing of teeth would indeed come to pass. For not enough individuals would be left upon the planet to assure mankind reembodiment, and many would have to wait for centuries in the wings of the great stage of life until the earth could be gradually rebuilt.

Also, if their activity became ultradestructive, it is possible that they could render the earth completely uninhabitable for so many generations that it would be necessary for us to transfer the lifewaves of this planet to another home in which to start all over again the arduous business of mastering life as you know it from the age of prehistoric man to the present day.

LIFE IS PRECIOUS

Look you well, then, to your victory. Look you well, then, to your life. It may seem to you that you are but a firefly flitting across the swamp of life and you may say, "But in a few short years, I, as myself, shall no longer be in this embodiment."

Let me tell you, precious ones, *life is precious!* Let me tell you, precious ones, that the gathering of opportunity is the summation of your life. Let me tell you, if you were to see the activity at inner levels that accompanied your birth, your natal day, you would realize that a universal conspiration* for the manifestation of each one of you caused you to come forth into this realm. It caused you to gather the substance of previous embodiments and focus all within the records of akasha and tie that to your four lower bodies so that you might move here to take advantage of cosmic opportunities and understand the need to draw yourselves into the fullness of cosmic purpose to fulfill the divine plan, the purpose of your All-Father.

Wise, then, is the one who understands the need to perpetuate and preserve life wherever possible, as long as possible, because each individual life is sacred. Sacred is the opportunity that gave you birth; sacred is the opportunity that gives you the opportunity to win your victory.

YOU NEED YOUR FLESH FORM

You must understand, then, that it is up to you to reinforce the great power of life within form. For life within form has purpose; life within form has divine purpose. While it is true that life is intended to be a schoolroom opportunity whereby you can master experience here to win your victory into higher realms (where you will not require this fleshly body but a new body of light), yet until you have won your perfection, I assure you that you have need for a flesh form.

Therefore do not take lightly the possibility of discarding the form that God and the elementals have so carefully and beautifully builded. You must understand that your body, which is the temple of God, houses an immortal soul intended to become an illustrious being of light as is your own Master Morya. If, then, you correctly understand your destiny, you will esteem the cosmic purpose for yourself individually.

O how treacherous is the thought—and I assure you that we teach this

conspiration: a joint effort toward a particular end

in our schools upon Venus—that robs man's immortal birthright from him and makes him feel belittled. Belittlement is one of the most horrible, awful and treacherous forces that has ever been generated in the universe by the nefarious consciousness of the sons of darkness.

Let me point out to you, then, that you should never attempt to belittle any individual upon this planet but attempt instead to raise mankind up, for so do ye the work of the Venusian masters and so do ye the work of the Lord Christ. The work of raising up mankind is perpetual and the help that cometh through you day and night is a work of magnitude that spans the foreverness of God.

YOU ARE INTENDED TO BE THE FULLNESS OF GOD

You must recognize that you are co-workers and co-servers with the powers of light, for so it was intended. You must recognize that you are children of cosmic love, for so it was intended. You must recognize that your destiny is to attain absolute mastery of self and the power to walk the earth as a God fashioned in the very image of God, for so it was intended!

You must recognize that you were intended to be the fullness of all that God is. And if this seems so high to you that you cannot imagine yourselves in this role, then call unto me and I will give you my momentum of victory that overcomes the world and all its thoughts of belittlement and smallness—its thoughts of limitation that seem to squeeze you into the mold of finite qualities.

I AM Victory! And I tell you that your victory is at hand!

[Audience rises.]

I AM Victory and I tell you that the powers of light and the cosmic councils are determined that mankind should escape from the awful traps laid to rob them of some of their rightful powers: the power to escape from all the traps laid in past generations, regardless of whether or not they themselves were karmically involved; the power to escape into the great Temple of Mercy at Peking and to understand that Kuan Yin sits there in this very hour and meditates on how she may draw to herself the souls of men.

She would send them forth into the world as her sons and daughters to create the quality of mercy and sustain that quality in life until all the cruelty was taken out of man, transmuted from his consciousness, and he was set free! (Won't you please be seated.)

THE SPIRIT OF OVERCOMING

O gracious ones, how lovely is the spirit of overcoming! The [powers of light] are they who have overcome. These are they who have overcome. These are they who have overcome!

What have they overcome?

Mortal thought, mortal density, the accretion and accumulation of years of wrong sowing. If this be true, we give no power to the opposition. But recognize it you must; you must recognize the opposition by turning to us with each thrust made against you.

If you cleave unto us, if you hold our hand, if you enter our consciousness, if you permit your consciousness to enter ours, if there is unity between us, then I do not think any power in heaven or earth can separate you from the love of God!

But you must understand that every positive statement must be reinforced by the power of action within your world. You must understand that it is not enough for us to utter a statement for and on behalf of your victory. You must accept that statement and believe in it, act upon it and be tied to it and united to it.

This, precious ones, is one of the reasons why down through the centuries and even as recently as twenty or forty years ago, various dictations came forth from our realm and octave promising victory unto mankind and giving them certain inalienable rights. These rights have indeed been given but they have not been claimed.

I want you to know, precious ones, that we have made our promises and fulfilled every one of them, but there has been and will always be a dual tie to all promises. We may not make our promises without having certain conditions met by unascended mankind.

You do not think, surely, that we are required to promise you that we will give you our support and assistance and then turn around and function at your level to receive that assistance, do you? You certainly do not expect that we should give you our energy and our love and then [be obliged to] move your hands to take it.

YOUR RESPONSIBILITY IS TO MASTER YOURSELF

I tell you, you have a very definite responsibility. Mankind's lack of awareness of this has been and still is to expect us to perform for them all the acts that were given to them to perform for themselves by *volens, volens, volens*—will, will, will!

Will must be generated within you for strength, strength, strength, and power, power, power until you become the master of yourself rather than let yourself be mastered by outer conditions. [These conditions] will bring you into bondage and keep you there if you do not watch out!

You have heard it said that parents would frighten their children by saying, "The goblins will get you if you don't watch out!" Well, I want to tell you today that this is more or less true, but the goblins are within the consciousness of man and they ought to be vanquished therefrom by the immortal power of victory!

Teach your children that they are required by the law of God to serve with alacrity, to understand as did Samuel of old that when God speaks, man must answer.[4] The compelling power of universal law is resident within man but it will not act unless he calls it into action.

God has implanted a certain segment of himself within you that is a seed of spiritual will. And every quality of God is within you although you do not realize it. It passes unnoticed and unrecognized while you look at your weaknesses and say, "This is me."

It is not you! It is not part of you! And I tell you today that if you do not rid yourself of those concepts, you will be placing yourself in the realm of stultification and stratification! And mankind will type you and they will say, "This is that type of individual." And it will be so. And they will cast you in a mold and it will be true because you will have done nothing to take yourself out of that mold.

Therefore, because the time is short and the power of light demands it and the great cosmic law requires it, we are hopeful that we will find responsive individuals who will have faith in my statements in this audience and in the student body who will hear and read these words. For I come from a mighty evolution of cosmic beings and from the realm upon Venus where the seven Holy Kumaras dwell and I know whereof I speak. I know whereof I speak. *I know whereof I speak!*

THE FLASH OF A COMET'S TAIL OF COSMIC DUST

The great council at Darjeeling, the Royal Teton Council and all the councils of the Great White Brotherhood, including the mighty Council of the Pleiades, have determined that earth shall receive the flash of a comet's tail of cosmic dust, as it were, which shall activate among mankind some of the divine principles, which they will then bring forward to be redeemed.

Those who do not redeem them may find that the power will act in reverse and that they will turn somewhat the other way. It will be almost a reactive power. But we are determined to release it because it is necessary, because the time is short for the era of the golden age to be brought in by those who have the wisdom to build it. And we *must* call mankind out of their lethargy and make them aware of the need to establish their victory within themselves as a focus of immortal life that we can use and use quickly! [Audience rises.]

You cannot know, it is impossible for you to know the energy the ascended masters have expended through the centuries. And I tell you, it is impossible for you to know the energy your Saint Germain has expended in this class, although he did not speak on the program, in order to generate within your blessed hearts some of the wondrous momentum of freedom that he has and that you need and that the Law requires you to keep.

I say to you, then, in the name of Almighty God, do not let this class pass by without making a resolve within yourself that cannot be broken! And note the word *resolve.* It means to re-solve your problems. It means to overcome the conditions that brought unhappiness into your world! It means to determine that your pursuit of life and happiness will bear some fruit upon the tree of life as well as upon the tree of liberty.

Men want liberty. They want freedom and they desire it and command it to come forth. But I tell you, one of the most important things for you to do is to recognize the responsibility you have toward liberty and freedom and to see that that liberty and freedom are keyed into the vibratory action of life! For life is God and God is law and God is love!

I hear people saying, "We have patience," when they have none. I hear people saying, "We have love," when they exhibit no love. I hear people say, "We are children and students of the light," when they have little light and the light that is in them is but darkness.

The time has passed when men can go on fooling themselves year after year. This is a year of victory by the power of divine love. And you had better get rid of all of the conditions that are affecting your world, your health, your mind and your status in life if you want to obtain your victory. Or the first thing you will know is that the sands in the hourglass will have run out and we will have no one to represent us, no one to carry our torch, no one to guide mankind who, dwelling in a darkened world of abomination and desolation, will find life not worth living.

THIS IS THE HOUR OF DECISION

I tell you, then, this is the hour of decision. This is the hour of affectation, not the affectation of little mortal things that do nothing for your soul but the affectation of eternity. If you were able today to see the Pleiades in all their brilliance and glory, to see the great temples of the Brotherhood at Shamballa, to enter in to the vibratory action of God in the secret and sacred places of the earth where you have never been, I tell you, your hearts would beat with joy and pride in the creation. There would be no mutterings against Almighty God and the Prince of Peace but only the receptive, humble attitude that would say,

O my God, let me live.
O my God, let me give.
O my God, let me strive.
O my God, I am alive.

Don't you see, precious ones, what your victory means?

Your victory means everything to you. Your victory is your life! It is the divine plan fulfilled for all the centuries of striving. Every angelic being has labored for this. Every one has strained until the very ropes themselves that connect the higher octaves are taut and tense with the hope of glory. Cosmic exhilaration flows over this great network, yet the response is small.

Let me see a change in you. Let me see a change in you. Let God see a change in you; he created you. Let Saint Germain see a change in you; he sustains you. Let Jesus see a change in you. He gave everything that mankind might have his teachings and [the example of] his life.

I tell you, the day is here when you must recognize that God has thundered as from Horeb's height and thundered in your midst. You may hear a mighty peal of thunder and I tell you, it is the mighty thunder of the apocalypse. It is the coming forth of the Four Horsemen. And I tell you that you must manifest your victory now or your victory will be gone for ages, ages rolling on and on.

I have spoken and God has spoken through me! It is the reflection of the solemnity of the council. Yet there is joy and mirth in us, for we hope there is worth in you.

God bless you. God sustain you. God love you. Assert your independence, for your I AM Presence is your independence. Depend upon it and let it depend upon you. In this mutual relationship such joy will come forth that will sweep the earth, and then this activity will flourish as a vehicle and instrument of God to be absorbed in the end as a mighty activity of light into the Great White Brotherhood, which gave it birth with hope, with joy, with worth, with mirth.

I thank you. And I say, Victory is my name.

July 4, 1966
La Tourelle
Colorado Springs, Colorado
MLP

11

THE SCIENCE OF LIFE

Peace, beloved ones. Is there room in the chamber of your heart for me? Are you receptive to your own God-directed consciousness of victory? Does the rhythm of determinate effort, consecration and reconsecration to immortal purpose beat within your heart?

I AM come this night to feed the flame of victory in your being, to consecrate your effort to Christ-illumined seeing. Peace, then, blessed ones, whose struggles to understand are legion. Let go of the struggle to understand and learn the science of life—the science of life that understands the Law [and is able] just to be.

Just be. Feel the love of the Creator's consciousness in descending currents of cosmic wholeness. The mystery of Christ-regeneration has escaped the age by and large, but it lingers and is nourished in the hearts of the comparative few who understand the meaning of devotion to the uttermost—devotion to a purpose that does not yield one inch of ground to the Adversary of infinite purpose.

Co-measurement is the word, the vital essence referenced by the Brotherhood that captures the mind and feeling of man and causes him to see and know that he is a son of God, destined to inherit the earth by reason of his meekness in struggle.

The victorious power of God rises into active pulsation when the human ceases to struggle. And then the Divine takes over and the fiber of the will of God infuses the mortal form and raises the corners of the mind until all four corners are exalted. No longer is there a sense of struggle but a sense of victory!

This is the very consciousness of the Master Jesus, both today and during his Galilean ministry of service to the earth. His demonstration of cosmic love did not begin with the appearance of the star in the East but was a promise long fulfilled, coming to fruition in the time of David. As the Psalmist declared, "Thou wilt not leave my soul in hell, neither wilt thou suffer thine Holy One to see corruption."[1]

What is the meaning of this for man? Men fear death, yet prior to birth, where were they? Where were they one hour before birth?

The physical form in the womb of the mother, quivering with the energies of her heart, does not pulsate to the divine rhythms of the individual's consciousness until the inflow of the holy breath from the heart of God. Then pneuma* begins and life pulsates within. And the flame of God within the individual consciousness is flung to the wind, which takes and bears that flame among men, wherever the individual desires to go.

THE MYSTERY OF SURRENDER

When a consecrated life is reached and surrender is born in the consciousness, one no longer desires to direct the flow of the life energies. One becomes aware that the will of God has from the beginning made inherent within the consciousness of each lifestream a destiny and pattern to be fulfilled.

Therefore the consciousness of God does command that those who are obedient to the purposes of life and the purposes of victory will understand the rhythm of the Divine One. They will understand that this is the power of the Sun behind the sun, the noble effort of God that will outbreathe and outpicture as that pattern in those who surrender themselves to the will of God.

---

*pneuma: soul, spirit

They will understand that surcease from struggle, when the consciousness is surrendered to God and not to any other spirit or consciousness, is a definite activity of light that infuses the soul with the consciousness of God-victory. God-victory, God-victory, *God*-victory, has a different meaning from that of the individual who declares to mankind, "I have won the race."

What is this spirit, then, that is acting within man? Is it the spirit of one who desires to assert his power over his fellowman? Or is it the power of God active within him that knows the way, every step thereof, and determines to take the child-son by the hand and lead him, not to keep him confined to the status of a child or a state of consciousness in which he is dependent upon God but to push him out of the nest of divine consciousness as a full-grown bird, a fledgling no longer, ready to fly with wings of infinite victory into the holy sky of cosmic purpose.

GOD DOES NOT BLUNDER

Men do not understand purpose. They do not understand the meaning of life; they do not even understand the meaning of themselves. They blink an eye and wonder why life does not obey them. And they are fully aware of the fact that they have blundered again and again, although people sometimes say to each other, "You must not think that you have blundered, for that is a negative thought."

Well, precious ones, if this is so, what man must understand is that God does not blunder. Therefore man must learn to decipher the engrams of God's thoughtforms and consciousness for and on behalf of himself individually, so that man may outpicture the life that was his immortal destiny from the beginning, that is his immortal destiny now and that will be in days to come the fullness of the life of purpose that God holds for each one.

Unless men and women are ready to surrender, there is no hope for them save round after round of mortal consciousness. And the struggle and the straying go on. And I think, if you will pardon the expression, the braying goes on rather than the praying!

I tell you, there is a time to smile and you can smile at the self you once were. You can understand that you need not be as you once were, as did Balaam the son of Beor who was rebuked by the dumb ass speaking with a man's voice.[2]

THE WILL OF GOD IS SUPREME

Understand, then, that the will of God is supreme. Had Jonah understood it, he would not have lain within the whale's belly and the great fish would not have been prepared to swallow him up. I have used this term whale because of your familiarity with it and I did not actually intend you to understand that Jonah was swallowed by a whale but by a great fish, which "the Lord had prepared to swallow him up."[3]

Understand, then, that what I have in mind for you is something greater than that. It is the process of initiation, which was mentioned this very day in the address of Holy Amethyst, who was, as some of you know, the angel of comfort who appeared to the Christ in Gethsemane's garden and assisted him when he "sweat, as it were, great drops of blood."[4]

How many of you have sweat great drops of blood in the struggle to understand, in the struggle to pray, in the struggle to decree, in the struggle to study to show thyself approved unto God? How many of you have, in this day and age, actually been in a state of consciousness that caused you to recognize that you must put forth a more than ordinary effort?

Now, do not be confused. Why do I say at one moment that you must cease to struggle and at another that you must put forth the effort?

I say it unto you because you must have faith in your victory. And the faith that is generated within you will inspire you to do the things that you know to be the will of God and to know in full faith that God is directing you even when you do not see his hands.

This faith was spoken of by Jesus unto Thomas when he said so clearly, "Because thou hast seen me, thou hast believed. Blessed are they who have not seen and yet have believed."[5] Ponder this mystery in your heart, blessed ones, and understand tonight that as I am addressing you, I am also projecting my consciousness into the great golden record room in the Grand Teton [mountain in the Teton] Range.[6]

A MEETING IN THE GRAND TETON

Tonight a solemn conclave is going on there, a meeting perchance, but not really per chance, for it was called by special decree. And, blessed ones, that meeting taking place right now is intended to bring about certain plans for the endowment of man and the endowment of the youth of the world.

[These plans would set forth] an understanding of the problems of this age and the power that true religion plays in releasing man from his sense of mortal obligations so that he can absorb the concept of his spiritual responsibilities. Do you understand what I mean?

If individuals would struggle for their spiritual attainment as they struggle for mortal bread and for status before men, their victory would be won quite soon.

CHRIST'S TESTS IN THE WILDERNESS

We come now to the forty days in the wilderness. When the Christ was an hungered after forty days of fasting, the Evil One came to him and said: "Command that these stones be made bread" and "Cast thyself down, for it is written, He shall give his angels charge concerning thee . . . lest thou dash thy foot against a stone."[7]

And the Word came back in ringing denunciation, without struggle, in a simple, forthright statement, for the Christ felt no sense of struggle or the desire to contend with the Evil One. He did not resist evil in the form of a vicious attack. He abode within the format of the sacred Word and he uttered the Word with firmness and his lips tensed with firmness as he spake out of the God flame of his heart and said, "Get thee behind me, Satan, for it is written, Man shall not live by bread alone but by every word that proceedeth out of the mouth of God."[8]

You thought I said that! But it was the Master Jesus who beamed these words to you so that you might hear the vibratory action of the firmness with which he spoke! It was intended that you should emulate him, even as we have done and have obtained our victory by the emulation of every avatar and every Son.

For all whom God has loved enough and all who have loved God enough have ascended, as did Elijah in a chariot of fire, back to the heart of God. Are these not, then, all worthy men? Worthy, that is, as spiritual men?

"THERE CAME TWO ANGELS TO SODOM"

And what of the angels who came to the house of Lot and entered into the house while the children of Sodom "encompassed the house around?"[9] What of those beings who, by spiritual power, caused blindness to come upon the [men of Sodom] and did lead Lot out of unrighteous Sodom?

They did carry him high up and out of danger while the atomic substance of the atmosphere was ignited by the Word of these great Master Presences who came forth from the Karmic Board to render judgment in the name of God to the cities of the plain, Sodom and Gomorrah. What of them?

They were manifestations of the One, as were the gentlemen who came of old to Abraham and spake unto him the words of promise saying, "Sarah thy wife shall bear thee a son indeed; and thou shalt call his name Isaac." And Sarah laughed by the tent. And the Lord spake unto her out of the voice of the Master and said, "Wherefore did Sarah laugh, saying shall I of a surety bear a child?"[10]

And she said, "I laughed not." And he said, "Nay, but thou didst laugh. And this thing shall surely be."[11] And it was. And the child of promise was born. But what thoughts filled the heart of Abraham when he was sent to the altar to offer this son of promise unto God?

What of that moment? What did he think when he raised high the dagger to strike a blow to the son of his heart? He stood ready and willing to obey. But has God required it? Did God require it? I tell you, nay.

And so, the sacrifice of identity men make, the sacrifice of self-reign that men make, consecrating themselves to God and his will, is not at all an act of desolation or of death. It is an act of consecration to life and life's purposes.

God will restore the reins of life to the individual who has demonstrated his willingness to achieve victory, who has become mature enough in consciousness to deserve to hold the reins. It is an act of mercy indeed that God himself stands ready and willing to assist each lifestream in attaining his victory and accepts the sweet surrender of his soul and rejoices because of his consecration and devotion to God's purposes.

You must understand, precious ones, how real all of this is and how unreal is the sense of struggle proclaimed by many of the adherents of the various religious faiths of the world who do not understand the teachings and tenets of the faith they seek to promulgate. They do not understand the meaning of vicarious at-one-ment.

They do not understand the meaning of faith. They do not understand the meaning of consecration. They do not understand yet their prayers rise and their hearts are touched by feelings of the Divine. A soul hunger is within them and they yearn to understand and to know more.

But they stand ready to rebuke the child of flesh who is attuned to the cadences of the spirit because the individual who directs to them the word of truth does not uphold the tenets of the faith that they were taught from their mother's knee.

But what of the Cosmic Mother? What of the eternal truth? What of the fruit of the Spirit? What of immortal life?

They do not recognize, then, that holy truth is not always readily perceived through the apertures of life manifestations. They do not realize that behind the appearance world is an invisible world of cosmic promise, and the life that stands behind the veil is more real and transcendent than all life standing here on the mortal side of the veil.

ACCRUE A SENSE OF VICTORY

Tonight, however, I have said enough on that subject and I am interested in causing you to accrue a sense of victory, regardless of whether it is by the acceptance of my flame of victory, by the acceptance of the flame of victory of Jesus the Christ, by the acceptance of the flame of any master anywhere, or by your own direct apprehension of the flame of victory from the heart of your I AM Presence.

We are not concerned with a sense of struggle over doctrines and tenets.

We only seek to illumine you and to create a concept of beauty in your hearts that will enable you to understand higher truth. If you desire to hold on to a particular tenet or idea that you have held for many a year and you choose not to relinquish it or cognize that there are greater revelations to be made, that is well and good.

If you can make your ascension and achieve your victory with the knowledge you have and the flame that now burns within your heart, heaven is not here to terrorize you or to threaten that which you desire to hold close. We only desire to expand the dimensions of your consciousness, because from what we can see of your life-record, we believe that you need the cosmic sense of victory of the avatars of God and the blessed teachers of the Great White Brotherhood.

We believe that you need the flame we proffer to you tonight. [Audience rises.] We believe that you need it and that it will provide additional impetus to the hunger of your soul and will help you to find your way to the eternal magnet of God's heart and the love that that magnet generates. (Won't you please be seated in God's name.)

A GOLDEN BALL OF VICTORY

Blessed ones, you stood for your victory tonight when you rose to your feet. Do you realize, then, that although there was a certain mimicry of motion as individuals followed others who were rising to their feet, by that mimicry of motion your Holy Christ Self consented to that which I am saying?

Therefore cosmic law permits me (in absentia, as it were, because you have not voted upon it) to give you a golden ball of victory. And I have asked that the great presses of heaven be struck and that there issue forth [for each one] a golden ball of victory. And I desire to give it to you tonight.

I do not intend that you should receive it during this service. I desire that you should receive it in the aloneness of sleep; therefore I have asked that an angel of record come tonight to those who have the faith to understand that I speak truly, and that they may then look to receive during the night within the forcefield of their identity a magnetic golden ball charged with the vibratory action of my victory.

I give you this gift tonight because you have made the effort to come here and have demonstrated by your faith in remaining that an activity of light and cosmic consecration is taking place. For the invincible cosmic honor flame of God intends that man should not vegetate or remain to become crystallized as Lot's wife did but should find his freedom, not through rebirth but through consecration here and now to the purpose that beats his heart.

Understand, then, that the flame of victory I wield is a tangible offering. Understand, then, that the flame of victory that I AM is a consecrated effort on behalf of all the mankind of earth. It is not a puny, paltry manifestation of someone's consciousness. It is not an activity of this messenger; it is not an activity of which he is capable.

It is an activity of which no man is capable unless he be in the ascended state. And it is an activity that should cause you to clench your fists and say, *"I am determined to win my victory, so help me God."*

This is a plea before the bar of infinite justice and it is heard by the Lords of Karma, who sit not so much to judge as to provide the impetus of opportunity to all.

HOLD IN ABEYANCE

May I say to you this night what would be a little mystery to the average individual? You do not know this and therefore I desire to proclaim it. So great is the karma-making apparatus upon this planet for most of the lifestreams embodied here that we find it necessary to enter plea before the Karmic Board again and again for a condition we call "hold in abeyance."

Consequently, individuals' karmas are constantly being held in abeyance and they do not descend except in part. This is to afford [these ones] an opportunity in the name of divine love to find their way back to the Father's house without the terrible weight of oppression of their own iniquities fully resting upon them.

However, the masters have found occasionally that some individuals seek to perform acts of destruction against the children of light. And therefore, knowing that the children of light could well go down because of the tremendous viciousness of human thought and feeling, we have found it necessary on occasion to enter [a second] request with the Karmic Board.

Such an individual's record is then brought to us and we write upon it "Put back into circulation." And at that precise moment the great hammer and judgment of the Law falls upon the lifestream and they find that there is indeed recompense from God. This is [the meaning of] the saying, "Vengeance is mine. I will repay, saith the Lord."[12]

Understand, then, that the law of love chastens and the Lord "scourgeth every son whom he receiveth."[13] He prunes mankind when they become too ambitious in an evil way, so that they may be curbed and that which they do may be stopped as the precipitate of a continually rising tide of evil in the world of form.

We desire to see the world free from evil, the terrors of black magic, the destructive activities of witchcraft and the awful brooding of mankind on the assassination of political figures in the world who may, in some cases, represent the will of God for the people.

Again and again individuals throughout the world have become victims of the terrible horror and blight of assassination. At the present time certain activities in this country are coming to light and shocking many individuals. I would like to say to you that this very messenger recently made a trip down into the South on behalf of the hierarchy in order to direct certain currents into circulation in world affairs that were instrumental in seeing that a certain indictment was returned.

THE BROTHERHOOD OF GUARDIAN WATCHMEN

You must understand that the Brotherhood has many messengers who perform various services but few who stand before you, as this one does, to give forth the living truth in vital, flaming substance from the octaves of light. Individuals may also consider themselves to be messengers of God in everything that they do.

They may consider that if they till the soil they are acting the part of the great Sower, who goeth forth to provide sustenance to mankind of earth. And yet I am certain that many of you are aware of the demographic problems facing mankind which, predicated into the future, reveal that it may be impossible without changes in mankind's habit patterns to sustain life, simply because there would not be enough food to sustain the projected population.

You must understand, then, that the mighty law of life is always activated on behalf of the mankind of earth for the governing of human affairs. The Great White Brotherhood is the watchdog—although I am sure that they would not care to be called watchdogs and I have used the term purely in order to fit the word pattern that mankind themselves use.

They are, then, and I choose to use another term, the guardian watchmen over all mortal affairs and they have a power that is known as the power of cosmic veto. It is an overriding power. When individuals continue to direct themselves on a course of evil and follow a downward trend, [the Brotherhood] is able then to use this power of veto and to direct cosmic currents of karma in such a manner as to change the course of history.

However, this power of the great Karmic Board is limited within the domain of mankind and balanced against human free will. It is a very delicate and subtle subject, scarcely understood by most among mankind and best understood by the members of the Karmic Board themselves.

STUDY TO SHOW YOURSELVES APPROVED UNTO GOD

Now, then, I have given you some instruction that I trust will be of some assistance to you in generating the fear of God that is the beginning of wisdom.[14] "Perfect love casteth out fear, because fear hath torment,"[15] but you must understand both thesis and antithesis.

You must understand that the Law and the science of words, human semantics and divine semantics, are able to convey a host of ideas to mankind in order to challenge their consciousness to study to show themselves approved unto God and to learn how to use the blessed mind that God has given them in a proper manner.

You must understand, then, that human deductive reasoning, when properly employed, teaches mankind to use the powers of the mind. Inductive reasoning is also effective. And so the syllogisms of mortal reason become exercises in consciousness.

However, there is a reason and a system of reason, which men can learn, which is far above the reason of mankind. It is the a priori reasoning of the soul of God. It is the reasoning of the soul within, which is not limited by the dimensions of the senses and very easily goes forth into space and comes back with an answer.

These are the arrows of light that fly through space to a cosmic goal and return unto the individual who sent them forth as boomerangs of light, conveying an essential message to the soul that shows the individual how he may obtain his victory through hope. And hope is a consecration of God's law, for hope, when it is properly identified, also enables man to objectify that which he had hoped for.

Understand, then, that the mind and heart of man can become saturated with the laws of God until those laws of God, by showing men how to hold a sacred vision, are able to magnetize and draw such love into the world of the individual as to sweep the earth and remove the currents of oppression and depression that are occasionally borne by the winds of deceit and confusion.

Men must understand that they ought not to be subject to any other spirit than the Spirit of God and the spirit of truth. They ought not to accept any other spirit save the spirit of victory. They ought not to accept any other sense than the sense of victory. And I tell you, this is not a case of playing a game of charades.

It is not a case of self-deceit or a case of mortal reason. It is a case of divine reason becoming encased within the human heart and expanding the flame thereof until a new and fresh start can immediately be commenced with every downfall.

The moment you fall down, the moment you feel a sense of weakness or oppression, the moment a cloud of darkness appears in your mind, the moment you feel that you are not expressing the fullness of the Christ, at that moment and not another you should seize the opportunity to assert the power of your divine victory.

CALL UNTO ME AND I WILL ANSWER!

Call unto me and I will answer! Call unto me at that moment and ask me to give you my flame of victory and see if I do not flood your being with light! Call unto me and recognize that I AM there! I AM here and I AM there and I AM ever responsive, coming from the farthest corners of universal consciousness to bring you that selfsame flame of cosmic victory that I brought to many, many sons of God in past eras.

Understand, then, that even before I ensouled the flame of victory, one [Son of God] went before me who is now a truly magnificent being in another system of worlds and another universe entirely.

I tell you that my name, Victory, is also my office. And I tell you that tonight I am willing to give you an opportunity to be of assistance to me in the world of form. [Audience rises.]

[I am willing to give you the opportunity] to spread the concept of cosmic victory everywhere you move, to spread the concept of Christ's victory—his victory over sin, his victory over death, his victory over shadow, his victory over all outer circumstances and conditions.

Will you accept the flame of victory I bring? Will you utilize it in your daily living from now on? [Audience responds, "Yes!"]

THE PURPOSE OF THIS ACTIVITY

Are you ready and willing to understand that this is not an ordinary activity? If it had never existed but to assert the power of victory at this moment, it would have justified its reason for being.

It has a greater raison d'être, however, and it will certainly be manifest as you, the adherents of this activity, understand that its real purpose is an invisible purpose: To fulfill the mind of God among men, to externalize the plan of God and the radiance of God to overcome the darkness of the world.

[Its purpose is] to let the light of God stand supreme, raining the golden latter rain of Cosmic Christ illumination from summit heights upon mankind so that the sons of God may indeed see the vision of Christ's perfection, that they may speak with a new tongue, loosed from the power of darkness, and clearly obtain for all who will, the power of freedom's flame and God illumination.

That Christ be glorified is now my desire and it should be yours. And if it be yours as it is mine, then the universal Christ, the light of the world, will be glorified in you now and forevermore.

I say, let divine intelligence increase and let it be multiplied. Go not forth to deceive mankind by the illusions of your consciousness as some have done. Be not harbingers of false doctrines or teachings. Go not forth to submit to spirits of darkness and shadow that masquerade in sheep's clothing. They are wolves, I tell you, and you must beware of them.

Go forth into the world of form and bring mankind the awareness of the clarity of our vision, of the clarity of your own. Represent us in the world of form as ladies and gentlemen of cosmic intelligence and make men proud of the work that is being done, even as men are proud of the work that your own beloved Saint Germain accomplished during his manifestation as Sir Francis Bacon and in his release of the Shakespearean plays.[16]

Make men proud of all that is of light and of the glory of God. [Make them proud] that they may come gladly and willingly into the fold, not thinking that you are deceitful people or foolish people deceived by the peepings and mutterings of some strange spirit but guided by the clarity of the vision of the living Christ that has arisen within you with healing in his wings and the vision of hope to a world that waits for the sunrise of its victory now and forever!

I thank you because I love you. And I trust that when my voice ceases to speak and my vibrations cease to activate your hearts as they are now doing, you will realize that just behind the veil of Be-ness I stand! And you can call to me and I will answer in the moments when you need me.

Victory to the world in the name of the living Christ! In memory of the Master Jesus, drink ye the cup of his consciousness, of his Spirit. Go forth in emulation of him and be lights everywhere you move. So shall God be glorified not by one son but by many and the hearts of the captives shall go free.

[The holy breath sounds.]

March 24, 1967
La Tourelle
Colorado Springs, Colorado
MLP

12

THE VICTORY WAY OF LIFE

The enveloping power of your victory is a marvelous gift of infinite capacity—[the capacity] to expand, to expand your thought, to expand your perception, to realize that you are not the limited but the limitless!

I AM come this night on behalf of the universal hierarchy to bring to your souls not only a sense of victory and its buoyancy but also the God-realization that this is the plan that was conceived from the beginning by the pure mind of God.

What joy is to be found in a happy child! How easily individuals can return, if they will only accept it, to the God-realization of the miracle of life, the pulsation of the sun's rays as a marvelous potion, as a lotion that will bathe the body and the mind and the being of man and wipe away from his consciousness all sense of doubt and fear and tribulation and human mischief, and produce in its place the God-realization that I AM Victory!

You must understand that this is no ordinary activity. It is an extraordinary activity of your own God Presence! And your God Presence will not be brought under the power of human hypnosis or the thought that the individual can control the God Self.

This is the trouble on earth today. Individuals want power and they desire to use that power, not for their freedom and the emancipation of other human beings but that they might be thought wise by men and surfeit themselves in their carnal longings.

We are aware of all this, but we refuse to give power to it. For we are concerned with the Spirit, which understands that man is the offspring of God and, as the offspring of God, he ought to open up the portals of consciousness of his heart and of his feeling world to say:

O God, give me your victory!
Give me your victory!
Give me your victory!

Will you accept this fiat in your feeling world tonight and accept the pressure of the light that intends to convey upon you all beauty and perfection? [Audience rises.]

Will you accept the thought that there is only a very thin veil between reality and man's illusions? Why not, then, either unzip the zipper or cut it asunder? Do something with it. Don't let it hinder you from realizing your God potential. (Won't you please be seated.)

ACCEPT OUR PRESENCE AND BE AT PEACE

We are aware that the very manifestation of our words and our thoughts, our feelings and our love, may be strange to some of you. But we also think that many among mankind, as they passed through the veil and the change called death, experienced many strange adventures in the other world and these did not seem real to their consciousness at the time they transpired.

Will you understand, then, that it is perfectly natural for you, who have not heard dictations before or realized the thought of prophecy in this day and age, to have some trepidation? Please, then, disabuse your minds of any unsettling ideas concerning it and be at peace.

Let the understanding of universal love from the heart of your own I AM Presence flow into you. Feel the mantle of God wrapped around your shoulders and his love pulsing forth in the flame within your heart.

If you do this, you will make it easy for the ascended host. They will be able to come into the forcefield of your world and drop a conveyance of their love; and it will be a gentle thing, a sweet manifestation, as a face of a lovely child or a rose or the sound of waters moving over stones.

TAKE COMMAND OVER YOUR PHYSICAL BODY

Please understand that you need never have mortal tension if you will call to your God Presence and recognize that you can have the victory over every rippling muscle within your body. We fully understand, however, that a buildup of mortal tension from time to time makes people as hard as a rock. And when this condition occurs, they seem to find some surcease from distress through the hands of the manipulators who are trained and skilled in the plastic arts of molding the human form and helping it to release its hidden tensions.

We think, then, that mankind should understand that this [service] is a great boon. But the day will come when individuals, through a higher degree of victory and a higher degree of mastery over their world, will say to the muscle in their big toe, "Relax," and it will do so.

Now, won't you smile just a little bit with me over that? [Audience laughs.]

YOU MUST HAVE A SENSE OF HUMOR

Precious ones of the light, you have to have a sense of humor, for it is very important on earth in achieving your victory. Some of the greatest masters that ever lived, when faced with the most terrible, scaring trials of their existence, understood that by a smile and the understanding that it was necessary were able to feel a renewal of the flame of victory within them, of the God-determination that said:

> *I will not stop!*
> *I will not accept the pressure of this mortal thing!*
> *I will not accept this shroud over my identity!*
> *I AM a son of God!*
> *I am following in the footsteps of the master*

And behold, the master is my example.
I will do as he did
And believe as he believed.
I will act as he acted
And I will feel as he felt.
And there is no power in heaven or earth
That can dissuade me from acting that way.

When this consciousness flows into you, you are accepting the pressure of the ascended masters' octave. I tell you, you will be surprised; it will be remarkable how a change in your consciousness will then be brought into manifestation.

Some ladies who are accustomed to thinking that something is just a little bit too heavy for them to lift and that they need to call for the assistance of a man (although the object is really not too big, when you stop to consider it), will find that by a call to their God Presence they can summon enough strength to be thought of as an Amazon. [Audience laughs.]

We tell you tonight that the practical aspects of life are to understand that the natural flow of energy pulsations from the heart of God is based on the humor of the mind. When the mind decides that life is full of death and sickness and disturbing outer conditions, it sometimes thinks that the whole universe is pitted against it and that Almighty God himself does not care for and has no concern for the soul.

I tell you, nothing could be further from the truth, for the uncompromising light of God, the light that never fails, is waiting to be called into action to assist you to your victory. This is a very beautiful concept, precious ones, when it is understood by a soul who seems to find himself stalemated in a pool of mortal emotion from which he seeks deliverance.

At that moment, what a boon it would be if one could just quiet the thoughts of the mortal self. "But this is quite difficult," you say. And so it is because you think it is; and, of course, it follows your thought and becomes more difficult by the moment, as long as you sustain the thought.

When you understand that the cosmic law of victory is waiting to be called into action, then you will see that all those little demons of mortal thought and feeling will be vanquished over the hill. We do not think that it will be a problem for you to see them running away; it is when they are running toward you that you seem to be in a state of trepidation!

EXPECT THE TRIAL BY FIRE

I tell you, then, you cannot expect now or at any time not to be tried by fire. We have won our victory in the face of all sorts of outer conditions and, as I read the record, I think that some were a great deal worse then than they are at the present time.

It is one thing to have to face all manner of human ideas and human resentments, human resistance and human doubt and fear; but it is another to face those conditions and then thirst for a drink of water and find that that water is miles away across a desert, or find that it is denied you because you cannot pay the price, or find that your garments are threadbare and you cannot find a sou to pay for new ones, or find that you are accused of a crime you did not commit and you have no funds to pay for protection or help.

I want you to know and to realize, then, that men can be in terrible conditions. In ages past, when transportation was dependent upon animal life and upon water, and men moved lugubriously across the face of the earth, the conditions were not as they are today and there was little easement from pain.

Individuals often had to face the burning iron when their limbs required amputation, for the only way to stop the flow of blood was by searing and burning [the flesh] in full, waking consciousness. The pains of childbirth were also very much with the womankind of earth.

I think this age has brought many mercies and gifts into manifestation, which ought to assist the race to gain something better than a condition of euphoria or [a tendency] to vegetate and let the energies of their life stagnate in pools of wrong habits, thoughts and feelings.

I tell you, the Gods look down upon mankind and the immortal presences of all life and say, "When will you find your freedom and your victory? When will you accept it? When will you be free?"

We know from past experience that it does not necessarily require hours and days and months. To start the flow of that specific energy requires a moment of dedication and God-determination to never again accept anything but your victory. And when that specific energy has started and is sustained and fed each day and men believe in it and love it, what do you think will happen when other conditions come up against the pressure of that mighty stream of victory that flows from the heart of your own Divine Presence?

I tell you, it will produce a miracle in your life that you will ever be grateful for and you will love to pass on to your children and to your children's children. It is a heritage of magnificence. It is something greater than the sense of struggle mankind has engaged in for so long—the sense of struggle that continues to produce the struggle, as Saint Germain has said.

WELCOME ADVERSITY AND LAUGH AT IT

Struggle is not what we want for you. It is not what you want for yourself and it is not what God wants for you. God wants you to have the joy, the joy, the joy, the surging joy of the reality of life. He wants you to understand that whereas you may have committed acts of karmic responsibility that must return to you by cosmic law, you can also welcome these conditions at every turn by saying, "I am grateful, because one more object is out of the way of my freedom and my victory."

Become not discouraged but encouraged by the flow of your karma and understand that when God sees your attitude as such, it will be [to your credit] for, as beloved Morya has said, "The devill that prowd spirite, cannot stand to be mokqued."[1] When you learn to laugh at adversity and to accept it and when you realize that adversity is something that can become a path to your freedom, you might even welcome it.

This in itself is an attitude of victory, for you can learn to overcome adversity, to mitigate it, to cause it to loosen its hold upon you and to ride up over it. This is the meaning of victory and the meaning of life. For when life is won and when attainment comes unto a son of God by his acceptance of the pressure of the Divine Presence, it is a beautiful thing to behold. Then he realizes that not by another's vicarious act but by his own vicarious act he has identified with the God Presence, and the God Presence has performed it through him. That is to say, performed it through the veil of his own flesh.

Thus the Christ becomes the divine Mediator, and the Mediator acts to mediate the difference between the human self and the Divine. When this is accomplished, what a magnificent thing it is, what a joy, what a perfect manifestation of your victory! For your victory belongs to you now. You do not have to wait for it until some far distant mañana. It is here with you, within your God Presence, in the pulsing stream of light that descends from your God Presence now.

THE VICTORY WAY OF LIFE

While you are seated here, will you try to understand that the very stream of energy that flows from your Presence and sustains your heart can intensify your desire to overcome your difficulties?

I tell you, it will produce, during your waking and sleeping hours, a changed man and a changed woman who will not be spineless creatures who decide to take the cure here or take the cure there or move here or move there and, perhaps, somehow or other, get a little joy out of living.

Well, life, as God intends it to be, is not that way. There is a whole lot of joy in living if you understand the victory way of life that I espouse. And I have espoused it not only for the people of Venus but for the people of Earth.

I have sustained a mounting momentum of my victory, which I wish I could bequeath to you tonight in its entirety, but I suspect the Lords of Karma would not quite wink at such a monstrous thing. For if I were to give it to you completely, you would not be able to obtain it for yourself, and I do not wish to rob you of the precious opportunity of doing it for yourself.

This is a do-it-yourself project, precious ones, where a man becomes a God and then sits back upon the throne of attainment and laughs. He laughs because he has attained! Do you see?

It is not a thing of weeping and affliction. Doesn't it say in your scriptures and is it not fully recorded, "God shall wipe away all tears from their eyes"?[2] What do you think that means? It means you should accept your victory and learn to rejoice in the victory that comes to you, in the fullness of knowing that that victory will also be your neighbor's. There will be no competition, for you will all be striving for the same thing.

When you attain it, what will it mean? It will mean that you have entered into the joy of God, nevermore to descend into mortal density. You will busy yourself working in the many sosophoric rounds of identification with the creative schema, producing inspiration on other systems of worlds in little hearts who are mutants of the spirit confined to the veil of flesh, not realizing who they are and fighting about it, wrangling all the while. And the Gods stand there with the mantles of their victory, waiting to drape them over their shoulders.

Don't you see it? Don't you understand it?

Well, understand it, precious ones, for I tell you, this is the key and the solution to all life. Because of the conditions of the world, we need a group of staunch and stalwart students of the light who will go forth in the understanding of what it means to wear the mantle of their victory.

It is not a condition of the outer. It is not a condition of which one says, "I don't think I am strong enough," or "I am going to get strong enough." It's a matter of accepting the strength you already have and moving forward into the light, refusing to accept the pressures brought against you that try to pull you down.

These pressures are brought against every son of God. They test the mettle of man and they produce a miracle in every age if they are adhered to. But if you do not overcome them, if you disregard them and say, "Well, it doesn't make any difference," then, of course, you will go the way of the mediocre.

You will then find yourself to be very ordinary, very much a lump of clay, very much disturbed, very unhappy. [You will find yourself] coming back again and again into physical form to struggle against the same odds and ultimately to come to the same position you are in now—face to face with [the questions]: Will I win my victory? Will I keep my determination? Will I accept the pressures of the light or will I go back into the dark or the realm of mediocrity? Will I accept a dogma that is not quite such a high tower?

A PRAYER TO THE MAHA CHOHAN

I do not believe this is what you want. I believe you want the fullness of your freedom and that this must come because of the cast of your mind, the set of your sail and the purity of the Holy Spirit.

I say, then, as a means of releasing a stream of freedom into your world tonight, I can do nothing better than to call to the Lord Maha Chohan. So I ask you to observe a period of stillness during which you may raise your arms upward with the palms of your hands turned up into the atmosphere.

O Lord Maha Chohan, thou representative of the Holy Spirit, place thy rays of love and light and victory into these lifestreams. O thou master of wisdom and divine love, let the essence of thyself flow through them. Bestow upon these children of God's heart the celestial dove of their purity and let them feel its joy in their heart as it wings its way to the Divine Presence and creates the miracle flash of the ark of the covenant.

[Master claps.] You may lower your hands. Fold both hands over your heart. Accept the treasure of these divine pulsations as a renewal of your energy from the Divine One.

There is but one God and all men are his offspring. And out of this monotheistic concept of the Deity we release the understanding that every son was intended to be that which God is. Behold, ye are gods.[3]

Let all understand, then, that you to whom the Word of God is given will receive tonight from my heart the ark of victory, the ark of the future and the ark of salvation for this planet. Bear it well. Carry it well. Love it. Cherish it! Raise it and it will raise you over the flood of man's mortal concepts, out of the domain of darkness and shadow and into the light celestial where the purity of the eternal One releases a stream of perfection from the Sun.

[Master chants in angelic tongues for 42 seconds.]

Out of the shadows have I called victory. Out of density and darkness has the eternal lily blossomed, the Buddhic manifestation, the budding of man's divinity.

Om Mani Padme Hum.

I thank you.

July 7, 1968
La Tourelle
Colorado Springs, Colorado
MLP

13

A MORE THAN ORDINARY RESPONSIBILITY

Be of good cheer, for it is I. I AM Victory. And out of the joy of my heart, I bring to each one of you the realization that the light, the unfailing light of God, is charged with the faith of your own victory over every outer set of circumstances that seeks to control or to direct your life.

You should understand, then, that man's thoughts are almost never still, at least for any appreciable length of time. Individuals constantly develop ideas or thoughts within the forcefield of their consciousness or they become subjected to the thoughts of others from the akashic records, from the minds of current, contemporary thinkers, or from loose thoughts and ideas floating in the atmosphere.

Some of these thoughts produce a certain amount of good, but many are but vacillations, imperfectly formed matrices, which the individuals who receive them do not at first recognize. The safest thing for each student of the light is to understand the need to protect himself from the tramp thoughts of others. The best way to do this is to simply invoke your mighty tube of light from the heart of your own beloved mighty I AM Presence.

You should recognize, when you invoke this tube of light in full faith that God has lowered it around you and that the energies of God are surging through its forcefield to protect your world, that when you qualify the very power of that tube of light with the added impetus of your own constructive thought, God then amplifies it almost without limit.

ASSUME CONTROL OVER YOUR WORLD

The students should clearly recognize that they have a more than ordinary responsibility to draw forth a stream of radiant energy from the Godhead. They should see that their qualification of the power of the light from God's heart is also essential in directing that energy from on high to absorb the stream of constructive thought they use as a matrix to guide the invoked substance.

When the students understand the statement I just made, it will show them that they have some regulatory influence over their own world. If they have some, then it becomes not a matter of how much influence is acting from their level, but that some is. They can always increase the span or the scope of that influence until, in due course of time, they become the masters of their destiny.

Now, because I realize full well that many students here will not at first grasp the full import of my statement, I hope that you will pause for a moment with me and reflect upon it just a little bit further. You see, by turning over the qualification of energy to you, the Godhead is charging you with a set of responsibilities, and the responsibility with which you are charged becomes your assumption of control of your world.

When you realize this, you will see that it is part of the divine plan. If God were human, he would be flattered to have individuals continually applying to him for assistance, but because the real purpose of creation was to make man the master of his world and take his God-given dominion over it, it is the full intent of God and the ascended masters that each one should ultimately become that master of his world and arbiter of his destiny.

REVEL IN THE IDEA OF EXCELLENCE

When you understand this, you will see why it may be very important that you absorb my momentum of victory and why it is also important that you learn to develop your own. We are concerned, then, that the students understand why so much help and assistance is given from higher octaves.

From the beginning, the higher has always sought to raise the lower; this is a natural and perfectly orderly manifestation of divine love in action. When individuals have a specific quality of grace, such as music or art or any other quality that manifests here below, their desire to share that quality with their fellowman is either a gesture of humility and service on their part or it is the exhibition of pride in accomplishment.

Those who are aware of the power of victory and the conclusions victory reaches when given a certain idea must understand that the best purposes of life are served not by abject humility but by the humility of dignity that understands that it is the delight of the universe to bring forth excellence at every point of manifest consciousness.

Men and women, then, should revel in the idea of excellence, for excellence is the divine plan fulfilled. But wherever individuals compete with each other rather than strive for excellence, they are not prone to manifest victory over the intelligent accomplishments of their lives or the talents thereof but are apt instead to have a consciousness similar to a yo-yo. One moment they are up in the throes of exaltation, for some have applauded their manifestation, and another they are down, for somehow they feel the expression they released was inadequate and did not fulfill the purpose they had intended.

God is different. When God lives in man and God's power is given dominion over man, it is never the intention of the Godhead to assert control over man but to relegate to the individual in embodiment the full power and momentum that God intended him to have in order to use the divine will as a guiding matrix for his life. Then he can draw forth from the Godhead the starry guidance he requires and appropriate it as his own. In fact, utilizing divine coordinates, he can ultimately bring forth from his own field of consciousness the blessed spirit of victory he admires in me.

It is the same with every ascended master. Whatever quality the master manifests, when the student understands that this quality can be and should be appropriated by him, he will recognize that his contact with the master is one of guidance, just as one goes to a wise master teacher, a musician or someone able to portray the correct movements of the hand in creating art forms.

But who can actually initiate the student into the idea of structuring from the heart those manifest art forms that will ultimately give to the planetary body its spirit of victory?

THE HARMONY OF GOD
AND THE DISSONANCE OF MAN

Color is magnificent and utterly important in the manifestation of the harmony of the spheres. Harmony in music is essential to help men to realize the harmony of God in higher octaves. Do you see, then, why the color wheel has been distorted by those dabblers in the sordid aspects of the astral and the occult?

Do you understand why they have also interfered with the musical patterns released from higher octaves and have brought forth patterns of dissonance that have created inharmony in human life? They threaten to literally tear apart the balance of the glandular system of man to produce distortions in future generations that will affect the seed of man so that man will produce in the womb a manifest distortion in form simply because that mutation is the result of an aborted consciousness.

We tell you, if man does not cease this activity in which he is now engaged, he will find repeated once again the creation of the monsters that existed before the Flood. Although the Flood did wipe out the matrices involved in the creation of those monsters, man, by drawing the patterns and negative records forth from the astral and by creating the dismal beats and so forth in the atmosphere, by creating distortions in color and tapping into the psychic records of the architecture of that age, is re-creating the matrices that the human consciousness can pick up to produce similar distortions to those created before the Flood. This, of course, is an insidious attempt by the powers of darkness to reproduce that which God in his mercy wiped out by the Flood.

We want you, then, to recognize the symbol of the rainbow that came forth after the Flood. Today the rainbow standing in the sky reflects to all mankind the purity of the white light. Its marvelous half shell, radiating in mankind's full sight, shows that the whole complement in the fourth dimension can manifest the purity of color that composes the angelic and cosmic realms, out of which is created the most splendid and beautiful forms that the heart and being of man can conceivably imagine.

THIS GENERATION'S RESPONSIBILITY IS VAST

We say to you all, then, that the responsibility of this generation is vast. Let men understand that each generation is a link with the past as well as an orderly progression into the future. This generation, invaded as it is by the spirits rebellious from the time of the destruction of lost Atlantis, does have a responsibility for the hospitality given to those discordant souls.

You may not understand how this is so, but when I tell you that a guest in your house, whether invited or uninvited, becomes your responsibility once admitted, you will understand that man has some responsibility for the orderly control of his world. And if this planetary body is to manifest the victory of God, it must be because victory is a wanted manifestation for embodied mankind.

Fortunately the great cosmic lords have a fiat on high in the books of cosmic law that states: As long as there is one individual upon a planetary body who holds the balance of light for a planet, that planet cannot be utterly destroyed.

We want you to understand, however, that this is the extent of the mercy of the Great Law. There is nothing in the codes of the ascended masters, in the books of the Lords of Karma, that will prevent the sinking of continents, the upsetting of large land masses, the manifestation of tremendous upheavals in the consciousness of the people and the destructive manifestation of fierce and awful pestilence upon the planetary body.

I come to you tonight to tell you, whereas it is not the will of God that any of these conditions should manifest and it is not our intent to make a prediction as to the probability of these unwanted events, the possibility thereof when invoked by the people must be considered as an ever-present possibility by you. You must see that the student's responsibility to call forth more light and to sustain the momentum of light already generated and active upon this planet is very great indeed.

Unless the students bring forth enough light to counterbalance these manifestations of darkness, I do not doubt that the balance of power could swiftly swing toward the side of negation. And Nature herself, in her rebellion against the imposition of shadowed forms of darkness and hate, would throw off those impositions by the natural activity of the upheaval of the earth, the sinking and rising of continents and the utter change of the positions of nature upon the planetary body.

Man has already seen with the passing of time the manifestation of burr, thistle and thorn invade the nature kingdom, so that the rose itself has taken on the sharp and biting thoughts of mankind. The crown of thorns that was plaited and pressed into the Master's head was a symbol of the crucified rose, for Jesus was a manifest symbol of the perfect life here below. His Christ manifestation was the Christ manifestation of every man, and the crown of thorns pressed into it was the world's hurtful, biting attitude toward spiritual progress in a world of mortality and materiality.

Infinity's power to raise mankind from the cross of matter, mankind's power to accept the gifts of divine grace from God's hand [are dependent upon] the requalification of all the destructive energy ever released upon this planet that is responsible for the creation of dinosaurs in days of old, of the tyrannosaurus and of all other animals and animal forms created in past ages. It was not the will of God to create a world in which these awful forms could tread. They produced the destruction that occurred in past ages to the hurt of mankind and the cosmic records of akasha that yet record those awesome days.

THE POWER OF GOD'S VICTORY IS WITHIN YOU

We, coming to you tonight with the fullness of our love, say to each and every one of you, the power of God's victory is within you; it will give you the spiritual exaltation to enable you to join our bands.

We are not concerned alone with the aspect of escapism whereby the students might be made to feel they ought to forsake the earth and leave this world utterly comfortless because of all the hate and hate creations here, because of the destructive activity manifested by mankind. Some individuals have been selected by cosmic grace to remain here and in some cases have sacrificed their ascension for a proscribed period of time.

Others have ascended, yet have elected of their own free will to work and serve with embodied mankind, to engineer and assist mankind in the utilization of the elements of freedom that the Law requires. I want you especially to pay heed to the marvelous manifestation of your beloved Saint Germain and to take note of the fact that while he was utterly free, he did descend from the ascended state in the era of Napoleon and act in the hope of producing a United States of Europe.[1]

We want you to fully recognize that the manifestations of Saint Germain's love have been very great indeed and his love remains in the world to the present hour as a rose releasing the fragrance of its power. We want you to know that not only Saint Germain but also the other ascended beings, such as your beloved Mother Mary, the Mother of Jesus, your beloved Jesus, the Great Divine Director, beloved Morya El, Kuthumi and all of the panoply of ascended masters known to you, have offered their momentum and service to embodied mankind.

Seeing that they have forsworn the nirvana of God and have forsworn their personal bliss and activity of reaching the mighty, higher onrush of perfection manifest on other planets in this system of worlds, I think that it is only fair that you should express out of the purity of your heart your gratitude to these mighty souls of light, whose love is brought forth as a bouquet in your midst tonight through the energies I am releasing to you.

[Audience rises.]

I thank you for your tribute and thank you in their name. (Won't you please be seated.)

I RELEASE A STREAM OF ENERGY

I AM Victory. And I will now begin to manifest the momentum and buoyancy of my victory in your midst. I will start the stream of energy from our octave trembling through your forms. I will start the activity of victory moving through the passions of your mind. But on the morrow, when you awake, will it be terminated? Will you once again enter into the momentum of a dying world or will you be able to retain the passions of our flowering hope?

Again and again the ascended masters have released their power, their energy and the beauty of their expression into your midst and have poured out their love as an unguent upon your blessed hearts. They have done this in the presence of many and in many parts of the world, yet the ingratitude and ignorance, the forgetfulness of those who have heard their words is almost shocking to the ascended hosts, even with all their knowledge of human depravity.

We say to you, then, tonight, that what we have done is for your salvation and your freedom. Won't you understand that the victory we give you tonight is yours now? It can be yours for all eternity if you appropriate it. But oh, how quickly men are prone to forget their blessings! How quickly they are able to enter into the vibration of deceit or doubt.

How easily they are moved from a position of security to one of shake-ability. We come to you tonight and say, let us replace shake-ability with shape-ability and let us hereby resolve that from this night forward, each one of you shall manifest a greater momentum of your victory than ever before. If you do, you will make it unnecessary for us to cover the same ground again and again, to make the same admonishments and promises, to release the same levels of energy, all to be absorbed by your flesh forms and bodies without producing one iota of forward movement.

WE WANT TO GET A GRANT FROM THE KARMIC BOARD, BUT YOU MUST MERIT IT

We come to you, then, tonight, because we want to get a grant from the Karmic Board for future classes wherein we may do some of the things you have called for—called for, it seems, almost for generations. We want to exalt individuals. We would even like to see someday the ritual of a public ascension performed in your midst as at the time of Jesus.

We would like to step through the veil and clasp your hands. We would like to show you the playing lights of power from the angelic realms. We would like to show you the akashic records and let you go back even to other planetary systems to see how they lived and to examine the history thereof. We would like to give you tremendous gifts and blessings, but the Law requires that you merit it.

As long as we must, as you would say, harp upon the same thing, then that is the way it will be. The stultification and the stopping of progress are occasioned sometimes by a few individuals. Won't you understand that God is no respecter of persons, that every one of you, blessed hearts, in this place as well as in the student body throughout the world, are greatly loved of God, and there is no exception. Simply because you made a mistake at some time in your life does not mean that heaven spurns you.

The love of God for each lifestream remains inviolate for that lifestream. But that one must understand the need to break the old matrices and habit patterns, to shatter all that is not of the light by the power of the light, to draw down from higher octaves enough of the light of his own victory to actually be self-illumined.

When this is done, I assure you that the momentum of every Son of heaven can be drawn to your blessed lifestream to push you over the hump that is the point of no return, for when individuals reach a certain point, the great magnet of God's love encircles them and draws them at that moment irresistibly to the light. When that surge of power comes into their vehicle, their flesh form, their mind and their being, when it builds up and the cells of the body become charged with it and it becomes a glowing light as at the creation of the earth, each cell is then almost a glowing world with continents filled with people.

All things seem to be a sea of light and the body seems to be transparent, like glass. Then the magnetism of God begins to pull the cells and the individual feels called back to the heart of God. And consciousness, pirated now these many years from the Divine, is called Home once again. "Thou art my beloved Son, in whom I AM well pleased" becomes the fiat that holds the sacred tone, the tone of infinite love that invokes in the soul the ray of the return.

The ascension flame springs up
And the individual knows that no power in heaven and earth
Can stop him from the light that flows.
From his very toes unto the top of his head,
Instead of human thoughts and densities,
The power of majesty glows.
The radiance of the victory of the flame
Will draw him upward in God's name.
He will see that no power on earth below
Can impede him or his flow.
He must return by sacred fire
To the cause of first desire.
His First Love, then, reborn again,
Will bring him to the freedom of the law of love,
The power from above
That breaks the bonds and shakes the sons
Until they are all one in light for light's own sake.

We say, then, as our parting word to you. The victory of the light is yours tonight, if you will make it so. A high resolve in soul, a high resolve in spirit to accept this love will give you, without fail, if sustained as a momentum in your world through all generations, the victory of Jesus, the victory of Mary, the victory of Saint Germain and the victory of the Great Divine Director.

And, in conclusion, it will give you *my* victory, for I AM *your* victory!

[Audience rises.]

I thank you.

October 13, 1968
La Tourelle
Colorado Springs, Colorado
MLP

14

INDOMITABLE GREETINGS OF COSMIC VICTORY

On behalf of a planet, may I bring you those indomitable greetings of cosmic victory! And may I bring that buoyancy and joy which I AM into the forcefield of your consciousness tonight in a more than ordinary way! I AM Victory! And I AM also the victory of every man, woman and child upon this planet—freedom in the light and freedom to be that which God already is. For when you were endowed with the majesty of the divine image, it was so that you could manifest it.

Will you then tonight understand with me that the manifestation of the image of God in the world of form is the highest glory which man can share in? As I come to you tonight, I come in an invocative spirit, because I am determined that the joy which I have shall be the joy of the world. Never in over ten thousand years has the planetary body seen or understood that experience which I am directing tonight by agreement with those cosmic councils and Solar Lords governing this system of worlds.

It is true that humanity have departed from the covenant of Asha,[1] the covenant of purity; but I want you to understand that in the hearts of men there is an anchor of both their victory and their purity, which I AM. Therefore, tonight as I descend into the atmosphere of the planetary body,

I bring with me over ten thousand legions of angels [audience rises], and I bring them in God's name to the earth to minister to the children of men because of their basic needs. (Will you please be seated.) I invoke, then, in the name of God and by the power of God, the angelic hosts of light for and on behalf of this planetary body. And they come with me in order to vest you and to vest humanity with an awareness of their victory!

What is victory? It is the overcoming of those outer conditions which you have struggled against with your mortal consciousness. Now I say, let us demand the reinforcement of that mortal consciousness by those immortal applications of cosmic joy, peace, and loveliness which shall bring to the mind a new domain, a new outlook not only upon this year, but upon all years to come as the immortality and the peace of your victory as a reality.

You have thought in terms of your victory as remote. Well, I want you to understand that the realization of your victory can be an immediate occupation of the total being of man so that people, instead of being involved in a struggle for this or that, can at last understand how they can enter into the immediate fulfillment of those cosmic wishes that are a part of the great cosmic light of God which never fails. I say to you tonight, the light of God never fails! And when I say it, I want you to reinforce that action as a tangible focus in your own hearts so that you can become the beneficiaries of that cosmic service which I seek to render unto you.

You have somehow or other had the idea that you are deficient. Will you please remove from your mind and consciousness tonight that you are a deficient person and enter instead into the consciousness that you are an efficient, God-free being determined to embark upon the course of your own cosmic victory? For then I believe that the focalization we can produce in the world of form will be a cosmic miracle of light's splendor such as the world has not hitherto seen—no, not for thousands of years.

I want you to understand that there is a law of abundance functional in every one of the ascended masters. And do you know what that law is? It is the law of the production of greater grace in the heart of those who are yet to come than they themselves have manifested. No matter how great the ascended masters' consciousness may be, in the world of finite form they are always imbued with the consciousness that God is and is functional within their own manifestation.

And therefore they understand the law of miracle transcendence whereby the consciousness in any given age can at last ascend itself into a higher vibratory rate, to higher spheres, and bring with it the consciousness of initiation into the world of form whereby the planetary body becomes transformed by the transcendent light of purpose which is the glow of the eternal power and fire of the cosmic being of God himself in the heart of the Great Central Sun.

Will you accept that? Will you allow yourselves to become enamored by that? Will you draw nigh unto that? Will you accept that victory as a part and portion of the Godhead that is tangibly intended as a gift for you? Well, dear hearts of light, I am offering it to you! Will you not take it? Will you not accept it? Will you not be it?

If you will, I am sure that the transformation that will occur in your thought processes will not so immediately decide that now you are at last going to go through some strange and undesirable negative condition. For how easily the human mind is able to accept that about itself because of the tremendous infiltration into the world of form and the life patterns and life records of so many, many people who have passed through undesirable experiences.

Well, all you have to do is let go! Let go of those old ideas! Arrange for the transmutation through the sacred fires and elements of God's own being, and then decide that you will have no more of that! Are you not tired of situations in your life that are less than victory? Will you accept with me tonight, then, a feeling of your own God-victory and make it a permanent part of your own world?

This is the manner in which I myself was able to attain not only to the title of Victory, but to the being of Victory as a part of God. You may say to yourself, "Ah yes, victory is a part of God and victory is a part of mighty Victory, but is it a part of my own world? No." Well, beloved hearts, as long as you say no, it will be that way, don't you see? But the moment that you decide that you will become a God-victorious person, a person—a pure sun—of great light and loveliness, then you have already started those fires of victory upon the great end hearth of your own consciousness, and from that domain it will *expand* and *expand* and *expand* until it covers the earth!

Humanity have for thousands of years accepted the principle that they need to rob their brothers, because they are not satisfied that the abundance of God's love has provided enough through the avenues of nature; therefore, they reach out and take that which is not their own. They do not understand the one fiat by which I invoke the angels. And now I will invoke them: *"The earth is the LORD's, and the fullness thereof!"*[2]

As I spoke these words, every grain of sand upon the planet recorded them. You think, perhaps, that these are being recorded only upon electronic tape. Let me tell you that every grain of sand, every drop of water, every portion of *all* substance has recorded my words tonight because I speak with the authority of God. And I have delivered unto the world this, my fiat: *"Victory, victory, victory, victory, victory!"*—billions and billions of times written upon the sands of the planet. You cannot handle a grain of sand or substance from now on without knowing that the word "victory" is upon it.

"Oh, what an ego he has!" you say. [Audience laughs.] Let me assure you that I have long ago dispensed with that. I have uttered this name as a quality of God-obedience, a quality you can make your own, a quality you can cause to stir those unregenerate energies in yourself and tell them to depart from you and to be transmuted into light and loveliness as those beautiful regenerate energies of God-happiness and victory.

What a triumph it will be, then, when humanity, at last accepting that spirit of cosmic understanding which I AM, will understand that it was the original intention of God from the beginning day that man should be an overcomer of darkness. Well then, let us get on with the business of overcoming!

How do you suppose it shall be done? First of all, by the buoyant, joyous, transmutative release which I am making tonight, I expect you to go out and literally beat the world into submission! You say to yourself, "Well, what do I do first?" And I tell you, it is to actually focus that consciousness of God-victory in your own individual worlds. And when you do it, I tell you if you will remain constant to that sense of victory, it will make a *wonderful* change in your world, a change that will cause those little obstacles that so long have become the stumbling blocks in the pathway of your life to literally yield themselves unto me.

"Oh yes," you say, "while the consciousness of Victory is buoyantly, joyously buoying me up, I am able to do all of that." Well, let me tell you something tonight: When you understand that the God-power of Victory is literally alive within you, when you keep that consciousness enshrined as though it were an icon upon the wall of your being, it will transform you!

But when you let slip from your consciousness all of these things because the bugaboo of human nonsense stands there and says: "Oh, you're a terrible person; you are an egotistical person; you are a person of darkness and deceit; you have this fault and you have that fault"—so long as you accept that, you probably will.

But the moment that you begin to understand that only by cosmic grace and loveliness—manifested by Jesus the Christ and the ascended masters throughout the ages—will you ever be able to shake the dust off of your feet and find at last that you can arise in those triumphant moments whereby the great cosmic spirals of the cosmic fire become a tangible manifestation for *you.* How do you suppose this will be done? Because the Spirit within you is made of the same substance as the Spirit of the ascended master.

Well, don't you see then? It is merely a matter of expressing those God-qualities which are already within yourself! And the idea and concept that you cannot do it is a concept of satanic lore, a concept of Luciferian strategy whereby humanity have accepted this and have not understood that at last the very cradle of God-victory is within themselves. When they understand this, then they are no longer a lone pine tree standing upon a lonely hill separated from the world and feeling so sorry for themselves.

Do you understand, then, that all of us are altogether with you, standing with you? How in God's name can you actually stumble any longer? Well, you say, it isn't exactly easy! [Audience laughs.] Let me tell you that it may seem to be hard to actually do the will of God; but when you accept the spirit of your victory, you will be transformed in thought! And whereas that action of thought may not immediately seem to percolate through to those decadent atoms which you have unfortunately not shepherded through the great cosmic fire often enough, then you will understand that that power of the Cosmic Christ that is universally within you and is now called into action will become a tangible manifestation from an ultimate standpoint and you will not be weary simply because you see some manifestation that is not already perfect.

This is one of the great stumbling blocks of humanity. It is the idea that they are not already perfect. Well, I tell you, they are! They have simply accepted imperfection, and this has become the fiat of their world. They have accepted the dissonant beat of drums from an idle jungle of human nonsense, and they have denied the immortal facets of cosmic light that actually breathes and glistens within them. What do you suppose beats your heart, beloved ones? Well, the power and energy that beats your heart is the power by which the worlds themselves are framed and by which they are turned in space and by which the glory of God becomes a tangible reality in the face of an avatar such as Jesus the Christ, in the face of an avatar such as El Morya.

All of these great ones—Kuthumi—they builded cathedrals; they struggled against the outer circumstances of the world. He became the divine poverello, as he was called, because he said: "I will give myself unto thee. I will give myself unto God." And what really transpired? Well, God already had him, but the devil seemed to have a hold of one foot; and somehow or other he was disturbed somewhat if that one foot was pulled upon. Well, I want you to understand that it doesn't matter if they have you by *both* feet [audience laughs] if you understand that God is inside of you and he that is in you is greater by far than he that is in the world.[3]

It is a state of consciousness; it is a matter of understanding; it is a matter of the recognition of that understanding—by you, not by someone else. It is not enough for El Morya, the great master, to have in his consciousness that he can overcome the world and the state of the flesh and the state of outer carnal manifestation. But when the Spirit of God takes *you* over, something else will happen. It will not be a figment of your imagination!

Now let me say to you, why do you suppose I say that? Because so many people have rationalized and brought out into the intellectual state of their being those very marvelous little tidbits of human knowledge that say that God is not, that Christ is not. Why, you would almost think, dear ones, that they would say they themselves were not! But you seldom hear them say that.

Do you understand what I mean? They will say that God is not—the great God of the universe. They will say that beloved Jesus is not, but the ones who say it don't say that *they* are not. They seem to consider themselves, then, to be of superior intelligence and power of rationalization whereby they can literally rationalize all of the ascended masters out of existence.

Well, thank God that they have not done it! For we are *here!* And our victory is a tangible manifestation within *you* if you will let it upon the altar of your heart and being! And I tell you that it is the fervor of God by which I speak, that it is the victory of God by which I speak, that it is the devotion of God by which I speak, and that I am come this very night from Venus to bring you the radiation of the sacred fire and the power of great invisible worlds even beyond that. I have traveled this very week to the very heart of the Great Central Sun! And there I have been charged with those solar energies by which the very hub of creation turns and radiates and pours out its victorious energies for the accomplishment of God ideals.

Oh, you say, the pralaya* will end. Well, let me tell you, though it may end, it will start again! And I want you to know that the hub of creation

---

pralaya: in Hindu cosmology, a period of dissolution and destruction of a manifested universe, preceding the new creation will keep on radiating and turning in the diurnal movement of worlds without end throughout all time to come and throughout all eternity to come. And never will it stop! It is like a top that is wound up forever because the energies of God are triumphant in it. And the energies of God are triumphant in you and they are a part of your own very soul!

Will you understand that? Will you smile in your heart as you recognize the truth in my words? For by this smile of acknowledgment, you will help to solidify in your world those buoyant, joyful, cosmic, radiant energies by which you were formed in the very beginning, and you will understand that those cosmic laws which enabled me to come here and speak to you tonight are the laws by which the universe is both guided and governed. And when you understand that, outer conditions are meaningless. Why? Because you have understood the higher Law, and the lower laws of human manifestation seem themselves to pale into insignificance.

Will you accept then tonight the idea of your own ascension in the light? Well, the moment you accept it as a premise, what do you have to do? Right away you start changing your life, because you know very well the consciousness you now have is not the consciousness of the ascension, nor is it the consciousness of your victory. So you set about the task of deciding for yourself that "I am going to do something about that and I am going to transform myself in consciousness."

What is the end result? The end result is a triumph for God. Every single soul that graduates from the schoolrooms of earth becomes a triumph for God. And strange as it may seem, this is one of the reasons why we sometimes display ascended masters in more than ordinary manners, because we want the whole universe to rejoice. As it was said in your own Bible, every sinner that repenteth causes joy in heaven.[4] Well, let me assure you that the moment a man repenteth or a woman repenteth and turns to serve the light with all his heart, the light turns around to serve him with all of its. And what takes place? Why, an entire transformation of course!

And you say to yourself—simply because you engage in a checkerboard consciousness, playing little games with yourself—you decide: "After all, I heard Victory; I was inspired. I heard this or I heard that and

I was inspired. But now I have all these tragic circumstances facing me and what am I going to do about it? I've got to do something about it right now!" And so you don't do anything about it whatsoever. You simply suffer the qualms of conscience, the regrets and the pains that you got yourself into hot water in the first place.

Well, I want you to understand that the pathway to joy and deliverance and victory is one that is strewn with a lot of human nonsense behind it. Will you recognize, then, that you'd better throw out some of that ballast so your balloon can go higher? [Audience laughs.] Well, if you will accept that, then I can do something for you, and you can do something for yourself. If you don't accept it, I want you to understand that you will more or less stultify yourself, stand still, and sometimes go under the quicksand. For the quicksand is there! It's waiting to absorb you! It wants to soak you up like a blotter or a sponge! It wants to take you and rob you of your energy!

And what happens to the quicksand? Well, down underneath, you see, they have a little tunnel. And you know what happens in that tunnel? They take *all* of the energy they can steal from all of you, and where do they put it? They put it out in the world to create negativity! And so it becomes a vicious circle, and humanity is constantly the victim of it.

Well, when men understand at last that their victory—their God-victory—is within them and they understand that every cell has the imprint upon it of the words of eternal, immortal, ever living victory, they will understand at last that that is the reason for rejoicing and they will no longer entertain those dark thoughts whereby their consciousness is dragged down as a whirlpool of defeat and darkness and sadness and their face grows long and becomes wrinkled [audience laughs] and they have all kinds of bad ideas and they can't sleep and they decide that the whole world is against them! Why, beloved hearts of light, the moment they begin to understand that this is *nonsense,* they will recognize that they can keep drawing that great sphere of cosmic victory!

You know what I am going to do for you tonight? I am going to answer your calls; that's what I am going to do! And I am going to answer them in this way. Sometime when you get these awful spirits of despondency that I described to you in part, will you just make a call to me very quickly and say: "Beloved mighty I AM Presence and beloved Victory: Help me, help me, help me! Get me out of this condition right away, right now!"

And you watch what happens: The first thing you know, way down to the very tips of your feet, you're going to feel that cosmic energy penetrating you and you're going to get that *smile,* and all of the darkness will suddenly creep away and hide because it has no place else to go! [Audience laughs.] It can't stay inside of you any longer, because you are a spirit of victory! You're a spirit of triumph! You're a spirit of joy! You're a spirit of God! And you flood that across the face of the whole green earth! And then after a while there won't be any more snow! [Audience laughs.]

You can melt it with divine love! Why, you can melt all of the ice crystals out of your world and you can find your freedom in that wonderful golden sun of the golden dawn of cosmic illumination. And you can bring that to the feet of humanity and you can cause humanity to understand, by the fervor of God and the faith of God, that God is real and that they are real and their soul is real and the joy within them is real, that I AM real, that Victory will seal you in a heart of cosmic victory forever if you will only yield yourself to that spirit of truth that is within you.

Begin to study to show thyself approved unto God![5] Begin to understand, to accept the great fiats of immortal life within you and recognize that forever. I have come to you tonight and I have come to the world with a special purpose. And I am going tonight to every continent upon this planet, and I am going to put a massive image of Victory into the etheric realm over that continent. And I am going to send an arrow down into every heart that is dark and black and deceitful, and I am going to say to that heart, "Don't you know that you beat because God lives?" And I am going to try to create a sense of abundance in the minds of humanity as has never been done before, and I am going to work with *you.*

Will you then recognize the power of being a catalyst? Will you recognize the power of being a catalyst? Will you recognize the power of being a catalyst? You can become a catalyst wherever you go, for I will make you an emissary of Victory to this planet! I will make whoever will accept it an emissary to this planet so that they can carry the light of victory to the dying world that you presently envision and revive it and restore it to life—and in three days it will walk again in the spirit of cosmic joy!

Do you know what I'm talking about? I'm not talking about three earthly days—Monday, Tuesday, and Wednesday—I'm talking about the victory of the eternal day of awakening humanity to make them realize the timeless beauty that is in the thought of victory! Why, you have only taken one quality of God. What will happen when you take them all?

I thank you.

January 3, 1971
La Tourelle
Colorado Springs, Colorado
MLP

15

THE INITIATION OF THE TEN

I AM Victory. I come with the authority of Alpha and Omega to challenge all that opposes the victory of the consciousness of mankind and of the entire planetary body. I come with healing in my wings and I come with a thousand legions of victory, each legion containing ten thousand angels of victory from out the Great Central Sun.

The testing of the hour, the testing of the planetary body, is the initiation of the number ten. And so I say to you each one, ask that ye might receive this initiation of Lord Maitreya, the initiation of the ten. Having asked, stand fast to receive, for the Lord will not fail to grant your request and you must not be found wanting when the test is given.

I am not interested in "C" students. I demand "A" students, "A" for Alpha. I am not interested in those who pass the tests by the skin of their teeth. I am interested in those who determine to pass the tests with flying colors. Sons of Alpha, "A" students, the cream of the crop, these are the ones we take and the rest we leave behind.

The test of the ten is the test of selflessness. Are you aware of self as human or divine? In the crucible of this test you will be called upon to decide: human or divine.

The sword of victory shall fall and on which side will you stand?

Will you stand to the left or to the right? This is the choice. It must be made in small things and great things—in all things. Daily and hourly, you must choose, and by your choice you will earn the mark of Alpha.

THE MOMENTUM OF
TEN THOUSAND-TIMES-TEN THOUSAND

I come, then, to bring the momentum of my legions who have passed the test with flying colors. These are the "A" students arrayed before you. They stand as golden pillars of fire, fires of illumination standing in the temple of our God, pure and undefiled before his throne. They are ready to bequeath their momentum to those of you who would pass this test.

Rise, then, I say. [Audience rises.] Stand erect to receive the momentum of the sons and daughters of Alpha, for the entire planet Earth stands upon the threshold. In the weighing and the judgment of the Keeper of the Scrolls in the coming six months, the final determination shall be made, based on whether or not a sufficient number of embodied individuals pass the test of the ten.

Let me say, then, that the earth is in the tenth house of her evolution as a planetary body. In order to ascend the spiral into the house of victory, a more than ordinary devotion and dedication must come forth in coming months. Will you, then, determine to be the balance in the scales of life that by the power of victory outweighs all the failures of mankind?

I say to you, this is possible, for when you place your momentum of victory in the balance, ten thousand angels will stand in the balance with you. That is the power of the light. That is the power of the light to magnetize greater light and to outweigh the darkness by the power of the ten thousand-times-ten thousand.

And I say to you, when you are victors in this test, to you shall be given the power of the ten thousand-times-ten thousand. And whenever you raise your hand to manifest the power of the divinity of self, the momentum of ten thousand-times-ten thousand will come upon you, will raise your right hand, will increase its momentum and will deliver the thrust of triumph to all peoples, to all life.

There shall be great rejoicing as the laurel of victory is placed not only upon your head but upon the heads of all who are tied to you in the cosmic antahkarana of victory. Keystones in the arch of being are you, if you accept this.

DO NOT FORGET MY WORDS

I must say to you, each one, the power of darkness to make you forget my dictation and my words is very great when it is weighed in the crucible of time and space. The legions of night, already arrayed against you to make you forget and hence be off guard when the test comes, are great indeed. I point this out to you, not as a point of discouragement but as a point of the power of the All-Seeing Eye in its discrimination so that you are forewarned and hence forearmed.

THE GOLDEN-AGE MAN AND WOMAN APPEAR

Now my legions are gathered and the ten thousand stand over you. Sealed, then, upon the crown of your noble heads, ladies and gentlemen, are the fires of victory. They are burning there as the golden-age man, the golden-age woman appears within you—fires of illumination burning through the brain, burning through the skull, burning through your physical forms. Your mental, emotional and etheric cycles are all receiving the purification of Mighty Victory and of Cosmic Christ illumination.

I want to tell you that it is my cosmic office and my authority to bring you this momentum of victory. I have given my all for a million years to be able to stand in this place and bequeath this momentum to you. It has been no sacrifice but a rejoicing.

In your octave, however, it would be counted a sacrifice. Therefore, I say, fear not to make the sacrifice of the little self to prove the groundwork of the Great Self so that you, too, can become the benefactors of the race, of the planet and of the solar system by the power of Mighty Victory, *by the power of Mighty Victory! by the power of Mighty Victory!*—whose mantle is given to you this hour to wear, as long as you determine to efface the little self and edify, glorify and resurrect the Great Self.

So, then, burn on, fires of victory! Burn on within the hearts of these children! Burn on within the hearts of the children, babes in mothers' arms across the face of Terra. Burn on, for I, Victory, declare it!

In the name of Alpha and Omega, I initiate the age of Victory.
Cycles of Victory appear!
Cycles of Victory appear!
Spirals of Victory descend!

Let the Holy Spirit, the Whole-I-Spirit of the Almighty One, come forth now and Helios and Vesta and the Great Central Sun Magnet—all are in position for the victory of planet Earth.

Now ye are no longer mortals but electrodes of victory.

Can you remember this identity that I transfer to you in this hour? Can you conceive of yourselves from this day on and forevermore as electrodes, as fiery sparks of victory?

Victory automatically conveys illumination. Victory automatically conveys power. Victory automatically conveys love. It is the spark that flashes 'cross the night sky of humanity's consciousness. It illumines the night, transforms the consciousness and raises all into the Christ-awareness that is the precipitate of gold from the Great Central Sun, the lodestone of the golden age and of the golden-age man and womb-man.

I, Victory, have come into your midst. If I spoke for another hour I could not increase the tempo of illumination, for that which has been released has been released by authority of the Cosmic Solar Logoi and the Lords of Karma.

It is given to you. It is given to you as fiery purpose, as a flame within your being. If you could see yourself this moment on the inner, you would see a temple transparent, with orifices that are the points of the chakras. And as you gaze into that temple and into that house of the living God, you will see burning from head to toe the fires of cosmic victory, the fires of illumination.

Retain them. Amplify them and use them to set the mark in the annals of time, in the sands of time, in the very earth, in the waters, in the air and in the fire of the earth. Set the footprint. Set the engram of the golden age and stamp the mark of victory.

Leave the mark of victory where'er you walk and then beckon mankind to follow after you, for they follow not after the mortal self but after the Divine Self, who has replaced the mortal. They follow in the trail of light left by the ten thousand angels who this day have espoused your cause.

Sons of light, daughters of light, be emblazoned with victory! Accept the calling and go forth to do the will of God!

October 15, 1972
La Tourelle
Colorado Springs, Colorado
ECP

16

VICTORY FROM GOD'S HEART

Flaming ones, I AM Victory! And the spirit of victory from out the Great Central Sun draws nigh the earth in this hour of triumph. I AM come with legions of light bearing the wisdom flame, sacred honor of light held in the heart of Christ. Light expands the domain of God's consciousness as wisdom's flame, as the light from far-off worlds, the power of the spoken Word.

I AM Victory! I AM Victory! I AM Victory! I AM Victory! In the four planes of Spirit, in the four planes of Matter, the flame of victory blazes, and those who come at the eleventh hour as well as those who come in the early morning shall receive the just reward for their labor.[1]

What does it matter if the Lord of the vineyard should pay them equally? Is it not the choice of the Lord to reward great and small as he sees the line of the past, present and future devotion of the soul and of the flame within the heart?

Therefore, I say to each one of you, whether you have labored in the vineyard of the Lord for an aeon or a moment, you can receive your just portion of light that is the fulfillment of the Law within your being.

THE GOLDEN LIGHT OF VICTORY

It is a matter of cosmic cycles, precious hearts. The light of victory is an ongoing light, a mighty tide of golden illumination swimming in a sea of white fire. Moving upon that sea, merging and folding within the sea, the waves of fiery light and golden-yellow flame now cross the earth and bring to mankind once again the memory of a former estate, a state of love and victory and mastery.

I AM a cosmic being spanning years, spanning centuries of attainment, of light's atonement, of light's fire in the heart of the atom. My legions are atoms of God, flaming balls of light, of fire, of worlds of consciousness, of truth that is the freedom of the Law.

APPROPRIATE THE LIGHT OF THE CHRIST

Thus, because it is the hour of victory, all mankind who attune with the consciousness of the Christ may receive the victory of that light. It is a matter of appropriation. It is like strolling in a beautiful garden where floral offerings are displayed by elementals to the glory of God. To admire the flower, to take in its fragrance is an aspect of the enjoyment of beauty, but to the initiate of the sacred fire who knows the foundation of the rose to be geometric design and fiery fohat is given the ability to appropriate, not only to admire.

Thus to appropriate the sacred pattern, the petaled pattern of a rose, is to take in that pattern and assimilate it, to become it, to outpicture it and finally to create it. Thus you see that the difference between the child-man and the man of maturity is the difference between one who gazes upon the Christ in admiration and one who gazes upon the Christ and appropriates his being, his consciousness, his law. He makes it his own, claims it as his own being in the oneness of love.

Did the Christ not say, "I and my Father are one"?[2] Can you not also say, "I and my Father are one" and thus appropriate the consciousness of the Father as a mantle of light that descends from heaven, as the mantle that was passed from Elijah to Elisha?

APPROPRIATION IS A SCIENCE OF INITIATES

Thus appropriation is a science of initiates, of advanced disciples in every age who have reached the age of responsibility, who will, in every task, respond to the ability of God to be in man, the ability of God to work his works through man. O impoverished ones who stand and admire the sun and stars and earth, do you not understand that the impoverishment of your consciousness, mind and being is ever the line drawn between child and man—between the one who observes and the one who becomes the fullness of God in manifestation?

Thus the angel of the Lord who came to John the Revelator would say each time the beloved disciple fell down and worshipped him, "See thou do it not; I am thy fellow servant and of thy brethren that have the testimony of Jesus. Worship God."[3]

Do you not understand the lesson of Jesus washing the feet of the disciples? The servant is not greater than his Lord. Thus the man Jesus desired to place himself in adoration, in service to the Christ in each disciple. This is the flaming spirit of the victors, of the overcomers—those who worship the Law, and in worshiping the Law see the need for action and for becoming that Law in manifestation.

> I AM the light of far-off worlds.
> I AM the light of victory, cosmic banner do unfurl!
> I AM the light right within you now
> Starting the sacred action of God's sacred heart,
> For I desire that you should appropriate this night
> The power of God's heart, his light, his energy,
> His focus from the Central Sun
> So that you can know that Christ, the only begotten one,
> Is Son of God in you, in me, in all of hierarchy.

The echelons of fire, flaming fire rising higher, also show the pattern, the weaving, the tapestry of divinity in all. Thus the tapestry of life is a great scenario, a mighty mural that shows the beginning of life unto the ending, for the origin of man in fire must culminate in fire. Between the beginning and the ending of Alpha and Omega is all mankind, wending the way of earth, of merriment and mirth, descending into the level of toil, coming to the place in time and space where Satan's wiles would tempt them and would foil.

THE HEARTS OF ANGELS

Precious hearts, the hearts of angels great and small do bleed as they observe the weariness of mankind upon this planetary home. Where angels serve the need of tiny babe, of child, of youth, so are the hearts inclined of those who come as emissaries from God to man to comfort, to bring compassion, to bring mercy and to unfold the plan.

When they see the effrontery of man to God, they come back to the center of the retreats of the archangels to be repolarized to the divine feelings, to the divine consciousness. And these angels in their great sincerity, in their great desire to raise mankind step-by-step, higher and higher, see the pitfalls, see the lack of protection, see the forcefields of trepidation that surround the little ones and they provide succor and comfort.

Often their hearts are heavy, for they see that the consciousness of mankind is tethered to unreality through television, radio, motion pictures and the great flood of books and publications that tear down the soul consciousness of the little ones.

Never in the history of the evolutions of this planet have there been so many guises to distract the consciousness of the little ones. From morning to night their attention is on something in the outer that pulls them away from the center of Be-ness.

I AM Victory's ray and I send the light of victory to each heart evolving upon the planetary body.

The light of victory is a buoyant joy.
The light of victory is gold without alloy.
The light of victory descends.
It descends to defend the consciousness of God in man.
It descends to give mankind a joyous determination

To keep on keeping on,
To move forward in the light,
In the progress to the starry heights
From whence I come and whence I go.
Thus, there is a cosmic energy called flow
And in the flow the cosmic cycles are fulfilled.
The cosmic cycles are God-willed in power, in wisdom, in love.
The joy of God reveals the hope, the worth, the faith, the charity.
Let all mankind rejoice this night
That opportunity swings wide the door
And heaven's portals open once more
For mankind to choose the right,
To live in the light, to live for God,
To live for the glory of his immaculate Son.

And so I take my torch of victory's fire. I touch it to your hearts. They, too, will burn with the fire of God's heart that you shall appropriate in part this night. For by dispensation of the Lords of Karma, a portion of that flaming, fiery victory from God's heart is given to you.

It can burn there for all eternity, uncontaminated if you will, if you determine that on the ground it will not spill. For do you know that you can spill God's light by releasing it into the human plight of strife and strain and persecutions vain? Thus, beloved ones, retain, retain, retain.

O fire of victory, as the golden petal of the lotus flower that in the heart of Buddha glows, like the flowers that in your garden grow. O hearts of love, hearts of love, be wisdom's fire to all mankind and know that I AM Victory.

I AM Victory and its flame everywhere in cosmos. And wherever the word *victory* is spoken, there is that release, that impetus to finish in the Christ and to manifest the victory of the light. I have come forth that you might be inundated with the golden fires of victory this night. I have come forth to seal this class, this seminar with the spiral of God-victory, anchoring, then, within the golden ball of light the victory of the legions of Venus, of Sanat Kumara.

Thus we seal the *New Atlanta* in the fire of victory, as it is an idea, a blueprint in the heart of God. All who are called and who make their calling and election sure will find that if they endure, a focus can be appropriated over this very place of victory's light by the mature, by those who are of a mind to do the will of God, to prove the will of God, to work the works of God.

Thus appropriate, appropriate, appropriate the fires of victory. Be Victory in action. Then you shall see how you are me and I am thee and we are one in eternity.

I AM Victory and I AM thankful.

September 3, 1973
Atlanta, Georgia
ECP

17

VICTORY: A CYCLE AND A FLAME

I AM the victory of the light in the hearts of all mankind!

I AM the victory of the flame and my legions descend in the golden flame of victory. They stand on earth this day to proclaim the victory of light, of peace and of the feminine ray. "There shall no evil befall thee, neither shall any plague come nigh thy dwelling"[1] when in victory you take your stand for the light.

It is the determined, invincible, victorious light of freedom and the sense of freedom that give mankind the victory over every unwanted condition, over all darkness. Faith in the victory, hope in the victory, charity in the victory are the components of victory. Did you ever see an army or a player win a fight without the sense of victory?

The great sense of victory overcomes in every struggle, great or small. Those among mankind who have the vision of victory every day, every hour, are those who triumph over the problems that arise daily. Arise with victory in the morning, retire with victory in the evening and consecrate the cycles of the hours to Victory's flame and you shall see the salvation of our God in this age.

Do not accept the defeatist concepts of the dark ones who enter subtly through momentums of condemnation and degradation. Do not accept defeat, great or small. That subtle acceptance at the level of the electronic belt is certain death, certain darkness. Do not accept to even contemplate defeat at any time, anywhere. Do not utter the word of failure. It cannot be; it must not be; it is only illusion.

Espouse the flame of God-reality. Pledge your energies to the light and guarantee the flow of light in the name of the Christ. Is not the I AM Presence, is not the Christ Self, the greatest guarantor of your life's destiny?

O ye of little faith, espouse the flame and be free to move forward in perpetual harmony. I AM the defender of your God-mastery, your God-harmony and your God-vision, for reality is the flame of the Holy Spirit that animates every cell of life.

THE CRUCIFIXION OF THE FEMININE RAY

Thus, as the malefactors hung on the cross with Jesus the Christ, so the malefactors among the Jews and Arabs come in the hour of the crucifixion of the feminine ray to be tried in the hour of their judgment.

Those who are ready for the crucifixion will have the reward of eternal life. "Today shalt thou be with me in paradise"[2] is the eternal hope that God maintains in his heart on behalf of the laggard evolutions and those who have perpetually sought to defame the image of the Divine Woman, of Mary and her Son.

Those who refuse to acknowledge the Christ are the malefactors who are not content at the hour of their own judgment and desire to crucify all mankind upon a cross of war, darkness and despair. Hierarchy will not have it. Hierarchy demands that voices rise from among mankind to challenge this infamy, to challenge the persecution of the Christ afresh and his crucifixion in this hour of tribulation.

WE SPONSOR THE FEMININE RAY

This is the age of the Divine Woman. And for the Divine Woman to appear in all mankind there must needs be at least one woman who will lay down her life that all may live—lay down her life so that it might be taken up again by God that God might be glorified through woman, through womankind. Thus the Mother flame, which you espouse and serve, is the flame that shall be victorious within you one and all.

As I speak to you in this hour of the earth's greatest travail, travail for the birth of the Christ Child, the great avatar whose star is appearing even now in the sky, be still and know that I AM God.[3] Know that the twin flames who have sponsored this movement (as Above, so below) shall continue to sponsor the victory and the sacrifice of the feminine ray.

As one messenger laid down his life that all might live, that that life could be taken up again in the second messenger, so it shall be as the two laborers laboring in the field; one is taken and the other is left.[4] Thus, it is ever the human consciousness that must be sacrificed and consumed for the divine consciousness to appear.

This symbolical rendering has been played before you in the drama of the two witnesses. The victory of love they brought to the earth is a testimony of the victory of life that you by your dedication can also bring. You see, precious hearts, on this anniversary of the test of the ten and the great surrender that is necessary,[5] you can look to your leaders and see how total surrender has been given in this twelve-month cycle and total surrender shall be given again and again.

Heaven does not require that you lay down your life in the fight nor that you die for freedom. [Heaven requires] that you live for freedom. In victory there is no death; therefore in the ascended presence of Lanello, behold the victory of your God!

THE DEATH OF THE HUMAN EGO
FOR THE RESURRECTION OF THE DIVINE EGO

The victory of the light of Jesus the Christ is the portrayal again and again before the eyes of mankind of the truth that the human ego must die on the cross that the divine Ego be resurrected in all. Do you think that Jesus had a human ego when he went to the cross on behalf of mankind?

I tell you, nay. Yet he was willing to make that public demonstration on behalf of all who would find the key to salvation, to eternal life, to the salvation of the nations, [in the understanding] that in the laying down of the lesser self, the greater might appear.

Therefore also learn that for your messenger it was not necessary in the sense that there was a human ego that should die, but that the mortal, the corruptible image, might put on incorruption.[6] He put on immortality to leave the mark of the example of raising the feminine ray for the next two-thousand-year cycle of the reign of the Divine Mother in the flame of freedom.

I AM Victory! I have come with my legions and they are legions of cosmic beings who have attained Cosmic Christ consciousness. We come forth in this hour as we came forth in the beginning of Saint Germain's dispensation in this century. We renew our pledge and our vow to stand behind the flame of freedom.

And so when you see the violet flame blazing across the earth, you will see, peeping through, the golden light of victory and the fires of victory. The legions of victory ride their chargers with violet-flame angels; together, two by two, they come, clad in the robes of righteousness and of the saints.

STUDY THE CYCLES

I would point out to you this day that in your analysis of cycles and the cycles of the stock market crash, you should realize that in every century mankind is given a hundred-year allotment of energy with which to prove the mastery of the Christ by the power of the ten-times-ten. To master selflessness ten times is the victory of each century.

Do you see, then, that the first thirty-three years of the century are critical? Likewise, the first thirty-three years in the life of man marks the attainment of Christhood or the lost potential for that attainment. In the perfect life lived by Jesus the Christ, you witness how mastery came to the four lower bodies through the four cycles of seven, [ending] at the twenty-eighth year.

This was followed by his going within for the five secret rays to bring his mastery to the thirty-third year and the hour of the ascension. Two of the secret rays were within; three of the secret rays were in public demonstration of the Law. This is a test and a pattern that individuals and nations must follow.

Therefore, learn well the lesson of the 1920s as the dark forces introduced their dark music, their dark rhythms, and mankind began to move to the sinuous winding of the serpentine force and the serpentine lie.[7] They opened their emotional bodies, their mental bodies to darkness and to the manipulation of the flow of harmony that no longer flowed to the music of the spheres and the stately movement of the waltz. [The waltz] had been given to them by Saint Germain in the previous century in preparation for the flow of freedom, for the flow of supply and gold in preparation for the Aquarian age—the golden age that should come to pass on American soil.

A DOWNWARD SPIRAL

Thus, with great subtlety, the Luciferians wove their plots to defame and deface the image of the Christ through the destruction of the American economy. What occurred in 1929 was the beginning of the downward spiral of opposition to the ascension of the Christ consciousness in a people and a nation.

Will you let it happen again? We will not.

Will you let it happen again? [Audience responds, "No!"]

Praise God for your fervent desire to pit your energies, roll up your sleeves and dig in with Saint Germain for the greatest invocation of light and victory that the world has ever known, for it is necessary.

What happened at the time of the crash, the mark of Antichrist?

Instead of the ascension of consciousness, suicides occurred by the hundred, by the thousand, as those who had welded their consciousness to materiality saw not the vision of the ascended Saviour nor the goal to be like him. Instead of rising, they leaped from the skyscrapers of New York into caverns of despair and hopelessness.

Precious hearts, how easy it is to analyze the plots of darkness after they are spent. After the failure, after the battle has been lost, then the historians go back and tell us how we might have won, how it might have been.

I tell you, the thirty-three-year cycle comes three times in each century. Beginning with the new cycle in 1934, you will see that 1966 is the culmination of the next thirty-three years. Precious hearts, America is on the eve of the victory of the two hundredth anniversary of the birth of a nation. Nineteen seventy-six marks two centuries of the test of the ten, ten times [each century].

Do you see, then, how the forces of darkness are rallying to deprive mankind of the victory of the declaration of the independence of the soul?

THE DANGER OF THE ELEVENTH HOUR

If you behold the chart of the cycles, you will see that the hour of victory, the eleventh hour, is fraught with resentment, revenge, retaliation. This is the dragon's tail of hatred of America, resentment of her good and her giving and her aid—her giving of foreign aid without limit until the Divine Mother has been milked of the very essence and energy of her life.[8]

That milk has been fed to the bastard sons of darkness throughout the world, who have taken that light, that precious light, and used it to pervert its energy to darkness for the betrayal of the very heart of the Divine Woman!

I would point out to you that neither in the Arab nor the Jewish culture does the Divine Woman occupy a position of ascendancy. Woman is not allowed to enter the sacred rooms of the Jewish synagogue and woman is at the lowest ebb of her evolution in the Arab nations, for even in Communist China and behind the Iron Curtain woman retains greater dignity. I say this to point out to you that this is indeed the crucifixion of the feminine ray.

THE WOMAN OF THE NEW AGE

The Divine Mother must appear in America as the crown of glory. The Goddess of Liberty must stand forth and be adored as the archetype of the woman of the New Age. Hearts of light, precious souls, stand forth in the victory of the woman of the New Age and perceive the dawn of the realization of the feminine ray within you!

Understand that the light of victory in America is the light of the victory of the Divine Woman clothed with the Sun.[9] As the Goddess of Liberty wears the crown of seven rays, symbolizing the seven rays in outer manifestation, so the crown of the woman in the apocalypse has twelve stars, symbolizing the mastery of the five secret rays and the seven outer rays.

This, then, is our desire: to train you to master both crowns. To this end the Blessed Virgin has released the sacred rosaries through the Mother of the Flame. Thirteen in number, seven and five, with the thirteenth in the center—the focal point or pivot point in the center of the circle that is the mastery of all twelve.[10]

Thus, by giving the rosaries of the seven rays and the five secret rays, you make your attunement daily with the consciousness of victory and the victory of the feminine ray. Four times seven, twenty-eight, is seven on each side of the pyramid of life (the four lower bodies) and five for the culmination of the victory of the Christ.

AMERICA THE VICTORIOUS!

Precious hearts, as a nation, America is destined to be the great example of victory. As Jesus Christ was the avatar for the Piscean age, so America is the pilot nation selected by the ascended masters. Here people of every race, nationality and creed may merge their energies, their very blood in the melting pot so that the threefold flame of Christ light may come forth in balanced manifestation, so that the Constitution of America, written by Saint Germain as a divine document, might find parallel in the constitution of all nations upon earth.

Precious hearts, ponder well that it is not America, her government or her people who are at fault. It is the infiltration of the fallen ones, the dark ones and their systems of chaos and disintegration, their failure to pass the test of the ten, their abuse of capitalistic society by the laggard consciousness of greed, their failure to uphold the Christ as the head of every business, every government, every household.

Thus America must return to the feet of our God. Americans en masse must unite to preserve the flame of freedom. Right or wrong, that which is unreal can be consumed; that which is real can be set on high as a goal, as an ensign for all nations and all peoples.

DEDICATE YOURSELF TO THE FLAME OF AMERICA

Renew your fervor and dedication to the flame that is the reality of America. We do not ask you to dedicate yourselves to the corrupt ones who corrupt others, to their flaws, failures or to darkness. Nay, we ask you to dedicate yourselves to the principles of the victory of the Christ light in this people who yet retain to this very hour the greatest light and the greatest love of any people upon the globe. And I say this as my analysis from inner levels.

Believe it and know that the potential for victory for the entire planet is here. Do not flee America as rats fleeing a sinking ship. Some have done this, retreating to other countries, other places where they felt the economic climate was better.

This is the time to plant your feet firmly on the soil of America, to let the hierarchies of light channel their energies through you to hold the balance in the hour of Libra when the hierarchies of Victory stand in the flame of the Holy Spirit that is the flame of the golden west.

America is the fulfillment of the flame of the Holy Spirit in the Western Hemisphere. The Northern and Southern Hemispheres must be united and serve together with the understanding of the threefold flame as power, wisdom and love so that the seventh root race might be born, that the archetypes of freedom might be etched in fire for the victory of an age—the Aquarian age of the lightbearers.

WE LEAD WITH THE FLAME OF VICTORY!

I AM Victory! The golden-white light burning as a flame at the point of the third eye upon my forehead is the sign that we lead with victory.

We lead with the flame of victory. I place that flame upon your foreheads now and I place upon you the helmet of peace for the protection of your mind from psychic attacks of fallen ones. Even at this very hour they are using mechanical equipment to project rays of disintegration upon the very mind, sensitivity, devotion and dedication of the elect of God. Therefore, the helmet of peace shall be unto the righteous and unto the saints the protection of the sign of Aries that the mind of Christ might be fulfilled in you, that you might answer the fiat "Let that mind be in you which was also in Christ Jesus."[11]

Thus the heart must also be sealed in a blue sphere, for your heart must be kept in harmony. I invoke that sphere of blue from the heart of Hercules. I, Victory, in the name of the Christ, do command the legions of Hercules to encircle your heart chakra with a sphere of blue so that the shock tactics of the sinister ones will not shock the hearts of the children of light.

The prophecy has been foretold that in the last days men's hearts should fail them for fear.[12] That is part of the shock waves of darkness that are projected by the forces of the night. Is it any wonder that our messenger, those close to her and those serving in our light brigade have felt the strain on the heart in recent weeks? The waves of darkness of these malefactors, these laggard generations, have determined to pervert the heart consciousness of the Christ and the Holy Spirit through the perversions of the fires of Aries and Libra.

Understand, precious ones, that you must apply the science you have been taught by Mother Mary through the Mother of the Flame. The practice of that science will be the salvation of the religion of our God. For I tell you truly, unless you watch as watchmen of the Lord upon the wall of the Lord, you will not be able to give the cry, "All is well!" when they say, "Watchman, what of the night?"[13]

You must, then, beware of cycles. Beware of the infliction of darkness upon the centers of light in your being. I call to Cosmos to seal the secret rays in your hands that you might receive the energies of those secret rays and go forth using your hands only for blessing and for service, not for bane or ill-gotten gain. See that you do not participate in the dishonesty of those who practice in the marts of human commerce without the Christ light.

I say, then, be *sealed* heart, head and hand. "Put on the whole armour of God"[14] of righteousness and truth and go forth to the victory.

I AM Victory! I have come forth to anchor victory in the earth. The victory is unto the faithful who know that they know the Law, who practice the Law, who entertain the sense of victory, who are reborn in the flame of victory.

I thank you and I am with you until the hour of the victory of Armageddon, when light stands triumphant and all the world bends the knee to confess the Christ as the true life of every man.

I AM in the flame and I AM One!

October 12, 1973
The Motherhouse
Santa Barbara, California
ECP

THE NAME OF THE GAME IS VICTORY!

Down the corridor of the centuries, cosmic beings are aligned with the geometry of God's mind. They stand as on a stairway that disappears into eternity, watching the overcoming victory of lightbearers on this and many other worlds. Cosmic beings are of such attainment, such timelessness as to make incomprehensible to mortal ken the vast identity contained within each one's beating heart, beating in rhythm with the heart of God.

You stand at a level of hierarchy on one step of those stairs. Vast numbers precede you, and countless numbers will walk after you, climbing to the summit heights—all impelled higher and higher in the cosmic scheme by the flame of victory that I bear.

I AM Victory. I AM the victorious fulfillment of the light within avatars, sun centers and evolutions of worlds beyond worlds. I come with legions of light. We come in the golden light of victory and the aura of this city is filled with our presence. Ten thousand of our band come to shower upon you the joy of victory for the celebration of the new year.

Why do mortals toil in their merrymaking? How hard they work to have the memory of a good time! How they sport the ego. How they laugh at the antics of the little self, parading in the latest fashion or the latest step, and so they come, two by two. Is it the zoo or is it the calling of the lightbearers?

One wonders, observing over the centuries, when mortals will free themselves from the striving to be mortal. They are mortal already yet they continue to reinforce their mortality as though they were about to lose it. Aye, alas, they shall lose it. They shall lose the mortal temple. Some perceive, as the years go by, how fleeting is what they thought was the flame of youth. Yet, were it truly the flame of youth, it would not be fleeting, for the flame of youth is the ascended master consciousness. It is the bubbling joy of crystal light, overflowing as a river, nourishing and sustaining body temples far beyond the allotted span.

LEGIONS OF VICTORY ENTER THE FRAY

I come with rejoicing. Angels blowing horns, you know, angels playing harps and all that! Mankind thinks that we have naught else to do in heaven!

We have time for merrymaking after the battle is won, after we have fought a good fight. Do you know that the legions of victory relish a good fight? Do you know that they are the first to leap into the fray or into the icy waters or into the fire, with their hoops of fire of flaming victory?

So they come. Whatever aspect of mortal consciousness must be brought low, the legions of victory have a means, a method and even a tool; it is as though they had packs on their backs. You should see these legions of victory as they enter the fray. Perhaps a wrench, perhaps a sword, perhaps a rolling pin, perhaps a purple fiery heart—nothing is too small or too great. If it works, it is used by the legions of victory.

You can see or imagine many hilarious scenes as the legions of victory outsmart the fallen ones who march against the Woman and her seed. Somehow, in the leaping, curling fires of victory, there is a joy, a sense of divine humor that carries us above and beyond the call of duty as we fight the good fight hour after hour, day after day, year after year.

Did we not hear one of you say, "Have we not been fighting against that force, that darkness, for sixteen days? Isn't it about time we stopped fighting the force for a while?" Yes, we listen as you speak and as you discuss the overcoming, the victory of a planet. And we remind you that our legions are in the fray twenty-four hours a day century after century.

Therefore, you see, of all the gadgets and the tricks that we use to let the ego fall and to let the pride go before the fall, we must retain and maintain that joyous spirit. Or else, you see, our activity could become a source of aggravation, of insanity, of irritation. This you must understand, you who, unbeknownst to you, have been enlisted in the ranks of Victory. Now that you are a part of our band, you must understand that too much seriousness in the fight will cause you to take flight, to have the fright that is common only to mortals and never to the hosts of light!

BY WISDOM WE OVERCOME

I say, then, *Victory, Victory, Victory, Victory, Victory, Victory, Victory, Victory, Victory* is the breastplate, the armour, the shining light, the yellow light—Cosmic Christ illumination.

When we thrust the sword, it is not only to pierce the heart of the enemy but also to thrust forth fiery darts of illumination, for by wisdom we overcome. When that sword is thrust, it delivers the divine mandate: "Come up higher and be the Christ consciousness. Surrender the human ego or be no more."

Can you imagine those who have dwelt in caves of darkness on the astral plane coming face to face with a member of our legions in the brilliant dazzling light? As they rub their eyes and come out with their dirt and their grubby clothes, they will hear the mandate: "Surrender to the Christ. Surrender to the Almighty or be no more."

Oftentimes, I am happy to report, they do surrender and they give forth a mighty cry that is the death knell of the ego, the last gasp of the ego as it goes down. Then, in the vacuum that is left, the Christ consciousness descends, and standing before us, we behold a son of light, a child of God ready to join us in the fight.

You ask, "What happens to those who do not surrender?"

They are escorted by the legions of Archangel Michael's band for the action of the final judgment at the Court of the Sacred Fire. There the Four

---

and Twenty Elders examine the record and determine whether or not an evolving soul is worthy of having another opportunity to register claims for good in the evolving planetary homes from whence he came.

CROSS THE LINE FROM UNREALITY TO REALITY

The name of the game is victory! There is no other status symbol in heaven but victory. From the least unto the greatest, those who enter the portals of heaven must be victors and all who claim that victory must use the flame I bear.

I AM the cosmic consciousness of victory. I AM God's awareness of your victory. Therefore, call to me in the hour of victory, the hour of the victory of the manifestation of the Holy Ghost within you. Victory is Reality and there can be no Reality without victory.

Do you think that you can cross the line from unreality to Reality without a fight?

Well, let me tell you, I AM come to disarm you of that illusion.

Do you think that you can cross that line without the challenge of the dark ones, without the mandate to manifest the cosmic honor flame, without a conscious choosing of the right? Do you think that you can remain in the veil (energy veil, or *e-veil*) of the hypocrites who say yes to the right ones and no to the right ones but never in all their life make a choice or take a stand for victory, for light and for the Christ? They are the appeasers. They appease the dark ones and they remain in the veil of illusion.

Therefore, to cross that line, be ready to bear witness to the truth, to stand on principle and to refuse by all the fire you can muster to submit to one iota of the lie of the dark ones: the lie that you are not whole, that you are not a son of God—the many lies that, one and all, are compromises with the flaming presence of Reality.

TAKE A STAND FOR TRUTH

Some among mankind hope to make the grade in life by an act of faith and to return to the heart of the Saviour without ever having had to take a stand for light. They desire to be popular, to be thought well of in their communities, to occupy positions in society and they mouth the mouthings of hypocrites.

They are not to be trusted and are never the representatives of the ascended masters. You see, to lie, to misrepresent truth, to compromise is to sin against the Holy Ghost. And that sin cannot be forgiven until it is forsaken, for in that sin you enter into a state of illusion and you can never come out from illusion until you forsake the gray areas, the small white lies, the misrepresentations.

I say, espouse truth; pursue truth and you shall find Reality. And when you stand in the presence of Reality and in the flame of Almighty God, you will have the gift of the Holy Ghost. With that gift you will have the power to bring forth at will the designs of the Creator, the scheme of that which is to be brought forth as the kingdom of God made manifest upon earth.

Do you see, then, that the action of the Holy Spirit is the initiation you must pass to take dominion over the earth, to master the physical plane, to master the earth and to return victorious to the heart of God?

Understand, precious hearts. God hath made man upright, but man has sought out many inventions. The inventions of the mortal consciousness are all compromises with the image of the Christ. If you align your four lower bodies with any of these compromises, you will find that your identity separates from the presence, the omnipresence, of the Holy Spirit and without that presence you cannot go far in conquering the earth.

WE COME TO REINFORCE DETERMINED SOULS

We are flaming victors of a cause. We are flaming ones. When we see a soul determined to have the victory, we rush in with fire and with an infusion of God-determination. Perhaps a thousand of our legions come to support one soul who kneels at bedtime and calls to the All-Father for the strength to face the dawn and the tasks and responsibilities of the day at hand.

Wherever there is prayer, the legions of victory come, for victory is the flame that makes mankind see that the victory can be the fullness of God-reality. Understand your sudden surge of feeling that affirms, "I can. I can make it all the way. I can do this thing for God today." That surge of hope, that surge of energy gives you the scope to see the vision, to be willing to pass the test. This is our high behest, our calling, our willing and our service to God and man.

CROWNS OF VICTORY

In the hour of the culmination of a year of service, in the hour of the fulfillment of the service of the Mother flame in South America, I am come to crown your efforts with victory. We crown the Christ with many crowns and that Christ is also the Christ in you.

The Christ in you is the King of kings and Lord of lords. However you exalt him and glorify him in Jesus and in others of our ascended bands, remember that the Christ and the prophecy of his coming must be fulfilled within you, must be accepted because you are worthy to receive him in the manger of your heart and to walk the earth as a Christed man and Christed woman crowned with the crown of victory.

The crown is the symbol of completion, of fulfillment and of the opening of the crown chakra. It is the symbol of the culmination of the spiral of Alpha and Omega, and, you see, without the crown your endeavor is incomplete; with the crown you have a permanent focus replete with energies of sacred fire impelling you higher and higher to greater and greater victories in the light.

SCROLLS OF VICTORY

I come also bearing scrolls of victory. These scrolls bear the record and the testimony of those who have overcome the world in the past twelve months. Counted, then, among these scrolls is the scroll of your own Lanello, who has ascended from your midst by the fires of victory. He stands with me tonight to proclaim the victory—your victory in the fight.

Among these scrolls is that of one whom you called D. Cree, our own beloved Denny Cree, who ascended in this year. Thus have no fear, for angels of record and Keepers of the Scrolls keep the scrolls of victory of every ascended Son and Daughter of light. They keep them as a record true that you may read to see exactly how the overcoming and the victory were won.

Do you understand, then, that by reading over, step by step, the victories great and small of ascended avatars you can see how you can follow, step by step, the same path to your own victory? For after all, the human consciousness, with its foibles, its fantasies and its failures, is somewhat the same through its dreary repetition of the same old temptations and the same old mistakes and the same old failures.

Do you see, then, that every ascended being has walked where you now walk, at some time, at some point in his evolution?

All who are victorious have faced the tests that you now face. You can, then, by invocation in the name of the Christ appeal to that specific ascended being, although the name may be unknown to you. You may call to the ascended master who has mastered the particular step that you are now on, the specific test that you now face. And you may say:

> *In the name of the Christ,*
> *O beloved ascended master,*
> *Whoever you are, wherever you are,*
> *You who have the victory over this test,*
> *I ask you to give me*
> *The full-gathered momentum of your victory*
> *That I also might overcome*
> *And leave a record in the sands of time*
> *For others who will follow after me in the victory.*

The victorious passing of the test of the ten, then, comes because you invoke victory and because you are determined to be victorious. If you slide into an exam without preparation, without considering the facts, the cosmic astrology and the activities of light and darkness that must be recognized for what they are—light to reinforce light and darkness to be transmuted—if you do not come to the test prepared, do not expect to pass the test. It is as simple as that.

You cannot assume that somehow by the smile upon your face or the clothes that you wear you will automatically by some magic formula pass through the tests of victory. It simply does not work in that manner.

STUDY THE LAW

The Law is the Law; it has ever been the same. If you expect to pass your tests, you must use every point of the Law that you have ever learned, every teaching of the ascended masters that has ever been given. You must study to show yourself approved unto God, rightly dividing the word of truth[1] and employing those words where they are applicable to your level of evolution.

Somehow the very definite teachings of the ascended masters that are pointed toward those who require them are often missed. Often the points on which we lecture in our dictations are taken up by devotees who have already overcome them. I say, then, to those of you who need the lesson and to those of you who know that you need the lesson, hear my words and apply them.

As you apply the teachings of the masters, you earn the right to have a higher teaching, and as more and more among you apply the precepts of the Law you will come to the place where collectively you will have earned the right to have more advanced dictations and more advanced revelations.

Because such a great compendium of knowledge is waiting in the octaves of light to be delivered to mankind, we have initiated the victorious spiral of the Ascended Master University. Those who by preparation, by submitting to the disciplines and the ascended master code of conduct have earned the right to hear the higher teachings will receive our advanced dictations and instructions in the higher levels of the Ascended Master University.

We must look far and wide to find hearts purified to receive the higher teachings. Therefore we have prepared a way for training, discipline and initiation that you might receive even as you have called forth more light.

SCROLLS UNFINISHED

I would also speak to you of the unfinished scrolls—scrolls that are your own—held by angels of the Keeper of the Scrolls, angels of record and by your own Christ Self. Upon each golden scroll taken now from the archives of the Keeper of the Scrolls is written a list of the victories you have won in every incarnation since your soul descended into form. Some were upon this planet, some upon other planets, for you represent a wide range of evolutions and backgrounds in cosmos.

For some of you the scroll comprises many pages, victory after victory after victory; for others there are fewer pages. I make this record known to you to give you an added spark of determination, so that you might know that every single victory, even if it is a victory of holding back the sharp word, the sharp tongue or the jagged emotional energies that tear the very garment of the tube of light of another or their forcefield of harmony—each such victory is carefully recorded in script, a beautiful script that is unique to the angels of record.

Do you know that in order to become angels of record, the angels must practice that script and must receive an "A" in penmanship before they are allowed to write on the scrolls of victory? And so they write in a language that you will one day know as the code of fohat and you can read in hieroglyph from the inner being of the soul the record of your own victory.

THE SCROLL OF YOUR OWN VICTORY

At this moment an angel of record stands before and slightly above each one of you. If you will look slightly upward, you will find before you (as you look with your inner eye) that the angel of record is holding before your gaze the scroll of your own victory. You will see that the victories are numbered and you will see that some of you do not have a victory inscribed next to the number. Instead there is a blank, an omission—call it a sin of omission if you will. As the angels of record turn the pages of the scroll, you will see, then, where you have been victorious and where you have omitted the calls to the flame of victory to pass the tests victoriously.

All this is now recorded in your etheric body, and although you may not have total awareness, your soul has the direct revelation this night of what it must do to complete the divine plan in this life for the remainder of the year, for the coming year and decade unto the turn of the century and beyond to the hour of your ascension.

Your soul knows, for it is impressed upon it. And in its awareness, your soul will also make known to your outer consciousness by a very definite action when you pass the tests victoriously and when you do not. Specifically you will be given the opportunity to fill in those blank spaces as you move with Helios and Vesta through the cycles of the year.

You will be given the opportunity to pass tests that were failed in centuries gone by. You will be given the opportunity to manifest the flame of victory and you will know when you have filled in one of those blanks. For the angels of record, in their delight, might be found to titter with joy, and you might perchance hear their bubbling laugh of victory in the hour of your overcoming.

Have you not also laughed when you have overcome, laughed because of the great release of tension, of joy, which bursts aflame as victory moves on? Have you not also laughed at the tempters and the fallen ones and the liars? Have you not also laughed at their lies, which are no longer something to be believed but something to be mocked and cast down?

So, you see, the glee of the angels is also released. Then, as the pages are filled in one by one, you will come to the place of the present hour of victory. You will see that all of your victories will be upon a new scroll and a new page of gold. Then, by the action of transmutation's fires, by the realization of God-reality that all that is past that is not of the light is unreal, go forth to reclaim the past, to reclaim the energies and then to build a glorious future of victory, victory, victory!

Now the angels of record withdraw. They step back one step and one step higher. They roll up the scrolls and file from this room to return them to the record room of the Keeper of the Scrolls. One day as I stand before audiences to come, I shall be able to declare to them that I am holding the scrolls of victory of Keepers of the Flame who walked before them. On those scrolls will be written your names, for you shall have overcome this world.

Is that not a glory to be contemplated? You will see how souls so very close to your own, who have walked among you, are now members of the heavenly hosts. This is hope. This is victory. This is the fire of other worlds.

I release to you my flame. Use it as you will for the victory of the planet, for the victory of elemental life, for the victory of mankind and for the ascension of your own blessed soul.

Wherever you are, wherever I am, we are one in the flame of the Father-Mother God. Wherever you are, call for victory and I shall come as the genie of victory, the genius of victory.

By God's grace, I AM the mind of Victory! I AM the heart of Victory! I AM the hand of Victory in action! I AM the genie with the lamp of Cosmic Christ illumination won by victorious overcoming!

[22-second pause]

It is done. I have impressed a record of victory in this city, in the angel.[2] Forevermore that angel shall be the flaming presence of victory for souls yearning to be free.

I thank you and bid you good evening.

December 29, 1973
Mexico City, Mexico
ECP

19

THE CIRCLE OF FIRE

While some contemplate the overthrow of light, I come forth to deliver the message of victory to the age. I manifest the flame of victory. I roll back the clouds of oppression. I AM the fullness of the light of God's victory.

I come to reinforce the ranks of lightbearers with legions of victory, with flaming gold, with light's potential to be free. I draw a circle around the lightbearers. It is a circle of fire and all upon the planet who have saluted the Christ flame, who have bowed to the light of God within every man are included within that circle. It is a circle of protection and a force-field of victory.

In the days ahead, each one of you and all souls whom I am contacting as the members of the true Church Universal and Triumphant will require this forcefield to retain the impetus of the thoughtform for the year, which is also imprinted upon the soul as the face of Almighty God.[1]

Victory is the light that overcomes revenge in the eleventh hour—the revenge of the dragon, the beast and the false prophet.[2] These must come for judgment, and the denizens of the pit will also be brought forth; for man by his perfidy has opened the pit and allowed the demons to rage madly through the world to taunt the feminine ray, to distort the minds of children and to overthrow the true image of Father.

REINFORCEMENTS ARRIVE

I say, then, reinforcements are arriving from out the Great Central Sun. They are lightbearers who have seen how the dark ones have contemplated the very destruction of the efforts of those who were called so long ago by Sanat Kumara to bring light, to triumph and to try the souls of mankind. And, you see, the coming of the lightbearers and the coming of the dark ones can mean only one thing—confrontation.

The decision, the choice to render the soul unto God is made by choosing light, forsaking darkness, living in light and in the cosmic honor flame. That decision is taking place in this hour, in every hour, every moment, every second in all eternity until you are locked in the Being of God as an ascended one.

I AM the law of cosmic abundance that overthrows all opposition to the manifestation of the light in Matter! I AM the cosmic flow from the Great Central Sun. I AM sweeping clean the highways of the etheric plane, the mental plane, the emotional and physical planes so that mankind might receive the action of the Holy Spirit, the waters of living flame and the light from far-off worlds.

THE WAVE OF LIGHT DESCENDS

I AM the action of that light consciousness. I AM that descending light. I AM that wave from the Great Central Sun.

You have heard that a great wave of light must inundate the planet ere the earth can proceed to the golden age of glory. That wave of light descends this day and you will see how the debris of the ages and the fallen ones will be swept away. Even now those ones challenge the authority of the Brotherhood and of the ascended masters and they heap vilification upon the heads of lightbearers. Their accusations are known and they come as the rippling of the dark waters of the night.

Let those waters be reversed. *Roll* them back! *Blaze* forth the action of the flame of cosmic flow! In this hour of victory, let mankind learn the mastery of energy in motion. Let them become energy in motion and see how God's movement throughout the cosmos is the light that transforms, the light of resurrection, of ascension—the sacred fire that is every man's calling and every man's home.

LET THAT WAVE REVERSE THE TIDE OF CHAOS

I say, then, let that light, let that wave reverse the tide of chaos and confusion whereby the dark ones have sought to pervert the Mother flame. *They shall not prevail!* They are stripped and demagnetized of their momentum and their authority in the government and the economy this day!

By the light of Alpha and Omega, by the light of the Cosmic Christ, by the flame of victory, so the fiat rings forth! It shall not be stayed. It shall not be withheld. It shall be, contrary to all the cries, the outrage and the weeping and gnashing of teeth.

The legions of light, the waves of light are ongoing. Coming from afar, they descend. All who are of the light and within the sacred circle of God's love will be in the billows and the spume of love, will feel the warmth and the coolness and the laughter and the glow of the bubbling waters of freedom.

Freedom is come. Freedom is the I AM Presence. Freedom is the light from far-off worlds. I AM that light. I AM Victory's flame. I anchor my flame in the heart of each one. And I come, following the release of fearlessness flame that you recently received,[3] to fill the vacuum with the glow of victory.

Victory is always enlightenment; enlightenment is enlightened self-interest. When you take a genuine interest in the God Self, then you begin to live. Then you begin to know what life is and what life can be on this plane. O joy! O love! O hymns of praise!

BE BATHED IN THE VICTORY OF THE CHRIST

I AM the rainbow and the lightning. I AM the sun. I AM the release of energy from stars above. I AM light descending—a spray and shower of light's magnificence in this very hour.

Mankind, be bathed in the victory of the Christ and prepare for the sacred celebration of resurrection's fires! Prepare to deliver unto the age the edict of Victory, the law of Victory, the love of Victory!

So is the Book of Life opened this day! So are written the names of the saints. So are they hallowed and consecrated within the circle of fire. Be still, and know that I AM God.[4] Fear not when the unreality of the world topples all around you, for it is then that you will stand and behold the reality of God's kingdom. All else is temporal, yet in the temporal domain is opportunity for victory and for great gain.

Waste not the hours, the precious moments that God has given thee for victory, for self-mastery and God-control. After all is said and done, after the sands in the hourglass have run out and you stand face to face with the emissaries of cosmic justice, all that will count is what you have gained as the mark of God-mastery, of initiation, of attainment, of love for your fellowman. For remember well the words of Christ, "Inasmuch as ye have done it unto one of the least of these my brethren, ye have done it unto me."[5]

THE MYSTERY OF VICTORY

Take, then, the mystery of victory. All humanity who stand before you are Gods in disguise. As you give freely of your life unto them, you gain your freedom from the wheel of rebirth, for you prove that you are willing to give the allness God has given unto you to the Allness of God in each one.

Remember the key: humanity—Gods in disguise, symbols of hierarchy, potentials of Christhood. Forget not, then, to entertain strangers, for thereby some have entertained angels unawares.[6]

Life is a great mystery. From day to day, opportunity is at hand. Look up and live, O ye hosts. Look up and live, O ye who would become a part of the Lord's hosts.

I AM Victory, and I have won that victory through countless ages of striving to be in the flame. I AM one in the flame. Come into the oneness of that flame. Find cosmic abundance! Find the City Foursquare! Find the ultimate fulfillment of Terra—a star to be!

March 3, 1974
The Motherhouse
Santa Barbara, California
ECP

20

SPIRALS OF VICTORY
FOR THE GOLDEN AGE

I AM Victory! I come forth with legions of light from the Great Central Sun, where the altars of victory that are the four pillars in the temple of being are blazing bright this night with the fires of victory, with the golden flame of illumination.

I AM Victory and I come to release from the heart of Alpha and Omega the spirals of victory for the golden age. These are spirals for the victory of a planet, a solar system and a galaxy—the victory of the white-fire core of being.

Now, at this moment, as angels of victory stand before you, a spiral of victory is released from your heart chakra resembling the spirals of paper that are thrown on New Year's Eve. And so the spiral of the fulfillment of your immortal destiny is anchored in Matter.

I come with a proclamation of joy, discovery and light for the golden age of your own soul manifestation. For the golden age must take place within you each one that the golden age might appear as the Second Coming of Christ universally in manifestation in mankind.

I AM the joy of victory. I AM the fulfillment of the light of victory in every atom, in every erg of energy. I AM the joy of victory rolling back the hordes of night and the fallen ones who would take from you your very life in order to usurp the joy of my flame and my coming.

Well, I am here! I am in this forcefield and I proclaim the golden light of victory within you!

WHEN WE WIN IS UP TO YOU

The question is not *if* we win; the statement is *when* we win. When we win is up to you; it is not up to the hierarchies of light, for we have already won. Your victory in this place beneath the sun is determined by your consciousness of the spirals of victory.

And so, you see, you can make a wide spiral whereby your attainment is won in a thousand or ten thousand years as you please or you can tighten the coils of victory and earn your ascension in this very lifetime by the grace of Almighty God.

Don't you appreciate that gift, O blessed hearts? Don't you understand that Saint Germain came forth to deliver the mandate of the age—the flame of freedom and the violet transmuting flame—for your victory?

And because he came forth on behalf of every man, woman and child on this planet with a dispensation for the age, I came forth to support him in that victory, in that mission of freedom's light. Therefore, if you are grateful for my presence here, you can thank Saint Germain, for without his conviction, without his faith in some among mankind and in the sure response of their hearts, cosmic beings, ascended masters would not have come forth.

I tell you, Saint Germain took a stand for light when many in embodiment were among the almost numberless numbers who had betrayed him in the past. Yet his faith was the faith in God, in God's Law in the heart of man.

DO NOT BE OVERCOME BY THE HUMAN CONSCIOUSNESS

And so I say to you, be not disillusioned with the outer consciousness and its patterns. Be not overcome by the human consciousness, by the darkness and the perversions of the flame of life and of the Holy Spirit in the hierarchy of Libra. All of the lies, treachery, intrigue and unreality that usurp the place of the Most High God in government, in the economy, in commerce, in the whole network of organized crime, shall be brought to naught in this hour.

I AM Victory and I challenge all that assails the cosmic honor flame in this nation, in this planet and in your soul. We will brook *no* interference with the victory of our chelas. Therefore I say to you who are weary with the burdens of life and the compromises that you have elected to take of your own free will in the human consciousness—in the name of Saint Germain, I say, be free this night. For I am here and I am here to support you in your commitment to the holy fires of freedom.

Lower that forehead with determination, I say, and lead the angels of light and the forces of light into the fray. Forward, I say! March to the victory. Accept *no* force, *no* consciousness, *no* circumstance in your life that would deprive you of one erg of God's energy of immortal love, mercy, justice or the flame of peace.

I CHALLENGE THE CARNAL MIND

Therefore, I challenge that carnal mind and I stand with Archangel Michael to proclaim the word of that challenge:

In the name of the living God,
In the name of Jesus the Christ,
In the name of the fire within you,
I challenge the carnal mind,
The Antichrist and all satanic power
In every man, woman and child on this planet.

I take another step: *I challenge Lucifer, the Luciferians and all the hordes of night who would deprive this nation, this land, this hemisphere and this planet of the fulfillment of the spirals of victory for the golden age.*

I stand in the name of the Christ consciousness of mankind.
I stand in the name of the I AM THAT I AM
And I challenge every foe, every tyrant, every woe.
I say, Beware! For the light of cosmic forces dawns
And you who have aligned yourselves with darkness,
Beware! For this is the hour
To align your consciousness with the Christ
And to proclaim your separation from the fallen ones.

A RELEASE OF KARMA

With the dispensations of the new year, the Lords of Karma are at this very hour contemplating releases of karma to the fallen ones and to the wicked on the planet. You will find that if your energies are aligned with or tied into them through economics, through the flow of supply, through interest in corporations that support the beast and the mark of the beast, then, I say, you must bear the karma of that tie.

Come out from among them and be a separate and a chosen people, elect unto God. Choose your election well and realize that when you support the tobacco industry, the liquor industry, the drug-trafficking industry, when you support organizations that betray the youth of the world, you have the karma of the betrayal of these little ones. And, I say, remember the words of Christ, "Whosoever shall offend one of these little ones which believe in me, it were better for him that a millstone were hanged about his neck and that he were drowned in the depth of the sea."[1]

I say, then, beware of the flow of energy, for you will give account of it. If you would have and retain the spirals of victory, then reinforce *light! light! light!* upon the planetary body and use the life God has given into your hands to proclaim the victory of every man, woman and child upon this planet.

THE JUDGMENT OF ABORTION

I say, let your consciousness be stirred this night!

I am determined that you go forth in the flame of Archangel Uriel to challenge the proponents of abortion in this land. I am determined that you take his dictation and distribute it to all who are involved in this crime against the Deity.

You see, this is group karma; mankind will be judged collectively and all who do not take a stand against abortion will be counted among those who did nothing and therefore did cast their vote for abortion.

I say, then, it is your responsibility to give forth the proclamation of Almighty God for the judgment of abortion and the abortionist. God will not hold guiltless those who continue to turn their backs upon souls and avatars who come forth from other spheres and are denied embodiment at the hand of this ignorance and this malice!

I CHALLENGE LUCIFER!

I say, correct ignorance with information; correct malice by challenging the Liar and his lie. I challenge that one, that Fallen One whose time is short. And I say, Go back! You are judged this day not only for the slaughter of the holy innocents in this age but for thousands of years.

Therefore, in view of the challenging of the messenger and of this company and of the hierarchy of ascended masters by Lucifer prior to this conference, another percent of energy is taken from him for the direct confrontation that occurred even this night and the interference with the flow of light.

Know, O children of the light, that those who challenge the messenger and the Christed one in manifestation will bear the judgment. Some of you have known that an immunity was given to Lucifer because of his attainment prior to the Fall. Therefore only those on this planetary body who can reach the level of attainment that he had prior to the Fall have immunity against his interference.

Many years ago, when the Great White Brotherhood inaugurated the mission of the delivery of the ascended masters' teachings to the age, the messengers were granted immunity from Lucifer's interference. He was then charged that any opposition taken against the messengers would cost him certain percentages of his momentum of energy used against the children of light.

To this hour, forty-four percent of that energy has been taken in addition to this one percent, which serves as a warning to that proud spirit: Thus far and *no* farther. And with the addition of that percentage, a certain portion of darkness on the planet is consumed in the sacred fire focused in the Christ, the Elohim, the archangels and the seven Holy Kumaras.

Therefore, I say, the percentage taken is concerned with the manifestation of the perversion of victory—that aspect of unreality that challenges the hierarchy of Libra and the manifestation of the Holy Spirit. Therefore, I say, let the exposure of the Liar, the lie and all crime in this nation be made manifest this night as the price that must be paid by the Fallen One for his attempt to deprive mankind of this light and this teaching!

THE WEIGHING OF HUMANITY

I AM Victory and my consciousness is the consciousness of God-justice. And in the scales of justice, the scales of Libra, humanity is weighed this night. As a result of that weighing, those who have aligned themselves with the Fallen One are judged; those who have aligned themselves with light may look forward to the hour when that proud spirit will step forth to challenge the ascended hosts and thereby lose his total momentum, his total area of operation upon the planetary home.[2]

Then you will see the purging of the carnal mind in all mankind. You will see the great day of choosing come, when mankind will be free of that one, free to make their calling and election sure. Therefore, in anticipation of that day, I anchor the violet ray and the spiral of victory in every human heart. In every forcefield that bears witness to God, I anchor *victory! victory! victory!* I anchor the will to victory, the love of victory and the wisdom of victory.

I AM Victory and I will have the victory of the light in Terra! Will you have it with me?

I am here and I stand before you and I challenge you. Will you claim that victory with me this night? [Audience responds, "Yes!"]

So be it. By the majority of God within you, let the earth be proclaimed victorious. May you remain vigilant in the discrimination of the Christ to see that you are not deprived of your abundance, your light, your faith, your hope, your charity by the fallen ones who come as wolves in sheep's clothing.

So, I say, beware. This is the hour of the excitement of victory when you are empowered by the Christ to put down the emissaries of the dark ones. I say, be fearless. Be wise. Be harmless. Be attentive. Go forth clad only in the armour of Archangel Michael.

If you give your invocations to the Defender of the Faith without fail as you have been instructed—fourteen times in the morning, fourteen times at night*—then you will have the seal of Michael the Archangel and he will go forth to do your bidding in the name of the Christ. He will go forth to defend your soul and that of all mankind against all enemies.

Hail to the light! Hail to victory! Hail to love! I AM the Word incarnate within you. I AM Victory.

October 11, 1974
Los Angeles, California
ECP

---

*In a later dictation, on July 5, 1992, Archangel Michael asked us to give decrees to him for twenty minutes a day.

21

A SPIRAL FOR CHRIST-VICTORY

Hail, victorious ones from out the Great Central Sun!
Hail, legions of victory!
Hail, legions of love!

Come now into this forcefield of Terra. Come in the flaming consciousness of victory and blaze forth that light of victory for the kindling fire of love in every heart. So is love the victory on the Path. Unless there be love, there can be no victory.

Love is an illumination of the fires of the Holy Ghost when the quiescent energies of the Divine Mother are awakened in the flaming Spirit of the Father. Wisdom, as the light of the dawn, projects the understanding of love, even as love begets wisdom. And in the twofold action of the golden pink glow-ray, the glory of victory is perceived; the mark of victory is perceived.

The goal, then, is seen as the fulfillment of oneness, the fulfillment of life, of energy, of consciousness, of becoming all that you are by letting the man that is within come out, express and be the God-victory, the God-dominion of your outer consciousness.

So then, O light of the soul, come forth in the flame of love. Come forth and be the reality of each one. Therefore, you see, illumination, the illumined action of love, is the pathway to reality. The realization of who I AM, who you are, is the consciousness of victory.

If you were to retain the continuous awareness of Self twenty-four hours a day, you would also retain the awareness of victory. For to know the Self, to realize the light potential of the Self, is to be aware of the unfailing nature of Selfhood in God that is victory.

Now let the darkness be swept aside by the oncoming tide of victory. Let the spiral of Christ-victory be imparted by angelic hosts unto the planet and the evolutions thereof. Let the flood tide of victory come forth from the Great Central Sun. So I am here and I have come to shatter the veils of darkness, temptation, sorrow and maya, and of being out of alignment with the inner geometry of being.

BEHOLD YOUR GOD

Now, by the magnet of the Great Central Sun of victory, let the forcefields of your chakras be drawn into the power of the immaculate vision of the Cosmic Virgin. Let energy move to the center of the All-Seeing Eye. Now, I say, behold your God.

Behold the God of Selfhood, and know that you are God in manifestation and that the manifest action of God is man, woman victorious. I AM the balancing factor of victory in the Libra scales of the plus and minus; I AM Alpha and Omega converging in this point in time and space for the birth of the Christ consciousness within you. Therefore, at the nexus of the cross, at your own heart chakra, I place the spiral of Christ-victory.

Blaze forth. *Blaze* forth. *Blaze* forth and let the golden light, as golden waves of peace, encircle the planet as a swaddling garment of living flame. Let the fires of illumination come forth.

I say, awake, O mankind. Awake! awake! awake! to your God-reality, I say. Be that reality. So, then, sunder unreality. Sunder unreality and let the razor's edge of the mind of God part the veil for the stepping through of your own beloved Jesus the Christ.

THE STEPPED-DOWN PRESENCE OF JESUS

In this hour of victory and cycles turning, there is a new stepping-down of the consciousness and the electronic forcefield of Jesus the Christ, bringing that beloved avatar closer to mankind's outer awareness. This stepping-down of his Electronic Presence is accompanied by a stepping-up of the awareness of the Christ consciousness in the hearts of the people.

Therefore you will see in this year, 1975, as mankind pursue the Holy Spirit in nature, in invocation and in love, a turning to the Master Jesus, the master teacher, World Teacher of the age. Mankind's hearts will be quickened by the presence of this beloved one of God penetrating through the etheric plane, preparing them for the Second Coming and the reign of the mind of Christ within their mental bodies.

Then there shall be a squeeze on the mental bodies of mankind, a squeezing out of the energies of the not-self, the logic of the carnal mind. There will be pressure from on high as the Christ Self becomes more real, more active in the lives of mankind, especially in those who respond to the Call, the inner Call of the Good Shepherd.

My sheep know my voice.[1] So shall mankind know the voice of Jesus and in his voice they shall hear the voice of the inner man of the heart,[2] their own beloved Christ Self, speaking with the tongues of angels and of ascended masters.

Therefore, let the coming of Jesus the Christ not be to the exclusion of the ascended hierarchies. Let his coming pave the way for the descent, the pressing-in upon the auras of mankind of the victorious momentum of the saints and ascended beings of all ages. So shall they come to receptive hearts; so shall all mankind know that the victory of the individual is in the inner reality, is in the Real Self. As Jesus is the Christed One, so is each and every one who is ready to receive the anointing of the Christ Self within.

AFFIRM YOUR VICTORIES

I come on wings of victory. I come to place the laurel wreath of victory upon the heads of the overcomers who are overcoming in all things, being tempted and tried yet still pressing on, dauntless toward the victory. These are they who are forging a new age.

Come then. Come in your souls, O hearts of light. Affirm your victory, for you have had many victories of which you are not aware, that I acknowledge and affirm in the name of your God Self—so bowed down have you become at times with the burden of Antichrist and the accuser of the brethren.

I say then, claim your victory. There is no more urgent call of the hour than the call to claim your victory. Therefore, speak that word:

> *In the name of the living Christ,*
> *In the name of Jesus the Christ and my own Christ Self,*
> *In the name of the I AM THAT I AM,*
> *I claim my victory now.*
> *I claim my victory now.* [Audience joins in.]
> *I claim my victory now.*
> *I claim my victory now.*
> *I claim my victory now.*

The acclamation of the angels of victory is upon you, and the only time—and I say the *only* time—that the forces of darkness and the heathen can take from you your victory is when you lose the sense of victory and when you fail to claim that victory.

Do you understand that in the claim of victory is the flame of victory?

That flame is invincible, victorious, invincible, victorious, *invincible, victorious*. We shall win. We shall win. We shall win. I say it once, I say it twice and I say it again, for I am the cosmic consciousness of victory. I ensoul that golden light of victory. Now let it blaze forth as the sun of Helios and Vesta, as the magnet of God's love and wisdom multiplies the power and momentum of victory that I bear from the heart of God.

Let us see mankind come beneath the rod of the law of self-discipline. In the true freedom of the Aquarian age, let each man discipline himself under his own tutor, the Christ Self. Let each man know the law of the I AM Presence and be that law in action.

So is victory won by the discipline of the cube, the square, the sphere, the triangle of light. So now, angel of the triangle, strike the triangle. [pause] The tinkling of the triangle sounds the note and the moment when other legions of victory who have responded to the light within your heart and your sense of the victory come from far-off worlds.

A VICTORY ON ANOTHER WORLD

Mankind shall know this year that as the flame of the Holy Spirit is released, so the defenders of victory and angelic hosts come. And do you know, precious hearts, that they come fresh from a victory on another world and system of worlds in another galaxy? It is a solar system with conditions similar to your own, where a certain number of planetary bodies within that system were perverted by certain fallen ones, where certain planetary homes and their evolutions retained the light and where one specific planet held the balance of light for a solar system.

And these legions of victory, anchoring the topaz of victory for that planet—the crystal fire of golden consciousness of Godhood for a people —were able to turn the tide whereby children of the Sun proclaimed their victory, claimed their victory and saw that victory won.

In that victory was the dissolution of microbes, germs of evil infesting the minds of a portion of the people. This substance was as a great dead sea floating in the atmosphere, threatening to overtake a planet and consequently a system of worlds because that planet held the balance. Therefore, I say, the flame of victory with its white-fire core of the Holy Spirit is able to dissolve the microbes that infest the mind and pervert the consciousness of victory through their sense of doom and failure.

These legions come fresh from the glory of that victory, which shall also manifest in Terra if you will but lift your heads on high to receive the conquering heroes as they come—legions of victory that will tarry with Earth and enforce the spirals of illumined action that mankind might see and know the path of victory.

I place within you a spiral of victory for the fulfillment of the organization of The Summit Lighthouse and, I say, let the consciousness of

God-reality be a crown upon your head for the fulfillment of the teachings of the ascended masters.

CLAIM YOUR GOD-REALITY

I call forth the illumination of the mind. I demand the burning through of all in consciousness that impedes the flow of sacred energy and sacred wisdom. So be it, in the name of the Holy Spirit.

I say, claim that reality and you shall win. Stand in the flaming presence of reality. Stand in the golden white-fire sun of Libra and know who I AM, who you are. Then let the disc of Self be reunited with the disc of God Self-awareness and your soul shall walk the earth as the conquering hero infused with the presence of Lanello, infused with the flame of the Divine Mother.

I ask you, with all of this, how can you fail? How can you fail to avail yourself of the opportunity for the victory of a planet?

This victory will turn the tide and manifest the victory of this solar system and the elevation of the frequencies of the planetary homes into new dimensions of etheric cycles, preparing the entire whirl of cosmic energy for fulfillment in the ascension and the return to the white-fire core. This is the joy and the fulfilling of the Law.

I invoke the law of your being. I invoke the light of your being to *burn* through all sense of injustice. *Burn* through the records of death, doubt and fear, anxiety, tension and frustration. *Burn* through and dissolve those energy forcefields that are not of this world, not of your God consciousness. They have no part with the eternal sense of victory.

YOUR ANGEL OF VICTORY

Legions of light arrayed in numberless numbers come forth and merge now with the individual auras of mankind. In this cosmic moment, I pronounce to you that every lifestream connected with Terra, embodied or disembodied, every man, woman and child in whatever plane of Matter receives now the ministration of an angel of victory.

That angel of victory steps into the aura of the individual to reinforce the rising spiral and momentum of victory. Let the armour of victory be upon mankind, the consciousness of victory, the love, wisdom and power of victory!

So the transfer is made of the Electronic Presence of the angels of victory. As you claim the reality of your victory daily in the name of the Christ, watch and see how mankind will have the renewed sense of the ancient motto, "We shall overcome." [Audience joins in.] We shall overcome. We shall overcome.

It is done. It is sealed. It is locked in your heart. Defend it with all your might, with all your main, with all your love. I say, defend the victory that is already won. Defend the light that shall overcome.

I AM the Spirit of Selflessness in you that sees with crystal clarity the attainment of victory, past, present and future. In the eternal Now is *Victory! Victory! Victory!*

December 29, 1974
Los Angeles, California
ECP

22

VICTORY OVER THE
DARK NIGHT OF THE SOUL

Hail, lightbearers!

I AM Victory.

I AM the victory of God within you. I AM that victory now.

I AM the bursting forth of the flame of your own God Self. I AM the release of the fires of victory unto the mark of the hierarchies of light and God-power. I AM releasing cycles and cycles beyond cycles, as dispensations come forth for the twelve aspects of the law of being and for the action of the Mother flame to be fulfilled in you and in Church Universal and Triumphant.

I come, and my legions come as numberless numbers arrayed in the white-fire core, in blazing golden helmets of light, swords drawn—the sword of peace that is a living flame that now cleaves asunder the Real from the unreal.

I come to proclaim the age of deliverance of the feminine ray within you. I come to release, by the action of the sword of living flame, the white-fire core of being.

So let purity come forth. I AM the victorious champion of purity. So I come, following the Goddess of Purity, and I demand the action of purity within you. In the name of the Cosmic Christ, I challenge every challenger of your own God-purity and I send forth legions for the binding of the forces of impurity that prey upon the children of this world. In the name of the Cosmic Virgin, I say, They shall not pass! They shall not contaminate this generation! For I stand, and Godfre and Lotus stand with me.

The ascended messengers of light come to proclaim the reinforcement 'of the cycles of victory of the golden age through this activity of light—through all activities of light that teach the way of ascended master law and the liberation of the souls of mankind by the action of the sacred fire.

LEGIONS OF VICTORY VOLUNTEER TO TAKE INCARNATION ON TERRA

Legions of cosmic victory come forth in answer to the calls of mankind, in answer to the pleas of those souls who, descending into form, found their form and their opportunity for life aborted. So they wait in the wings of life. Pray, then, for fathers, mothers to be raised up to receive these souls who are determined to come forth for the victory of the age.

Now, I tell you, by dispensation of the Lords of Karma, certain flaming ones from my band, from the legions of Victory, have volunteered to take incarnation upon Terra, for their joy, their light and their determination has been heightened by your joy and your light determination. They see victors here below and so they come forth because you have given your light, your sacred calling unto the Lord's hosts.

Therefore, unto you who apply and unto all who apply to the Lords of Karma to receive lifestreams in the coming year, the opportunity to give birth to the legions of Victory is at hand.

VICTORY OVER THE DARK NIGHT OF THE SOUL

So, I come as an angel of annunciation and as the angel of deliverance. I come in many guises, but my name and my flame is Victory—victory on the brow as the golden flame that illumines the mind, victory as a spiral to overcome defeat in all mankind. I AM Victory! Victory! Victory!

By the action of my flame I draw all that substance into the light. I cause those negative spirals of defeat to be turned upside down and inside out, inverted now to become spirals of victory within you. Feel the joy, the crystal white-fire light pouring forth from my garments of light and know that I come to proclaim your victory in the Dark Cycle[1] and in the dark night of the soul.

Some of you have wondered about that dark night. It is a time that comes to every avatar, everyone on the path of the ascension. It is the hour when the momentum of your devotion to the living flame as concentrated energy here below in the aura must suffice for the momentum of victory.

It is the hour as in the final hour when Jesus was on the cross—the hour of calling forth, "My God, my God, why hast thou forsaken me?"[2] In that moment the cutting off of that blessed one occurred so that he might prove his victorious overcoming by light's momentum. That moment of separation from the God Source can seem as an eternity and can be prolonged by misunderstanding and misapplication.

In that moment, in that hour of testing, you must have on the wedding garment lest you attend the wedding feast and the lord of the feast come unto you, saying, "Friend, how camest thou in hither not having a wedding garment? Bind him hand and foot and take him away and cast him into outer darkness; there shall be weeping and gnashing of teeth."[3]

Outer darkness is that space into which the soul not having the momentum of light is cast in the hour of testing, in the hour of the dark cycle that is the dark night of the soul. Heed, then, the teaching of the Brothers of the Golden Robe for your mastery of the aura and the auric light, for herein is your opportunity to reinforce the light of the causal body here below for the ultimate test of victory.

TERRA'S DARK NIGHT OF THE SOUL

Terra, in this hour, passes through the dark night of the soul. So we come as legions of light to stand guard for a planet in distress, a planet crying out in travail, giving birth to the Christ consciousness.

O Mother of the World! Thy soul, a flaming light, does now give birth to the Christ consciousness for mankind. So let the Christ consciousness be born. Let the Mother be delivered of the Manchild and let the Christ consciousness go forth as a babe in arms to become the Christed one.

Now, O children of the light, sons and daughters of God, let the Mother flame within you, united with the Father image, give birth to the Christ consciousness. So let it be. As the dawn's early light must come on Easter morning, so let it be that the Christ redeemed, regenerated, resurrected within you is that light and that momentum of victory for the salvation of a planet and a people.

Let your light be as the corona of the sun in the moment of the eclipse that is the dark night of the soul of the planet. "Let your light so shine before men that they may see your good works and glorify your Father which is in heaven."[4] So let that light, as the light of victory, reinforce the path of overcoming and hold the balance for evolutions who come to this point in time and space without the seamless garment.

A MOMENTUM OF LIGHT
FOR THE MENDING OF THE GARMENT

I send forth light and the light of purity for the mending of the garment. This is mercy's flame that the garment might be mended to serve again for a time, times and a half a time[5] until the soul can erase the seams and the mending and preserve a seamless wedding garment.

Now understand that Victory is delivering a momentum of light from the Great Central Sun for the mending of the auric forcefield of those who have rent the garment by the use of drugs, by the penetration of the astral plane through forcing the chakras, by all manner of perversion of the sacred fire and of entering into necromancy and spiritism.

You who have torn the garment of the soul, to you I come with light, with purity, with victory. And so you will wear the mark of the mending until the hour when you, in the light of your own heart flame, can face that dark night and that dweller-on-the-threshold and in the momentum of victory overcome it all for the ultimate reunion that is the ascension.

To those among mankind who *will* to overcome, who *will* to be resurrection's fires, I ask you, what more can you ask of Victory than the healing of the garment?

I say, do you not rejoice in Alpha and Omega, in the beings of the great cosmic councils who have conspired this day to deliver unto mankind this opportunity of victory through the hand of one who has long served the blessed Knight Commander, Saint Germain?

Precious hearts of light, by the very mention of his name you ought to stand in honor of this great soul who has delivered unto mankind the flame of mercy. [Audience stands.] By his flame I am called forth, and many cosmic beings have come because Saint Germain has laid down his life, his causal body, his light momentum, that you might receive the impartation of the Word.

Even the training of these messengers is a dispensation of El Morya and Saint Germain that the Word might be continued, that mankind might have renewed opportunity from the hand of Portia and her cosmic flame of justice.

Oh, the love of the hierarchies of heaven is beyond all loves, beyond all life, yet so tangible and so near!

YOU CAN NEVER PLEASE THE HUMAN CONSCIOUSNESS

Precious souls of flame, you have the friendship of the hierarchies of light. To have a friend at court, at the Court of the Sacred Fire, is greater by far than to have the popularity of the world and the mass consciousness. I say, laugh at the consciousness and the mockery of popularity—here today and gone tomorrow.

Mankind is on a treadmill of pleasing the human consciousness. Well, I tell you, I for one know that you can never please the human consciousness, so you might as well cease your struggle and have the consciousness of victory over every aspect of the human. Merge with the God flame and, as Morya says, "Let the chips fall where they may."

Let the human consciousness become a little disturbed, a little heated in the presence of the flaming ones. Let some have their reactions; they also have their karma and their accountability. It is time, then, that you took your

stand for the light and ceased your concern over the opinions and the pining
of family, relatives and friends who are pining for you to come home.

Have they ever been concerned about your coming home before? Not
until you came into the activity of the ascended masters. Now, you see, they
long for the consciousness that used to be, that has gone into the flame.
And when they see you, they say, "What has happened to you? We don't
know you." Then they have to admit, "You look wonderful!" [Audience laughs.]

BE NOT ASHAMED OF THE FIRES OF VICTORY

Victory is a flame to be worn in the heart, on the brow and on your
sleeve if you will. Be not ashamed of the fires of victory. Impart the joy of
victory and remember the moment of our cosmic communion, for this is
a moment you will cherish for all eternity. This is the moment when you
planted your feet squarely on Terra and declared, "In the name of God,
I will have my victory in this life. I AM Victory! Victory! Victory!"

So will you make that proclamation?

[Audience affirms with Mighty Victory:]

> *In the name of God,*
> *I will have my victory in this life.*
> *I AM Victory! Victory! Victory!*

So be it. That *is* the Call that compels the answer. My flame reinforces
the fiat of your soul and is now a whirling, golden fire, twining around
your forcefield in the action of the braiding of light as the caduceus of
Alpha and Omega.

So you stand in pillars of flaming victory. So come the legions. Now,
will you say, "In the name of the Christ, I reinforce my victory by the
legions of Victory"? [Audience affirms with Mighty Victory:]

> *In the name of the Christ,*
> *I reinforce my victory by the legions of Victory.*

So you have opened the door of consciousness; the legions step through
and you stand in the Electronic Presence of the golden ones with their

golden helmets. These are the hosts of light. You can stand in the aura of a legion of angels and of a member of a legion of angels in any moment, any hour of the day or night, when you affirm and acclaim that you give yourself unto the hosts of light and that you consecrate your victory by Victory's legions.

I tell you, my legions are rubbing their palms with delight, ready to jump into the fray because you have ordained it by free will. Now see what these conquering heroes can perform through you as you walk the earth as victors of light.

See how you will take the earth and how you will take that spiral—that string that is on the top and pull the string. How the planet will whirl at a new momentum and frequency of light. See how you can increase the spin of the top—the top of Terra—by your consecration of Victory's flame.

I come from out the Great Central Sun. I return to the heart of the flaming yod. I return to the Great Central Sun Magnet. Think upon me and by the arc of love I will flow as a cosmic being who comes down over the arc on the sliding board of cosmos. So I come down that slide into your heart's chalice in the very moment you affirm, by your determination to be victors bold, your Christ-victory here and now.

Whenever you proclaim the victory of your inner vow, I AM there. I AM here. I AM in the Great Central Sun. I AM in the fiery core of Terra. I AM the momentum of victory for the passing of the Mother flame and the children of the Divine Mother through the Dark Cycle and beyond, into the golden age of enlightenment and peace.

I AM Victory! I proclaim victory for you and for all mankind! Invictus, we are one!

March 27, 1975
Los Angeles, California
ECP

23

THE WAVE OF LIGHT FROM SHASTA

Hail, legions of light! Hail, angelic hosts! Now descend in the flame of victory! Now descend! Now descend! I call you forth from the Great Central Sun. Now encircle the devotees round about with the flame of victory and let that victory be anchored within the soul!

Hail, children of the light! I AM come in the flame of Venus and in the flame of Sanat Kumara. I come with great joy! I come with victory! I come to inspire you unto that joy of victory which shall surely be your own if you will plant your feet firmly on Terra and plant your hands into the air raised up unto the star of your own I AM Presence. I say in this moment, this cosmic moment, claim the victory of the light! Claim the victory of your ascension! Claim it now I say, for this is the holy day of decision! [Audience rises and responds with cries of "Victory!" and "I AM America's victory now!"]

Ladies and gentlemen, I thank you for your response. May you know that your response, heartfelt, reaches the angels of the Great Central Sun, who have come forth on a special mission this night to seal your inner vows, to seal your victory. And therefore by that decision and by that confirmation of the victory of Terra, so you seal your heart flame in a coil of fire, in a coil of energy that shall go forth to fulfill its cosmic purpose.

And so the Goddess of Liberty is redeemed and her call for a thousand faithful decreers to save this nation and save this planet has come home, for you have faithfully decreed in these days of victory and you have shown the cosmic councils what you will do for light. Now show me also, as the days pass into the years, how you will retain the fervor of victory!

ANGELS OF VICTORY

Do you not feel the joy of my company? Do you not feel the great release and surge of angelic hosts who have known naught but victory for thousands and thousands of years and years and cycles beyond your ken? And their momentum is victory, victory, victory! So let it be your own; for these angels come forth in adoration of that flame, the threefold flame within your heart which they also used for the victory. And therefore they worship the flame as the flame of victory, for they know what that light can do.

Now see then how you have come from north and south and east and west; and many have not known even my name or even that such a being as Mighty Victory existed before this conference. And many have not known of the violet-flame angels or of the gracious Sanat Kumara, our hierarch of light. You see, then, you have proven to the Lords of Karma what I said in my request for a dispensation of victory, that it would be possible to draw to Shasta 1975 souls sincere, souls yearning to be whole even though they knew but a small aspect of the law, and by the fire of the Brotherhood to draw them into the lodestone of the light of the Mother and the light of the I AM Presence.

And thus you have responded! And so by the alchemy of your fervent love, most precious to behold, there comes forth this night a momentum of victory for your soul. And I have stood before the altar of Almighty God in the Great Central Sun and I have made a pledge on behalf of every soul who has given of his energy and his light in this conference. And I have made that pledge that my momentum of victory shall be as a mantle of protection, as a sphere of light, and as a momentum that will draw not only your soul, but the souls of all whom you contact into the joyous flame of victory. So be it! It is my calling. It is my offering. It is my honor to bring to you the flame of my heart.

SCROLL FORETELLING THE DAY OF THE ASCENSION

And now angels of victory release unto each soul the scroll that foretells the day of the ascension in the light. Do you not know, precious hearts, that the day and the hour of your ascension as opportunity has been written by the Lords of Karma? And *if* you fulfill your calling and your election and *if* you apply your energies in devotion and remain in the center of the flaming will of your own I AM Presence, if you fulfill all that is required by the Great Law for your soul, you will come by the spiral of victory released this night to the day and the hour that God already knows for your victorious ascension in the light.

Think of that! The goal that you scarcely knew before you contacted the teachings of the Law! Now you understand that God has first perceived the plan, that God has placed within your soul the conception of that plan. And now by the joy of victory with freedom's fire, you are free as the dove that soars unto the heights to move into the center of that mandala which the LORD God has so lovingly, compassionately created as your very own. (Precious hearts, won't you please be seated.)

AN OPEN DOOR FOR VICTORY TO FLOW

With the announcement of Alpha of the judgment of the Fallen One, I come to announce an open door, an open opportunity for the blazing light of victory to flow across Terra unobstructed by the shadowy figure of that Fallen One who in that cycle was wont to challenge and to test and to accuse and to oppose the children of the light so blest.

Now then, the cycles roll! And I would also tell you that that one, that Fallen One that is called by the name of Satan, a number of cycles ago was also bound and remains bound. And therefore, for that thousand-year period of the binding of that one, there is hope, there is opportunity, there is the most tremendous momentum for the expansion of the flame that the world has known for thousands of years. Now see how opportunity, as the golden door, stands before you! And you standing before that door may know that the knock and the opening and the entering-in is that which you have been called to, that which is your hope, that which is the fulfillment of hope, that which is a present reality here and now.

See then that you understand that Victory's flame is the momentum whereby you challenge every lie and every remnant of the seed of the fallen ones. Do you understand that now is the moment to rush into the battle-field, to take the victory, to take the land for Saint Germain, to claim Terra for the light? Now is the moment when the general in the field gives the command "Onward! Onward! Onward to victory!" Now is the moment when the fallen ones will scatter at your footstep, at the drumbeat.

Mine eyes have seen the glory of the coming of the LORD! And I give to you that vision of the coming of the LORD's hosts. This is the time when although there is the rumbling and the grumbling and the raising-up of mighty armies in many nations and nuclear power and wars and rumors of wars—this is the hour of victory! This is the hour when light goes forth by the power of the spoken Word, when light goes forth! And in your name, the name of the I AM, in your name, in the name of the Christ, the fiat "I claim that energy for Saint Germain!" will cause the ones of the night to tremble and to falter and to fall. And then the inrushing of the angelic hosts as they bind the tares and take them to be burned at the harvest, the harvest of the LORD's hosts, the harvest of the children of the light.[1]

CHALLENGE ALL THAT OPPOSES
THE CHRIST CONSCIOUSNESS ON TERRA

This is what I am saying. I am saying that by the fiat, by the command, challenging all that opposes the Christ consciousness on Terra, all that you see as threatening woe, will go! I say it will go down before the authority of your I AM Presence! Now try me and see how that Light will swallow up the Darkness! See how the light of your Presence is able to restore the planet to the golden age! I AM Victory and I know whereof I speak! I have seen the conquering of worlds, of maya and effluvia by light, and I have seen worlds come into a golden age that many an ascended master had long crossed off the list.

I say this for you must understand that at any moment, at any hour, no matter how far the children of light have been taken into the lie of the fallen ones, when the truth is acclaimed, when it is spoken, when our light goes forth by the spoken Word, the souls of those children of the light know the voice, know the vibration, know the Call! And they run and they leap and they come and they forsake their former ways and their former lives! And overnight you will see how the youth of the world will claim Terra for Saint Germain!

THE WAVE OF LIGHT FROM SHASTA

So be the wave of light going forth from Shasta! Carry the light of Ra Mu and the golden oil of the crown of chakras! So be the wave going forth north, south, east, and west, even as you have come! So go forth as rays of the sun and claim Terra for victory, victory, victory! Victory, victory, victory! [Audience joins the Master:] *Victory, victory, victory! Victory, victory, victory!*

So be it in the name of the living God! I AM that flame. I AM your flame to claim. I AM with you unto the end of the cycles of error and to the fulfillment of the cycles of truth. Be thou made whole in victory!

July 6, 1975
Mount Shasta, California
ECP

24

VICTORY'S TORCH PASSED UNTO THE MESSENGERS OF TRUTH IN SCIENCE AND RELIGION

How came thou into the midst of the sacred fire? How came thou, O soul of God's desire? Came thou by love, or by the flame of truth, or by the presence of victory? By the light of God came thou in, O soul of fire. Therefore, soul, do not lay claim to thy accomplishment in that sacred fire, but know that it is because the Lord thy God hath led thee into the place hallowed by the flame of victory!

Know, then, that all are come into the One because the Call has gone forth as a mighty light ray to draw you into the center of the One. Know, then, that even the very first step on the path of freedom is a step empowered by the Almighty One. This for the moment of pride in attainment—now for the moment of humility. For the moment of humility, then say,

I, O God, AM one in thee because thou art my very own. I AM one with thee, O God. I have come into the center of thy sacred fire by thy grace. I AM God in manifestation. I claim that God as adornment for sacred life aborning and for the moment of love. Because thou art, O God, I AM love.

Precious hearts, I come with legions as always—legions of flaming victory, flaming, God-victorious Christ-illumination, Buddhic-illumination, and the illumination of wisdom in Mother's name. I come in the great glory of the Great Central Sun with that vision, the far-off vision of the dawn of victory. I come as the hymn is sung to that name and to that origin of my flame.[1] Ah, how the flame has gone forth as God has cycled the mighty fire of victory across a cosmos. And curving, it has returned as the mighty arc of life to envelop, to enfold, to be the manger and the abode, the cross and the crown of the Comforter and the initiate on the path of comfort's flame.

The goal of the ascension is to impart comfort to life. The comfort is the certitude of victory. Sometimes it becomes necessary to manifest the victory of the ascension in order to give comfort to life, and sometimes it becomes necessary to forgo the ascension to give comfort to life. The Lord will tell you himself whether the Alpha or the Omega current is unto you the calling in this hour.

There have assembled now in this hour at the rear of the auditorium, balancing the flame of spirit, those souls of light who have come forth from the Temple of the Resurrection—unascended souls of magnificent countenance who have stood with the evolutions of Terra, who have stood with the saints and as the sages. They have stood to retain that flame at the etheric level to give comfort to life. They hold the polarity of the Omega cycle in Mater. They are the consciousness of the ascension, yet unascended. You might say they have reached that plane of *samadhi,* of eternal communion with Mother light, and from that communion drawn forth even the light of nirvanic planes, anchoring that light here below. They are the perpetuation of the Word.

Now, then, salute these precious ones, among them your own beloved Yogananda and Babaji and Mataji who retain in Mater the flame of life. Salute them with your heart's love, precious ones, for they have come to enfold you. You may stand and face them and see the glory [audience rises], for they come with light, trailing the light of the garments of East and West. See them as they stand. They stand to ennoble the race; they stand for the meeting of the paths of East and West. And among them are those saints of the Church of the West also, and even the Eastern Church, who have been claimed as saints and yet who have not taken the full measure of the ascension, for they have been waiting, waiting for the hour when you would come into your own.

See that light, those of you who have learned of these great ones. See how their love is of the brooding presence of the Mother, how they do nourish life. They are accompanied by unnamed, unnumbered souls of the East who have remained in the hidden fastnesses of the Himalayas. They are accompanied by souls who are your brothers and sisters on the Path. And so you see, the path of the East has come to the West, and the way has been forged by Ramakrishna and Vivekananda and all those who have made the trek to deliver the word of the sacred teachings. Now see then how all of the children of Israel find a meeting in the heart of the Mother, find the place of consecration and, above all, the definition of purpose, of mission, of will, of identity.

O sacred identity of the newborn Christ, sacred identity of the masters of the Himalayas who pay tribute to the messengers in the West, to the witnesses who bring forth the teachings of the ascended masters. Now let the paths of the masters ascended and the masters unascended converge as the cross of light in the heart of the Mother. And let the teachings of both schools be combined in the great mysteries, for thereby those who have studied with the unascended masters will have the benefit of the Spirit corps of the ascended masters, and those who have been the students of the ascended masters will understand the mastery in the Matter plane of the unascended ones—the bodhisattvas becoming the Buddhas, becoming the Mother in the way.

Now, will you not turn and face the ascended masters who have gathered on the platform as the chohans of the rays, the Great Divine Director, and the Maha Chohan, sponsoring the path of the ascension— the path of the ascension that arcs, then, from the side of the South in the unascended avatars to the side of the North that is the fiery core of the Spirit plane.

Therefore, you who have come in the way of the ascended masters, stand to give forth the teachings of the ascended masters to the chelas of the unascended masters. Do you see, then, that this intertwining of East and West and paths of Alpha and Omega is once again for the caduceus flow and the fiery action of the Law? Do you not see that by the eighth ray of the Buddha and the Mother there is the integration of fiery worlds above, fiery worlds below?

Yo! Yo! I say. *Yo!* Come forth, legions of Mighty Victory! Come forth now to impart to the messengers of truth in science and in religion that impetus of victory whereby we go forth to win, we go forth to conquer!

Each one of you is aligned in science or in religion, for these are the polarities of Alpha and Omega. Understand, then, that to bring truth in Spirit and in Matter through paths of East and West, there must be the understanding. And those who have majored in religion—that is, that *religio,* binding the soul to the Spirit—must now consider that science of the Spirit and that science of Matter in many forms, in many ways. Therefore, for the balancing am I come that those of you who are people of science may now learn to converse in the terms of religion; those of you who are people of religion may now learn to converse in the terms of science.

Messengers of truth, you must be ready and able to speak in every tongue, as Charity and Chamuel have said. You must be ready to speak to souls who cannot understand aught but the language of science or of mathematics or of the teachings of the East. See, then, that you become fluent as linguists of the Spirit in the terminology and in the understanding of the peoples of this earth. You must speak to them in a way that they can understand. This will demand study on your part of the religions of the world and of the newest discoveries of science and allowing the inner flame of the Christ within you to correlate, point by point, these manifestations of the inner law.

You will be able to prove that living truth. And I tell you also that the reward for your study will be that your Christ Self will transfer to you those clues and those keys that come from the Cave of Symbols where

Saint Germain presides to hold those necessary inventions and interpretations of the Holy Spirit that will be given by the alchemy of Aquarius to those new-age disciples.

See then that you must have a matrix, a certain matrix of understanding, in order to receive the interpretation of the Word for the great multitudes of the peoples on this earth who will be drawn into this teaching. See then that you have the sense of victory, for it is the victorious sense of cycles spinning, whirling to the white-fire core of being that will take your mind across the paths of the golden consciousness of the mind of God whereby you will increase your intelligence; your very IQ will be intensified.

And have you not already observed how your minds have been quickened and you are not as slow and sluggish as you used to be or as your friends, you find, still are—who have not taken up the path of light? You can move with dexterity, you can think with the mercury diamond-shining mind of God! Therefore, let it be so! For we desire to expand now the chalice of your consciousness in preparation for the coming of Jophiel and Christine, who will sponsor the glorious release of illumination's flame.

And you who will not be present at this quarter of Summit University, I say to you, wherever you are, you must make the daily call to arc that light of the mind of God from the trinity which we will form from this focal point of light in the City of the Angels. See then that you realize that all are students of the law of the Most High God and you are never excluded from our sessions at Summit University, but you only exclude yourselves when you fail to make the Call for the angels of light to bring to you the latest dispensations of the teachings that come through the hand of the Mother.

Therefore, everywhere you are in time and space, know that the Buddha and the Mother can transfer to you by God's grace that energy and that teaching, and that you must and you can be, by journeying to the retreats of the Great White Brotherhood, au courant of the latest discoveries and the latest releases of light. They are indeed for the salvation of souls; they are indeed for the two-thousand-year cycle of Aquarius.

And therefore, let all be diligent to assimilate the Word, for the only repository of the Word is in your heart and in your soul and in your mind. Secondarily, it may be recorded in books. But after all, the worms may eat the books, but the worms can never, never, never eat the fiery sacred heart of the repository of Mother Mary and of Saint Germain.

And so you see, the torch is always passed by the heart; and as we stand before you, we release that fire of the heart and so you release the fire of the heart. It is all well and good for you to pass the book, but you must endow the book with the flame of your heart. It is the cup, it is the chalice, it is the instrument, it is the Matter cycle. It is the bowl of your sacred flame of Summit University.

You must not feel that that book has been fulfilled only in its writing and its printing. It is fulfilled when you wrap it in love, when you charge it with your life's devotion, and when you give it with full understanding. Do you know what is in the book that you give? Shame on you! You must know that book ere you give it. If you would give it away, you must give a portion of yourself with it. You must be able to confer that teaching and not simply the paper.

Precious ones, when you have entrusted to you the illumination for an age, it behooves you to study, to learn, to carry with you the sayings of the masters, to have your little cassette tape recorder and to punch that button and to hear those tapes whenever you have a spare moment. When you are having your meals, is it not possible for you to enjoy the teachings of the masters? Is it not more important for you to hear the conversations of the angelic hosts and the teachings of the Lord than to engage in idle chatter that does not lead to the evolution of the God consciousness on earth?

I speak this to you because it is necessary for some among mankind to sacrifice these little pleasures because we are dealing with a very dense evolution on earth, as some of you have observed. [Audience laughs.] This evolution is a perverse and stubborn evolution, infiltrated by fallen ones who have dedicated themselves to Darkness rather than to Light, and they will not give up their stranglehold on humanity all so easily.

And therefore, I say to you, when you go forth to cut humanity free, do not expect to be welcomed by the archdeceivers or those who have been referred to as these "experts." I tell you, they will not welcome you with open arms, but they will use the full power and the money and the energy that they have amassed away from the Mother and her children to deter you from your path. And they will cause all manner of grief to come upon you, and every method that is available in their hands, as it has been done already to the messengers and the prophets and the teachers throughout the ages.

And therefore, expect no hilarious reception. Become accustomed to the fact, therefore, that the sword of illumination's flame will cut to the quick those ones who must rely on the carnal mind and its game. The sword of illumination thrust, thrust to the core of the error and the lie, will so take those fallen ones off guard that while they are reeling from the blow, the precious children of the light will go free! And you will stand and with the Lord you will be in derision. You will laugh in derision,[2] for the fallen ones, you see, have not accelerated consciousness. And therefore, in the day of the judgment, of illumination, they will not stand, but they will stand wondering, "What has happened? Mankind are no longer in our grasp—here we stand alone!"

Do you not understand that those who have amassed the power and the wealth of the world are only standing on the pinnacle of the people of God, that they are taking from them their daily work, their daily bread, their daily supply, and that when these are withdrawn, they will simply plop! [Audience laughs.] Well, this is the mighty cosmic sense of victory that I bring to you this day, the understanding that the foundation of life on earth is always sealed in the hearts of the devotees and the people of God.

Well, I daresay, some of you have come into your own. You have finally remembered who you are in this conference. Isn't that wonderful! [Audience laughs and applauds.] Well, it is indeed wonderful and we are joyous, for we know that when the soul remembers who I AM, then that soul will soar. And do you know, some souls of light have attained such an awareness of who I AM that it has exalted them even right out of the very spheres and planes of Mater. I tell you, then, for some who are advanced on the Path, we must veil the awareness of who I AM for that awareness is so great that it will actually act to tear that soul from this very octave.

And therefore, we keep the balance for our messenger; we keep the balance for those who view the messenger. And the veils that are worn are so that not all will recognize who that I AM is, who the I AM THAT I AM is. And so the messenger will have identification almost in the human sense for the guarding of the identity, the guarding and the watchfulness of that identity of God in this plane.

Do you understand that once the soul has so totally identified with God in the cosmos and in Spirit, that soul is simply swept up into that awareness and is no longer among you? As we have said before, when the vessel is perfect, the vessel disappears. Therefore, be grateful for imperfections in the vessel, be grateful for chinks in the armor and dents in the cup, for by these there is yet recognition in Matter of the flaming Presence of the living God. And so within yourselves, you are a people fashioned after the image of God, yet you also retain your identity in family and community and even in your tribe. So understand, then, that these identifications are the coordinates in Matter whereby you win that victory for Spirit in Matter.

We adore mankind. We adore the flame within the children of God. We adore that flame. We do not desire to see robots or tin soldiers or perfect people marching about. These are not the people of God. We desire to see that individuality that comes as creativity, that comes as the difference whereby you are not gingerbread men cut out of the cookie cutter of the fallen ones, but you are individuals who have forged an identity that can be seen and known; and therefore, by those differences you are recognized against the bas-relief of the divine consciousness.

Therefore, take care. Do not strive for human perfection, but strive for the divine perfection as the infusing of the flame of life. For when that perfection comes upon you, it fills in the nicks in the cup, the chinks in the armor, and all of the imperfections in the vessel, and you find the overlay of the radiance of the light of God that never fails is the perfection of life itself.

And therefore, you can see in the face of all—the faces of the little ones, the faces of all people of God—the very beauty, the holiness, the exquisiteness that is never, never found in the imitation, in the imitation creation of the fallen ones—that robot consciousness and that chemical creation that walks the earth not as sons and daughters of God, but in imitation, in the false imitation, of the Christed ones.

Let the imitators, the counterfeiters be exposed! Let them be exposed by truth! Let them be exposed by the flame of Mighty Victory and by the messengers who are yourselves, your very own selves, our messengers in science and in religion. Let both Liar and lie[3] be exposed that the Liar may have the opportunity to choose to separate himself from his lie. This is the coming of the judgment. There must be the separation of the Liar and the lie, for that individual also has the freedom to choose, the freedom to be that flame of truth!

Therefore, I have come to transfer to you that flame of Mighty Victory, that flame that is the sponsoring flame of truth in this year of truth on earth. Understand, then, that when you come with the flame of truth and you give your invocation to Pallas Athena, the Goddess of Truth—and I am wondering why you have not given more of that invocation in this class—when you give that invocation, I say to you, you stand before the people of earth and through you and through that sword of truth is the judgment.

For when truth comes, the individual must choose then between truth and error. And I must tell you this great fact of life: that every soul on earth bears the record of truth deep, deep within the fiery core of being, and when confronted by that truth, that soul knows the truth and that soul makes the decision either to confirm or to deny that truth.

You will watch, then, as people will hear you speak the word of truth. And you will see the hesitation, you will see the inclining of the ear to the spirits of error, you will see them listen for the counterpoint view, you will see them search their outer minds for explanations. And then they will weigh truth in the balance with error, and I tell you this is wrong, for truth can never be weighed in the balance of error. Error is the yin and the yang of unrighteousness, truth is above all error. And therefore, it is not the decision between truth and error, it is the decision for truth alone and truth as the victory.

Therefore, you will see that deliberation, and some will choose the way of error and some will choose the way of a relative truth. Neither of these is the correct position. Relative truth is not the answer in this hour, but it is the absolute law of your God-free being. Therefore, speak the truth and as Morya says, "Let the chips fall where they may!" Those are the chips of the human consciousness. Let them fly! Let the soul be carved free by that flaming sword of truth!

Speak truth, that out of the mouth of Christ did manifest and by Buddha was thrice blessed. *Speak* that truth and go forth with the song and the poem "Tell Them."

> Tell them of the coming, then, of that age of Aquarius.
> Tell them of the coming of the messengers of truth.
> Tell them of the law of the inner guru.
> Tell them of the Real Self and all that is true.
> Tell them, for they will know, they will hear.
> They will remember the voice of the Elohim
> And of the elder days and of those manifestations of the avatars.
> Tell them, for they will remember.
> And in their remembrance will be their choice,
> And in their choice will be their judgment,
> And in their judgment will be eternal life or eternal damnation.

Understand, then, when I speak of eternal damnation, I only speak of that damnation which is sustained as long as the individual chooses error. For the individual is his own judge, and the individual Christ Self must sustain that judgment until the individual chooses the path that is the way of righteousness.

Therefore I AM come. I AM that mighty descending flame. The flame of victory is a giant *V.* So it descends by the arc of God. It touches the point of the flame in your heart, and immediately it ascends. Therefore, you see, if you follow the flame of victory, it will be for the going out and the coming in of your soul, day by day the rhythm of Mighty Victory. That *V* can be that impetus of motion from out the Great Central Sun to the heart of the threefold flame on earth, back to the Great Central Sun, back to the heart again, until you are focusing the mighty diamonds of Mighty Victory. And those diamonds of Victory are indeed the manifestation of the sign of the *V* pointing toward Matter and pointing toward Spirit.

So is the diamond formed! So is that the manifestation of my action of the Buddha and the Mother, my action of the flame of the figure eight! So it is coming! So it is the light of the six-pointed star! So it is the light of the five-pointed star where you are! For you see, you must earn that sixth point, you must earn that point of attainment, you must earn the point whereby you balance the threefold flame within your heart and you balance the energies of life. So let it be for the coming of the victory! So let it be for the manifestation of love!

We come in the victorious sense for the laying of the foundation for the coming of the Lord of the World. We give to you that impetus of fire that you might receive the emanation of the consciousness of the Lord Buddha, that you might have already the golden bowl within you—the golden bowl of victory, illumination, and truth, that precipitated bowl that comes from the Royal Teton and is the very bowl of the soul. Into this bowl, then, let Lord Gautama pour of himself and of his sacred fire.

We have come then as servants of the Mother, as servants giving to you the necessary manifestation, the container, the cup for the energies of Lord Gautama. May you keep the golden bowl. May you take the sword of truth. May you march with legions of truth this year.

You will recall that, on this occasion last year, Ray-O-Light stood before you to tell you of the testings of doubt and fear that would come in this year.[4] Well, I see that you have survived. [Audience laughs.] But I see that some among your members have not survived, for they have been taken far afield from the energy field of truth, of self-mastery, catapulted out of the midst of the company by their own doubts and fears.

Some have been rescued by our legions and some have rejected our legions in the very way. I tell you, I must even cover my eyes when I see children of God resisting their deliverers, resisting the angels of the lightning mind of God. And yet it has occurred. I say, pray for the sons and daughters of God and children of light on the earth, for they are beset by the many complexities of the human mind which, in order to be free of its complexities, must surrender itself, must be dissolved into the mind of God, there to find the simplicity of the eternal truth.

And so I stand in the place of Ray-O-Light to give to you that flame of truth, that energy of truth. It is the focus of your victory over fear and doubt and all of the endless questionings of the Law. With that flame of truth, go forth once again with legions of victory, go forth with legions of Ray-O-Light, and vanquish the fears and doubts of a planetary body. Let them be put into the center of the fire by knights and ladies of the Table Round.

I will be with you this evening in celebration of the coming of the Court of Sacred Fire. I AM always in you the shining star of hope, of victory! I AM reborn in you!

December 31, 1976
Pasadena, California
ECP

25

VICTORY'S STAR

Hail, sons and daughters of light! I AM come with my legions of victory to stand in this hour of victory with Saint Germain and El Morya and your blessed selves. We come to anchor a mighty flame unto the earth, a spiraling pillar of sacred fire that is the energy of God this day from the heart of the Great Central Sun.

I come to anchor it in the very midst of the forcefield of this altar of invocation, whence the word of the Mother and her children will ring into the very elements of the earth, proclaiming the hour of victory and of the I AM THAT I AM, truly the coming of the Lord for the alchemy that shall melt the old order of heaven and earth and bring in the new heaven and the new earth upon this planetary body.

My children of the Sun, I salute you! Oft have I watched you from far-off worlds as the twinkling lights of your invocations lit up an otherwise darkened star. And I have sent a light and my twin flame has sent a light and we have said, "We will multiply that light. We will travel down that mighty sunbeam into the hearts of the chelas. We will come into the temples of light and we will start Victory's fire!"

And so the hour has come when the Cosmic Council and the Lords of Karma have agreed that a greater impetus of victory might be endowed within the earth, within the children of the Sun during this epoch of the Dark Cycle of the descent of the misuse of the light of the hierarchy of Scorpio. A darkness such as you cannot imagine is programmed to cover the land—programmed by the fallen ones, who always scheme to multiply the darkness of mankind's karma unto the destruction of souls of light.

My children of the Sun, won't you be seated in Mighty Victory's flame?

A GOLDEN OPPORTUNITY

I am here because I am here. [8-second applause] And you are here because you are here. And inasmuch as we are both here, let us make the most of a golden opportunity for light to increase magnitude upon magnitude until this planetary body becomes a blazing sun.

It is time, then, for those fallen ones to go to the Sun, to spiral into the white-fire core of Alpha and Omega and there to be no more. Time and space is for the reading of cosmic astrology and the cosmic clock, yet for all of their getting, these fallen ones did not get understanding.[1]

They make their psychic predictions. They read the astrology of the Jupiter Effect.[2] They make their predictions for 1984 and not once have they included the mighty prophecy of the coming of the hosts of the LORD!

Well, I am here to give you the prophecy that you can make certain by your performance. Therefore my performance shall be yours and yours shall be mine and we will march with the legions of victory. Is it not so? [Audience responds, "Yes!"]

LEGIONS FOR THE VICTORY OF THE EARTH

Hail, my beloved! Armies of the LORD are arriving from the quadrants of being on the rays and lines of the twelve hierarchies. The angels of Archangel Michael, legions of light, come in a May Day display upon the celebration of the Knight Commander, Saint Germain's coronation for the Aquarian age.[3]

They come and they march and parade in full dress to demonstrate their light, their prowess and their skill in dealing the deathblow to the enemy at will in other systems of worlds. They come wearing laurel wreaths of victory for having fought the good fight and won. They are winners. We are not betting on the losers but on the winners in this race of light accelerating light!

And so you see legions of violet-flame angels under Zadkiel and Holy Amethyst and beloved Omri-Tas. Their numberless numbers fill the sky. They fill the cosmos. The solar system cannot contain the numbers of legions who come for the determinate victory of this earth and this solar system!

YOU MUST BE EMBOLDENED

Beloved ones, you have been told by ascended masters bold that you must be emboldened with a will to win. And the Great Divine Director has come to increase your forcefield of blue lightning as a manifest presence of your identity. Thus he has bequeathed to you his momentum of willing to be in God an identity not tampered with, inviolate.

I am come to reinforce that determination. I am come to charge you with the enthusiasm of hosts of light whose time has come yet whose prophecy is unknown. You who can read the signs of the times and of the heavens know that this is the hour of the cosmic cross of white fire, of the Pleiades' descent. The hierarchies of the Pleiades and Surya come and challenge darkness wherever, whenever, in the body of the earth, but they must have you as their mouthpiece. They must have you wielding the pen and the sword deftly.

My beloved, we are certain of your cooperation. It is because you have already given it that we are here, and we therefore applaud the embodied lightbearers, the Keepers of the Flame and all chelas of the living gurus.

THE HEROES OF THE AGE

Planetary body, I salute you. Children of the Sun, Helios and Vesta, I, Victory, salute you in the name of the ascended Lanello, who has carried unto his ascension the white banner of victory and peace with the golden fleur-de-lis of your own heart's balance and victory. Thus he becomes one of the heroes of the age, side by side with Godfre and the key saints who gave their lives that you might serve to the finish.

They have taken their leave because they placed their trust in God in you, in the God within you. They had the ultimate certainty that men and women of good faith would follow after them and not let down the banner or the torch of light. And you who run and read and see the Word of their presence and sing of their light in your midst, you are the visionaries. You are the sages and seers, East and West, who impart to the children of earth the mighty vision entrusted to you by the purity of your devotion and your heeding of the Word now given to you these many years by the Mother.

Therefore we must salute her lifestream for staying and still staying midst the onslaughts incomprehensible you know not of that are a daily battle upon her soul. Yet the chelas who surround her have also been the recipients of those arrows of outrageous fortune. And it is the Mother's request that I pay tribute to them also, for they have been the rings of fire and the legions in embodiment and in all octaves who have stood to defend the office of the Messenger that is so vital, so absolutely necessary, as the link in the chain of octaves.

NEW LEGIONS FOR THE VICTORY

We speak of the chain of octaves; we speak of invincible victory. We speak of the light and we are come to bow to the light within you and to let you know, dear hearts, that the Cosmic Council, ratifying the decree of Almighty God, has this day sent legions on every line of the clock, all registered in the Great Causal Body of the Great Divine Director. In his name you may also invoke all the legions serving under a particular hierarchy of the sun on a particular line of the clock with a particular ascended master who also serves on that line.[4]

You need not know all the names of these hosts of the LORD, but wherever there is a problem, such as the hatred of the incoming Christ Child on the one o'clock line of Saint Germain in abortion, in all manner of desecration of Saint Germain's teaching, his beauty and his light of freedom, you may then invoke the legions of the hosts of the LORD who have come marching this day in his name on that line of the clock under the hierarchy of Aquarius.

Instantaneously those legions will go forth, do your bidding and take action. You will not know until you try, until you see, and ultimately you will not know until your ascension in the light what tremendous power has been added to the side of right and light in this moment on this day of Gemini 1979. [17-second applause]

SANAT KUMARA'S TEACHING ON THE RUBY RAY

Beloved ones, the Four and Twenty Elders are standing in awe of Sanat Kumara, the Ancient of Days, who himself, upon the great white throne, stands and bows before the Nameless One, the Almighty, who bequeathed to him the opportunity for the salvation of earth. The hosts of the LORD and the Cosmic Council have given all that can be given thus far in answer to your calls for the increase of the spin of this earth planet you call home.

Beloved ones, when you implement these forces and hosts of the LORD, who can know, who can tell what is in the heart of the Almighty for continued reinforcements, until truly the transition into Aquarius may yet be known as the coming of the golden age upon earth. Not in a decade has there been such hope and such promise through this activity and through the hosts of the LORD as there is this day, my beloved.

Now, as you take every advantage of this opportunity, I ask you to become diligent in combing the earth for facts, for figures, for names. Do your research carefully, for although we may see—by the fullness of the crystal ray, the mighty X ray, the All-Seeing Eye of God—that which is acting here, we cannot intercede unless you make the specific calls. There-fore, these hosts of the LORD, encamped round about the hillsides of Los Angeles, San Francisco and the chakras of the nations of the earth, are ready to spring, ready to move, ready to march.

They are the disciplined ones; they are intense beings of love who, one and all, have passed their initiations on the mighty ruby ray, which Sanat Kumara hastens to bring to your attention through the *Pearls of Wisdom*. The Ancient of Days can hardly wait to transmit to you these teachings so that you may enter in to the correct and not the incorrect use of the ruby ray.[5]

In his name I am therefore authorizing this messenger to release these *Pearls of Wisdom* before their date so that students of the light may have these dispensations and move forward swiftly to invoke the light of the ruby ray, not to their hurt or to anyone's hurt but for the swift and sudden descent of light that will act! act! act! in the heart of the earth to set aside the conditions that for far too long have held sway in the very midst of a sincere and noble people.

The majority of the people upon earth desire freedom, peace and the abundant life and they have been fooled and manipulated to believe that the path to these ends lies through Marxism, socialism and the conspiracy itself. Therefore the action of the ruby ray is designed by the LORD God to strip the children of earth of an overlay, hardened over the centuries, of a pseudopersonality and a pseudoanalysis of the problems at hand.

Only the action of the ruby ray possesses the All-power of God to perform a certain work in the midst of the people of earth. And this is why, even though you have given ultimate decrees to Astrea and the violet flame, it is necessary that this action be added unto the calls. The ascended masters have not been able to release this information to you until this hour because it required a certain number of students to support our messenger with the calls and dispensations already given in order for the next step to be released unto you.

If we had not had that support in protecting our forcefield, our movement and our teaching, we could not have brought you the advancing initiations that will come. They will come so swiftly it shall be as the fulfillment of the prophecy "As the lightning cometh out of the East and shineth even unto the West, so shall also the coming of the Son of man be."[6]

You, every one of you, I say, is that Son of man. And you shall come with the swift lightning of the ruby ray and you will see how your calls will make the difference—all the difference in the world from this moment on.

I LAY MY STAR OF VICTORY UPON THIS ALTAR

Now I stand at the altar of invocation here in the sanctuary of the Holy Grail. And I raise my voice by the authority of Sanat Kumara, Hierarch of Venus.

I, Mighty Victory, stand and I invoke a mighty pillar of the ruby ray. I invoke a mighty pillar of victory and I invoke the mighty pillar of the crystal ray given unto the great prophets and leaders of old. So these intense rays of light shall go forth, shall *seal* the earth, shall *roll* back that darkness if and only if the souls of light will ratify my call this day.

O LORD God Almighty, Brahma, Vishnu and Shiva, by the I AM THAT I AM and the sacred Om, I pledge my life and my attainment, as so many cosmic beings have done this day, that neither this messenger nor the true chelas of Saint Germain will let us down until that victory is indeed a *Victory! Victory! Victory!* won in every continent, in every nation, in every heart of light, in every soul who breathes the air of the Holy Spirit.

Therefore, I invoke these flames. Therefore, I lay upon this altar, in the very heart of the Mother, my own star of victory that I give to the Cosmic Council. I place upon their altar this momentum of my victory to hold the balance for the light that shall now be entrusted to Keepers of the Flame.

Beloved ones, you have often heard how the ascended masters have paid the price ahead of time for a dispensation for their chelas. Well, I come forth in the name of Sanat Kumara to do something for that great Being, as he has done so much for me and for so many evolutions.

I give my star of victory in the name of Saint Germain and for his flame. I give it for every service ever rendered by the angelic hosts, the Elohim, every ascended master of the Great White Brotherhood, worlds without end. And I give my star in the name of a certain number of chelas whom I visited in the past two-week interval, whom I know to be staunch and stalwart servitors of light. And to whom I said: "I see your light. I see your devotion. I will give my star for you and for those who are the living immortals—the saints who have gone before you in the building of the true Church Universal and Triumphant."

Therefore this light of God that I anchor here is my momentum of victory, which shall indeed turn back the darkness that some have attempted to put upon the messenger, the organization and the true believers of this hour of the coming of the LORD I AM THAT I AM to the earth.

Therefore this light shall repel, shall turn back, shall send forth the acceleration of karma and of evil intent that is pitted against all lightbearers upon the planetary body. Invoke it, I say! Always remember to invoke it in the name of your mighty I AM Presence and Christ Self, Sanat Kumara, the Ancient of Days, Lord Gautama Buddha, Lord Maitreya, Lord Jesus Christ and Saint Germain, the twin flames of the two witnesses and the hearts of the saints.

I desire that you should use this order of invocation as it is taught by Sanat Kumara and as it will be released to you in the coming *Pearls of Wisdom.* For by the descent of the pillar of victory, the pillar of the ruby ray, the pillar of the crystal ray, you will ensure and safeguard that the descent of these intense energies will bring harm to no one, least of all yourselves.

THE PRAYER OF THE LEGIONS OF VICTORY

Legions of Victory, stand now! One hundred thousand angels of Victory are in formation with you. They stand in, among and around you at Camelot this day. And they say,

> *In the name of the Lord, in the name of the prophet, in the name of Saint Germain:*

> *Here I AM Lord, send me!*
> *Here I AM, son of man, chela of the light,*
> *By the Word incarnate within you, send me!*
> *I AM an angel of Mighty Victory.*
> *I AM committed to fulfill his promise unto the Ancient of Days.*
> *I AM a bearer of his flame*
> *And the three pillars that he has enshrined here.*
> *I AM an angel of Victory!*

Here I AM, O chela.
Send me! Send me! Send me! Send me!
O send me where'er you would send me.
And I will go and I will start that glow of sacred fire
Where'er you send me.
And whenever you make that call,
O chela of the light,
Not one but ten thousand of us will respond,
For our reinforcements are gathered
Around the world on every continent,
Not only here at Camelot.
But we are here,
And we are here to stay
In the name of our leader, Mighty Victory,
Unto the hour of earth's victory in the light!
O chelas of the flame, this is our mantra:

> *Here I AM LORD, I AM THAT I AM,*
> *Word incarnate in the chela,*
> *Send me! Send me! Send me! Send me!*
> *Send me! Send me! Send me!*

O beloved ones, there is such excitement in the hosts of the LORD as they are now given the release to act as they have never acted before—to act! act! act! in the name of the sons and daughters of God.

No other name shall be honored but the name I AM THAT I AM and the Name behind the name and the Sun behind the sun. Only the pure in heart may invoke the name of the Ancient of Days and all who serve him in the great cosmic spheres.

I AM light! I AM the light of victory in you! I place a replica of myself within you. And there is no crowding of the secret chamber of the heart, for truly the image of every ascended master, worlds without end, can come into your heart and still be the only begotten Son, the universal Christ.

Therefore unabashedly, I AM that Manchild in you. I AM being born in you by Lord Maitreya, and the light of the Cosmic Virgin, the light of Alpha and Omega descends. We come to give birth to a soul, to a nation, to a planet and to the goal of universal Christhood for the offspring of the Most High God.

In the name of Alpha and Omega, I am sent. I have come and I have established the purpose to which I came. And to all darkness I say, It is finished! Om.

June 3, 1979
Camelot
Los Angeles, California
ECP

26

VICTORY TO THOSE WHO LOVE!

O mighty work of the soul forging God, forming the reality of the mission in the very heart of the Self! O mighty work of the ages wrought by the spirit of love! O devotion to the cause that continues without being held back by any lack! This virtue of the soul centered in the rose of the sacred labor is the one I extol.

I come as a champion of the outworking in the heart of the chela of the very light of love. Love is my way. Love is my victory. Love is the ray of victory that I AM. This is the love that I behold in the heart of the chela who sees the goal as crystal fire mist and determines that the crystal fire mist shall not remain in the etheric octaves unheard, unknown, unspoken, unwritten—the chela who says: "I have seen God. I will see to it that millions see him and know him as I AM."

O the one who has the courage to unveil the vision of his soul. Fearless, dauntless, unconcerned that the vision, that precious treasure, might be trampled upon, he reveals the vision because of his ultimate faith in that vision. The vision is greater than he is; it is all consuming. It has become the passion of being.

The vision is ultimate truth. The vision is that measure of God the soul has been accorded in grace; and the soul who truly sees the portion apportioned unto him knows that the geometry, when translated into the Matter sphere, will of itself defend itself, preserve itself, perpetuate itself, as the music of Beethoven, chela of the Great Divine Director, reveals.

It is untouchable. It cannot be stolen. Though mortals have attempted to pervert it, they have only bound themselves further by the sacred fire that pours through it. It is the poetry of sacred fire plucking the harp of the heart. It is the sound of Elohim.

There is one initiate called of God who will one day appear in Matter to deliver the conclusion, the finale, of six other symphonies that continue the path of initiation of the ruby ray. But that one of Cosmic Christhood shall not appear nor shall the music be heard until a retinue of lightbearers has so incorporated this mighty music of the spheres as to have assimilated it as the Body and Blood of the Cosmic Christ, Lord Maitreya.

When every atom of your being whirls to this music, when the fiery core resounds it and transmits it from the Great Central Sun, when you stand as a pillar of fire of ascension's flame and the ruby ray and the sound of freedom emanate from you to drown out and swallow up all dissonance of the betrayers out of the pit who have spread abroad their anti-music, anti-art, anti-dharma, polluting the sound waves of the earth and the soul, when the force of the music within you can swallow up the anti-light and the anti-freedom, *then* you will understand.

When the sound of Elohim, of the ruby ray and its initiates is heard in physical Matter and the balance is held as pillars of fire proclaim the name I AM THAT I AM, the Word and the sound of the Word in the music of freedom, *then* will the music descend. Then will that one descend to record it.

You will know that in the beginning was the Word,[1] and by the Word spoken and transmitted as the music of the spheres of Elohim, by the Word transmitted as the sounding of the soundless sound, the intoning of that music will spell the final round of the consuming of evil within the spheres of this solar system. And there will be no stopping that sound across a cosmos when it is emitted from initiates of the sacred fire, from the sacred heart of souls comfortable and comforting all life in heaven and earth by the intensity of the Blood of Christ.

BY HARMONY WE WILL PRESERVE FREEDOM

Therefore listen, O children. Harmony, O blessed harmony, is your challenge for the preservation of your freedom. And you will note how accurately he, [Beethoven], said, "I do not write noisy music."[2] Noise, the noise of dissonance and discord, side by side with the veritable sound of fiery vortices of moving galaxies, of Elohim humming the sound of the *HUM*, the *OM*, the *HRIM*—all the sounds and tones of the universal Ma can be heard in those nine symphonies of the Word.

Therefore, note well that those who manifest anti-freedom are inharmonious to the core. They have subverted the life force of Alpha and Omega in every atom of being. In physical Matter they are the irresponsible purveyors of the misuses of the energy of the atom and all manner of misuses and abuses of deadly substances and poisons, radioactive energy, and on and on.

Mark the individual who is discordant and you will know that man to be anti-freedom, anti-Saint Germain. He may cover over his discord from subconscious levels with an aura of peace or sanctity or apparent support for the causes of freedom, but ultimately, when face to face with the Great Divine Director or Saint Germain or a chela or the embodied messenger, a rupture occurs and a volcano of psychic discord comes to the fore with the demands of the fallen ones for their right to be discordant, their right to be tyrants, their right to be free to be Antichrist.

GOD HARMONY IS INDISPENSABLE

Well, my beloved ones, we see in the release of God Harmony in the past year the beginning of the harmonization of the forces within each chela. We see that the whirling of the sun centers, accelerating the light to throw off discord, originates in the harmony of the inner soul, the balance of Alpha and Omega.

We see that for the freedom of the earth, God Harmony is an irreplaceable, indispensable cosmic being. For Harmony transmits to you the initiation whereby you overthrow the invasion of invisible tyrants into the world of the self. All sorts of conditions, all sorts of physical manifestations from drugs and alcohol to sugar, nicotine and poisonous toxins contribute to the inharmony of the body—not to mention the pollution of the astral plane, the unseen pockets of rage and anger and the subtle, deafening beat of the demons and their rock beat that resounds on the astral plane and bombards the emotional body and the solar-plexus chakra even when the physical ear does not hear it.

Thus the dire pollution of the planetary body in the astral and physical planes is designed to thwart the descent of the magnitude of the light of freedom that comes forth from the Great Divine Director and Saint Germain.

MY NAME IS NOT AS IMPORTANT AS MY MESSAGE

Thus, I come. No need to wonder who I am. Listen to my message and you will know. By and by I will tell you who I am, for you hurl your questions to me, "Who are you? Who is speaking?" And so you cut across the message that does flow. You see, my name is not nearly as important as my message. We are the nameless ones and our names are given as a point of reference for unascended chelas who need a name to know a vibration. Truly the vibration is in the name but the vibration comes first and the name second.

Therefore I give you my vibration today, and by tuning into that ray you may become myself. Then before you leave, I will give you a name tag that you can wear to say, "See, I AM THAT I AM." Well, they shall know you by your fruits, not by your name or by my name but by the good works of the sacred fire of the ruby ray.

What does it matter if his name was Beethoven? His vibration is the light of victory, freedom and joy! Victory is his flame! Victory is that vibration! You can be it too. You can choose to be that flame if you will. Or you can sit and still wonder who you are, who I am, who anyone is.

Perhaps you do not even know the name of your own God Presence. Perhaps we should begin at the beginning and therefore know that behind the name I AM THAT I AM is the sounding of the Word and the sounding of the name. The name I AM THAT I AM is also a vibration of the victory of being and of life. It all depends how you read the word. Some read it as power, some as love, some as wisdom, some as the white light of purity. I have always read it as victory.

I have always been that God-victorious flame, worlds without end, for when I look into the sun and the smiling face of Helios and Vesta, I see God-victorious, God-free beings. And I say:

> Let freedom ring in the hearts of souls in the earth.
> Let them receive a spin and a shake.
> O world, awake!
> Let their atoms spin!
> Let their souls be enfired with freedom.
> Let them accelerate!

BY GOD-HARMONY WE WILL OVERTURN
THE DISCORDANT ONES

Therefore, heed my message. We will overturn the discordant ones by God-harmony. Let all understand that what is perceived as harmony today may be perceived as inharmony tomorrow, as you refine your inner ear and tune in again to the sounding of your own celestial tone and bring your forces and your vibes to that pitch.

Thus, beware of those who come speaking of freedom's song but harboring in the folds of their garment a wrong, wrong vibration. They are for freedom that they may have the freedom to impose bondage upon others.

Now I stand today and my legions stand with me and we are determined that those individuals upon the planetary body who demand equality and freedom simply to manifest the greater and greater degradation of the not-self shall not stand. No, they shall not stand in the holy place of the congregation of the righteous! No, they shall not be allowed to purvey their abominations any longer because we stand—because we stand in you and we have heard your calls and your cries for freedom.

And so we have taught the Mother the lesson of the deadly force of condemnation that is the anti-harmony that besets the decent, honorable people of earth. Therefore, we match her vow [to bind the forces of condemnation].³ We will come each day to reinforce her calls and we will stand with the heart of every friend of freedom to multiply those calls and the clearing crystals that descend by the "terrible crystal"⁴ invoked by the Mother.

We will intensify them. We will burn and consume the demons and discarnates and they will not have a chance to survive, for their dance is the anti-dance. They cannot perform their dance in the presence of God-harmony, God-victory, God-direction, God-power!

I AM here and I AM come and I will match your vow. You have considered how you would make your vow. Well, whatever vow you make I vow to match, as long as it is in accord with the will of God. You see, I will come and I will give a spin to everyone who is determined to win and to accelerate.

Now arise, I say! For I would prepare your temples for the coming of the light of the Cosmic Christ. I direct my ray now into the cause and core of all misuse of the Mother light within your base chakra. I AM Mighty Victory and I come for the victory of your soul and the victory of the Mother within you.

I come to bind the deceleration of death that has held back the rising of that Mother light, but I will not allow it to rise without your God-determination to keep the flame of purity. For I am a champion of the World Mother, worlds without end, and I will not let the Mother light be desecrated in anyone.

Therefore I come with a blue flame from the heart of the Temple of the Blue Lotus. I come with Himalaya's flame; I come with a blue energy of protection. Let the veiled goddess of the Kundalini's sacred fire be veiled in blue lightning, in robes of blue. Let your white chakra forevermore be sealed in blue lightning! And let Archangel Michael, the defender of the Woman, *defend* the base chakra, *defend* the ascension flame, *defend* your path to victory!

This is my gift. And I have meditated long upon how I would accelerate the Mother light without the danger of violating that light through the violations of the untempered chelas. Beloved ones, this is my deliberation.

Therefore, as I stood before the Great Central Sun, the dispensation went forth that Lord Himalaya and his devotees of the blue lotus will now stand to give protection to the white light of the Mother chakra throughout the planetary body.

This means that the white chakra in the Middle East and in the very center of the earth, the white light of the Mother, the ascension flame, shall be sheathed in blue lightning from all the legions of light back to the Great Central Sun. The Great Teams of Conquerors and the mighty Blue Eagle, Archangel Michael, the legions of the will of God and devas of the diamond heart—all have pledged to protect the white light and to protect those who use it.

A MEDITATION ON THE VEILING LIGHT
OF THE BLUE GODDESS

Now, beloved ones, this is indeed a dispensation from the master mind of God, the Great Guru. And I am grateful that he has placed in my heart this meditation on the veiling light of the blue goddess.

Thus, souls who invoke the white light, let there be upon you the mantle of the universal Mother to rise safely. Let the seat-of-the-soul chakra be *purged* by the sword of Kali. Let it be *purged* by the swords of the legions of victory. We will not leave the soul of light where we find that soul of light if only that soul determine to flee the dens of the psychic hordes.

I send forth a ray to melt the allure and the magnetism of the psychic plane, for too many children of God are caught there. Therefore I challenge their pride and their ambition to cavort with psychic entities. *Burn* through, O ruby ray from the heart of Sanat Kumara, Gautama Buddha, Lord Maitreya, and Jesus.

Burn through, O ruby ray, by the hearts of the messengers and the saints. *Burn* through, O ruby ray, into the cause and core of the pride of Lucifer that is upon those individuals who insist upon being psychic channels for all manner of effluvia and degrading vibrations. *Burn* through, O sword of living flame! Cut them free! Cut them free! Cut them free!

Now, if you still resist me, O soul of God, I must hurl and fling my challenge right into your very soul! Therefore I challenge you to stand before me to declare that these psychic hordes are more real than I AM, than Sanat Kumara is in the very temple of this messenger.

Burn through! Expose the false hierarchy! Expose the false impostors and the entities. *Burn through,* O ruby ray. *Burn through,* O light of God. *Burn through!*

Now, souls of light caught in variance and witchcraft, you will be forced to look upon me once each day, for you will have to compare my reality of ultimate God-victory in love to your own paltry offering. I will stand before you and I intend to remind you every single day that *every single day* you postpone your surrender of the deadly practice of witchcraft you make karma that will bind you for thousands of years to this evolution until you have finally surrendered and brought the message of Victory to the children of God!

THE JUDGMENT OF THE FORCES OF WITCHCRAFT

I am in the earth and I fling my challenge through the messenger and the chelas. Therefore, every practicing witch and warlock, black magician and Satanist this day, every psychic channel must give answer to the Mother flame, to Sanat Kumara, to the legions of Venus and to every chela who is dauntless with the thrust of the jaw, the glint in the eye and the seizing of the sword of Lanello! For we come and your judgment has come and we invoke the judgment of the Lord Jesus Christ upon you!

You can no longer serve without our challenge every twenty-four hours. So, then, tremble if you will. Tremble in your boots. Tremble if you will. So is the coming of the Mother flame of victory. So is the coming of the flame of freedom. If you would be free from fear, then forsake your misuses of the Mother flame, for you will not live another day upon this planet without coming face to face with the infamy of your malpractice against the body of God.

I *expose* you in all of your infamy and sodomy and perversion of the Mother light! Therefore, come out of the woodwork and be exposed, you worms. For I will have you; either you will become a soul worthy or you will melt in the very heat of the ruby ray. This is the hour of decision—to the right or to the left.

There will be no more derision or mockery of the Mother flame without the intensification of compensation, of return of karma. Therefore, look upon me, for my face cannot be erased by your sorcery. I am here and I am here to stay, because I love the chelas of the light.

I love humanity. And I perceive that psychotronic energy, for want of another word, that psychic hatred that penetrates both from physical apparatus and from the very apparatus of the chakras themselves, as individuals, using no apparatus, use their own chakras to transfer the astral, psychic force that you have called psychotronic energy. Indeed it is real, because men have willed it so, but we will steal that energy and turn it upon them.

The children of the light will not go down in disease and cancers of the body and soul because of that force. No, not as long as the lion roars, not as long as the message of the Word goes forth, not as long as the chelas utter the call of light, for this is our triangle of victory: Almighty God in heaven in the Great White Brotherhood; the mouthpiece of the Word; and the millions who have heard and repeated that Word. Thus is the cycle, Father, Son and Holy Spirit, complete in our community of light.

RISE, O MOTHER FLAME!

Therefore *rise*, O Mother flame! Rise within these temples, and as the Great Law allows and as free will allows, purge each one of every absence of surrender that has drawn about the soul chakra any perversion of the living flame of freedom.

Now *rise*, O Mother light. Rise into the desire body. Light a light so brilliant that every soul may see and know what is the anti-desire, the desire that conflicts with the God within.

Now, O soul so illumined, I speak to you at subconscious and super-conscious levels even beyond your outer awareness, for you see me and you hear me. Soul who hears my word, who sees, then, by the brilliant light of the Mother within the desire chakra, take thy stand to surrender that which is at hand that is not the hand of God.

Whatever you can give, give this day and let your giving increase until you go all the way with the ruby ray.

So ascend now, Mother light, into the heart.

Here in the heart I come for one purpose, to clear the records of death of previous incarnations and the experiments with death as wrong thought, as preoccupation with death and dying that goes by many other names. I come to clear the heart of the burden of the death entity.

Burn through! Burn through! Burn through, by the action of the ruby ray. Let the decelerating spiral dissolve and let the accelerating light of the ascension flame blaze through! Blaze through! *Blaze through!*

RISE TO THE THROAT CHAKRA

Now for the clearing of the will of God, now for the clearing of the will of God and now the anchor point in the spoken Word of the chela becomes the sword of Maitreya. [pause]

Now the blue veiled goddess ascends through the throat chakra and I, with the goddess, give you the spin of life that you might determine to get on the whirling merry-go-round of the will of God, the soundless sound of the Word in the throat chakra of power, the vortices of power from Almighty God.

Now you may summon that light. Now you may accelerate, O soul. Take flight safely in the arms of Mother.

The acceleration of the Word within the throat chakra is the power of Hercules and Elohim. It is the sealing of your life as the authority of that flame.

Now we rise for the clearing of the All-Seeing Eye of God. Let it be cleared of all ulterior motives, all impure seeing, for that emerald ray is a penetration, my beloved. That emerald ray is a penetration of the geometry of God.

O seraphim, mount! Mount with the white light of the Mother and take these souls by thy wings of light, rustling wings, vortices of light. Take them to the vision of the New Jerusalem.

THE VISION OF THE NEW JERUSALEM

Beloved ones, the Great Law will not allow the entire clearing of the third eye, for this is a work of love and of your soul's devotion to the dharma. But I may give you the gift of a vision—the vision of the New Jerusalem. And by that vision I secure a flame of hope, which I now place within the third eye of each one, and that flame of hope is a white light of ascension fire.

The flame of hope will carry you higher and higher and give you the God-desire to transmute all lesser seeing, lesser goals, lesser planning, limited consciousness. *Burn* through, O lasting flame of hope. *Burn* through, O Archeia Hope. *Burn* through, O Mother flame of Hope!

Now, my beloved, I will seal you in the All-Seeing Eye by Victory's twofold flame, for only to this level may I rise in this hour. We will now establish a balance and an adjustment of your vehicles and continue with our initiation when you have stabilized at this level of awareness. [pause]

Because of this initiation, my beloved, we cannot allow new students to enter the conference following this dictation, for we are now about to accelerate with those who are here, those who are willing to go all the way with the Christ and the Buddha.

Yes, I am Mighty Victory. But I am more determined that you know my vibration through this dictation and this transfer of light than that you know my name. For, you see, impostors will come to you and they will say, "I am Mighty Victory," but they will not carry my vibration, my light, my joy, my animation and the energy of the transfer of a cosmos of Cosmic Christ illumination.

Therefore, not in the name will the game be won but in light! light! light! of the Great Central Sun and the smiling face of Helios, who winks and says: "There is only one Mighty Victory. There is only one I AM THAT I AM. There is only one Son. All others are impostors of that flame."

Dwell, then, in the consciousness of oneness and you will always know the singular initiate of the sacred fire who has the authority of Almighty God to bear the name I AM. O my beloved, understand the mystery of the One and none will ever distort your vision—your vision true of Saint Germain and Jesus Christ, El Morya, O true blue!

You will never believe another liar, for the lyre of your heart, blessed instrument of our music of the spheres, will be the measure and the only measure of the voice of the Good Shepherd and the message of our Word. Our Word is a two-edged sword revealing good and evil, cleaving asunder absolute Good and absolute Evil.[5]

I AM come. And I come to send that sword and not to send peace[6] until I have carved in pieces the dragons of the anti-will. I will not send peace but a ray of harmony that will disturb all inharmonious atoms and I will intensify that ray of harmony and thereby they shall be exposed and they shall have no peace until they come in a whole piece to surrender before God.

Think upon this and be free in the God-reality of the Great Divine Director.

Victory to those who love!

July 3, 1979
Camelot
Los Angeles, California
ECP

27

THE SIGN OF THE GOLDEN V
DRAWN IN THE
CRADLE OF THE INNER RETREAT

Hail! O mighty Liberty—wonder of the age, goddess of our love, and threefold flame held in the hearts of a mighty people.

We are come, our legions in full array, to pay homage to the light of that Woman who has held the flame of liberty for all of our brothers and legions of light—even the Goddess of Liberty who now takes the lead as the spokesman of the Karmic Board to dispense light and a quotient of liberty, the liberty whereby each one may expand and expand again a cosmic identity and yet see the light of day by the aperture of the soul.

O happy hearts afire with a vision and a devotion that comes from the mild eye of Pallas Athena! O happy hearts who rejoice in a victory anticipated even as faith is the substance of things hoped for![1]

You have learned our lessons and we have been a part of them all. For our flame—as leaping, golden-yellow fire tongues—has been even the instrumentation of a greater perception, a greater expansion—and, above all, it has been the joy of Nada and of Kuan Yin, even the very joy of Cyclopea, even the joy of the Great Divine Director!

Blessed hearts filled with that truth, come forth then and realize that we would set the seal, not only upon this conference but upon thy life. For why do we then hold a conference for the entering in to the inner retreat of the heart? Why do we gather together the hosts of the Lord and the sons and daughters of God? It is not for a moment, but it is for a moment that shall become an eternity.

This coming together, then, is to set the mark of your own individual fiery destiny. And we have not overlooked any one of you. But we have come to your heart of hearts, we have taken you into our own, and we have set before you the goal of victory!

> Victory! I say.
> Victory for the fullness of the light!
> Victory for your tenure on earth!
> Victory for the flame of God!
> Victory for the ascension of self within the planetary sphere and spiral!

I am *indeed* Mighty Victory! Well, after all, who else did you think would come to set the seal of victory on Saint Germain's Inner Retreat?

Well, I am here in full array, with ten thousand of my own saints and angels of living fire! And this is certainly a mighty dose of yellow fire that I release to planet Earth—far more than you would expect on the Fourth of July. But after all, this is indeed the fifth! And therefore, we must augment our yesterdays. We must multiply them! And by the power of the four and the five, we can make the nine come home—the three-times-three for the victory of the decade of the nineties where all that is counted that has gone before will be that fruition of life!

Yes! I am here!—and you have never seen me more physical before. For the rain that falls is the rain from heaven. And it does carry with it many of us who have remained high at inner levels and octaves of vibration. As you go within to the inner heart, so you prepare a place that is ensconced in the physical temple for our own descent and for our own release of light.

We are here, then, to consecrate the victory—all past, present, and future victories—of the light of freedom within you. Therefore, it is an inner retreat into the experiencing of past, present, and future freedom for all who love that freedom even as we do love the heart of freedom in the Goddess of Liberty.

Realize, then, that this has been an experience transcending (even as it has followed) even the planes of life. Therefore, we have taken you back that you might bring forward momentums of light and bring into the flame those conditions of consciousness that you would not have remain on your application for the Inner Retreat.

And therefore, we come with the cosmic eraser of Saint Germain! We come with the violet flame. We come with golden illumination that sparks hope—that allows you not to mope but to leave behind you those dread, depressing burdens of the past that have no part with the higher air of the higher mountain!

Therefore, let us climb. Let us climb a mighty stairway of light. Let us determine that no soul will take flight from planet Earth without passing through the mighty arch of Chamuel and of Archangel Michael[2]—the mighty arch that does align the inner will with the outer will and the mighty will of Elohim!

Let us determine that this earth will spin a mighty fire, that there will be a resolute impending and a momentum of light that will determine that Christ-victory for all!

We must increase—we must increase momentum, we must increase the vibratory action of all life upon this planetary body! And this is the necessity for this Inner Retreat, this dispensation, this going forth.

Beloved ones, earth has come to a crossroads. And you know, as the proverbial top that will fall over when its spin is not great enough, we come to that place that—for the equilibrium and the balance of planet Earth—there is required a greater spinning of light, a greater acceleration.

And this means many changes within and without. These changes, beloved ones, are calculated to be the transition into the great golden age. Therefore, you can hear in the acceleration of light and in my voice and in all that has gone forth here that there is indeed a stepping-up of your four lower bodies, a stepping-up of your soul and of your heart!

I ask you to *leap* into the very heart of my victory flame! I ask you to dance with my legions of light! I ask you to acquaint now yourselves with the saints who have come with me. For there is a mighty God-momentum of determination that, once and for all, these souls of light who have descended with the Ancient of Days *shall* forge and win, *shall* manifest that place in the sun, *shall* produce a victory that shall allow every member of those twelve tribes to come home to God!

We are determined, blessed hearts! And I tell you, rare is the moment when heaven has opened itself to reveal to the children of the light just how determined we are that *you will win in this fight!*

And I tell you, beloved ones, sometimes we do not always show our determination—because, you see, then perhaps you might become *less* determined thinking that we are *more* determined—and therefore we allow you to think we are *less* determined so that you will become more determined! Such is the psychology of the ascended hosts of light!

[Audience applauds.]

Now we would take you into our heart of hearts, not as those who are unknown to us but those who are known to us and of us—those of you, then, whom we would call friend, compatriot of freedom, and ones who will cooperate with our cause for the victory.

Therefore, we open up our council chambers. And we let you know what is the determination of Almighty God so that you can ride it as a wave of light! so that you can feel invigorated! so that you can feel your own God-determination coming forth from your very heart and soul, from your very causal bodies!

Blessed hearts of light, that God-determination is *fierce!* And you will see the chiseled faces of my legions with their piercing eyes, how *fierce* they are with that God-determination to beat down every foe of self-indulgence, procrastination, and all that hinders you from the victory of life!

Why, beloved hearts, there are among you many who have won in past cycles for the very appreciation of timing. Timing has spared your neck and spared the nations.

Timing, then, must be reconsidered in this hour. For if we accelerate, then your previous assessment of timing may not be at the point of precipitation.

> If all is in acceleration,
> You, beloved hearts,
> Do not want to see yourselves left behind
> In a proverbial cloud of dust!
> Well, blessed hearts,
> Let us be where we must—
> At the head of the line.
> And let those who shirk behind,
> Let them have that dust until they eat the dust
> And eat the dust no more!
> For they will come to the fore
> And they will surely be a part
> Of the legions of light!

Blessed hearts! We have seen the violet flame. We have seen the violet-flame smoke and balloons and action of your ingenuity at the parade of Camelot.[3] We rejoice—for it is a victory parade! a victory celebration! a victory garden! and a victory Inner Retreat!

So you see how we place our prefix on every word and manifestation of your life. For all that you do is a victory, victory, victory manifestation! Else, why would you do it? There is no reason for doing anything except for the victory of the God flame! Is it not so? [Audience responds, "Yes!"] And so a victory cannot be half-baked, else it is not a victory!

Blessed hearts, consider this. As I have said before, the sign of the *V* is the sign of the descent and the ascent of the soul. Well, when is the *V* formed?

We have discussed this, blessed hearts, for the legions of light love to discuss the philosophy of victory! And they have come to the conclusion that the victory is formed the moment that the soul begins to ascend. And until it begins to ascend, there is only a single descending line. Do you see? And therefore, for the victory of the light to manifest, you must be on the upward path. And *the only way to go is up!*—if you would have your victory coil follow you and transport you into the very heart of the Sun.

Therefore, the *V* for victory is a triumph already won. For from the moment that that line is formed, it is actually complete in the inner eye of God and in the mind of God. And therefore, the ascent will be the manifestation of the momentum of the descent. For by the momentum of the descent is the ascent, and the perfect lines are forged and won in God.

Therefore, beloved ones, when we make the sign of the double *V,* it is the double *V* of the double victory of your twin flames by the power of the Word—even the spoken Word. And therefore, the science of the spoken Word is always for the victory—for the victory of your life.

And as you affirm that Word, you are always affirming that victory for your counterpart and for the mighty causal bodies which you share. And therefore, those twin causal bodies may deliver to earth in this hour the momentum of Shamballa, the momentum of Gautama Buddha. And you may see how twin flames may multiply the light and the fervor of devotion, even when your twin flame is ascended.

And, I say, especially when your twin flame is ascended, you must remember to mark the sign of that double *V,* that you might have the full action and the power of two causal bodies of light to deliver the abundant life to planet Earth!

This is the glory of the Lord multiplying again and again and again! Therefore, we would send you with the sign of victory and with that brand of life itself, even the double *V,* for the moving together again and the return to the very heart of the One.

So let there be the Alpha. Let there be the Omega. Let there be the victory of life. And let each and every one of you take with you that soul of light—that great causal body of your divine counterpart—to the Inner Retreat. And therefore, the visible and the invisible life of your soul and your being will there be able to precipitate the divine plan and the original purpose for which you came forth from the very heart of God.[4]

As the Mother yearns, so I yearn for you to place your feet upon that soil, that you also might feel the physical touch with the flame of Shamballa and the arcing of Shamballa unto the West[5]—so that you might also feel the divine memory of the first time that you placed your feet on planet Earth, when you came forth out of your root races or out of your legions of light or from the very starry bands of Sanat Kumara.

The touching of planet Earth, beloved ones, in the early golden ages, was a moment of supreme joy and promise and hope of victory. And the touching of planet Earth in dark ages by those of you who come as saviours of the world—this also was a moment of promise and of hope and God-determination for victory. Therefore let Hesper, the mighty star of love, and the legions of Sanat Kumara and of Lady Venus send forth now this final release of the activity of divine love—divine love of twin flames, divine love of the Great White Brotherhood, divine love of every chela unascended for all who are the lightbearers of planet Earth.

For, beloved hearts, love is truly the key to the opening of the door of the Inner Retreat. Love is truly the key to the opening of the door for the understanding of yourself as the God Self manifest within you.

Therefore, there comes from Venus a mighty love-action. It is for the melting away of all that would come under the category of anti-love. And when you think of it, all that is anti-love is anti-victory, anti-life, anti-wisdom, and anti the fullness of the will of God made manifest!

> For love and victory are one.
> No victory without love.
> No love without victory.
> For love is the fullness
> Of the consummation of thy soul's reunion
> With the mighty I AM Presence.

O blessed souls of the sacred fire, therefore we are come—we are come for the anchoring with you now of a single angel of light, an angel of victory, that shall stay with you and teach you and show you what are those downward-spiraling momentums of defeat, of anti-victory! Let them be exposed! Let them go into the flame!

Beloved hearts, if I could tell you, I would tell you of all the joys that await you when you have got the victory over the last enemy—which is your own self-concern and self-love, manifesting ultimately as the entire coil of human creation.

Blessed hearts, you can, with this dispensation of acceleration, now accelerate the putting of that entire momentum into the flame. For with the holding of the balance of the ascension flame in the heart of the Mother and her own balancing of that karma, lo, this year[6]—we, therefore, come to the dispensation where you may also accelerate and move beyond the stars to balance an incredible amount of your own personal karma as you continue into the service of the planet.

Beloved hearts, you know of the misuse of indulgences[7] in the Roman Catholic Church over the ages. But, I tell you, there are definitely dispensations given to those who transfer from their hearts the very foundation of life that will enable others to pursue the Path. And though this has been distorted in the past, I cannot withhold from you the great truth that by your laying of your offering upon this Inner Retreat, you yourselves will find dispensations of light and the opening of the way to the greater glory of your own goal appearing through the mists and becoming clearer and clearer every day of your life.

I admonish you, then, to pursue the flame of community—even as you see the crumbling, as it were, of an old order of civilization where individuals have lived apart from one another and apart from God, in a certain sense. And there has not been enough of the sacred trust or of the presence of hierarchy of the archangels for individuals to truly trust in coming together in community in that supreme interdependence that underscores independence, individuality, side by side with the dependence upon Almighty God and the heart flames of one another. Community is a glorious concept when there is a focalization of the Divine One in the midst.

Blessed hearts, let us face a single reality: that without your trust in the messenger and of our Word, there would possibly be factions and disagreement even among the chelas of the ascended masters. Therefore, I say, pray that the office of Messenger might always be filled and that the filling of that office by divine ordination might carry, then, the momentum of this union and of this light and of the blessing of Alpha and Omega.

Therefore, let the trust be not alone in the messenger but in the Messenger behind the messenger—who is your own I AM Presence and Christ Self, and all of us at inner levels.

Blessed hearts, our voice is indeed one. Our vibration is one. Our harmony is one. And what we have hoped to accomplish over these many years through the messengers' service is to teach you not merely how to obey the laws of God but how to interpret the laws of God, how to act upon them from the standpoint of your own individual Christ Self, how to arrive at that point of equilibrium and divine harmony where you find yourselves—through the wisdom of God and the love of God and your devotion to God's holy will—at that point of cosmic agreement.

For this cause, councils of the Great White Brotherhood have been established on earth and in heaven, that agreement might be reached whereby numbers of souls coming together through the attunement of the Cosmic Christ might arrive at that just and lawful decision that bears upon the moment and the needs of the hour in time and space.

Let us realize, then, that the foundation of the Inner Retreat is based upon the dispensation of the coming of Lord Maitreya in this age, upon the Cosmic Christ who has sent forth his emissaries—emissaries that carry a mantle in many different ways and in many different levels of attainment.

Let us realize, then, that that which endures is the great causal body of the Cosmic Christ! That which endures is the threefold flame that beats your hearts. That which endures is your own soul's communication through the Christ Self to the Great White Brotherhood—confirmed by the messenger, directed by the messenger, but always drawing you into a greater and greater oneness by the Holy Spirit.

The Holy Spirit, then, be upon you for the victory! For, blessed hearts, many times two million right decisions[8] will be made by you collectively at the Inner Retreat. Have you thought about the very concept that it would be impossible for one individual in embodiment—namely, the messenger—to make all of those decisions or to review all of the plans and projects and all of the administering of such an endeavor?

You see, therefore, that there is a need for the light of your own Christ-discrimination to shine, for you yourself to rise into positions of responsibility and leadership whereby, through a gradual vestment of your lifestream with a limited authority, that authority might be increased to greater and greater authority.

And therefore, you may find yourselves interacting in greater and greater concentric spheres of light—as Above, so below. And the meshing of your consciousness with that committee of ascended masters responsible for your project and your endeavor will be the very means whereby there is "one accord in one place"[9] and there is the merging of your lifestreams in the very heart of the Cosmic Messengers, the Cosmic Christs, and all of those who go beyond this form unto the octaves of light—who, one by one and step by step, are the emissaries and the messengers and the witnesses unto the Most High God!

Understand, then, that the dispensation of messengers is always to reestablish the condition of your consciousness whereby you yourselves are receptive to the mind of God. And therefore, inasmuch as the messenger is in need in this hour, I say: Fear not! For the messenger is here and here to stay as long as that requirement is.* And I tell you, heaven understands the needs of the hour.

And therefore, rather than have you continually affirming the ascended consciousness or the ascension of the messenger, we would far rather have you affirm the victory of the Mother flame on earth at the physical level—both in the body of this messenger and in your own dear temple where God would breathe upon you the sacred fire breath of the Holy Spirit!

Therefore, let us dedicate the Inner Retreat to the *physical victory of life on earth*—to the *physical* golden age, to the *physical* consummation of love in the holy family, and to the *physical* incarnation of the avatars! And let us not be otherworldly. For I tell you that the angels in heaven and

---

*Our beloved messenger Elizabeth Clare Prophet made her transition to realms of light on October 15, 2009, and is now an ascended master.

Almighty God hold a very clear vision of your ascension into the light. And therefore, let us now go down to the very cup of the V, to the very cradle of life, to the very heart of the Inner Retreat!

I enfold you in my arms. And my legions of light carry this entire company in a great sphere of light to that very heart where I have stood with the messenger this very past week for the opening of her eyes to the great multitudes and lifewaves who will gather there—even those who are now, even now, being sponsored by the seven mighty archangels!

Did you think that the archangels came for a small purpose?[10] I tell you, it was no small purpose! They are preparing the planetary body and the root races and the embodied angels for the captivating of their souls into the mighty upward-swirling light of their seven causal bodies times two, making the manifestation of Alpha and Omega, for the action of that fourteen.

Blessed hearts, the archangels have come to dedicate that Inner Retreat to the ascent! For the archangels presided over the descent of the early root races and have acted as manus, lawgivers, and teachers for millennia of earth's lifewaves.

Therefore, they come now for the consecration of the return. And, I tell you, it is a solemn moment—as we are now in the very cradle of the Inner Retreat together—as I draw the sign of the V. And Archangel Michael and Jophiel and Chamuel, Gabriel, Raphael, Uriel, Zadkiel stand with me for that mighty action of the drawing of the V. And therefore, it is the dedication of earth, her evolutions of light, to the return, to *The Homing*. And there is a swinging of the cosmic age.

And at inner levels, the precision of this cycle is known and the hour is known. And it is known at the Royal Teton Retreat. And it has been known for several millions of years that this gathering would take place in this very hour and this would be the moment for the striking of the great Cosmic Clock for the dedication of every soul of light that has ever descended upon earth to take the opportunity for the ascension! And as the divine plan is, so this will be consummated in the victory of planet Earth herself.

Blessed hearts of light, I can only intimate to you by my description and these few facts what a cosmic moment it is and how the energies are shifting in the very core of the earth and how the weight of planet Earth is also shifting and how there is a lowering, ever so fine, an approaching—a 'rapprochement', if you will—of the mighty I AM Presence and causal body of the lightbearers closer to that soul. There is a polarity twixt the soul (sealed in the inner retreat of the heart with Christ) with the I AM Presence. It is this polarity that we have desired to establish by having you present at this *Inner Retreat!**

And therefore, we have urged you to be with us. And we urge you again and again not to miss these quarterly conferences, not any hour or any day—whether you think it is important or no, or whether you think you have other business or other things to tend to. For we cannot build a consecutive spiral within you when you pick and choose and come and go and do not tarry in that flame.

For the hierarchy of light is real! And these conferences have been dedicated to *seal you in the victory of your causal body!* And your causal body is only *Victory! Victory! Victory! Victory!*

And why can you not contact that causal body? It is because you need to build mighty, moving, upward spirals!—golden spirals carrying all of the substance of self and solar awareness into that nucleus of fire in the very heart of the living Christ, that the polarity, the spiritual polarity, of Spirit and Matter might be established, fortified, sustained, and held in balance for your mission upon earth.

Blessed ones, every soul of light affected by this ascent of the *V,* this turning of this cycle, is in conclave at the Royal Teton Retreat and does participate also at inner levels in the setting of that forcefield in the cradle, the very heart of hearts of the Inner Retreat.

Now we pause as every lightbearer upon earth contemplates the mystery of the Holy Grail, the mystery of the path of the ascension—contemplates the inner vision and makes a heartfelt determination to make contact in the outer with yourselves who are holding the physical focus of the physical flame of the Inner Retreat. [90-second pause]

*Refers to the 1981 Freedom Class, *An Inner Retreat,* held at Camelot July 1–5, 1981.

And I am meditating upon each victory
Of the lightbearers,
Lifetime upon lifetime.
I cannot know defeat.
Therefore, I meditate on the love that is complete
In the twin flames of Victory.
And I see a chain of victories
Not yet assembled, not yet reinforced
By the thread of the Divine Mother
Who takes her needle,
Passing through each one of these records,
Pulling through the thread.
And voilà!
A string of crystal beads for a Golden Crystal Age—
Each crystal of the rock containing a fire of life,
Each crystal the complete record of your victories.

I must tell you that it brings more than a single tear to my eye as I see the lightbearers, in the presence of the Divine Mother and the Cosmic Christ, bringing to bear the fullness of each one's God Presence and Christ consciousness so that the soul—even in outer, physical awareness—might have more than an intimation but a very real sense of *ongoing Self-worth!*

Not the self-worth of the moment that rides a single victory of yesterday and then falls again on the rollercoaster of today's defeat. No. It is that confidence born of the understanding of the long cycles and the sine waves of victory where you may contemplate mistakes, not in an isolated sense but in the context of many victories by the learning of the lesson of the single mistake.

Heaven is not against mistakes. Heaven understands that in order to learn the correct exercise of free will, lessons must be learned—the most important ones: what not to do and how to avoid doing it.

You have all had such lessons. And by them, you have given upon the altar of God and of your nation, truly, a gift of victory unto Saint Germain. It is these that count!

These, then, are a part of the momentum of the downward spiral of the descent. Descending with clouds of glory and then becoming physical progressively, you have manifested your physical victories in a more and more concerted and concentrated way until, in the very bed of the earth itself, there have sprung forth yellow flowers of the field signifying your passing as a conqueror of life and your victories of the ascent.

And many of you have terrific momentum of victory in the upward current! So much so, that you will take little children and those more mature by the hand and lead them and multiply their victories! And that is the very heart of this community: that each and every one's victory should multiply every other's until that rising momentum will instill in each and every one the confidence of the indissolubility of the community—the confidence, the trust, the faith of heart with heart with heart.

Blessed ones, I would like you to know that this movement, this love, this trust—all together here—is an achievement of considerable import! You must understand that very few groups are formed anywhere in the world today that can boast of this number of lightbearers who are in harmony, in love, and consecrated to one central purpose.

Blessed hearts, we give credit where credit is due: to your own heart flames—above all, to Alpha and Omega and Helios and Vesta. But we would also say—on the occasion of this anniversary celebration of the meeting of the messengers in conclave in Washington, D.C., for the first time[11]—that we also extend our gratitude to their twin flames, their understanding and their understanding of the path of discipline that has led, by example and by manifestation of their causal bodies as well as by the transmission of the true Spirit of the Great White Brotherhood, to this union, this unity, and this love.

Let us, therefore, note well that this part of the mission of the two witnesses is most important. For the victory of all else, dear hearts, does depend upon community and the profound love that is here.

If for no other gift of your heart, Saint Germain and Portia rejoice in this hour that this understanding, this oneness, this permeation of your aura of the sense of Lanello and Mother with you—this is the cause of our great rejoicing! And this is the cause whereby heaven may truly lean upon this student body.

And lean we do. Lean we shall! For we understand that the necessity of the shepherd's crook and the shepherd's staff is that the entire causal bodies of the inner hierarchy might funnel through that staff and that crook into the very focal point, the focus of light, that is the synthesis of hearts.

Yes, indeed! *This* community has a heart!—a heart that beats as three-fold flame of Shamballa enshrined at the Inner Retreat. And, do you know, that inner heart is composed of the very fibers, the very devotion, the very components and the quality and strength of all of your heart chakras! It is one great heart. And the nucleus of the heart upon earth must, of course, be the hearts of the messengers.

Therefore, we pause and we consider how life is good. And life is good to us and life is good to you. And we are found together in the great miracle causal body of Almighty God himself.

Dear hearts, though the hour is late, we would tarry. For our angels are yet passing into your chakras substance of the divine memory, substance of the sense of your own continuity in life, substance of vision, O substance of the strength of the Word.

How we love to prepare your finer bodies for a greater release and a greater oncoming spiral! How we love to be with you! Why, you are making us feel most welcome on a planet that has not always welcomed us. This indeed is a joy!

Let us seal the Inner Retreat. See the beauty of it—hills and valleys, streams of light, fairest flowers, rivulets and lakes.

Let us seal it.

Almighty God, our Father Alpha, our Father-Mother Presence, our Mother Omega—now in the very heart of the Great Central Sun, send the light for the sealing action of each one.

Draw the circle of fire. Let there be all that is called of cosmic purpose suspended there. Let the victory appear! And if it is thy will, Almighty God, swiftly then defeat the enemies of righteousness upon earth and the enemies of the witnesses of the truth and of the messengers of light! For they have borne the burden of their strife. They have borne the burden of their infamy and their betrayal. Let them be bound, O Alpha and Omega!

I AM Victory! I intercede on behalf of the messengers ascended and unascended! And I would lay upon the altar of the heart of the messengers my gratitude for victories won and my own imploring of the Word that now, in this hour, the hosts of the LORD intercede. And by the binding of the enemy of the Word incarnate, let there be a staying action of the LORD God!

I, Victory, invoke it! And I ask it that souls of light might come into alignment, might find the Path, and that this movement might be built solidly upon that foundation of love and might expand! and expand! and expand!

Thus, my Word echoes over the ethers and is transmitted by the Holy Spirit. It bursts into flame at the feet of Alpha, with the sign of the golden *V* and the flowers of my heart as accompanying offering unto the LORD.

And, you guessed it!—they are fairest flowers picked at the Inner Retreat, that Alpha also might rejoice and be reminded that we have convened there and set, one and all, our footprints on that soil. And we declare it—by the very pressing into the heart of the earth—a place for great encounters.

Beloved ones, you are all cherished in my heart. Each and every one of you, by nobility of soul, has a precious marker there. And when I touch that marker with my finger, I am sensitized instantly to the entire condition of your life, your consciousness, the increase of light, the unseen burden as well as the unseen enemy.

In case you didn't know it, I AM your champion. I AM the champion of your right to be God-victorious! And if that is not enough, then I AM also the champion of your right to be the fullness of the mind of God and the fullness of his love.

And I AM the champion of your right to have on earth yet private property which you hold under the name of the Inner Retreat and which does belong still to that private entity, that corporation which is manifested for this purpose.

Thus, in the collective sense, by being members of this body, you are a part of the ongoing flame of our defense of the right of individuals—one by one and coming together in societies—to lay hold to that portion of planet Earth that you may dedicate by your free will to the highest cause of your understanding.

I am dedicated to the victory of earth and the freeing of earth from all holds and strongholds of the fallen ones. Our legions move with the mighty archangels and the Elohim. Our legions move with the forces of light and we are determined to wrest this entire planetary home from every force that is anti-Christ and anti-light. We have set our God-determination to this task.

And inasmuch as you now are the authority for earth,[12] I ask you—as my only request of this conference—that you also address a letter to Alpha and Omega for the restoration of this earth in its entirety to Saint Germain and to all who are the lightbearers, and that it be wrested from the hand of all who are the workers of iniquity.

This is so very important, because the only way that there can be a victory and an ascension for every soul of light upon earth is for the earth to be the Lord's and the fullness thereof, and all they that dwell therein to be the Lord's and the Lord's unto them![13]

I seal the earth in the sign of Victory! I seal the earth in the action of the sacred fire! I *seal* it! O blessed hearts of light. May you also rise with it as a rising, flaming, golden ball of light!

Lo, I AM that action of the sacred fire!
Lo, I AM Victory!
Lo, I AM Victory in your heart and in the Heart of the Inner Retreat!

Therefore, I set the date. I mark the place. And I say, let us be there for the great encounter of the freedom conclave July 4, 1982! Therefore, we shall stand where we have stood this hour in physical manifestation for the physical victory of the age!

I salute you! I send you forth as I *hurl* you, even in the spirit of the 'hurling' of the mantle of Jeremiah![14] I *hurl* you into the very midst of the people of the earth! And I will galvanize to you, even by my very heart flame, every soul of light upon whose brow the sign of the ages will sing *Victory! Victory! Victory! Victory* to life, to light, and to immortality.

I seal you. And I sign off in a rising spire of victory!

July 5, 1981
Camelot
Los Angeles, California
ECP

28

THE MIGHTY CIRCLE OF VICTORY

I AM in the heart of the victorious sense of Christ!

I AM Victory, and with me are legions of light, kindling a cosmic flame of illumination. I come to transfer to you the victorious sense of the disciple in the very hour of ignominy that is manifest by the betrayal even of the one who denied that he would ever betray.[1]

Beloved hearts, realize, then, the proximity to the Word and to the Christ of the fallen ones who would crucify him. For it was not the people but the fallen angels, even the Watchers, who determined to put out the candle of the living flame of love in Christ Jesus. And therefore, they had denied him in heaven and were cast out—those Nephilim gods.[2] And on earth, the Watchers who had taken dominion would see to it that his power, that his light, and that his name would not be exalted. But the more they denied, the more they would crucify, the greater the light of Christ became as a fire in the hearts of millions.

Therefore, beloved, though that disciple that denied him was long on sacrifice and very short on obedience, you also must realize that the temptation to enter into sacrifices for the LORD as a substitute for obedience must be faced by every individual who would walk with him through the cross and beyond to the resurrection. But before that, the descent into hell must also be the way of the fervent disciple.

Thus, I come with my flame of victory for you who would follow him. To each of you I give the understanding that when all is quiet and you are alone with him—free to love, free to promise, free to obey—it is something quite different than when you stand in the presence of these fallen ones and in their auras literally charged with the light they have turned to darkness and the power of darkness.

And therefore, it is as though there were a scrambling of the mind and one's sense of identity. And one's balance is lost and the base instincts of self-preservation come to the fore. And the last thing in the world that is thought of is the very life of the One Sent. This we have seen again and again through the ages.

Therefore, I come in this hour, that there might be a record in the earth of the path of discipleship, where these disciples who have been so long with the avatars of East and West in so many incarnations will have the mantle of victory on that path to lay as a mighty track which those who come after you may follow.

And therefore, with practice comes perfection. Practicing therefore in the very presence of the adversary, challenging these fallen ones who move against the holy innocents, dealing with the power of their darkness on a daily basis will produce in you some adeptship, some mastery of the sword Excalibur and the lightning mind of God.

And therefore passing through this hour of darkness many times over, you will then know what is the exact vibration and manifestation, and you will have such a momentum of victory, multiplied by our legions and my own heart flame and the disciples who have ascended and the Lord Christ himself, that you will fool them, these ones who are so accustomed now to manifest their terror, their acts of violence, their anger, their tirades, and their abuse of the Word, and the momentum of their planetary chain— that they cannot believe that anyone would survive to challenge them, that any community would endure.

Is it not written that they *all* fled[3]—all of them? And these were the closest to his heart. Did he not in that moment think of his mother and of Magdalene?

And yet he bore the flame of that mighty God consciousness. He knew that he came from God, he would return to God, and he would pass through even the valley of the shadow of death, even death itself, entering hell, there to preach to the rebellious angels, and he would rise on the morning of the resurrection. On the third day he would appear.

And thus, you shall also—first passing the tests of discipleship to maintain the oneness of the mandala, not to scatter out of fear, not to scatter and leave the place of El Morya in quest of a Holy Grail that is not thine to quest.[4] The leaving, then, of the citadel of light and its defense, whether of the Person of Christ or of his community, becomes therefore the breaking of the mandala of the Whole.

Let true friends of Christ in this hour therefore form a white-fire core of the one hundred and forty-four—twelve disciples for each line of that cosmic clock.[5] May you also volunteer to fill those lines, selecting the one on which you have, in your own heart's deliberation with your I AM Presence, the greatest momentum of diligence and service, faithfulness—not necessarily the brilliance of the highest light, but constancy, patience, and endurance, and a fortitude beyond all temptation to stray to the right or to the left.

I AM Victory! And I desire to seal with the signet of my ring those who are qualified to stand on the lines of the clock, guarding the center as the point of the ascent and the descent of the Christ, and therefore guarding the very circle of hierarchy and its community so that not only does Christ descend into the heart of the One Sent, but the avatars may descend through this spiral. And therefore, we will beat back the foes of the avatars that cast their shadow and threaten to cause dispensations not to anyone's desiring!

Thus, I speak of the word of the archangel Gabriel as such that cosmic councils should perhaps determine that avatars and advanced souls should no longer incarnate due to the great damage done to them by all manner of drugs and abuse. Therefore, these dark ones are in fact setting themselves against the circle of light and against the initiatic ring guarding the point of the One, guarding the descent of Sanat Kumara in form.

Therefore, we see that the center of the circle is the place and the point of the Christ consciousness. And it is also the point of thine own, for it is the meeting place of Master and disciple and Guru and chela. And therefore, it is a fountain of love which must be tended, must be ensconced, must be seen as the beauty of God incarnate.

Therefore, I come and I show to you the way of the victorious sense, the love of the Lord, and the love of obedience. For you see, the path of sacrifice that neglects obedience is taken by the untransmuted ego that says, "I will do this wonderful thing! I will pick and choose what I will do for the Lord. And when I have done it, he will notice me and give to me a reward."

It is a psychological factor of control, beloved ones, to put oneself in the driver's seat and say, "I will do this and that, and they will render praise to me. I will choose what I will do, but I will not do what I am told by the authority of the Word with us. I will not obey the voice of God within me. I will not hear the call of the Ancient of Days through my mighty I AM Presence in the day that the Lord hath need of me, but I will give to him as I pick and as I choose."

Thus, beloved ones, the path of sacrifice without obedience is a path of idolatry to the nth—the idolatry of self and the idolatry of the One Sent. But then, so many of you have already recognized this foe of your Great God Self for what it is, and you understand that the greatest joy of life is to be with Mary in a state of listening grace, listening to the voice above, listening to the voice of the one in embodiment that bears the authority of that Word in your life.

And therefore, to fulfill the mandate of the Law becomes the delight of that one, and he meditates in the law of God. And in that meditation, it is as though he were one with the Manus, the great Lawgivers of the races.

For in the meditation of the Law, he identifies with the eternal blueprint of the I AM Race—and in joy and in love, in action and in service, an immense creativity is born. For oneness in the will of God opens the doors to the vastness. Having access to cosmos and the cosmic mind, the fulfilling of the will of God is seen as having a far wider latitude for the expression of true Selfhood than any picking and choosing of sacrifices might bring.

Therefore, beloved, understand that a greater affection, an understanding of love in action, an understanding of staying with the LORD in this hour of betrayal was, of course, needed and it was absent.

One asks, Why? Why is it so that these individuals so lost their hold so easily that the Master could be betrayed and taken from them?

Beloved, consider again the absolute nature of Evil and its power incarnate unto those who have dedicated themselves to it by the very drinking of the blood of Christ and of the holy innocents, by the perversion of all of the chakras and the life-force. These have a momentum from aeons of movement against the light, and these fallen ones are the practitioners of black magic.

It is necessary, then, that Jesus Christ should indeed have been crucified and resurrected and ascended to open the Path for other disciples to follow him and to ascend, and for the dispensations of Saint Germain in this age to assemble many sons of God in the fullness of the Spirit of the Great White Brotherhood, that these might stand in the day of the challenge, standing with Enoch and the hosts of the LORD to pronounce the judgment of these fallen ones even in the very midst of the power of their darkness.

Thus, it is understood that those who will stand against them in this age of their final judgment must have the attainment of light equivalent to the attainment which they had when they fell. Thus, you understand that Lucifer himself was an archangel.[6]

And so you see why the archeia Mary was chosen to bear the Christ. For she must withstand, with her blessed Raphael in heaven,[7] the onslaughts of these fallen angels of high rank against that child before it was born and in the early years and on and on through his entire lifetime.

Thus, one having the attainment equal to and beyond the Watchers and the Nephilim must stand in the earth and must hold the flame of the hosts of heaven to multiply your own hearts. For if you yourselves do not have the equivalency, your spoken Word in the science of Love is therefore the open door to your I AM Presence and Christ Self, to all the hosts of God, holding therefore the balance and being held by the love of the messenger in embodiment to stand therefore and to not be overcome—neither by one or by an assembly of the many of these fallen ones.

Now understand from this viewpoint of the "Good Friday spell" that it is indeed a spell of black magic. And this is why they could not hold open their eyes in the hour of prayer, nor could they resist Satan placing, therefore, his poison in the heart of Judas. Nor could they resist the entire circle of energy. Therefore, it acted as a repellent, the black magic of their concerted auras, and they all fled. And He alone stood with perfect understanding and compassion that He had come to stand with them against the wiles of the fallen ones, and they, too, must also learn to do the same.

They must value, therefore, the One, multiplied by the heart of Christ over and again. They must learn to value the Christian community, the community of the Holy Ghost, and ultimately the Union that would be born and a land promised that would be given.

This union of hearts in these fifty states in America is an amazing union. Seldom on earth has there been established such a oneness by so many people in such a large geography. Realize, then, that it is the memory and a very point of the tears that fell from the eyes of Peter[8] that has remained with the sons of light who have recognized that holding the flame of the Union is upholding the Christ in the heart of this nation, and upholding that light against all of the onslaughts of the seed of the wicked. The memory of the Union and its necessity is born of this very hour when the powers of darkness succeeded in breaking the band of their union.

Thus, beloved, in every age where the avatar has stood alone, the fallen ones have seized their opportunity to strike that one down. But where the wisdom and love of the faithful has manifested a harmony that would not be broken no matter what, *there* has been the victory, *there* has been the enormous victory!

Consider this very nation in World War II, betrayed by individuals at the very top levels of this government—all the way to the office of the president. Yet the people themselves would not be deterred from the victory, not by the betrayal of the leaders at home or abroad. They moved against the hordes of darkness and the victory was won.

And yet, the Watchers compromised that victory in the greatest compromise seen in these two thousand years as Churchill and Stalin and Roosevelt made their pact and gave away a land and a people whose victory had been won.[9] And this, too, was the influence of the fallen ones at inner levels. But, you see, all three of these were Watchers themselves.

And this you must understand: the betrayers of the people in office did themselves undo the mighty heroic deeds of the disciples and of the Christed ones.

You must know these things! You must know that the one who is upheld as a great president, Roosevelt himself, was a betrayer of America. And Churchill was a betrayer of Britain and of Europe. And so Stalin was a betrayer of all of the heart flames of Mother Russia. And all three together stood *against* the twelve tribes reincarnated, to attempt to divide them in the very hour of the victory of the promised land in America.

I tell you these things because in their respective nations, even to this day, these Watchers have remained heroes of the people. You are appalled that the people could consider Stalin to be their hero. Well, beloved ones, you ought to be appalled that the other people consider Roosevelt and Churchill to be their heroes! For they posed as liberators and destroyed the victory. They were the destroyers of the victory as surely as the Christed ones who won that victory were themselves disciples in the heart of Christ who moved forward and knew that they came from God and would return to God.

Let us understand that many of these fallen ones today appear in the guise of good. They do many seemingly good things, but they withdraw, take a step backward, or simply miss where they should fill a point with light.

Thus, it requires the astuteness of the mind of Christ ever seeking purification. Forget not to fast, to clear the senses and the mind. Your own beloved Mark did diligently follow the practice of fasting and designated one day a week for that purpose. Saturday is the preferred day when you have the violet flame passing through you, when you have the light of victory, when you have the action of the sacred fire preparing for the receiving of that illumination on the day of the sun's ray.[10]

Realize, then, that I AM Victory! I AM a light of victory and I have sought on occasions to contact some of you either with a warning or with instruction or with a penetrating light, and because your senses have waxed dull by overeating and overindulgence, you have not heard me and therefore a blessing was lost.

I come not to condemn, for my heart is filled with a compassion for your lifestreams. But I should say to you, beloved, that the joy of God does flow when you can discipline yourself—and not cheat—to pass that twenty-four hours in a cleansing action and then invoke the Holy Spirit to fill the void. For nature abhors a vacuum. If you empty yourself, God will fill you with light. And then your perceptions will increase and you will be meet for the battle of the LORD.

Now therefore, this is my day. This is my gift of the transfer of the victorious sense to the disciples of Christ, of the ascended masters, and those who have vowed to be his friend in the hour of betrayal—those who have vowed to be the friend of the messengers in the hour of the betrayal and the hour of the glorying of God within that very temple, within that very soul and heart before you.

And so it is with yourself. As the one is glorified, the hundred and forty-four are glorified, and all of the multitudes who eat the crumbs from the Master's table, assimilating some of the Word but not all—they, too, can perceive his glory in their flesh.

Because this victory lives, because it lives in heaven and on earth in the entire Spirit of the Great White Brotherhood, I come with that mighty announcement that *you, too,* can win and you can be, with Christ, alive forevermore!

You can affirm with Lanello,

Behold, I AM everywhere in the consciousness of God!

Behold, with Jesus, I AM alive forevermore! Death and hell have not touched me at all, for I AM the God-victorious one, as Above, so below!

My I AM Presence with me is the power of attainment that overcomes every foe of the Christ on earth. I take my stand on earth and I make myself the instrument of *flood tides* of light, of victory in Christ!

I AM the victorious sense of Mighty Victory!

I AM the victorious sense of Mighty Victory!

I AM the flame of victory in action!

I AM the flame of love unto the last.

I AM with Christ in the beginning and in the ending.

Lo, I AM where I AM in my very heart—Alpha and Omega—I AM the bearer of the Body and Blood of Christ.

I AM truly the burden-bearer of the LORD. I bear his light and his light swallows up the burden of earth as world karma.

I stand and I still stand! For I AM THAT I AM, and I know it! I AM it! I feel it! I think it! I work it in action physically in me.

Lo, I AM the victory of the light where I AM, here and now! Victory! Victory! Victory!

By the power of Brahma, Vishnu, and Shiva, I AM victory in the earth, and I AM pressing that victory into the very earth beneath my feet, beneath that soil and under the earth—all the way to the very white-fire core!

I AM the victory in the earth.

I AM the victory in the air.

I AM the victory in the water and in the fire.

I AM Victory!

I AM the victory of the light of the resurrection flame!

I AM Victory all the way!

Now, beloved hearts, can you not also be creative with me, creative in your heart, and affirm your own mantras of victory daily into the teeth of every manifestation of the absence of the love flame?

I AM the victory of this job!

I AM the victory of this work of my hands!

I AM the victory of the mind of God in me to figure out the Way and make it plain for others.

I AM the victory, by the mind of God, in all that I must do this day to bring God's kingdom on earth as it is in heaven.

And the I AM in me *is* the victory!

My mighty I AM Presence *is* the victory!

Mighty Victory in me is the victory!

Mighty Victory is where I am. I cannot fail, for God is with me now.

I AM Victory! I AM Victory! I AM Victory!

And I *roll* back defeat! I *roll* back failure! I *roll* back death and hell! And the mighty circle of victory on planet Earth shall begin in the dot in the center of our circle, and it shall press out from the very heart of the One who has sent the messenger, from the very hearts of those who are sent by the messenger.

And the circle will widen, and it will widen its borders through the hundred and forty-four disciples that one day become the hundred and forty and four thousand. And therefore the circle of Victory shall be wider and wider and wider until it shall take in the whole earth and naught shall be left except the flaming presence of Victory!

I AM the center of that victory. I stand in the center of Christ, and Christ in me is the center of my victory and I AM one and we are whole. I abide in him and he in me.

I AM Victory, I AM Victory, I AM Victory! I AM the victory of the resurrection and I AM the fullness of its power *here and now.*

Blessed ones, I open the ethers and hallowed space for you, each one, to *leap* to your feet now and *shout* your individual mantras of victory!

[Audience leaps to their feet and shouts mantras of victory.]

And this, too, is a joyous shout of victory—a tumult not crying out for the death of Christ,[11] but a tumult of victory affirming the everlastingness of Almighty God *where* I AM.

Feel the I AM in your heart! Feel the I AM Presence of you now in the beating of your own heart and in my golden flame for the age. For my legions bear illumination for that path of Christhood, and it alone shall be the path illumined. And all who step upon that path will come now to the fore with a new perception of Christhood and of their I AM Presence.

And the illumined teachings of the Word and the flame of the Royal Teton Retreat, of Lord Lanto and Confucius and the Elohim of illumination and the mighty archangels and all of the Buddhas and bodhisattvas and Christed ones, will *expand* and *expand* and *expand* this flame of golden light of victory! And we will expand it by the very same mandala of the center and the hundred and forty-four that we have commended unto you.

And therefore in the etheric octave, by the voice of Gabriel, by the voice of Alpha and Omega, the circle of golden victorious light of the Christed One, even the Lord Sanat Kumara in the center, *will* expand and expand by the heart of Gautama, by the heart of Maitreya, by the heart of Jesus, by the heart of all ascended masters standing at the level of Jesus.

By the level, then, of Lanello and by the stepping-down of Lanello into this octave, the mighty circumference of victory will be as a giant level of an ovoid, and beneath it another. And you will find that the center will be that fiery coil of the golden stairway—and you will see the octaves of heaven and earth open for the passing through of the saints to the higher octaves in their full, waking consciousness and their descent again to perform the LORD's work in the physical octave.

Therefore, we also push back now the darkness. And the light of illumination, the light of the crown chakra, does *indeed* now illumine a darkened world.

May all make their way to Victory's fount of illumination here this day, God's way!—in the heart of everyone who will stand and not deny their LORD, the Christ Self, and not deny the LORD, the beloved I AM Presence, and not deny any one of these little ones who come in his name.

I AM Victory *always!* I AM *Victory!*

Victory! Victory! Victory! Victory! Victory! Victory! Victory!...

[Clapping and chanting the name of Victory continues.]

March 31, 1983
Camelot
Los Angeles, California
ECP

29

THE VICTORY OF THE SONS OF GOD

Most gracious ones, I salute you in the flame of victory that burns brightly in the heart of the Central Sun as a golden flame so brilliant that all of cosmos moves by the very hum and the sign and the heartbeat of God's own victory!

Beloved ones, I am that victory in manifestation. I am the victory of God's glory. For I have chosen to display to all evolutions and lifewaves everywhere that the sign of victory and victorious overcoming is the power to reach the top every time, to reach the top of the crown chakra with each effort and joy and pulsation of the ideas of God put forth into action.

Now, unto a people that is called holy,[1] unto the ones prepared I come with ampules of victory; for I desire your understanding that wisdom, as wise dominion in all the earth, *is* God's victory. And victory itself can only come to the wise.

And therefore your golden victorious light is your crown chakra *blazing bright* the glory of Almighty God! It is the power of his mind! It is the pulsation of his spirit! It is the raised light of the Mother. It is a God consciousness that permeates the form and the formless nature of the One that is with you.

Beloved ones, golden waves and ribbons of light spanning cosmos in celebration of the victory of one son of God, and of the daughter of Zion who is the soul of the people of reality, are blazing forth and blowing in the cosmic breezes. For angels of victory one and all, though they come in full armour and with shields, have this day, in celebration of light's victory here and now, tied those golden ribbons of victory to their garments. And thus each one is streaming ribbons of light that become in their auric emanation as flames of gold leaping.

I tell you it is a cosmic sight to see these ten thousand-times-ten thousand legions of victory descending to the heart of the earth by the power of the spoken Word and by the fiat of the LORD God! For we are *determined* with God-determination that all that has gone before in this retreat and all others in all the years of our service with you shall be crowned this day with the power of victory, shall be *sealed* by that victory, shall be *known* in the earth. And you will understand the Christ in you as your conquering hero! And you will yet live to worship him, to abide by him, to be in the very heart of that Christ and not to be set back in any way, shape or form by any thing, any creature small or significant.

Beloved hearts of light, I tell you victory is a *spirit!* It is a determination! It is the launching of God-good within you. It is a drive that will not be set back. It is that *intent* of the forehead of the Aries mind of God that does move against the enemy by the very power of *victory* in the third eye, *victory* in the crown, *victory* in the heart, *victory* in all the body temple, *victory* shimmering as a garment of light that will not be stayed, will not be set back!

This power of victory must be yours. And therefore victory as a golden illumination overcomes all indecision, all confusion, all absence of right action. It is the power of determination and it is the wisdom that does precede right action.

And therefore, in the meditation of the heart and in the musings of your soul upon the LORD God Almighty you understand, beloved creatures of the Most High God—and I call you the "creation magnificent"—that it is the ongoing presence of this momentum of victory that claims the victory every hour and every moment, that does not allow defeat and therefore does not allow you to become prey to any force passive or aggressive that would otherwise set itself against you, from a fly to a mosquito to a demon to a remark that is not called for or anything that comes in your way.

Beloved ones of light, understand the thrust of victory! Understand the ribbons of glory! Understand the power of the sons and daughters of God in the earth and *be no more* those who are defeated, those who are the cynics, those who are the ones who go down in defeat at the least little crisis in their lives. *Be* the ones who have the sense of victory, who know no defeat, who will not even identify any defeat anywhere, anytime; for they are the living presence of our God!

And as you are in the earth, as I AM in the heaven, beloved hearts, so I swear to you in the name of Almighty God as I bow to him in this hour that the presence of victory that is in the Great Central Sun can also be yours in your hearts in this very moment! And you can walk the earth in the power of the Great Central Sun Magnet and in the power of victory! And victory can consume all selfishness. Victory can consume all indeterminate acts and all inaction.

Beloved ones of the Most High God, *victory* is the power of love! *Victory* is the power of God's power itself and the will to do and be! *Victory* is the absolute presence of the LORD our God with you for the overcoming of every single splinter of error on this planetary body and the astral plane!

And I tell you, when I deliver this message in all worlds the entire false hierarchy *trembles,* for they know that they cannot stand against the living flame of victory. For it is the crown of rejoicing, and it is the bedrock and foundation of all of your service and all of your life. And they know that if you take this message from my heart and receive it by the Holy Ghost whereby it is given, that you will *nevermore* be subject to their preying upon you. And you *will* be God-victorious! And they *will* be swallowed up by the light and they *shall* be no more! And death and hell *shall* be cast into the lake of fire![2]

And it shall be because you have taken to heart my [message] and understood that I come here with the full God-determination that I mean business, that I will have the Lord's work on earth and I will have it in you, and that our legions of Victory will stand by you and will coach you and will coax you and will move you toward the God-victory that is called for, that *must be* in the face of all of the complications of the tyrants and their woes and their planetary conspiracies and all that you have heard about for so long. I say they have *no* power in the face of one little child who knows that he is God's victory in action.

It is so! I tell you it is so! Do you believe it?

[Audience responds, "Yes!"]

Saints of the Most High God, the hour has come for the fulfillment of the prophecy of Isaiah read to you in this hour, the power and the fulfillment of Isaiah.[3] Take these chapters to your heart. Read them! Respond to the Call! Accept with gratitude the message of salvation and triumph of the daughter of Zion. And accept the mission of the Christ in this age, begun by Jesus, fulfilled in your Holy Christ Self, fulfilled in the presence of Maitreya, fulfilled in the Second Coming of Jesus descending on Ascension Hill[4] and delivering his mandate of The Lord Our Righteousness unto all people everywhere.

Beloved ones, children of Zion and of the true Israel, the House of Reality, I speak to you and I tell you, if you would but read and affirm the prophecy of Isaiah and Jeremiah, if you would but affirm the great mysteries in the life of Jesus as [the means to] your own salvation here and now, if you would but read the Psalms as though you had written them yourself as prayers to your God, you would discover that the Bible is an open book and a living book and it is God speaking directly to your heart.

Every promise that is made is yours to claim! Every warning that is given is yours to understand and avert by the power of the dynamic decree. Every calamity that is revealed as prophecy can be undone by the power of the spirit of victory in this age, by the power of the mighty archangels and the Elohim called forth by you! And every lesson learned by every individual is a lesson that you need not go through yourself but [that you may rather choose to] learn from the experience of others, especially those of a karma-making consideration.

And therefore, by studying the lives of those who have faced God, who have learned from his law, who have been put down by that law and raised up by that law, you may understand the way in which ye ought to walk! The way in which ye walk this hour must become the way of the prophet, the way of the disciple, the way of the Christ, the way of the revelator, the way of the ministering servant, the way of the holy people, the way of the apostle, the way of the progenitors of mankind, and the way of the holy angels.

Pick your character or mighty hero out of the Bible itself and become that one for a day and put on that mantle and call forth that causal body, even as you who have been Catholic are used to praying to the saints. I tell you, *pray* to the mighty causal body and the power of Almighty God in these personages and learn to love and know them. For, beloved hearts, they are the pioneers; they have carved a way! And the way they have carved is the path all the way up the mountain to the very crown chakra where you sit at the feet of Lord Maitreya, Lord Gautama, and Sanat Kumara; and you finish up the course of the raising up of the ascension flame, the Mother light, from the base unto the crown.

Beloved hearts, it is all *here!* And it is the hour when a God-victorious people who are victorious in Spirit must become victorious in Matter! And I say there must be a translation by your own Holy Christ Self, by your attunement, by your determination to work *change.* For you understand that all must change daily, all must move toward the center of the Sun, the mighty I AM Presence, the Divine Monad, the I AM THAT I AM, the living Word. All must say:

> I shall become the New Day!
> This human consciousness is not acceptable unto the LORD our God! Therefore I move toward the center of the One. I move as a discoverer of the great New Day and I shall become that day. And I shall leave behind all of those personal preferences of my outer personality, and I shall draw [my soul] into the center of the living Christ.
> And I shall *dare* to be different! I shall *dare* to be outspoken!

I shall *dare* to challenge and to preach the Word, for I have nothing to lose except my own ascension if I fail to do so.

And thus I stand with the living Word and I *fear not* to speak into the very teeth of those devils and to pronounce their judgment and to give them the warning to cease from their nefarious and destructive deeds. And I *fear not* to challenge those [forces of the Evil One] great and small.

For I AM in the heart of Saint Catherine! I AM in the heart of Saint Clare! And I take my stand this day against all principalities and powers of fallen angels who have attempted to seat themselves in the seat of authority throughout this planetary body.

I *challenge you,* each and every one who moves against the light of freedom and of Saint Germain! I challenge you in the physical! I challenge you with the Spirit of Almighty God! I challenge you by the power of Victory and his legions and I say:

You shall not pass! You shall not move with this infamy against mankind any longer! You shall not move against the holy innocents! And I stand in this hour and I call forth your judgment for your heinous crimes against the people, against the little children, against the State, against the Church, and against all manifestations of constructivism sponsored by the Great White Brotherhood. And I stand in the earth.

And when they say, "Who are you?" you may say:

I AM an emissary of the flame of God. I AM the representative of Mighty Victory. I stand in the earth by the authority of Jesus Christ and Saint Germain. And I AM an evangel going before the mighty archangels and proclaiming their word and their power.

Well, beloved hearts of light, you may tremble and consider, "How will I ever say such words?" Well, you may begin by speaking them in the very closet[5] where you ought to pray and to speak with the power of Almighty God against the foes unseen out of the astral pit and develop your momentum of challenging the dark hordes. And the most fearsome ones are the invisible ones. For those that are visible you can see and mark, and you can trace them by their own noxious odor, which they leave across the earth as a path of soot.

Beloved ones, you can know those that are physical and you can know what they do. And therefore, let us have a victory of Armageddon over the astral hordes and the dark ones that come to taunt, to maim, to distort, to cause insanity, and to be the spoilers of your joy. Let the victory come over your mind and heart and speak to those enemies within your own temple and let them be bound!

And I tell you, when you have a momentum of thus speaking, you will not care anymore and you will throw all caution to the winds. And you will speak with as much God-determination to the physical enemy as you have spoken to the invisible fallen one, [forasmuch] as you have seen that they have no power over you when you exercise the [power of the] spoken Word. And until you do [exercise that power] they appear as giant monsters.

And then, when you give forth the cry and the absolute call to Mighty Victory and you call to the Cosmic Christ and you call to the mighty archangels and you affirm the I AM THAT I AM where you are, you *behold* how the sun comes out and there is the mighty clearing and you see the rainbow of your own causal body. And you see the double rainbow as the sign of you and your twin flame one in heaven. And as in heaven so on earth, the combined forces of the Alpha and the Omega of your souls are the manifestation of a victory that is not capable of being defeated. It is unconquerable! It is dauntless! It is a victory of the ages.

And the golden sun of Helios does now enfold the earth in the flame of victory. And charging the very atoms of the earth and the very grasses of the field is that power of that golden sun, beloved hearts. And you see it and you understand it and you know that the day of our God is nigh and the day of his glory as well as the day of his vengeance.[6] For there is no greater power of judgment than wisdom itself and the power of God-illumination and the power of wisdom!

For when all see and know and are enlightened in the full glory of God, therefore there is the isolation of the criminal mind and the one that is set against Almighty God. And all may see outpictured that which is the denial of God and that which is the affirmation of God. And thus the angels may quickly come; for all cast their votes, then, according to the enlightenment of the I AM Presence and the Christ Self. And they no longer cast their votes for the fallen angels because they are in a state of idolatry, because they are in a state of spiritual blindness, because they have not the flame of victory.

Do you see, beloved ones? Illumination is the absolute God-awareness of what is and what is not, of what is truth and what is the lie. And therefore the coming of illumination is the crown of all-seeing! It is the power of vision and the purpose of the people to proclaim it! And in the presence of that enlightenment of the Holy Spirit you will discover that all will vote for the living Christ and none else. And none will be able to deceive by their sophistry, by their politicking, by their outright lies, by their relativity, changing this way and that for the pleasing of the mass consciousness.

In the name of the God of Freedom, in the name of Victory, I AM come that you might understand just how limitless is this very fountain of light to secure your own glory, the glory of your mighty I AM Presence where you are!

All that I AM, *all* that you hear is accessible to you! *All* of the Holy Spirit can be upon you. *All* of the God Presence can be with you. But you must lift yourselves out of a twilight zone of semi-action and self-concern and fly with the wings of the morning[7] and know those wings to be the mighty power of Mercury, of the caduceus raised, and on the brow wings of illumination, wings of vision, wings of the mighty crown chakra.

Thus, as I now place around and through and in your aura the light-emanations of the angels of victory, I bid you meditate upon the "Victory Symphony." [Excerpt from "Wellington's Victory, or the Battle of Vittoria," Opus 91 by Beethoven is played.]

I have addressed you in the power of victory, and in the transfer of that power I have come. Take this portion of my address you have already heard as a lesson in the vibration of the power of victory and what acceleration is required as in the launching of a rocket, as the thrust of the heart to drive through in the victory of every holy purpose. If anything is worthwhile doing, beloved hearts, it must be done with this power of victory. And unless it is worthwhile it ought not to be engaged in or to engage your energy or your life or your attention.

And therefore, it is the moment and the hour in cosmic victory to evaluate all of your occupations and preoccupations and realize that every investment of energy is an investment of God's light, which is inherently God's victory and God's power. When you invest that which is his gift to you in those lesser experiences, those things that are not worthy of your calling nor fulfilling thereof, then you create a counterforce to victory in your life. A part of you pulls in a degrading direction and a part of you is pulling for the mark of the high calling of Christ Jesus.[8]

There must be no division. All things must be to the point of holy purpose. For then, you see, all of your actions become a habit of victory, all are begetting a greater victory and manifestation. And the lines are clean and there are no smudges in the aura and no clouds of confusion floating in a configuration that seems more like a swarm of wasps on a summer day than it does like the mighty Blue Eagle of Sirius in formation and on the march toward victory.

Do you understand, beloved ones? You are composed of many forces, cosmic forces, and all of the movement of your being and your thrust must be to that one God-pointed direction of the crown chakra realized in the [Great White Brotherhood's] activity physically manifest on earth. For here is the challenge: not to ascend to the mountain but to come down from the mountain and to maintain the mountaintop consciousness in the valley. Here is the challenge! Here is the light, beloved ones! Here are the overcomers who will *not forget* the vibration of victory when inundated with the vibration of death. And though you may feel death all around you, yet in your heart is the flame of victory and the memory of love's victory.

Thus, when you need the power of locomotion, when you need the power to go and to gain that mark, play this first portion of my dictation and call to me and my angels. And we will re-create the divine circumstance of thy coming to earth and of all of thy life's thrust of positive good and give to you once again a noble start, as when you ignite the match, as when the fire burns and you have that impetus of all-consuming purpose.

Now then, when you hear the "Victory Symphony" you hear the balance of victory in the threefold flame. You hear victory's power. You feel victory's love. And you also are called as from far beyond the veil by victory's wisdom.

Think not that you can get here and there on earth what the masters are able to give you from above and in their retreats. Therefore seek the highest teachers and be the best taught among earth's evolutions. And qualify yourselves to become teachers of men by pursuing the Corona Class Lessons.[9] For the corona of the sun is a corona of victory. You see how I behold in all of God's creation victory itself!

All that I see is victory! All that I know is victory! All that I AM is victory and this for a purpose, that I might have infinite victory to impart to those who have taken on, to a certain extent, the defeatist vibrations of a civilization.

Now, therefore, beloved ones, I am seated in the throne of wisdom here with the living Christ of cosmos. I am in the center of that Christ, that universal Christ that is the Christ of your heart, and I deliver to you a message of consummate wisdom so that you may understand how we have drawn together this activity of light.

Planning is the key, beloved ones. Planning is the key. Thus, looking through the vast aeons to this moment where, you might say, infinity cuts through the lines of time and space, we have determined long, long ago that in this hour there should be assembled a circle of lightbearers, the circlet of the crown of the Virgin, upon whose shoulders we might place cosmic purposes and in whose hearts there might be room for that Christhood, who is the governor and overseer of the Lord's vineyard.

My beloved, planning is necessary lifetime by lifetime. Our plan has included you, if you will it so. We always maintain the contingency of free will. Thus it is written: "Many are called but few are chosen."[10]

Each niche in hierarchy, each office of Christ must be filled. And each office may become a mandala of many, yet singularly filled by the one if necessary. Some of you have held the heart of the daisy waiting for the petals to form. Others have magnetized numbers yet not quality. As you send forth, so you draw in; this is the line of the fisherman. Send forth the quality of heart and you will assemble heart-quality chelas. Thus we look to the one who may fulfill the office of Christ for each facet of the divine plan.

I speak, then, of a company of lightbearers already gathered here and in other parts of the world, a very different formula of the causal body of God than we saw twenty-five years ago. Some who have been among you have ascended and others, keeping the flame, toiling in the night, victorious in the day, are determined that your victory shall be physical every step of the way! I commend you, beloved hearts; for physical victories are the most difficult. And I recommend [that you make the Call to Sanat Kumara that this company of lightbearers shall] bring into an organized, physical manifestation a single idea for the cosmic good and the commonweal and rejoice in that victory.

Now then, beloved hearts, we have called many lifestreams. And as I look into this company I see those of you who have stood and held a flame of illumination in past ages, whether in China or South America. I see many who have stood against all odds, many who have been martyred.

And again, I see those who just before the moment of victory allowed themselves to be overcome, to decide that they were distraught, overworked, incapable of bearing the burden. Multiplying this fear in their beings, they became hysterical and fled in the night and said, "I cannot do it. I cannot face such crisis. I must go where there is peace."

Though they might have been peacemakers, they understood not how to hold the line, had not the remembrance that our God would send his Christ and his holy angels to reinforce the right step and the right decision if only it be made and taken. Thus you are also here to fight through with a victorious spirit those momentums of insanity and the easy retreat to the nervous breakdown rather than [placing yourself in a posture to] stand, face, and conquer with a mind of steel.

Yes, we may all decide we are sick on the day of the battle. It is easy. But I will tell you a secret. It is easier to be well! It is easier to be whole! It is easier to fight than to lie down and be taken and go down to the pits of self-despair. That is the hard thing indeed. Thus, let us not take the broad way[11] but the way of the simplicity of the Christ, which is not the complexity of the dark ones but it is [the way of the light ones who go] straight to the mark.

Beloved ones, we consider the causal bodies of those who are already a part of this worldwide movement and we say that within your lifestreams there is the sufficient attainment and ability and momentum of victory for the task at hand in this year. What is required, rather, is the decision to allow that attainment, that mastery, that momentum to descend the crystal cord through the Christ mind into the nexus and lever of the devotion of the heart and be expressed in wisdom by taking one's hands and using them to extend from the heart what is most needed for the accomplishment of the obvious calling at hand.

Therefore, let it not be said, "They have such a potential for victory." But let it be said, "They knew their potential and came to the altar and laid that fruit of past achievement before the flame of cosmic victory, before the flame of Almighty God, and said: 'I will be the physical incarnation of the movement toward the victory of this community of the Holy Spirit, of this settlement in Montana of the emissaries of the Great White Brotherhood. I will be there. I will have my physical victory in this hour. And I know that the only victory I can know is the victory of the now! And there is no victory that is procrastinated, for procrastinated victory is a certain defeat.'"

Do you understand that when victory is in your hand it is a coil of light? If not unleashed, it will be spent in a lesser manifestation and not be there when the fruit of victory is necessary. Thus, sense the rhythm of your days by the movement of the symphonies of Beethoven. Sense the rhythm and the moving onward, for all of cosmos is in rhythm and in victory.

Thus, beloved hearts, I reveal to you who have placed your trust in God and in God's representatives—for it is time that you ought to know that your trust surely is well placed and that ample initiations have been given to the two who lead you—that as they do not fail God, God surely does not fail them or you through them. . . .

Beloved hearts, I am grateful for your acknowledgment of victories won. For we desire you to know that there are indeed heroes on earth and heroines and that they live and breathe among you as very natural people, not perfect but [people who] in their hearts are perfecting the expression of the Law as their highest quest and goal. Beloved, there is a brotherhood and a love and a community that cares for and loves those who have stood for truth and been maligned and martyred, and who've been alone in past ages.

Thus all of you may know that I single you out in this moment. And the angels read the record, as I have read the record of one son of God, of your finest hour in all of the history of your embodiments. And it is read in this moment that you might know that you are *here,* for you also deserve comfort and the praise of God as your soul has allowed that God to be in you. And now legions of victory do applaud that moment of the finest expression of your wisdom. And you may applaud with them for one another. [31-second standing ovation]

Beloved ones, be seated in the authority of your Christhood. For that seat as the seat of wisdom is a mantle you can claim and one you can be certain will be yours if you have earned it. I speak of the earned mantle in the causal body that must certainly come upon you if you claim it in the dignity and bearing of your Christhood.

Thus you must come to the point of self-worth and not only the education of the heart but self-worth to be worthy of one's own Christhood of past ages. For once one has achieved a level of [Christ] attainment, beloved hearts, one must always keep the flame and the work with the Father to maintain that level and not to compromise it again.

Beloved ones, there is a mighty task to be performed. We have called you to it because [the community of the Holy Spirit] is necessary, not merely as an experiment or as a means to your ascension but as a necessary alternative to civilization as it is on earth today, a necessary stronghold of the wisdom of God and its practical application, and of men, women and children who have determined to embody that light. In other words the example must be present, the witness, the ensign. Zion must come again in the mountain of her God, and the seed of light must gather.

And there must be an example of courage. There must be those who engender in all others on earth this spirit of victory, of freedom and of courage. I need not tell you, for perhaps you know it better than the messenger, that you meet not so many in the world that have the courage of her heart or the determination of her mind and being.

There are not so many who will stand and not compromise. But there ought to be! And there shall be if you shall also reflect that spirit of your own Christhood, as is the spiritual example given that must also now become physically apparent [in yourselves]. For many fear, and when they see your love and courage their fear will dissolve in that perfect love. And they will also take heart and join the ranks [of those who will stand and still stand and not compromise nor be compromised].

Beloved ones, I speak, then, because you ought to know that when you give your life to a cause and a service and a community you have the highest backing of the Great White Brotherhood and the best representatives we can find.

Therefore I speak now of the mantle of King Arthur and of Camelot. And you have known of Mark, the soul who returns from having been in the lists and at his king's side as Launcelot du Lac. You understand the fire of his God-determination to let his sword and expertise become the spoken Word and his riding and his horsemanship to be the riding of your human creation, [in other words] the subduing of it. The knowing of every muscle and every move of the horse becomes the knowing of every part of your soul.

And thus he (Mark), who felt deprived in not being a horseman in this life, was truly a champion in like manner, yet translated spiritually. For all who knew him knew that he would probe the very depths and find that one thing that must be exposed and removed for the soul to continue [on the spiritual path].

And you have also been told that his twin flame—embodied in that hour as the chela of El Morya (King Arthur), Guinevere—has come to you in the person of the Mother and the messenger.

And you also realize, as you realize in your own heart, that each soul mounting the path of soul liberation does increase and put on a greater light through striving. And thus, it is not Guinevere you see or Launcelot or other knights but the souls of those who have gone through trial and separation and longing and the immense burden of the division of Camelot and have come together again, having passed through many initiations since then and achieved a greater nobility and been empowered by the might of the Lord himself.

Thus, should we point to you as having been the knight or lady then, we should also point out that since then you have walked over many bridges, overcome many problems, and gained the bouquet of flowers from the Blessed Virgin, Mother Mary herself. Beloved hearts, role playing in Camelot then and now is our objective for you.

The causes of witchcraft and of the fallen angels and of divisions [at Camelot, our mystery school of old,] can be studied and known at inner levels. For the full story has never been written of that age of chivalry and of the nobility of the quest and the true understanding that was held by the initiates under the tutoring of Merlin (Saint Germain) concerning the Holy Grail. . . .

Remember, then, the call of the transfiguration. Remember, sons and daughters of freedom, when Jesus took Peter, James and John into the high mountain.[12] The mantle is bestowed then and now upon the son of God and it is the reward for many, many, many lifetimes of service; it is not given for potential but for the actual manifestation and God-determination in love of that attainment in the physical octave.

Thus, by example you can understand that your Holy Christ Self, your Master, your Teacher, also waits to give you this anointing. And if you become all that you really are, you will also know the day when you will be called to this altar, called by the ascended masters to receive the mantle and the blessing and the sealing of your mission unto the finish.

As you lay the physical foundation, God then seals in the upper chakras the spiritual attainment, the bringing up of the Mother flame as the return of Omega unto God, and the drawing down of the spiritual fire. Thus in all ages those who must complete their spiritual attainment in physical embodiment must be sponsored by the Great White Brotherhood.

Thus was Godfre sponsored. Thus have the avatars been sponsored East and West. And you, [one and all,] also have the anointing as you have received it in these many dictations to now bring all things together for your final spiritual and physical victory.

What one has done, all can do. And recognize that it is to the one who is here and now in the present the master of the hour that all must look for the timetable, for the release, for the call to battle, and for the summoning to the harvest. . . .

I speak to you the advice of a father to a son and I remind you of Siddhartha and the victory of Gautama and the magnificent saints. As the heavens and elemental life and the angels proclaim the victory of the son of God, so the forces of hell also break loose to put down the ascending one.

Let all recognize the glory of the victory and its requirements. Let all understand that *the Union must be preserved*, of America, of the I AM Race worldwide, and of this community and of your individual heart and soul and mind within your being. Let no division enter either in the macrocosm or in the microcosm, and many sons shall come into the captivity of the Godhead and many daughters of Zion shall know the triumph that sings love's victory.

Beloved hearts, *light* is in the earth, *light* is the catalyst for your victory and for the Lord's vengeance! And they know it, both the exalted ones and those who have debased themselves.

Thus I say, let us return, then, to the integrity of the One. Let us support our leaders, raise up our followers, comfort our children and our families, and be all things that a community of the Holy Spirit must be to all people, its members, and the stranger at thy gate.

And let the glory of the Lord be the redemption of every one of you who has been slain and who has fallen in the way by some dark spirit that dared to taunt you. I, Victory, say: They shall *not* pass! You are triumphant this day and the triumphant ones! And this is the Church Universal and Triumphant. So be it!

All hail, legions of the Sun! I AM the victory of love!

[1-minute, 36-second standing ovation]

July 8, 1984
Heart of the Inner Retreat
Royal Teton Ranch, Park County, Montana
ECP

I AM YOUR SPONSOR ON
THE PATH OF THE RUBY RAY

*I lifted up mine eyes again, and looked, and behold a man with
a measuring line in his hand.*

*Then said I, Whither goest thou? And he said unto me, To measure
Jerusalem, to see what is the breadth thereof, and what is the length
thereof.*

*And, behold, the angel that talked with me went forth, and an-
other angel went out to meet him,*

*And said unto him, Run, speak to this young man, saying, Jeru-
salem shall be inhabited as towns without walls for the multitude of
men and cattle therein:*

*For I, saith the Lord, will be unto her a wall of fire round about,
and will be the glory in the midst of her.*[1]   Zechariah 2

Sons and daughters of victory, I claim you for my flame!

I am your sponsor in the hour of your full acceptance of the path of
the ruby ray. I desire you to understand that I come in the name of the
Cosmic Christ. I come with my legions who are initiators in this path.
And my legions have victoriously fulfilled this path—and that is the requirement for joining Victory's legions!

Therefore I promise you that the torch of victory, the crown of victory and the laurel wreath are within your grasp. You are reaching for the enfiring of the sacred heart, and some of you are so very close to the bursting of the flame of the Holy Spirit within you that, I tell you, I must announce this to you because initiates of the sacred fire always must receive notification by their teachers when they are at that point of realization of the Word.

I encourage you, then, not to turn back, not to lessen the intensity of the Call or the striving. Some of you are, as it were, carving a tunnel out of the rock of the earth. Three feet more, six feet, you will come to the other side—the other side in the Buddhic sense of the word, the other side of the River, the other side of the darkness of samsara.

PATHS TO THE HOLY SPIRIT

Therefore, beloved, I speak of this quickening and I tell you there are two ways and paths to the Holy Spirit:

One is by the gift and the bestowal of the Maha Chohan whereby you receive an impartation of the flame, not having the attainment of that flame or its God-mastery but having the love and the faith and the desire to speak for that Spirit.

The second method of impartation, the path upon which your feet have been set by Saint Germain, is the gradual assimilation of those cloven tongues of fire until, beloved, you attain the level of the mastery whereby both the flame and the vessel have the same vibration.

When this power of the Holy Spirit is upon you, it cannot be lost, taken back, or removed. And I say "cannot" but I explain that there is always the element of free will. But, you see, in this individual the free will has already been expressed—the affirmation of the God-mastery that is the equivalent of the requirement to be the bearer of the flame of the Maha Chohan.

I counsel you, then, to strive for this calling. For when you have this divine garment with you, you will truly go forth to awaken the nations, to cut free the lightbearers and to have the power of conviction that begets the power of conversion. Neglect not, therefore, the first and fundamental principles of the Father, the Son, and the Mother. For the Holy Spirit is the fire needed for the Coming Revolution in Higher Consciousness.

THE SENSE OF VICTORY

I, then, am your coach and more—joint teacher with Maitreya. Victory is the power of the star of the crown chakra. And the sense of victory abiding does defeat, in the very teeth, every enemy! The enemy who is arrogant and proud and believes he has won a round—he has won nothing, absolutely nothing but his own judgment. So I pronounce it! It is done!

But those who continue, those who persevere, those who endure, they are the ones who are truly God-victorious. The world is no judge of the victors. How many has it ever acclaimed of those of us who have gone marching into the kingdom?

We are not concerned if they have condemned us while they have guillotined us or put us out of the way in this or that manner. What matters is I AM real! We are real! Our initiates becoming the sacred fire are real! You are real, Keepers of the Flame, when you embody the flame of victory! God Victory is the name of Elohim. God Victory—let it be emblazoned on your heart. *It is your name.*

AN HOUR OF COMMITMENT

Therefore, let those who sincerely and with God-determination are ready for the tests of the ruby ray so then give the sign in their hearts at some hour or moment before this conclave is concluded. We must have your word. And if you care to inscribe it on paper and burn that with physical fire and call to the Lords of Karma and to the Royal Teton Retreat, we shall receive it formally.

Beloved ones, it is an hour of commitment and we do not allow the dalliance of the fallen ones who come to sip our nectar that they might go out [following] another round of pleasure. This path is a path which once taken you must not turn back, you must not fear whatever comes. You must know that you will gain the victory over fear itself and death and hell.

THE CHURCH OF GOD

And this is the church of God—your holy temple, the secret chamber of your heart. And in that condition of the sacred heart of Jesus one with your own, you will know the prophecy that is spoken is true of the living temple of the sons of God: Against this church the gates of hell shall not prevail![2]

Sons and daughters of Victory, in the name of Saint Germain, I challenge you to go forth in this Spirit of Victory and conquer!

I thank you for your presence and your hearts. [Audience applauds.]

July 6, 1985
Camelot
Los Angeles, California
ECP

CONQUER IN THE NAME OF VICTORY

Ho! Ho! Ho! Elohim of Victory's flame, I AM here!

I AM Victory in the full-bodied manifestation of those who entertain perpetually the majestic sense of victory whereby Lanello did win his own.

Beloved of Victory's flame, I AM come for the glorious Central Sun Magnet that you have built and are abuilding for the victory of all life. Thus, in the fullness of the resurrection's flame of the sun in Aries,

I AM THAT I AM Victory in the cloven tongues of fire!
Victory unto the seventh age!
Victory in the heart of Saint Germain and Portia!
Victory on the path of freedom!
Lo, I AM! Ho! Ho! Ho!
And the forces of anti-victory are repelled.
And they go down!
And they go down to defeat!
And they are bound!
Therefore, rejoice and say with me now:
Ho! Ho! Ho!
The forces of anti-victory are bound!
The forces of anti-victory are bound!

(Once more.)

Ho! Ho! Ho! The forces of anti-victory are bound!
And the Church Universal and Triumphant
   is God-victorious this day!
And the Church Universal and Triumphant
   is God-victorious this day!
And I AM God-victorious, for I AM Victory this day!
And I AM God-victorious, for I AM Victory this day!
I AM a son of Victory!
I AM a son of Victory!
I AM that daughter of Zion!
I AM that daughter of Zion!
And I AM that New Jerusalem, God-victorious,
   which cometh down from heaven!
And I AM that New Jerusalem, God-victorious,
   which cometh down from heaven!

Thank you, beloved Keepers of the Flame. Be seated carefully, for you sit now in the flame of victory.

Bright flames of gold and sacred fire leap around you. And you now understand the seat of authority of Christ-victory. And from the seat of victory in the threefold flame, you now reign in your own individual Christhood, the Lord of your domain—fire, air, water, and earth.

Praise the LORD I AM THAT I AM Elohim! For the builders of creation do rebuild now, rebuilding not only the temple of man, the manifestation of womb-man, but, beloved, they are rebuilding now the sacred fires of the heart. It is an hour of resurrection's rejoicing. And it is an hour of resurrection of the Divine Mother and her flame within you.

And all the earth does rejoice this day. All elemental life receive with praise and hosannas the coming of the Divine Mother into the very midst of the earth to claim the Word, to claim her own, to preach the mighty teachings of the LORD God Elohim. For the hour of fulfillment is indeed come. And this hour of the Palm Sunday is the celebration of the judgment of the powers of this world and the fulfillment of the Divine Mother and her Manchild in each and every one of you, sons and daughters of the Most High.

Therefore, rejoice now and do acclaim this mighty Word. For in the Word that is incarnate in the one and in the many is truly the path of affiliation—of assimilation of the Body and Blood of that universal Christ.

Praise the LORD I AM THAT I AM Sanat Kumara!

In the living flame of this moment, I with my beloved twin flame therefore spread now the laurel of the crown, do spread therefore the palms. And there is the carpet beneath the feet of the Divine Mother, for truly the age of the universal Woman is upon this earth, beloved.

Let it be seen. Let it be recognized. For this hour of fulfillment is the release. It is the taking away of the bonds and the barriers to every son and daughter of God. It is a day of rejoicing, for the light is come. And the people are ready to receive the message and the messenger.

Therefore, understand whose message you do deliver. For it is the message of the One who has sent you. Therefore, other messages contrive not, but take the message of the altar that comes to you out of the flame of the ark of the covenant. Dilute it not, for the spirit of prophecy is again in the land. And a piercing sacred fire of that prophecy, beloved hearts, must come forth in this pure and undiluted form. For the light must penetrate. And the sharper-than-the-two-edged-sword must go forth.

Therefore, listen well. And beware of deviations whereby the teaching may be used to promote other social or materialistic or economic causes, thereby forgetting that we entice not the people to find the teachings and follow those of the ascended masters for outer benefit but by the sacred fire for the purging of the soul and for the path of eternal life.

Thus, I behold you an order of the ancient priesthood of Melchizedek.[1] And I have shown the messenger in this hour of rejoicing as you have appeared in ancient temples, as you have come, priests and priestesses in past ages. And I have shown her how, in tending the altars, you were given the initiations of the twelve gates of the City Foursquare. And in some instances, as you desired to press on to higher levels of initiation, you therefore did not have the pure perspective of the force of Evil—the anti-force moving against that seventh-ray order of the priesthood of Melchizedek keeping the flame in all ages for the hour of Aquarius and of the Woman that is come.

Therefore, beloved, in your lifetime, leading to this moment of my appearance to you this day, you have been faced with the very same testings of your priesthood, of your holy vows at inner levels. And some of you have fallen into the same traps of the misuses of the light of the seven chakras that took you far from that special gate of the City Foursquare where you must now enter, where you once desired to enter and did not.

Thus, in this spring equinox, I tell you that the entire movement of the Keepers of the Flame, who function in the capacity of the thirteenth tribe of Christed ones in the center of the circle within the City Foursquare, must in this hour and in this cycle of the fourteen months of the blue sphere of the Will of God[2] pass the initiations of the entering in through the door of the East—the East Gate of Eden, beloved ones, where the angels keep the flaming sword to guard the way of the Tree of Life,[3] the East Gate where the dawn of Christ-realization must come in the name I AM THAT I AM, ancient name for the newness of the Everlasting Gospel appearing again and again as the needle has woven the teaching in and out of the fabric of the divine garment.

Thus, the needle and the thread appear and disappear. And the coming again of the threading, therefore, and the weaving of the teaching is the sign of the outer manifestation of the inner thread of contact of the Divine Mother.

Therefore, I blaze the light of the Buddha. Therefore, let the shield of the Woman appear. Therefore, let the light prevail, as you may know, beloved hearts, that your initiation must be under the hierarchy of the sun—the sun of Helios and Vesta in the sign of Aries. And by these initiations of this sign of absolute God-control, you must also come to master the signs of the cardinal points of Capricorn, Cancer, and Libra.

Beloved ones, this is the necessity for the protection of your role of priest and priestess of the sacred fire. Thereby, when you come to those other testings of the lines of the clock and the gates of the city, you will no longer enter into those misuses of the light that have set you back also in this lifetime and on this Path.

I AM Victory. And in the heart of hearts of our twin flames, we come with an extension of resurrection's flame to rejoice in victory, to enfire with the true spirit of the resurrection, and to tell you that the hour of the invocation of resurrection's flame is now. Let it be until the culmination of the Easter conference, therefore—let it be the keeping of the vigil of the resurrection of every son and daughter of God, every child of light throughout the Church Universal and Triumphant and all who are destined to be resurrected in the glory of the LORD in this life.

Therefore, let the centers around the world be called immediately following my release. For I am extending a grid of fire, resurrection's flame— now the pure gold and the ruby and the purple fires mingling—across the planetary body. And this grid of light, beloved ones, is the means whereby the inauguration of the etheric body new to the earth[4] will become a physical manifestation.

This grid of light that is intricate and strong around the world, that is being placed in position by my legions of angels, those of Uriel's bands and others assigned to the task, will be as the nexus of the light flowing from the heaven of the etheric plane to the earth of the physical. And it does therefore rest between, at the point of the Divine Mother—at the point where the grid of sacred fire must pass through the mental to the astral, hence into manifestation.

Beloved ones, this means that the holy order of the priesthood of Melchizedek, those who are a part of the Christed ones, must raise up the full power of their Christhood—"And I, if I be lifted up from the earth, will draw all men unto me."[5] Let this "I" of the sacred fire as the pillar of resurrection's flame, as the pillar of pure white fire of the Divine Mother, be found in you rejoicing and rejoicing and rejoicing at the coming of the LORD, the I AM THAT I AM, to your temple, the coming of the Lord Jesus Christ, whose representatives and disciples ye are.

Let the world be ready, therefore, and let it be readied. For we are readying the place for the release of light. So we send the messenger who bears the mantle of the Mother of the World. So we send you as her sons and daughters, so close as one in this mystical body. For truly the world is ready. Let the forces of darkness know that the hour of the judgment is come.

And I, Victory, have drawn my *V* in the sky from the beginning. I shall draw it in the ending. And I shall be with you, in Christ the victor over death and hell, until the golden age is the golden light of victory, of the sixth ray, of the saturation of earth in resurrection's flame.

Truly, O beloved, the light *is* gone forth and the New Day of your oneness is at hand. May you be vigilant and understand that the victory at inner levels can be won on earth only through your heart and soul and mind as one voice.

In the name of the beloved Virgin, who does guard, then, the holy purpose of America and every nation, in the name of her crown and her standing with you—let light prevail! Let victory be known! And let the mighty archangels deliver you unto holy purpose fulfilled.

May all the world rejoice that you indeed have kept the flame of victory, that you have desired and submitted to the testings of your souls, that you perceive the Real from the unreal and therefore have been the standard-bearers and the ensign of the people until this hour when all should know me,[6] the universal Christ, as the I AM in every man, woman and child.

Let all things be known. Let all things be fulfilled. Let the sharpening of the mind and the word and the action become the challenge of all those who miss the point of the nexus in their service and may now be fortified and strengthened by the grid of light of resurrection's golden flame.

Beloved ones, may all Keepers of the Flame the world around feel the summoning of my heart for the building of the Inner Retreat, for the preaching of the Word. May all things desired in this heart become the possible, for the fires and the momentum of cosmos are with you, builders in the temple of our God, initiates in the heart of Shamballa.

Priests and priestesses of the Order of Melchizedek, Zarathustra calls! Zarathustra commands!

O ye who are the body bulbs, O ye who have the sacred fire of Zadkiel, remember the power of Saint Germain from the beginning unto the end. By the seventh ray of victory, by the legions of the seventh ray, therefore, tarry here and conquer in the name of Victory. I say, conquer in the name of Victory!

I bid you God-speed.

Palm Sunday, March 23, 1986
Camelot
Los Angeles, California
ECP

32

THE PURGING OF CHICAGO

Hail, legions of victory!

I AM Victory! Welcome to my heart of God's victory!

Keepers of the Flame, rejoice. For I AM come to this city to establish an intensity of my flame that shall be as a mighty pillar of fire inundating and counteracting all forces of anti-victory and moving out by the power of the LORD's Spirit and his hosts to counteract that defeatism that is abroad in the land today. [28-second applause]

Indeed I AM Mighty Victory. And the LORD hath said to me this day, "O my son whom I have called Victory, no other flame but victory can defeat the forces of death in America and the earth. Go, then, to my city of light, ancient focus of a golden age. Go forth to unleash that Word!"

O beloved ladies and gentlemen of the heart of freedom, I say to you, with hearts noble as these and many more let us see how in the twinkling of God's eye the spirit of victory may infuse this land! And so I place my flame in the heart of the Goddess of Freedom above the nation's capitol.

And I cry, as the LORD God does cry, as the archangel Michael has cried, and the Angel of Unity does stand: O beloved, go forth north, south, east, and west and remind them, "O brothers, ye are indeed brethren. Remember ye are brethren in the light!"

Therefore, O brothers of the Holy Spirit worldwide and sisters of the fraternity of the Woman of the Sun, come forth now, I say. For in this land there is a fire of heart ready, then, to burst. And so may it be said of this generation of lightbearers that they saw the vision of a golden age and they did indeed see the forces of darkness pitted against it and they did solemnly choose and vow before the LORD God Almighty that the *darkness shall not be!* [18-second applause]

O beloved ones, fail not the spirit of victory. Fail me not, for I am thy brother also. And I come in the name of the Lord of the World to lend my spirit and my legions with those of the seven archangels to see what can be done, to see what keepers of this flame of liberty might do in this hour leading toward that hour of Wesak for the turning of the tide.[1]

O beloved, let your determination match the saints robed in white and those who are under the altar of God[2] for a season waiting, waiting, I say, for ye all to also enter that life that is power, that is wisdom, that is love.

Blessed hearts, receive, then, by the inverting of the baton of the Great Divine Director. As there is the inversion of this rod of power, then, heaven comes to earth to meet you in this hour, even as earth has a taste of heaven. So, in the presence of the Great Divine Director, I say to you, let your auras absorb the electromagnetic fields of the legions of victory! And let that victory be truly the word of the age.

There is a victory of the flesh. There is a victory of the spirit. One enters the other, and the soul who is the bride of Christ does enter the transfiguration of her Lord. I quicken, then, the memory of the soul and reason for being.

Beloved, all have come to this hour of victory. So many know it not. I regret that more cannot hear this word.

Beloved, the hour of victory is that for which you have been prepared and for which you have prepared yourselves diligently. And yet you have reached the ceiling of the offerings of Church and State—the politicians, the economists, and the wolves in sheep's clothing everywhere apparent and nonapparent yet most transparent to us, for you see, beloved, they lack the spark of victory! There is no victory where the joy of the Holy

Ghost in the full fusion of the soul in the living Word is absent.

Thus, mankind have reached a ceiling of human solutions. And few there be who can lead them to the divine solution. In fact, most have become so cynical as to suspect that there could be any mouthpiece of the heavenly host who could deliver any message that could assuage the grief, the fear, the doubt of the people of God in the earth.

Therefore, in the name of the Almighty One I enter the arena and I come, beloved, with the assistance of cosmic beings of light. These are not dead spirits! But we are they who are alive forevermore in God, who have not worn mortal form for tens of thousands and hundreds of thousands of years.

Blessed hearts, have you contemplated that you are also as old as God is, who conceived you "in the beginning" a living soul and sent you forth?

Thus, we are determined that this ceiling of limitation of self-knowledge of the sons and daughters of God shall be driven back by many hosts who have gathered, responding to the determination of fervent hearts in every religion or outside of the religions of earth.

Blessed ones, many see the handwriting on the wall and do read it. Many understand. But I say, it is the response that counts! And when the response of the people is limited by their leaders, I say, of all conditions this is most tragic in the earth.

Thus, I see losses of territory in this century that ought to have been dedicated to freedom by those who were free and could have done something about it. We cannot look back except to learn the lessons of history. And let us learn well that the enemies of the light in the personages of the fallen angels—they have come, they have played their roles of infamy, and they have gone down in ignominy.

Yet, beloved, by the actions of individuals few in number, the course of the downward spiral of history was set. And now you who have come again in your hour of victory must deal with deeds that others have sown. And the harvest is nigh! And the reapers come and they not only reap the works of these fallen angels, but they seize the tares as well—genetic strains of evil.

Thus, beloved, just at an hour when the LORD's hosts do intercede to bind those dedicated not to life but death in the earth, there is that moment when the seas and the lakes would overflow and the mountains would tremble and the earth should shrug. And in that moment a people have arisen—torchbearers of an age.

The question, then: Will they understand the timing of the hour? Will they understand that as in all battles of history those who could endure have saved not only their nations and families but the course of a planet itself?

Will those who have known Saint Germain cease, then, from their toilings and revelries and understand that in a matter of weeks and months the fate of history may be decided?[3] By thinking man,* but him not alone. By spiritual man—by those who work, those who love, those who know that God is nigh to deliver a people who will appeal, who will apply themselves to the urgency and not fail.

Blessed ones, if you will understand how the presence of angels of victory can press into the earth and yet some (who are of the earth) in the very pressure of our presence can feel more that spirit of anti-victory in themselves and defeatism, depression and cynicism, you will also understand how they must, then, make a decision by the lever of the mind and the will and the heart to say, "I will not be defeated, in the name of God! I will fulfill my destiny!"

Some have said this, beloved, without a shred of recourse to things beyond the empirical—yes, courageous hearts who have endured the centuries of barrenness of the religious tree of life. Yet the spark has ignited. It has become a flame. And that all-consuming flame is a passion for peace, for freedom, for the art of love, not war.

Blessed ones, others have made the decision to let the embers die. And in them the spark has gone out. And they have become what is known as a castaway:[4] as the Lord said, empty, empty houses full of dead men's bones[5]—that is, possessed by other ghosts of Christmas past who have taken up their lodging in that emptiness. And thus they have no rudder,

*Homo sapiens

no compass, no navigator. They are without Father or Son or Holy Spirit, and the love of the Mother has waxed cold.

Blessed ones, at some time in life there comes to every individual the pain of knowing a loved one that one cannot help, for the loved one has stubbornly refused to let go of the force of anti-victory.

Beloved ones, to the victors belong the spoils of the spiritual tree of light. Understand that anti-victory as defeatism must be defeated *by you* within yourself, within the mind and the subconscious, by an act of will and a decision that says, "I can do all things through God, who strengthens me." There is no victory without him. And in him you live and he in thee, beloved.

Surrender to this one idea: those who determine to succeed by the pride of the mind or whatever else and leave out that Holy Spirit, that power of the immortality of the soul in God—they shall not pass in this age. For the darkness has waxed gross in the earth.

Blessed ones, ye are the light* of the world. The light† of the heart of every Keeper of the Flame of liberty is the primordial light of a planet largely in darkness. Remember the key word of the Son of God. I remind again of it that you will not forget who you are. He said, "So long as I am in the world, I am the light of the world."[6]

Beloved, you are in the world, not I. You cannot say that Mighty Victory is the light of the world. But you can say, "I am the spirit of Mighty Victory incarnate! And the I AM THAT I AM of me *is* the light of victory in the earth."

When the responsibility for turning the tide of a nuclear age is put upon the heavenly hosts, blessed ones, a grave mistake based on ignorance of the true divine doctrine is made. You must act, knowing that all things depend upon the Spirit of the LORD in you.

This earth was given to those who wear these bodies that you wear, beloved. Remember this. We may intercede by the authority of your decree, but this is not our battle except you enjoin us by your call. The battle is to the Lord and the Lord of you, the Holy Christ Self.

---

*Christ consciousness
†threefold flame

Very few are in the driver's seat. Thus they accept the ceiling of cynicism in life. "Someone else must solve the problem," they say. The government, the Congress, NATO, the UN—always someone else is left to deliver a world.

There is only one God you can know and he is the God whose voice speaks in your heart. Oh, I beg you on behalf of all who have ever lived on earth and ascended and all who are scheduled to ascend in the next thirty years, respond to that voice! Some of you do not even speak to one another in love, let alone respond to the most loving, the most wise and powerful voice of all—the voice of the hidden man of the heart.[7]

Blessed ones, to the ingenious will the spirit of victory come. And by the power of the Cosmic Christ, may God truly deliver this nation and earth through you and so many others who receive the ministrations of my angels in this hour yet are ill-equipped to receive either me or my messenger or this creed.

Is it not wondrous that we can live and let live; and that knowing the power of this form of prayer we can acknowledge that others, too, reach God and that this is a mutually reinforcing system whereby the greatest lightbearers of all walks of life do supply some need, some support while receiving the same from others?

A fiery vortex of light is abuilding now and has been for some time, preparing for the release of the spoken Word into this city. It is composed of millions of angels, beloved, and of the fire they have brought from the Central Sun for this occasion of our communion of saints as Above, so below.

My eye is upon the corruption of this city, its former political machines and those who have survived in organized crime or racist groups of all sorts or militant groups. Blessed ones, the day has come, and it is the day of reckoning when this city should be, must be, and shall be purged. Let it be purged by Light, beloved, that can absorb the Darkness and leave a people in peace. Let it be so, for the vortex is set. It is in position to the very depths of the earth under the city.

Beloved ones, I tell you the truth. The purging shall come by light

[*Christos*] and violet flame, guarded by your own God-harmony, else one day, if it is not transmuted, the purging shall come by water and by fire.

Let it be known, then, that the Almighty has set to you this day a task which you and others like you can fulfill. Recognizing the seriousness of the necessity for Light to increase and for Darkness to be bound without a violent reaction or overreaction of the forces of nature, know, beloved, that responsible sons and daughters of God in the earth who see the course that is set and take their stand create new levels of opportunity for a dispensation to others yet to be awakened to their own Christhood.

Therefore, I, Victory, draw a circle of fire. It has a radius, beloved, of one hundred miles. Its center is in a particular place which I show to the messenger in downtown Chicago. Therefore, you may easily take and draw this circle and see on the map what the areas of concentration are.

Let it be known, then, that a people whose hearts were afire for God one day on the first of February in Aquarius 1987 did receive an impetus from the Central Sun, did receive an awakening, an enlightenment, and did determine to act before it was too late.

May you know the profound meaning of life and the protection of that life when life is ultimately threatened. Beloved, may you know that those things which threaten life on earth are so intense and intensifying in many hearts—from abortion to suicide, from dread disease to drugs to totalitarian movements to brainwashing to encroachment upon the body and the mind by toxins or vile thoughtforms and sounds.

Beloved, it is not difficult to understand the meaning of the Fourth Horseman, to observe life and what it has become. Will you not understand, then, the daily challenge of death that comes knocking at the door to convince you to surrender some portion of your personhood in God rather than take a stand for life.

O beloved, the demons of death are of the ultimate subtlety. Can you believe that a planet could be convinced that those things prophesied shall not come upon the earth? Yet this is what the forces of anti-victory, defeatism, and death have done. Those who have lived a little while remember when it was not so.

Therefore, act. Rouse yourselves, beloved! For this is, you might say, a final opportunity for this city and area. Let it be for the turning back of all that which was plotted on the graph of karma by the deeds of mortals —some who knew not what they did and some who entered the league of conscious Evil.

In this day, in the Holy Spirit of God, I, Victory, plant my rod in the center of this vortex. May it blossom as Aaron's rod. May it bloom as the rod of Joseph. Thus, Saint Germain and Joseph of Arimathea—let them have, then, the green branch and new life.

In ye all I place a portion of my flame of victory, and not alone my flame but my heart. All else I have laid upon His altar. Thus, beloved, the vortex is sealed—and ye also if ye will it so.

Call, then, to the angels of victory. They will comfort, they will enlighten, they will heal! They will rejoice with you day by day. They will strengthen and transfer from the heart of the Father new life.

Here, take, then, my heart and my flame. I am with you in Christ always unto the end of your karma, my beloved.

February 1, 1987
Blackstone Hotel
Chicago, Illinois
ECP

33

THE VICTORY OF FREEDOM

Victory is my name! And I AM here to seal *you* in *your* victory name!
[15-second applause]

The fires of victory descend, for my legions of light have not spent their allotment of illumination's flame given unto them in the heart of the Great Central Sun aeons ago for the blessing and the kindling of those already kindled by Victory's flame.

Therefore, the capstone of Freedom is Victory. And freedom without victory is no freedom, beloved! And that is precisely the state of consciousness in the United States of America today. There is freedom but no victory of freedom. Therefore, I say to you, What kind of a freedom is that?
[Audience responds, "No freedom!" (3-second applause)]

Thus, my beloved, shafts of white fire and yellow shall pierce this gloom and doom until those who think they are free wake up one day and find out that there is a people in Montana that is free. But [those who think they are free] are not free, for they are bound and bound again by the calamities of civilization that are as that which implodes from within and is not known or understood until it is too late. Blessed hearts, whether an Exocet missile[1] or a cancer in the side, undetected, there is calamity abroad in the earth.

Now that the trumpets of the seven archangels have sounded,[2] I must be present. For the victorious ones must have that extra flame upon the crown, the raising up of Victory's fire.

I AM Victory. And I am probing, therefore, the folds of your garments. There I snatch from you defeat and doubt and depression. Then there are those *p*'s of procrastination, possessiveness and, beloved, powerlessness. There are those misuses of the light of the first ray, all forces of anti-victory.

I AM Victory and where I AM there is no other vibration than victory. So it is of my legions. They multiply every day. They come from star systems, for they know that Victory's light is this same yellow/white fire. Oh, the glory of this coloration, beloved! The glory of the base-of-the-spine Mother light rising to restore life. Oh, how the presence of victory can fill your microcosm, can give that spin and health and God-awareness!

I AM Victory, come for the battle. Will you join me in the mental belt now, beloved? [Audience responds, "Yes!"]

Oh, my legions can fair contain themselves for desiring to sweep you up, put upon you their armour golden and take you, therefore, into those octaves where these fallen ones are ripe for the picking, beloved! They are rotten, I tell you, and ready to be cast into the fire. O blessed ones, this is not the field whitened to the harvest[3] of saints. This is the field neglected where the rotten fruit is no longer of the matrix of God. Therefore, it must be burned and the stubble that remains taken off the planet.

O blessed ones, the hour has truly come. For the opening of the seventh seal[4] is the true sign of the call of *FREEDOM 1987.*

Go to the root as John Baptist did.[5] Go to the very root with the axe to take it out completely. For this axe of victory is truly laid at the root of the Nephilim gods who have placed themselves first and foremost in education. There I stand! And there we are! For all life proceeds from the education of the child and youth.

Heart, I say! Take heart! Expand heart! Educate heart in the twelve lines of the clock. When we say educate the heart, we speak, then, of a sphere of wisdom of the heart chakra not outpictured in the physical heart that must pump the life of a system. Therefore, knowing has been relegated to the brain or nervous system, but not any longer. The profound wisdom of the Holy Christ Self is the wisdom of the heart.

Victory, then, is the release of the Trinity. Victory, then, is drawn in the sky. And though the horizontal bar be not drawn, spheres of solar rings drawn mark the sign of a protection peculiar to a people peculiar.[6]

Weary not, beloved, for the buoyancy of victory shall carry you to the star of Alpha. Blessed ones, our presence in these night hours has been to give you the sense of awareness of Self apart from time, space and physical body.

My legions come to seal in your beings, then, all given at this conference, both the gift of knowledge of events in the earth and the gift of wisdom of cosmic awareness. Cosmic awareness does flow from the Royal Teton. Victory is cosmic awareness! And cosmic awareness is only God-victorious.

I seal your projects and your service in victory. I seal you in the heart of Helios and Vesta. I seal you for another round of service to Saint Germain and Portia. I seal you for the great joy of bringing to Alpha the gift of posies of flowers gathered in the Heart.

O my beloved, I AM Victory in the heart of earth, in the heart of you and in this cradle, yes, of a new civilization. I say it, beloved. I embrace you. You are our own.

God-victorious legions, tarry with earth! Pour out now that which you have saved of the original dispensation of Victory, saving it for the hour when these should be drawn up by the power of Victory, by the wisdom of Victory, by the love of Victory, by the action of Victory! Victory! Victory!

So, beloved, you are in good, good company with so many angels.

Receive me to your heart. For I, Victory, encapsulate my Electronic Presence to a very small height that I might abide with you as the impetus to the balance of your threefold flame.

Just call to me and say: *"Victory's impetus is mine this day for power, wisdom and love in balance!"* So I shall be that inner helper with the Maha Chohan.[7]

To you my love forever.

Hail, Saint Germain! On yonder crest I salute you, my brother, and extend my hand. Thus, hands clasped, this is the sign of our oneness.

July 6, 1987
Heart of the Inner Retreat
Royal Teton Ranch, Park County, Montana
ECP

KEEP THE FLAME OF VICTORY

O light from the Central Sun, here am I, Victory's son, come to this city for the sole purpose of establishing in this place a living spiral of the flame of God's victory.

I AM an angel of victory, so called by my dedication to that light of victory in you all. God has given to me legions of victory in my command. And unto the living Christ of each son and daughter of God we serve to liberate life.

This flame, then, of God's victory is indeed a mighty pillar ascending far into the upper atmosphere and beyond. Blessed ones, it is a pillar of golden-white light. And therefore, its involuting action as the fire infolding itself does create a vortex drawing all into the higher victory of the Lord Christ in all people.

Blessed hearts, this impetus unto life, unto the raising of the sacred fire to the crown chakra, even in your own body temple, is delivered to you by the loving hearts of those who serve at the altar of the Most High God: seraphim of the light who tend these altars crying, "Holy, Holy, Holy, LORD God Almighty, thou alone art Holy!"[1]

These do deliver to you the golden ampule of oil from their auras which they have received from the altar of God, that you also might partake and quaff that substance now, beloved, knowing that ye are chosen of the light.

O people of earth, rise to your calling in that highest sense of life and liberty vouchsafed to you. Indeed it is the end of an era. Let it be the end of all human error and strife as well.

Understand that in order to articulate the Word, we send to you our messenger as a reminder from ancient times of your destiny and joy and love.

O awake, America! Awake, O people of the heart of Victory!

For long ago you have chosen that flame. And therefore your excellence is quickened now.

Did he not promise the sending of the Comforter?[2] Know that the heavenly hosts who deliver their word in this age are here to comfort, to strengthen, to warn and to deliver a people who would be delivered by the right hand of the Almighty.

Blessed hearts, take that hand and walk with God in this hour. For surely your voice in the power of the spoken Word, aligned with his own, may be the instrument for the saving grace that is needed in this hour when the blind leaders of the blind would take this nation far afield from the flaming sword of Victory, even the two-edged sword that does proceed out of the mouth of the Faithful and True, thus dividing the Real from the unreal.

Awake, O thou that sleepest![3] Awake! I say. Awake! in the name of God-victory! And hear the marching of the Faithful and True and the armies in heaven. Are they not come to deliver a people?

Shall a people not rise up and join them? Or shall they sleep and sleep away until they themselves and all they have built are taken from them?

The hour is perilous. The light is available and oncoming. May those who know the gift of free will and a path of light[4] not neglect to hear our cry.

Thus, all that can be done by heaven is being done, beloved. Let us hear the response of all in the earth out of every nation. Let them arise to know that earth is destined for a golden age in Aquarius and can meet that timetable if her people will it so.

Not here or there, not in this or that testimony but in the living kingdom, the consciousness within, do you find deliverance and surcease from all outer strife.

O expand, victorious threefold flame upon these hearts' altars! Expand with quickening fire!

I, Victory, messenger of Almighty God, am pleased to seal you in the heart of the living flame of victory. Let the love of many angels know your own heart and be known of you, O beloved.

O beloved, hear the voice of the Son of God! See him and live forevermore.[5] I AM in the heart of the flame of victory, evermore the servant of the light within you.

Hail, O legions of Victory! I send you now to every city, town and hamlet across the face of the earth to find some soul of light who shall be a bearer of the light of victory, a kindling spark to all.

Keep, then, the flame of victory.

October 22, 1987
Hilton East
Louisville, Kentucky
ECP

35

ILLUMINATION'S POWER RESTORED

Hail, sons of the Sons of God! I AM Victory and you are suspended in the golden sun of my causal body in this hour!

[29-second standing ovation]

O golden victorious flame of the God consciousness of the second ray, I AM Victory, victory, victory in the Three Jewels of initiation to which you shall attain if you are at all diligent and shun the dullard consciousness!

I AM Victory! I have come to see to it that you are not left in the ignorance and the twilight of a world that is neither here nor there. But I AM *here* and you are *here* and we are in the center of a sun of Being.

And surely you must have understood by this hour that we have come for a single purpose alone: to see to it that in the permanent seed atom of thy being there is that nucleus of the rod of illumination's flame, that it shall develop, that it shall be connected to the electronic and electromagnetic field of our aura, and that you shall endure as an integrity in the Divine Whole of God—even through the sun of the yellow sphere of your own causal body of light.

And by this display of the fireworks of the Fourth of July, which are a white fire and a golden-yellow illumination of the universal Christ, so be it known that we are absolutely God-determined that if you will make even a halfhearted effort to embody this light, you will discover that that ascending process does find you, then, so sealed in the shaft of illumination that you shall feel as though you were ascending in an elevator shaft of Victory's own house.

I AM the house of Victory. I AM the house of Victory. I AM that house, beloved, and in my house there is not a mouse. There is neither a dullard. Neither is there one who does waste time.

Now, if you come to my house, you may devour time but not as a mouse but as the Great Kali. Understand the principle of devouring time. Devouring time is devouring karma. Devouring karma is devouring ignorance. And as you become enlightened you dwell in the timelessness, the spacelessness of our realms, having absolute God-control of *kal-desh*.[1]

Therefore, in the heart of *kal-desh* where one meets the other, where both are neutralized in that very center of being, *I AM Victory and I AM Home with my own!* [18-second applause]

Being so loved, beloved ones, being therefore so tenderly cared for, you must surely know that if you will merely put one foot before the other, you can arrive at the gate. We are determined that no folly or foolhardiness of fallen ones nor brashness nor despot should ever, ever again compromise the beloved of the light.

Our effort is a supreme one. We have seen your own [effort]. We have seen that of Saint Germain and all the hierarchy of light. Therefore, those who go beyond these spheres through their embodiment of illumination's flame do converge on planet Earth for a harvest of souls who treasure the illumination of the Christ and the Buddha.

In this thought and thought realm, be seated.

I come with a fiery discipline of excellence. I come through the spheres of the God and Goddess Meru[2] to neutralize all patterns of witchcraft misusing the light of your four lower bodies. I come to neutralize all ancient misuse of the arts of light. Records of the black arts must disappear and they do so by the displacement afforded you in the presence of such beings of cosmic dimension who are of the Logos.

Know, then, beloved, that an arc of seven stars does appear in the heavens, though perhaps not to your sight. And this arc of seven stars is the sign of the coming of those Solar Lords and of the Holy Kumaras.[3]

All of hierarchy is determined that those who have the inner potential, those who have the past momentum and the desire [for a path of personal Christhood unto God] will now receive attention in the most needed areas of their consciousness, will now receive the tutelage of the Cosmic Christs and Jophiel's angels.

These angels of Jophiel are tender teachers. But make no mistake: if you have valued and prized the discipline of the first and the fourth rays, I can tell you, it is only preparation for that of the second. For the discipline of the second ray, beloved, is the precision of every petaled vibration of a thousand-petaled lotus. Truly the perception of the Gemini mind of God is unto you an open door.

Surely you will never be so blind nor forgetful nor allow density to encompass you about so as to have removed from you the vivid memory of this moment when a hierarchy of light cared so much for an evolution of light stranded, as it were, on a planet in the throes of convulsions whose end of chaos none can predict.

We come to assist our own, and our own are all everywhere who espouse illumination as a spiritual flame—and as a spiritual flame wherewith to nourish life.

My speaking to you bears the brevity and the punctuation of a cosmic moment that has come and that comes but rarely. Everything about this night is rare, even the place so long ago envisioned, so near to the place of the descent of the root races at the Grand Teton. The land is unique and the temples beneath the earth's surface are unique, as are the waters, as are the elements. Truly you have come Home to a place that contains *all* the ingredients for victory—and even myself.

I say it with a smile, beloved, for am I not most blest to bear the flame that in this moment of the history of an evolution is most prized above all flames—the golden flame of victory for a victorious golden age, for a victory in Armageddon, for the victory of your mind and soul and heart, for the victory of your beloved?

Indeed, my friends, I now desire to see a golden flame upon the brow and your visualization therein of the Amitabha. May it be so, beloved, for I do give you the opportunity to so increase in wisdom that the very momentum of the crown itself shall magnetize the Buddhas and raise up the Mother in you to fetch a starling[4] to become a star.

Seven Holy Kumaras, Eternal Youths,[5] reverse the clock in every lifestream, for Victory's hours are not counted. Thus, every hour that is Victory does not cause the aging of the vessel. To turn back time does not recede experience but only increases it, for thou art nearer thy point of origin in the Central Sun.

Now let us see how a marathon of illumination's golden flame properly protected, flanked by violet flame can change a consciousness of a planet through the lightbearers whose spirituality may hold the light you invoke. Let resurrection's flame resurrect the victory of illumination within you and may you prize our presence.

May you prize our presence as a unique moment in your fiery destiny—one you have long awaited and anticipated. And I will tell you when you began to anticipate that this hour should come. It was in a moment when you realized that wisdom had gone out of you, that light of illumined action was no longer thy domain. But it was too late. You had followed those compromisers of the second ray who absorbed but never did reflect back to you your own loving wisdom.

Therefore, beloved, sensing the bondage being forged of an ignorance [that descended upon you as nightfall] through a light lost and a law ignored, you said in your heart: "Though I have sinned against the law of wisdom, yet I know and I believe, I trust and I have faith that I shall pursue. And as I pursue the law of my God, so one day by an equality of co-measurement I shall be received again into the courts of wisdom's master to begin again to weave the coil of light that I did forgo in the presence of these spoilers."

Blessed ones, those who have perverted illumination's flame are angry this night. They are not happy in the least to see the restoration of so many pure hearts [to wisdom's holy fount].

May you recognize what power is restored illumination. May you recognize what you lost when you lost it and the great gift you now have for having regained a portion of it—[the increment of light] that is sufficient for you to multiply [illumination] by the action of your own heart flame.

So great a loss for so great a time ought to make you contemplate, beloved, and determine in all discipline registering upon your life that you will indeed make [your own] application for the sealing of the crown chakra that it may nevermore again, by the grace of God, ever tie in to the fallen ones by even the slightest expression by you of any criticism, condemnation or judgment of any part of life and especially not of any part of the Great White Brotherhood.

So as Gautama Buddha so carefully gave to you his message on the law of chelaship and the Guru-chela relationship through the heart of Sanat Kumara,[6] may you realize as you review the content of these days together that all that has been spoken and exercised of the Word and learned, all facts and figures, all that has been said is designed to enable you to avoid various types of pitfalls within and without upon the planet, that you might not lose the glory of the golden day of your ascension and that you might, in recognition of the dangers on the planet in this hour, secure the bastions of your cosmic consciousness through Maitreya's oneness and through him [the oneness of] all those of the spherical body of the second ray.

Out of the sun of victory I have come. And there is no other sun but Victory, for every Son is a God-Victory.

O my beloved sons, be, then, the light of a world. *See* what you can do. *See* what you can do. See what *you can do!*

July 5, 1988
Heart of the Inner Retreat
Royal Teton Ranch, Park County, Montana
ECP

36

"ALWAYS VICTORY!"

Hail, Chelas of Victory!

I salute you and I claim you as my own! For no other chela but the chela of Victory shall have the day and the say in the winning for Morya El and all the hierarchy of the Great White Brotherhood this battle of light unto light unto light unto victory!

Therefore I AM Victory! And I come with my twin flame and we stand as twin pillars in the earth. And we are the annihilation ray into the very cause and core of every force of anti-victory, every force of defeat, delay, procrastination and the no-win situation.

Therefore, chelas of the first ray, know, then, that I claim you as my own. We claim you as our own chelas of Victory! For, beloved, only the chela that descends in blue fire and ascends in the shaft of victory's golden flame shall have the triumph that is meet for all of heaven that has placed these things under your feet.

Therefore we say, Hail, Chelas of Victory!

[Audience responds, "Hail, Mighty Victory!"]

Blessed hearts, no matter what the hour, we would not leave you without our living flame of victory—*victory* for the spoken Word, *victory* for the Work of the Lord, *victory* in every nook and cranny of the mind, every cell of being!

There is a rolling stone and it does roll from octaves of light and it does become that boulder that descends. And it is that descending stone of victory that does part the way, that does separate the nonvictorious ones from those who are God-victorious in the flame of the universal light!

So, beloved, we come in this year and we demand that it be a year of victory in all quarters, in all areas of life, in every heart where there burns a threefold flame!

Our legions charge from the Great Central Sun, from the Sun of Alpha and Omega and your own sun of Helios and Vesta. We are in the heart and the center of sun systems, for we declare the hour of the release of victory that is a sacred fire that will consume all unlike victory, all unlike the love of victory! It shall consume all doubt and fear, all procrastination, all absenteeism from the center of the white-fire cross of victory.

O beloved, we have come for this moment and we are determined that this rolling momentum that we bring shall be the momentum of victory clear through the decade of the nineties, clear through until that moment when all does return to the point of rest and even quiescence—for earth shall have fulfilled the turning of cycles and the turning of worlds for that return to the centerpoise of new beginnings.

Thus, let the endings be fulfillments. Let them be fulfillments of all cycles, for surely it is the hour when the fulfillment of the eighth ray does bring about the sealing of all efforts and the planting of the seed of the tree of everlasting life.[1]

In you, then, we place the seed of victory. We place it in the very seat-of-the-soul chakra of all who are the chelas of the will of God worldwide. And as their numbers increase, so shall the seed of victory be deposited in that chakra; for from that very point, beloved, the soul will rise and rise by the *impetus* of Victory, by the *nearness* of Victory, by the *presence* of Victory!

For, beloved, we desire and we do place with you the Electronic Presence of the twin flames of Victory, which all twin flames may appropriate, all may take on, all may determine to fulfill.

And therefore the very fire of self-determination of the first ray does intensify as the most brilliant sapphire, cobalt-blue flame that does grow and move and go before you, beloved, clearing the way—clearing the way, we say, for the restoration of El Morya to the fullest stature of being and service midst his own.[2]

We are midst our own in this hour. And our determination and our presence and our shafts of yellow flame and our 'aurora borealis,' which we bear and carry as our own Electronic Presence, beloved, is the impetus of victory which we bring to add to your own and to give you the momentum for the rolling of that stone of the human self right up the very staircase into the level where that human is no more and the soul has reached the ultimate of Cosmic Christ illumination.

Blessed ones, never before in all history of the planetary spheres have you been anywhere that so great a momentum of victory could be your own. And as you receive us to your heart, to all of your chakras, as you receive this golden illumination flame, beloved, clearing the way for the clear seeing and clear knowing of every step of the victory of your life unto that ascension, so victory shall beget Victory. And you shall have the electrifying effect to impart to others the desire for Victory, the desire for Victory's illumination, the desire for the illumination of the bodhisattva, the disciple, the Buddha and the Cosmic Christ.

So, beloved, let illumination be the hallmark of the victory of the violet flame in this century and in this age. Let the full power of Aquarius now be enlightened by the victory of the golden victorious ones standing in the golden victorious light.

Behold, beloved, as there are numberless numbers of legions all clothed in the golden flame of victory and illumination, all clothed in that Cosmic Christ awareness, angels and those graduates of earth's schoolroom who do fill all of this court* and well beyond and do cover this property. For the legions of golden illumination's flame from all areas of the cosmos do gather for the victory of the lightbearers of earth.

---

*King Arthur's Court

And, beloved ones, there is a profound gratitude that ripples across the galaxies for the calls you have sent forth, for the calls of the messengers, for the steadfastness in the challenging of darkness and the dark forces, even against the odds of the fallen ones. Therefore fearlessly and in full faith of the protection of the Great White Brotherhood have you and the messengers taken your stand against Evil in any and every form. And therefore do the cosmic reinforcements come.

See the cornucopia of Victory's flame and light descending! See the bowers of fruit and loveliness! See, beloved, that even before you have passed through this very vale of tears and darkness and karma how you can sense at the level of the crown chakra how that victory does descend upon you, and day by day you literally step in and up into the garments of Victory. You step up into the great wings of Victory. You step into the very presence of the crown chakra of the Buddhas and bodhisattvas who attend you.

Blessed hearts, we come with the miracle golden light of victory. And we are determined with the profoundness of our being that earth through you and all chelas of the will of God shall know, *shall know, beloved,* the intensity of the light and the fire of that action! O blessed ones, let earth intensify that sense of [the God consciousness of] victory and let victory consume all ignorance and density and darkness and the weight of the very mortal mind and mortality itself!

I AM Victory and I salute you with legions of victory. Blessed ones, such an occasion is this that these legions of victory in formation stretch from this place to the heart of the God and Goddess Meru[3] and to the heart of the Temple of the Sun in the very center of this solar system.[4] If you can imagine numberless numbers of legions of victory, so imagine them, beloved, across the wide expanse from this place to the great throne room of Helios and Vesta. Now see and visualize legions of victory.

Do you know, beloved, that it is very difficult to fail in the presence of millions of legions of victory? Yet I must tell you, it is still possible to fail in their presence. It takes more than proximity! It does take *appropriation* —to *appropriate* the *spirit* of victory, to *appropriate* the *flame* of victory, the *joy* of victory, the *mood* of victory, the *momentum* of victory!

Blessed hearts, this is yours to activate in all of your chakras by free will. O let those tapes of golden illumination's flame roll! Let the momentum of victory roll and that of the bodhisattvas and the disciples and the legions. For, beloved, we desire to see you light up the whole sky with illumination's flame and thereby in illumination you will see many who could not enter this path by any other means but by the quickening of the mind, by the transmutation of the lesser mind, with its displacement by the universal Christ mind, the universal Buddhic mind.

Let golden illumination's flame, let the teacher within you, let the World Teachers, let Maitreya speak through you, beloved. Let this become a year so filled, so saturated with *light, light, light* of golden-yellow hue penetrating through you and going forth from you that the whole world might be touched by the radiance of the dawn of the New Day of Aquarius.

Beloved hearts, the violet flame [Omega] that is sent forth, the action of the blue-flame will of God [Alpha] together with Archangel Michael's Rosary,[5] all of these calls lay a solid foundation of the Alpha-to-Omega [yang-to-yin and back again]. And from the base to the crown [chakras] and [back] again there is [established through the joy and the fiery intensity of your decrees] the firmness of the violet and the blue rays.

Therefore, in the center [of being], beloved, there is the spanning of arcs of illumination chakra to chakra. And the Elohim join us and the Solar Logoi. And we are determined to peel away even the very capping of the mind [hence the crown chakra] by the fallen ones and those dense layers of programming [of the mental body] that come through all misuse of all types of waves upon the planet.

Blessed hearts, let us see a new birth of Cosmic Christ illumination, and let us know in this hour that it does begin with each one of you. It does begin with our being sent forth from the Great Central Sun. For blessed indeed are they who have responded to the Call, who have offered the calls and who have refined their sense of honor and the cosmic honor flame and the will of God and the coming to grips with those things unseen yet present in the mind.

So, beloved, we are Victor, we are Victoria,[6] we are Mighty Victory! We are the action of the sacred fire from the *a* to the *z,* from the alpha to the zenith, from the omega unto the horizon. So, beloved, know that the cosmic cross of white fire which we draw is golden illumination's shafts.

Call unto us and our legions of light, beloved, for Victory is on the march. And we are determined to see that each and every one of you does become the full realization of the absolute God-victory of your I AM Presence forever and forever and forever.

Surely that which is past of the old year and decade is into the flame, for you have sent forth the Call. Surely in this hour there is room for Victory's flame to saturate the earth, to fill in the fissures and to allow all that is born of God's own intelligent mind to receive that increment of multiplication from our heart.

After all, beloved, it is the heart of Victory that is ours to cherish and to give to you. And the heart is the seat of victory, for victory begins with the desiring of the heart. It is multiplied by the purity of the heart and the directness thereof. Therefore let pure hearts know the pure fire of Victory and may you bring that fire to every endeavor.

Blessed hearts, our joy overflows. Our cup does run over. And we are filled, we and legions of angels of the second ray, with the cosmic spirit of victory that will not be turned back. None can stay the hand of this victory, beloved, save the misuse of free will by the individual.

So let the gift of God to you allow you to maintain contact with Elohim and Elohimic levels and Alpha and Omega and to be in the heart of Jophiel and Christine and to banish all doubt, all fear, all that is less than the perpetual joy of victory.

Make haste, beloved, to run for the Sun; for the Sun of your I AM Presence is home base. And henceforward unto your ascension may you visualize that Sun as a golden spinning sphere of yellow fire continually emitting the light of the mind of God, of Cosmic Christ illumination, continually spinning, beloved, and like the fire infolding itself drawing all of your members into the intelligence of the universal One that you might transfer to those who have been deprived of learning and true learning, what for* the fallen ones who have moved against that light.

Blessed ones, I assure you, their day is done. *They cannot stand in the light of victory! Victory! Victory! Victory!* So it is known. So it is done. So it is manifest. So we connect with the heart of the earth and the Buddha of the Ruby Ray.[7]

And there does pass through the center of the earth to the other side [Victory's beam] and there does form an ovoid, an ellipse, if you will, of the fire of Victory's beam passing through the heart of the earth, passing through the heart of the sun of Helios and Vesta. And this orbit of light, beloved, does become a track that can be followed by you to the sun and back again to the heart of the earth, to the heart of the Buddha of the Ruby Ray, to the heart of Surya and Cuzco, to the heart of Helios and Vesta.

Always, always victory.

Always Victory! Always Victory! Always Victory!

May I say to you, beloved, if you will remember me, if you will remember us and if you will remember to say to one another, rather than the proverbial hello, "Always Victory!" "Always Victory!" with your handshake, with your farewells and with your greetings...

[Audience affirms with Mighty Victory:]

Always Victory! Always Victory! Always Victory!
Always Victory! Always Victory!

...And when you say it, beloved, will you see that golden light that is more brilliant than the noonday sun that you almost cannot look upon even at inner levels save with the closing of the eyes? Will you exchange the light and the greeting of the Sun of Victory and the greeting of the causal bodies of our twin flames, which we now conjoin with the causal bodies of the God and Goddess Meru over this place?[8]

Blessed hearts, we are determined for you to have this victory and we are determined to be a part of it! We are determined that no more heaviness or sadness or burden of any kind shall be upon you *but always victory and the sense of victory and the spirit of victory and the love of victory!*

*because of

Blessed hearts, with the legions who come be assured that that fire of victory that you choose to bear shall be a determination many times over what you have had. It shall be a sword of Cosmic Christ illumination that cuts through all density, all blocks, all perversity, all time-wasters, all that would take you from that victory. Therefore "Always Victory!" becomes a mantra. It becomes a mantra to *defeat* defeat itself and defeatism.

Blessed hearts, we come, for you have need of us. We come because we love you. We come because our God has sent us. We come because we want to spend the coming months and years of our heaven on earth with you.

In the *love* of your victory, in the *love* of your victory we come! We come to stay, beloved. We have no desire whatsoever to depart from this place or space or from your hearts. O blessed hearts, only receive us and welcome us and remember to call to us, for we must obey the Law that says,

"THE CALL COMPELS THE ANSWER!"

And we are compelled by love to help you, to help you and to help you!

All of our love, beloved, more than is expressible, so we give. May you be up and doing now to follow the star of Victory.

Always Victory!

[Audience affirms with Mighty Victory:]

Always Victory! Always Victory! Always Victory!

January 2, 1989
Royal Teton Ranch, Park County, Montana
ECP

37

A LETTER OF LOVE FROM
THE FATHER-MOTHER GOD

Victory is my name! And so I shall be wherever the son, the daughter
of God does raise up the flame of victory in the triumph over all that is
the nonvictory spiral in the earth! [23-second applause]

Your God-victory does impel my Presence and magnetize it, beloved,
and so I rejoice. For this *is* a God-victorious conference! It is a God-victorious manifestation of wisdom's flame. And *you* are the God-victorious
ones! *You* are the shining sons bearing mirrors reflecting light back to
Alpha and Omega and saying, "In the darkness of this dark star, *here*
are flashes of those who are illumined and loving and in the logic of the
Buddha!"

I AM Victory. You call me Mighty Victory. And I AM with my legions
and my twin flame, and we are determined to put in the heart of each and
every one of you that victory flame multiplying the threefold flame each
time you give that call to balance the threefold flame, to blaze that threefold flame.[1]

Come forth, beloved ones, for I would show you the mystery of passing through the eye of the needle. For when you understand the mystery
then you shall truly pass through it. (Won't you be seated, beloved.)

I desire you to know that this is an unscheduled appearance on my part which could only be approved after the fact. [1-minute 39-second standing ovation; audience gives the fiat *Always Victory! Always Victory! Always Victory!* . . .]

So great a tumult does reach the ear of Helios and Vesta. And you do carve out a tunnel of light whereby the ascending and descending angels may be in your midst, beloved. This is a great grace that you have offered unto heaven throughout this conference and many weeks of devotion. Blessed hearts, the opening [from the etheric] to the physical octave has been made secure by you by this effort; and I trust you will know that as it is secured it must be protected, defended, and re-created day upon day.

Blessed hearts, do you remember how difficult it was [as recently as] at the autumn conference to even receive the dictations of Elohim? How an entire day's work had to be done only to hear from those who spoke?

Blessed hearts, so you have gained this carving through the astral plane; and where the entire planet experiences that rising of the astral plane[2] the walls of the Inner Retreat do keep it out [from this consecrated place]. And in the center, therefore, there is reestablished a greater momentum—a momentum greater than ever before for this contact. And thus, beloved, you give an entrance whereby the angels can descend.

For you see, at that time, at that fall class, it was difficult for the legions of light to penetrate through such intensity of the astral plane to reach you and to reach the messenger. And so a very great burden did come upon her and upon yourselves and this burden you will not understand until many years hence. Therefore see what a difference a momentum does make, and may God bless you that you know the meaning of the words "Always Victory." Therefore, be seated, sweet hearts.

The rolling momentum of the victorious ones on the planet does evoke the rumbling of the unvictorious ones, and some can erupt in violence over the victory of the saints. It has ever been thus, beloved, but in this hour it is more serious than ever as decisions made on all sides are final ones for lifestreams.

For this is the meaning of the conclusion of many thousands of years of your incarnations upon earth, and we shall be releasing this teaching through forthcoming publications by the messenger. So you will come to understand, then, that the cyclic nature of events and the cosmic cycles are what make this year, these months and days, this coming decade so key in the life of every member of the planetary evolution.

Our Presence is to magnetize a sphere of victory—spheres of our twin flames. It is to place that momentum, that momentum of buoyancy, of joy and determination that is all a part of this golden ray that we serve. In the spheres of victory are the spheres of the mind of God. In the spheres of the mind of God are the Buddhas and the Divine Mother.

Angels of Alpha and Omega bear greetings and a proclamation. It is a message to the faithful and the true who serve with the one who is the Word of God:[3]

To you who have been faithful, to you who have been true, we, your Father-Mother, extend a right hand of strength and a left hand to hold you, even in the hour of your God-victorious over-coming. We send new contingencies* of angels from the Central Sun to minister with and to those in the service of the God and Goddess Meru who do carry our flame upon earth.

These angels come with a mission. It is to fully awaken your soul to the need for salvation, to the need to withdraw from all worldliness and materialistic consciousness, to master the elements and not to be enslaved by them, to manifest abundance and yet to be nonattached to the things of this world, to be just stewards of the kingdom of God upon earth and of all that is the inheritance of the saints, to be tender and loving and yet to know the fierceness of the flame of the Ruby Ray and to know how and when to wield it, to apply it.

We send forth this proclamation as a statement of our aid to all who call upon us that for your faithfulness and the flame of truth you bear we shall send to you covering cherubim, principally anchored in this community. And the legions who are under these

---

*i.e., angelic hosts sent at this time on a specific mission, to minister with and assist those on the spiritual path

great beings may also serve you where you have erected your individual altars. But the Call must be made in answer to the Call we send, for there is a wide gulf across the face of the earth betwixt our realm and that of our children.

Thus, we remind that we have established this place as a place apart for mutual reinforcement and love and action. Know it as the haven of light. Guard and protect it. Resolve all differences as they arise. Do not allow any subtle discord between one another to linger. The price is too heavy to pay for you or for us.

We therefore expect preparedness and diligence to that end. We expect a greater awareness of spiritual preparedness and spiritual self-discipline. And we do expect, above all, the setting aside of lesser activities which are yet amongst some of you too strong in their momentum. Observing the gain for your stick-to-itiveness in these five days, you may surely comprehend how greater gain can be won by a similitude of devotion.

We, your God Parents, bless you through the spirit of Mighty Victory. Our archangels of the crown chakra who are ready to crown you shall indeed crown you when you shall have endured to the end[4] of your human creation and karma and the very end of the dweller-on-the-threshold.

We say, *endure!* With fire we send the word *endure!* Never give up but endure. Do not indulge! Do not indulge! Do not indulge the base elements of the human nature else you shall forfeit the prize and be in a karma-making status. And some of you have allowed yourselves to slip into it.

Be not proud in your station but humble before your God and you will not be blinded by pride or stubbornness or even the wiles of the attempted self-perpetuation of the carnal mind. The [Christ mind and the carnal mind] cannot coexist. Therefore, cast out [the carnal mind] with fire and you shall see how suddenly the Lord shall come into your temple[5] and how the flame shall ignite and the Holy Spirit shall become your life, your joy, your love, your health.

I draw the line, we draw the line round each one and this place. It is a place you have provided, for the Law has declared that chelas of the will of God in the earth must do this. You have done it in 1981.* You have increased your holdings according to our direction.

Keep the flame. All is for a purpose. But ere that purpose is fulfilled you must pass through the eye of the needle.

How is it done? Blessed ones, we shorten the distance between question and answer by saying, one passes through the eye of the needle by riding the thread. Thus, beloved, one must conform to the thread. One must place oneself as the thread.

Apply to Confucius, Lord Lanto. Apply to the Buddha. For it is time and we, your God Parents, tell you that you may begin to learn the rearrangement of atoms, cells, and electrons for the purpose of the God-mastery in Matter. Thread the needle with strong thread, with all preparations. Make it long enough and taut enough. Pass through one by one and emerge. It shall be as though you have gone between two worlds, and it is so.

Approach the difficult with ease. Approach that which is easy with caution and concentration. Approach the impossible with the miraculous sense and the Call and with the mind one with the mind of God, for only with God is the impossible possible.[6]

As we have remarked on a number of occasions, remember that you are not sponsors of the Great White Brotherhood but that you are sponsored by the Great White Brotherhood. A place on earth in the land of Saint Germain and Jesus Christ, a place of holiness and even some vastness in itself has been set aside for the Great White Brotherhood. This act by awakened Keepers of the Flame who were awakened by Lanello has secured the dispensation of Divine Intercession as it could not have been given without such sacrifice or such vision.

Know this, beloved. For in the hour of great need America and

*the year of the purchase of the Royal Teton Ranch in Montana

the lightbearers of the world will need that Divine Intercession as no other people have needed it. And you will know in that hour that because you have laid this foundation we by the Great Law may act.

Therefore it is our divine decree that this land shall be further purified and solidified in the light, further accelerated in the etheric octave, even in nature's atomic structure. Thus being so dedicated, may you who have seen fit to found and establish it, defend it. And defend your right of freedom of religion, freedom of speech, freedom of the press, freedom to assemble, freedom to own and maintain private property. Thus the rights of all future generations shall depend upon your determination to defend here these [inalienable rights].

This night every square foot of ground that is under this ownership shall be occupied by legions from all bands and all octaves—disciples, angels, bodhisattvas. And they shall sit in meditation in commemoration of the Lord Gautama Buddha, who determined to sit under the Bo tree until he should discover the cause of human suffering.

Thus came forth the Four Noble Truths. Human suffering, then, is caused by inordinate desire. The cure is the Eightfold Path. May you recognize this Eightfold Path through the seven chakras and the secret chamber of the heart.[7]

May you know that where each one shall sit there shall be the consecration as holy ground and the erasing of past records of past eras, making this land even a greater magnet for those who must study here. These who have assembled for this purpose of this ritual shall also remain until they have ascended into the causal body of Gautama to reach that enlightenment that he did also reach in his second period of meditation.

These are your brothers and sisters, angelic comrades. These are your friends. These are the saints who comprise the Great White Brotherhood. We, your God Parents, tell you that you are closer to them than ever before.

Press on, then, to reach the mark of this high calling in the heart of Christ Jesus our Son,[8] in the heart of Gautama our Son, in the heart of the seven Holy Kumaras, in the heart of the beloved Melchizedek, who does keep the flame of Alpha and Omega in the retreat of Lord Zadkiel.

This document is signed and sealed on this date earth time and at this hour[9] that you might record it and know when this parchment was transferred to you.

Our love is with you. Remember that you have raised yourselves to an extraordinary level of an exalted state in the etheric octave. The test will be to retain it both within this place and wherever you shall journey.

Strive to do this, beloved. Strive to do this. And when you feel yourselves slipping, return to the dictations of *Only Mark.*[10] Return to the recent dictations and the decree tapes and call for this very same forcefield that is here in this moment to be duplicated.

Beloved, this is the ending of the reading of the parchment, truly a letter of love from the Father-Mother God.

Thus I, Mighty Victory, with my twin flame and legions of light do pledge to you to assist you to keep the flame of victory! to keep the flame of Alpha and Omega! to keep open this stairway to the stars, for the ascending and the descending angels that will prepare you for your victory and for the arc from Sirius to earth and the return!

This is the great gain of the Easter conference 1989! May you by your own devoutness earn the opportunity to have such another conference. It is up to you, beloved, for this planetary body in this hour is placed on the same notice, which notification Lord Morya gave: Pay as you go.[11]

You have abundantly placed before yourselves "money in the bank." Thus, may God bless you and multiply this light forever and forever and especially on the morrow and the morrow. We shall see, then, what your next step and choice shall be, what your decision shall be, what new levels of commitment you shall unfold.

Heaven will always answer; Saint Germain does tenfold.

Let the flame of victory blazing here tell the tale of victory, past, present, and future, projected of your lifestream. As we recede into the flame (and you yourselves also recede into it to regather and to continue) we are here at the Royal Teton Retreat. Come to our Great Hall that your decrees might go forth and the second ray intensify.

We seal this conference in a golden shaft of victory protected by all the archangels and legions of light.

The Divine Mother cometh, the Mother of the World cometh, and divine love shall be the magnet to draw her own Home.

March 27, 1989
Royal Teton Ranch, Park County, Montana
ECP

38

BREAK THE SPELL OF NON-VICTORY!

H*o,* legions of the Great Central Sun!

Ho, legions of the Great Central Sun!

I AM Victory! And I AM *here* to break the spell of non-victory in the lives of the lightbearers of earth! [47-second standing ovation]

Ho, I AM come! And I am here to put down these fallen ones who have determined to pervert the very life-force, the lifeblood and the beings of the servants of God.

I am here, beloved ones, for the spirals of victory descend!

I respond to Alpha and Omega. I respond to all the legions of the second ray. I am responding to and representing the mighty bodhisattvas who dwell on the inner planes of the etheric octave and desire to take embodiment. I come to you brimming with a joy that we can meet together the expectations and even the demands of Lord Lanto and all who serve with him, who read as we do the handwriting on the wall.

Therefore, beloved sons and daughters, be drenched in the flame of Victory! Be drenched in the flame of Justina! And know that we are one and that we add the momentum of our twin flames to those cloven tongues of golden fire that descend upon your crown chakras now. And they are meeting a certain amount of density and therefore we feed them our fire as the light does penetrate through the etheric sheath, through the mental, through the desire, through the physical.

O beloved ones, help us with right diet. Help us with pure thought. Help us with meditation. Help us with doing your *pranayama.** Yes, beloved, we will remake you in the image and likeness of God if you will cooperate. *Therefore, will you cooperate?* [Audience responds: "Yes!" (22-second standing ovation)]

I speak quickly and with a mighty fire, that I might inject in you the sense of acceleration. You have been on other worlds and systems of worlds and in higher octaves where you would think more easily and more quickly, your motions would be more direct and mercurial and you would accomplish so much more of the penetration of the mind of God and the drawing forth even of the engineering and the design and the architecture of the golden cities of light in the etheric octave.

Yes, you have lived in those levels, you have known a greater communication and now, I say, the forces of anti-victory, the forces of non-victory have heaped upon you a momentum and a burden and a weight, beloved ones. *And you must listen to me!* You must know that it must be challenged by you and you alone!

And the fire of you is the fire of God in you, for you are God-victory in manifestation! And I see you as manifestations of ourselves, of Victory and Justina, in the God flame of victory. And I see you in your mighty golden robes and golden winged sandals of victory. And you are that victory and I affirm it now!

And therefore I say: Take the fire of victory in your souls! Take the fire of God-victory that is the God-victory of your own mighty I AM Presence and *jump* out of those snakeskins, *jump* out of that density and go forward enjoying the vastness of the universe. For your own mind can tap it because you have chosen to develop your heart and meditate in your heart, and therefore the rings of fire grow—and therefore the bodhisattvas may come to you, they may touch you, they may quicken you!

---

pranayama:[Sanskrit] control of the vital energy through the practice of breathing exercises. See "Djwal Kul's Breathing Exercise," decree 40.09, in *Prayers, Meditations and Dynamic Decrees for Personal and World Transformation.*

Beloved ones, come into balance. Come into balance, I say! And cherish nothing in this world more than your own individual equilibrium—your equilibrium in your own tree of life, in your own mighty I AM Presence.

Let us say that everything that detracts from that equilibrium south, north, east, west, beloved ones, does detract from your mighty victory. And I say, a mighty victory you must have! And you should not make it [merely] by the skin of your teeth in the hour when your name is called at roll call at Luxor. Yes, beloved, you should [graduate] with flying colors and the highest honors! You should be ready for your ascension *tomorrow*, if necessary, or the next tomorrow or the next year or the next five. Yes, beloved, be ready now, and then walk the earth as that example that others may see and follow.

This *is* an hour of cycles turning. Whether we can turn them around depends on the response of every lightbearer on this planet to my message given this day! And therefore I ask you to communicate [your response] through prayer, through decree, through [the dissemination of] information, through giving to individuals the *Pearl of Wisdom* that shall be printed of my dictation and [telling them] of the work and of the calls of the legions of the second ray.

It is a moment, beloved, when all could be won and all could be lost. Do not discount your Godhood! One individual who is God, and knows it, is the pillar of fire, the rod in the earth that shall be the focus of the Great Central Sun Magnet. And many coming together in this place, even once a year, beloved, does produce that concentration of fire whereby we may penetrate and probe in the earth and place our probes, allowing the light you invoke to penetrate more deeply and more deeply.

Therefore I say, prepare for coming here again next year, starting the day that the conference has concluded. Make your plans, determine to have the funds and the means and decree for the absolute God-victory of souls.

Now I will tell you what we did with these earthquakes this day. We have taken the opportunity of your holding the balance for the earth in this place to allow these earthquakes to happen (as they would have inevitably happened) but with the least amount of loss of life and damage because *you* have kept the flame, because you have tarried these days, because you determined to go and you did go to the Royal Teton Retreat last night.

And therefore you did journey with legions of light and you did perform a mighty spiritual work over Yugoslavia.[1] And it did come to pass that you established a coordinate in that nation and other coordinates upon the planet with other servants of God whereby these earthquakes[2] might be for a mitigation [of world karma], a balancing [of planetary forces] and a release of pent-up [misqualified] energies in the earth.

Therefore, understand how much we can do when we have a body of lightbearers who can remain at the same place for a period of ten days or even more, but for any amount of time we are grateful—even if you determine to do a twenty-four-hour marathon in your study groups and teaching centers, where you can hold the flame of harmony and make of that flame one of God-illumination with the violet flame and all the calls that you give.

I will tell you, beloved, the [volcanic] release in Alaska[3] has the same [portents]. And some of you who are "old-timers" have seen earthquakes of this dimension (yet not of this magnitude) happen from time to time during conferences and it has always been because the student body has been able to hold the balance for a release. And without that holding of the balance, there could have been far greater calamity and destruction to life.

You know that earth changes are in the planetary plan, but how and where they shall manifest and what degree of burden or loss of life shall be upon the people surely rests upon the individual decision that shall be made each and every day by the servants of God on earth.

I say, become fiery electrodes! Love the wisdom teachings, pursue the path of the mystics, be together in the light and therefore convey a spiritual teaching and a spiritual consciousness. Read the books and the foundations of these mystical paths of the world's religions and thereby understand all people. And when you give your Ashram rituals, beloved, you will be able to contact in a deeper way so many souls of light because now you will understand their path. And when you understand their path you understand their vibration.

(Therefore, be comfortable by being seated.)

Beloved ones, in order for me to speak to you I must have a dispensation from the Lords of Karma, from the Four and Twenty Elders and beyond that the Solar Logoi. Therefore, I deem it a great privilege to be with you in this hour.

It has been weighed time and again preceding conferences and it has been decided that I should not speak. For the power of victory is great and the power of victory can unleash such tremendous enthusiasm and fire of purpose that when it does descend on the unenlightened evolutions of a planet it can stir up the urge to go out and do those things that are not the will of God.

Therefore we have created a trusted chalice, as you are that chalice and as you have placed your trust in God and made yourselves available to Lord Krishna and the hosts of the LORD. I desire, then, to continue to release this night the power, the wisdom, the love of victory! And to do so I need your cooperation in harmony. I need it, beloved, because if the light I release is so easily misqualified by those who are among the most advanced in the outer world today, then, you see, I will make that karma and I will again be limited in coming.

Consider, then, all those areas of your life in which you desire to be victorious. You would do well after this session or in the morning to write down each point of your personal lifestream and activities where you desire *victory*. You can chart it on a map, beloved, a map of your life, and you can put those golden ribbons at that place where you are determined to have your victory—*victory* over self and every condition, *victory* in this Church, *victory* in the dissemination of the teachings, *victory* in the nations, *victory* in the governments, *victory* in education, *victory* in every area of life!

Beloved ones, look all around you in this hour, and what do you see?

You see *defeat,* beloved hearts. Everywhere people are being defeated by their own ignorance, by their own absence of the fiery coil of the Divine Mother, of the sacred fire rising up within them. They are being defeated on every hand—in the economy and in business and in life. There is a world depression that is not as apparent as it might be. For if the world could know the state of world depression that is upon the people, perhaps they would determine to do something about it.

Well, I will tell you, your violet flame marathons in this conference, sprinkled with the intensity of the yellow fire, will awaken and quicken some. They will awake as from a deep slumber and they will begin the quest and they will search.

And when they search, *who* will they find?

They will find *you* as myself and Justina, and we will be there with you and we will be there to bring home the victory!

Let America awake! Let Americans awake! And let the fire of the entire Spirit of the Great White Brotherhood go forth from your hearts.

I, Victory, with my beloved consort, greet you in this hour! And we are transferring to you increment by increment that which you can spiritually assimilate of victory. Therefore continue your calls and affirmations to me this night and see what we will do together!

There are other events in the planet in store during this conference. We desire to see a mighty action for the right, for the feeding of the hungry and the liberation of souls and the exposure of the dark forces that are yet intent upon global warfare. These must be bound on the astral plane, and those in embodiment [must be bound] as well, by legions of Victory, legions of Jophiel and Christine!

We come in anticipation of Alpha and Omega. Now, precious hearts of light, so rise to that mighty occasion.

June 28, 1992
Heart of the Inner Retreat
Royal Teton Ranch, Park County, Montana
ECP

39

BECOMING MORE OF GOD DAY BY DAY

Hail, legions of Victory's light!
I summon you to draw nigh!
Enter, then, the Heart of the Inner Retreat!
Enter the hearts of those who bear the victory flame in the threefold flame of light!

Blessed ones, legions of my bands of victory approach in concentric rings of victory. I ask you to welcome them in this hour. [47-second standing ovation, salutations to legions of Victory's bands]

We also applaud the presence of the Lord Christ Jesus this day and of the Maha Chohan, and we are grateful for all of their words. For we, too, come and we come in an accelerated pace. And I tell you, legions of victory have always been accelerated! We see what the Lord has said, we see what the Maha Chohan has said and we quicken your minds and hearts that you might identify with our legions.

Now, beloved, as you are standing, remain standing. For one member of my legions whom I have singled out does place his Electronic Presence over you from this hour to the hour of midnight your time. Therefore you shall know what it means to be in the power of victory, the love of victory, the determination of victory, the truth and the wisdom of victory.

And you will see why it is that that shining golden-yellow flame of God does announce our coming. For we know that *none* can have the Victory, beloved, except they have enlightenment. For the forces of fallen angels, in all of their machinations, do move against the lightbearers and prey upon their willful ignorance.

With this understanding, know that the angel I have chosen from my bands is holding over you and around you a sword of illumination. Thus the duration of my dictation is an optimal time for you to absorb the qualities of victory. (Thus be seated, beloved.)

As I come to speak to you, I review the record of who was present at my last dictation[1] and at all my dictations, all the way back to those delivered earlier in this century by Guy and Edna Ballard. Yes, beloved, I have come in this century and my twin flame has eventually come also.[2]

I have seen some of you accelerate beautifully on the Path and I commend you, for you have made as much progress as is possible, given your karma and the circumstances of your soul. And I have seen others, who are not here at all, who have gone this way and that way. Is it because God has stopped up their ears and not allowed them to hear what they must hear if they are to be saved, as is taught in both the Old and the New Testaments?[3] Or is it because of a willful and very rebellious decision on their part to quit the walk with Mighty Victory and his legions?

What a pity, beloved! Opportunities come and go. I tell you, all is recorded. And thus, decisions not made and roads not taken are recorded on the ledger of your life and you will come full circle and encounter them again.

This is not a threat, beloved. This is a loving reminder. Do not take it as a chastisement but truly as a loving reminder that the way is up, and the way to go up is to keep on keeping on.

Thus endure, I say. Thus endure your karma! Do not be moved by it as though the tides of the sea and the winds could change your course moment by moment. Do not be moved by anything! You are more powerful than your astrology, than your psychology, than your karma, than all of the ruts in the road and all of those distractions that carry you astray.

You and the God within you are above all of this!

I say, how dare you subject yourself to simple astrological notations! Look at them with a glance, beloved, and then do the decree work so that you transmute the cause and core of your negative astrology.*

Then move onward and upward! Onward and upward!

The legions who come with me today are fierce! And we are fierce on the ray of wisdom. And in that fierceness we say: We will brook no interference with our mission to bring enlightenment and victory to all servants of God. We will brook no ignorance. We will not dillydally and we will not have you dillydallying!

We desire to see every single soul of light in the earth saved but, alas, we know that without your cooperation and the cooperation of the most advanced souls on the planet, this will not come to pass. And souls *will* be lost, as the Blessed Mother has said,[4] and they will not be found again.

Thus, we who make up the forces of Victory are all serving with a sense of urgency. We are all serving with a sense of immediate concern for the imbalances in the ecosystem of the earth. These imbalances do not bode well for the future.

Therefore, that thou and thy seed might live to take dominion over the earth and bring in a golden age, you must come into the centeredness of your own sense of what is worth having. That is the message of the day, beloved, brought to you by Jesus Christ and the Maha Chohan: You need to determine what is worth having and what is worth postponing for a greater purpose, a greater cause and a greater gift to be laid on the altar of God.[5]

I come, then, in the full light of the presence of the flame of victory that burns on the altar of the Court of the Sacred Fire, where Alpha and Omega await your Homecoming. That flame of victory, beloved, must be lowered deeper and deeper into the channels of the earth.

We desire to see you pull down that flame through your prayers to the Dhyani Buddhas, through your mantras, through every decree that you

---

*Your negative astrology also computes either as your negative karma or as the fallen angels' attack on your integrity, i.e., your soul's integration in God.

give. Call for the flame of victory to be anchored deeper and deeper in the earth that it might separate out those who are willfully of the vibration of non-victory, those who squander the life force and the sacred fire, who mock the Divine Mother and debase their four lower bodies in the misuse of the saving grace of God.

Blessed ones, I ask you to challenge the forces of an addictive materialism as well as those who are attached to them, those who perpetuate them, those who have come from other systems of worlds to be on this planet only for the pursuit and enjoyment of materialism. These have no desire to receive the Christ or the Buddha, for they have no desire to come up higher but rather to maintain the status quo of materialism as an end in itself.

It is the flame of victory that will move them, that will unearth them, that will also bring to them their positive and negative karma and break up the associations of individuals who horde money, horde supply, horde the goods of this world and thereby insulate themselves from their own karma.

What can we say, beloved? We can say that the dark forces of other planetary systems as well as planets such as the Twelfth Planet yet move on. Although they see the signs of their ultimate defeat, they also see the weakness and the cowardice among some who have had the teachings for years. And they mock these self-styled students. They mimic them. They make fun of them. For the weakness and cowardice of such students are of a truth chinks in the armour of the Great White Brotherhood on earth.

Look at those who have had the dispensations of the ascended masters in the Theosophical Society, the Rosicrucian Order, the Agni Yoga Society, the I AM movement and other forward movements that have begun to unveil the presence and teachings of great adepts in the earth. Look at the members of these organizations, beloved. Some have almost become intellectual snobs, for they do not use the teachings to challenge the forces of darkness in the earth but only to elevate themselves by their knowledge of the hidden wisdom.[6] They think of themselves as the wise ones, for they have such and such teaching that other earthlings do not have. This was never the Brotherhood's intent in the founding of esoteric organizations.

By contrast, here at Maitreya's Mystery School you are alive with the teachings, the masters are alive with the teachings and there is no need for you to crown us with laurels, nor for us to crown you. For we know who is God, we know who is the *one* God and we know that we are the vessel for that God and that we of ourselves are nothing, unless we are becoming more of that God day by day.

You, then, are on the right course. You have received what the nineteenth-century unascended adepts wanted you to receive. And now that they are ascended masters, they are well pleased that you have got the message, that you have understood the mystical paths of the world's religions and where those paths lead the soul. They know you have understood that the true teachings of the Old and New Testaments still stand and that you seek to act from the point of humility, for you know that humility is the point of the igniting of the fire of your victory.

Is that not so, beloved?

[Audience responds: "Yes!" (32-second standing ovation)]

Yes, beloved, review the messenger's lectures on Taoism and find the point of humility whereby you understand why the meek shall inherit the earth.[7] It is because ultimately those of pride will be judged and bound and removed to the levels of their karma while the meek stay centered in the eye of the T'ai Chi. And they in their meekness, in their humility, in their centeredness will therefore attract the greatest power of all—the power of the Almighty One.

There is, beloved, a certain enlightened self-interest in being humble. For the wise ones know that it is by humility that they will ultimately conquer self and the fallen ones, whereas those who rant and rave and come with their swords and their spears and ignite and reignite the wars that have gone on on this planet ad nauseam will never inherit the earth. The selfishness of the fallen ones leads to a false humility, whereas true *selflessness* leads to true humility.

Thus you have discovered the key. Keep it, beloved. Keep it.

There are many who have these teachings but who do not decree, do not invoke the flame of God, do not invoke the power of God. And therefore they and their organizations descend into a personality cult and they cut off the saving grace and the path of the Holy Spirit that is alive, that is burning, that is full of excitement in the joy of the New Age of Aquarius. That presence of the Holy Spirit escapes them and they descend into lower levels of the astral plane.

This is what has befallen many members of the New Age movement who see themselves as the vanguard of the age of Aquarius. Yet they have put aside the true teachings of God for something else that is distinctly not of the star of Aquarius rising.

And what is that something else? It is the adornment and lifting up of the human ego, exalting the ego as God. What a pity that any should spend a lifetime dallying in the psychic, or astral, state, beloved! It would be better for such a one to join the Pentecostals or the charismatics. Yes, beloved! For then that one would at least be anchored in the Holy Spirit and in the anointings. (You are welcome to be seated, blessed hearts.)

Our coming, then, this summer to Summit University with the Lord Christ and his legions[8]—*and he does come, beloved,* as the Faithful and True with armies of light[9]—is to support those legions. Our coming is to work with them. Our coming is to continually wash and bathe you in this glorious victory flame, this golden-yellow flame of illumination.

All retreats of the Brotherhood in the earth do keep the victory flame burning, no matter what the theme of the retreat. And they shall amplify that golden-yellow flame. . . .

Therefore understand that you have great good cause to support the activities of the Great White Brotherhood. For you see, if this movement can uphold the standards of high beings of light, then those high beings of light will have a secure place in which to be born and to carry on their missions on earth.

Where else shall we place these beings of light but in the community that most clearly reflects the etheric octaves and has the clearest pane of glass through which the teachings of the ascended masters may shine?

We cannot entrust high souls to an environment where they will be bruised and battered and beaten and suffer all manner of burdens from their parents and society. We must have adepts on earth and we must have a mystery school that is worthy of those adepts so that they can come into your midst and support you and lift you up. These high souls, as they are born to chelas of this community throughout the world, will assist in your healing and give you that joy and that buoyancy whereby through your invocation of illumination's flame you shall absorb their light.

Therefore I say to all parents and those who are awaiting El Morya's sponsorship to have children: You must seek the Holy Spirit, and have in hand the gifts and anointings of the Holy Spirit, so that a contingency* of advanced souls who have volunteered to descend to earth can come into such a dark age as this Kali Yuga. And when they come, you must guard them from the ways of the fallen angels, their rock music and the abuses of the media and from all that saturates the brain and the body through wrong diet.

You must comprehend, beloved, all I have said. You must see how important it is and you must know that one of the priorities of the Lords of Karma is not to allow souls to embody through parents who either cannot or will not be accountable for them, who do not have the spiritual strength to sustain their own marriages, let alone harmony with their children.

The Lords of Karma are unwilling to send highly advanced souls until highly advanced parents make it their calling and their business in life to see to it that they are fully prepared to be parents to these children. I ask you to accept that challenge, to prepare yourselves and to work on the karma of your psychology, beloved, for the earth will rise according to the number of souls of caliber you and others may sponsor.

And if the Lords of Karma do not allow these advanced souls to come in, then who will lead the way for mankind?

Who will show them the way?

And who will be their examples?

---

*i.e, a group of advanced souls waiting to descend to planet Earth until there are parents fully prepared to receive them

Highly advanced parents are the greatest God-solution that the Lords of Karma and we of Victory's bands can propose to you this day for the problem of highly advanced souls incarnating midst the chaos of this era. We ask you to ponder this God-solution and to get serious about your own adeptship that you might either bear these souls or be their teachers, their wayshowers. I ask you, beloved, to give deep thought to this proposal and see how you can be a part of the team that implements it. Then give the Lords of Karma your response.

I come with this message, which is of profound importance. And I tell you, the Lords of Karma are very serious about not letting one of these little ones enter the scene only to be betrayed by their caregivers and then to be lost. It has happened again and again and again. And the Lords of Karma have said to you: "No, we will not send them only to see them set back on their spiritual path. Far better that they be in the higher octaves with Lord Maitreya awaiting the manifestation of the golden age than that they come in these hours when even some among you who have children are allowing them to be exposed to those influences of the media which they should never be exposed to."

Let a word to the wise, then, be sufficient. For you are indeed the wise ones but not always as wise as you might be in your care of the precious ones that are already in your arms.

Now, beloved, as we turn to the problems of the decade across the earth, keep yourselves informed and make the calls that challenge those situations which threaten the integrity of the youth. Challenge whatever you perceive to be an out-of-line state of consciousness on the part of your leaders in every nation. *Challenge that state of consciousness!* Call for right mindfulness and the perfect geometry for the God-solution to every problem.

The solutions that have been proposed, I tell you, are the product of the deplorable mess the human consciousness is in; for the squandering of the life force takes from the minds of those who ought to make right decisions the necessary energy that they must have to attune with the mind of God.

When politicians make decisions for the sake of being popular and not for the sake of wisdom and the survival of the peoples of the earth, I can tell you, it is a sign that civilization is at the level of the last days of Atlantis, as has already been said.

Thus, beloved, in the fullness of the vial of victory that the attending angel now holds in his hand, so receive that precious oil at the hour of midnight, when your day is through. Receive it whether your soul is in or out of the body (in sleep). A vial of victory is a vial of illumination's flame. It is the oil of that flame and it is the oil of wisdom.

Be the wise ones, beloved. For where shall we go to find other wise ones except among those who have gone beyond the physical and the mental planes to probe the etheric octaves, who know deep within that they are a part of the legions of Victory?

Hail to you, my beloved! Hail to the light of God!

Be still and know that where you are is God, and you shall fulfill all that you determine to fulfill.

[64-second standing ovation. Audience gives the salutation:]

Hail, Mighty Victory! Hail, Mighty Victory! Hail, Mighty Victory! Hail, Mighty Victory! Hail, Mighty Victory! Hail, Mighty Victory! Hail, Mighty Victory! Hail, Mighty Victory! . . .

June 30, 1994
Heart of the Inner Retreat
Royal Teton Ranch, Park County, Montana
ECP

40

GO FORTH AND DELIVER THE FIRE

Now I AM come! I plant seeds of victory into your hearts, into the heart of the earth as sparkling fire, as yellow lightning. And so my legions come. We move throughout the planes. We move throughout the centuries past, the centuries future. And we arrive here at the Heart of the Inner Retreat to greet you as the victorious ones or the ones who are determined to be victorious. [33-second standing ovation]

Thank you. (Won't you be seated.)

We thank you for this opportunity, an opportunity to be with you, to assist you, to strengthen you and to call you to identify with your own calling in life. This you must define even if you accomplish it by novenas to the Great Divine Director[1] or to the All-Seeing Eye of God.[2] Can anyone tell you what is your calling except the still small voice[3] within?

You may know many individuals and professionals who may guide you, counsel you, open the way to a certain path of learning that culminates in your having a profession that can defend even the very citadels of the lightbearers. Blessed ones, it is tragic that some among you do not know or seem to know who you are or where you should go or why. Blessed ones, it is important to do something rather than nothing. Let your *somethings* be very worthwhile, always toward the good of your fellowman, also toward your honor in caring for your families and your nation.

DETERMINE WHAT YOU SHALL CONTRIBUTE

Blessed ones, you must take steps even if they are first steps. For El Morya has said to me: "These souls must permanently become that balance of the yin and yang whereby they have the sense, the inner strength, the sharpness of the mind to say, 'I will take these steps and then I will see where they lead me. And I will pray each step of the way and I will do something rather than nothing.'"

That is the message that El Morya would leave with me to give to you. For you see, beloved, life moves on and it moves quickly and you must engage. You must engage your teeth. You must engage your body and your mind and say: "I will study *this* so that I may have this certain accomplishment, this skill, this art, this application of technology. And therefore I will make something of myself for my community, for my family. And as a parallel road I shall also seek my spiritual destiny; and I shall place that first but not necessarily foremost, for I have responsibilities, and those responsibilities have to do with my karma."

Now, beloved, it is absolutely necessary that when you go forth from this conference you determine what shall be your handiwork, what shall be the expression of the mind, what shall you contribute to coming generations as this world is turning and technology advances almost faster than people can compute what is happening.

So, beloved, I make these my opening remarks. For I would say it is high time that you got on with something rather than nothing, those of you who are so uncertain in your destiny. Well, I will tell you, your destiny is to become an ascended master. And since you have trouble figuring out how to do that, I should say you should run to the heart of the messenger and apply to be on staff so that you can realize that you are a part of a much larger and vaster calling in God. This is a destiny of ages and it shall reach out throughout the planetary body. Thus, become a part of community if you have not found yourself, and attempt to do so while you are here. For the ages move on and the challenges are great.

USE THE SCIENCE OF THE SPOKEN WORD
TO TALK TO OTHERS OF WHAT YOU KNOW

Therefore we, the victorious ones, speak of all people on earth and specifically the lightbearers who have the violet flame. I am certain you realize that many in the 1930s knew of the violet flame.[4] But with the passing of the Ballards, there has not been such a proliferation of the violet flame except through this activity and through this messenger. Others have taken it up but we have not heard in another place such a fire, such a delivery, such an energy as the messenger has put out to you, not only in the violet-flame decrees but throughout this conference.

You must understand that this is what the meaning of determination is: Whether you are well, whether you are sick, whether you are weak, whether you are tired, you go forth and you deliver that fire, beloved, and that fire will never fail you. So, beloved, it is determination—not necessarily tremendous brain power but an absolute will, an absolute focus that says, "Saint Germain needs me for this cause. I am going."

Now, *we* like to hear that from yourselves also. And if you are not able to figure it out, well, join our teams this summer. Go out and hit the road. Come and meet people who need what you have. Feel that self-worth when you can deliver the teachings of the violet flame. Those who would rather remain here, that is wonderful; you will learn a great deal also. But, I tell you, there is nothing like meeting people to decide *what* you want to be, *who* you want to be, and who you do *not* want to be like, based on your interactions.

If you have not had public speaking or have felt shy about even talking to a few people, I say, overcome that. For El Morya is your champion. He, along with Saint Germain and the Maha Chohan, has given you the science of the spoken Word. Yes, the science of the spoken Word—you can use it in decrees, beloved, but you must also use it to talk to others of what you know and what is inside of you.

Don't second-guess people. If your Holy Christ Self moves you, if you feel that impelling in your heart to bring up the subject—perhaps a simple subject of the violet flame, perhaps a subject of the inner presence of God, something that you can talk about that is not too deep, not too complex, that will not frighten people away—you will begin to break the ice within yourself. You will begin to know how to talk to people, at first simply, perhaps even haltingly. But as you see how people respond to you and receive your message, you will realize how much more you know just by knowing your I AM Presence, the law of karma, the law of reincarnation, who you are and who you think you might have been in a past life.

MERCURIANS BOTH INSIDE AND OUTSIDE THIS ORGANIZATION

People all over the world have not even touched the hem of the garment of this teaching. Therefore, there are many Mercurians in this organization. There are Mercurians who are in the service of God Mercury; Hermes Trismegistus is his name. There are other Mercurians who live in their own pride. These you will see also. Some of them are newscasters or newspaper writers: they are usually in the communications media. They also use their position and their power but they may use it to manipulate politics, to manipulate the government, depending on what they put out in the evening news or in the newspapers across the country. . . .

They enjoy that pride and being looked upon as great men, but one day they must go the way of all flesh also. And one day they must return to bend the knee before the living Saviour Jesus Christ and know a humility that they have not known in this life. Well, beloved, such it is in many professions of the world when those who climb to the top think that they are, so to speak, the very best. They may lord it over others. They become proud, and their pride goes before their fall and often they fail.

So, beloved ones, as we return to the power of the spoken Word, the written word, the communications, that which you can receive on email, that which you can do with your computers, realize that there is no place on earth that you cannot reach when you have that connection. Understand this, beloved. Saint Germain has brought to you this communication system. Use it for all you are worth, for you never know when you meet a soul of light. And you never know when you will be called upon to explain what is reincarnation and karma, what is the second death, what is this, what is that.[5]

So, beloved, as you go out and share the deepest feelings of your heart, the greatest love of your being for so many people that you see and know yet you cannot reach, then call upon me. Call upon the legions of Victory. We will open the way, we will open the mouth, we will open your heart. And you will find yourself being one of the rescuers and then joining the bands of Victory.

CALL FOR THE BINDING OF THE PRIDE
OF THE FALLEN ANGELS

Yes, beloved, there are great victories to be won. There are challenges to be met. And the days coming may be dark days for a while—we hope not for too long. Yet, beloved, many must have their votes on earth who know nothing of the future. They have their votes; they spend them every day by misusing the science of the spoken Word in anger, argumentation, aggravation and all sorts of movements within the subconscious that erupt on the surface, revealing their true identity. And then you realize, Well, just how many fallen ones can there be in the governments of nations around the earth? And you begin to ask yourself, as you see the way the nations are going, how much evil there must be in those very ones who began on the first ray and then turned their back upon it, for they would rather follow Lucifer or Satan or Beelzebub.

Yes, there are many fallen ones who fell because they were on the first ray and they then took up their stations of pride. And they consider themselves greater than all other human beings, all other peoples on the planet. This is how they got that way, beloved. And this is how they have moved through the earth, destroying the governments, the economies of the nations, all of which does fall under the first ray.

How important it is in your labors to go after the fallen angels for the binding of their pride. When their pride is broken, beloved, what do they have left? It is almost as though it were a bag of sawdust, and you cut it open and that is all that is there—pride and sawdust and nothing else, yet they move about with such pomp. That pomp, beloved, betrays the LORD God but it also exposes them. Beware of the proud, beloved; beware of them.

A DISPENSATION FROM THE GREAT CENTRAL SUN

Now, in my sealing words to you in this conference, I would touch upon the subject once again of the children—of the children, beloved, and your prayers for them before they take embodiment, while in the womb and as life moves on. These are the tender vines, the tender vines.

I have received a dispensation from the Great Central Sun that all children in the earth shall have a single, powerful, mighty presence of an angel victorious from my bands. This aid shall continue [with them] through the age of thirty-three, beloved. One victorious, powerful, God-free angel of Victory—this I send to you. And these I send with you to your homes and places of worship that we might see the brightness of golden-yellow flames transforming every nation from whence you have come.

With this greeting and gift, beloved, I bow to the light within you. Call upon your angel. Give him the name you desire. Then call and call and call upon the LORD God.

I AM Mighty Victory in your heart forever if you will have me.

[1-minute applause. Audience gives the salutation:]

Hail, Mighty Victory! Hail, Mighty Victory! Hail, Mighty Victory!
Hail, Mighty Victory! Hail, Mighty Victory! Hail, Mighty Victory!
Hail, Mighty Victory! Hail, Mighty Victory! Hail, Mighty Victory!
Hail, Mighty Victory! Hail, Mighty Victory! Hail, Mighty Victory!
Hail, Mighty Victory! Hail, Mighty Victory! Hail, Mighty Victory!
Hail, Mighty Victory! Hail, Mighty Victory! Hail, Mighty Victory!

July 7, 1996
Heart of the Inner Retreat
Royal Teton Ranch, Park County, Montana
ECP

EPILOGUE

The Victory Consciousness. Incomparable. Unstoppable. Indomitable!

Now that you have experienced its buoyant, fiery essence in these forty messages from heaven, the choice is yours. The earthly way or Mighty Victory's way. The failure consciousness or the Victory Consciousness.

If these messages have touched your heart, if you've tried the victory affirmations and felt their powerful thrust, if you feel drawn to Victory's accelerated spirals and can't wait to unleash them in your life, say farewell to the status-quo and join us for the upward trek.

Behind these messages stands an organization and a movement, The Summit Lighthouse, that is committed to sweeping the earth with the Victory Consciousness.

Here, you'll find many choices.

Read our classics on a wide range of spiritual topics to become more familiar with the teachings of the ascended masters and learn more about the science of the spoken word, the spiritual science behind the mantras and affirmations in this book.

Study cosmic law and the truths of life at Summit University®, which offers a plethora of transformative online courses as well as fascinating seminars held yearly around the world.

Become a member of the Keepers of the Flame Fraternity®, dedicated to keeping the flame on behalf of a mankind sorely in need of a deeper understanding of the purpose of this beautiful thing we call life.

Each of these options is described in detail in the pages following the notes. We hope you will join us—because the strength of a forward thrust lies in the united heart flames of those who believe in that thrust. Nevertheless, if you'd rather go it alone, we applaud you for every step taken towards the Victory Consciousness and we say, Godspeed!

So yes, the choice is yours. May it be for the Victory, and may you win all the way!

NOTES

Prologue

1. *The "I AM" Discourses*, by Mighty Victory (Chicago, Ill.: Saint Germain Press, 1949), pp. 3–4, 279.

2. Ibid., p. 272.

3. Exod. 3:13–15.

4. "Aum Tat Sat Aum" is an ancient mantra in Hindu texts and worship. *The Encyclopedia of Eastern Philosophy and Religion* explains that these Sanskrit words literally mean "Om! That is Being." *That* refers to brahman, absolute Being, which is manifesting as the creation (p. 255).

A Primer about Mighty Victory and the Ascended Hosts

1. Godfré Ray King, *Unveiled Mysteries* (Schaumburg, Ill.: Saint Germain Press, 1982), p. 247.

2. *The "I AM" Discourses*, by Mighty Victory, pp. 3–4.

3. Justina, "The Forgiveness of Eve," Part 1, 2000 *Pearls of Wisdom**, vol. 43, no. 20, May 14, 2000.

4. "Always Victory!" chap. 36, pp. 316–17.

5. "The Name of the Game Is Victory!" chap. 18, p. 162.

6. "Indomitable Greetings of Cosmic Victory," chap. 14, p. 134.

7. "A Spiral for Christ Victory," chap. 21, p. 187.

---

*Throughout these notes, *PoW* is the abbreviation for *Pearls of Wisdom*.

CHAPTER 1

1. Mark Prophet taught that the story of Ruth and Boaz in the Book of Ruth symbolized the correct relationship between the soul and the I AM Presence.
2. John 14:12.

CHAPTER 2

Introductory quotation: II Peter 1:3, 4.

1. See Paul the Venetian, September 3, 1961, "O God, Help Me!" 1992 *Pearls of Wisdom,* vol. 25, no. 53, December 29, 1992, pp. 489–94.
2. Ps. 82:6; John 10:34.
3. John 8:32.
4. The ascended masters teach that it is not necessary to actually raise the physical body in order to ascend. The soul itself may take flight from the mortal coil and be translated through the ascension process, while the physical remains may be consigned to the sacred fire through the ritual of cremation. Although there are instances of a physical ascension noted in the scripture (Enoch, Elijah, Jesus Christ; see Gen. 5:24; Heb. 11:5; II Kings 2:1, 11; Mark 16:19; Luke 24:51; Acts 1:9), the physical ascension does require a 100 percent balancing of karma; whereas through the dispensation of the Aquarian age the Great Law exacts the 51 percent balance of karma, thereby enabling the soul to balance the remaining 49 percent after the ascension. In this case, the ascension process is almost never a physical one, but it is just as real and can be observed by the clairvoyant or those caught up in the extrasensory perception of the Holy Spirit. See Serapis Bey, *Dossier on the Ascension* (The Summit Lighthouse); and Mark L. Prophet and Elizabeth Clare Prophet, "Your Ultimate Destiny," in *The Spiritual Quest,* Sacred Adventure Series 1 (Summit University Press), chapter 7.
5. I John 3:2.
6. The civilization and lifewaves of the planet Venus have long ago attained to the enlightenment and peace of a golden age. Their consciousness and life evolution exists in another dimension of the physical plane corresponding to that of the etheric octave. Many of the most enlightened among earth's evolutions—inventors, artists, and seers—have come to earth from this higher plane of consciousness to transfer the blessings of God-dominion to the lifewaves of our planet.
7. Here the devotee is instructed not to adore the lesser self, but the God Self, or mighty I AM Presence—the Presence of God individualized for each son and daughter of light.

CHAPTER 3

1. Matt. 6:28; Luke 12:27.
2. Mighty Victory is referring to the painting of himself that is in *The "I AM" Discourses,* by Mighty Victory.

CHAPTER 4

1. John 1:29.
2. Phil. 4:7.
3. Mark 4:39.
4. Gen. 6:4.
5. Emile Coué (1857–1926), French psychologist.
6. Matt. 8:10, 9; Luke 7:9, 8.
7. John 14:2.

CHAPTER 5

1. Luke 2:14.
2. John 14:27.

CHAPTER 6

1. Matt. 28:9.
2. Gen. 1:27.
3. Luke 15:7.
4. Ps. 2:7; Acts 13:33; Heb. 5:5.
5. Mark 1:11.
6. The Cuban Missile Crisis was resolved in late November 1962 and significant progress was made toward a Nuclear Test-Ban Treaty that was eventually signed on August 5, 1963.
7. See Luke 18:5.
8. See Rev. 3:20.
9. Matt. 24:40, 41.
10. John 5:25.
11. Mighty Victory refers here to a six-pointed star of yellow chrysanthemums that was mounted on the altar.

CHAPTER 8

1. In a dictation delivered by Elizabeth Clare Prophet on March 19, 1995, Saint Germain said: "My precious one is present today, my beloved Anita Buchanan, who celebrates her ninetieth birthday. She does know the meaning of the days and the times and the seasons, and it was she who, as Queen Isabella, did provide the funds for me to make that voyage to the West Indies. Therefore I bow to this blessed soul of light. And I give to her my love and my commitment for the hour of her victory."
2. Acts 9:5; 26:14.
3. For the story of David Lloyd see *Unveiled Mysteries* (Chicago: Saint Germain Press, 1939), pp. 236–42.

CHAPTER 9

1. Ps. 121:1, 2.
2. Deut. 6:4.
3. Scripture records that Jesus was taken up by a cloud into heaven. This is commonly referred to as Jesus' ascension. However, the ascended masters have revealed that Jesus lived many years after this event and made his ascension after his passing from Kashmir at the age of 81.
4. Matt. 28:20.
5. Acts 1:11.

CHAPTER 10

1. Jude 13.
2. See Rev. 1:16, 20; 2:1; 3:1; 6:13; 12:4.
3. On July 2, 1966, Orion, the Old Man of the Hills, spoke about the intent of the dark forces to undermine both the economy and the values of America. He pointed out that if the eternal values were not kept, the children of God in America would not be able to keep their freedom.
4. I Sam. 3:1–18.

CHAPTER 11

1. Ps. 16:10.
2. II Pet. 2:14, 15.
3. Jon. 1:17.
4. Luke 22:44.
5. John 20:29.
6. See "The Royal Teton Retreat," in *The Masters and Their Retreats*, by Mark L. Prophet and Elizabeth Clare Prophet (The Summit Lighthouse).
7. Matt. 4:3, 6; Luke 4:3, 4, 9–11.
8. Luke 4:8; Matt. 4:4.
9. Gen. 19:4.
10. Gen. 17:19; 18:13.
11. Gen. 18:15.
12. Rom. 12:19.
13. Heb. 12:6.
14. Prov. 9:10.
15. I John 4:18.
16. Two ciphers, contained in the works of various Elizabethan writers and in the orig-

inal editions of the Shakespearean plays, reveal that Francis Bacon wrote the plays attributed to William Shakespeare. See Virginia M. Fellows, *The Shakespeare Code* (The Summit Lighthouse).

CHAPTER 12

This dictation by Mighty Victory is published in the form of affirmations as decree 22.04, "The Victory Way of Life," in *Prayers, Meditations and Dynamic Decrees for Personal and World Transformation,* available at the bookstore at www.SummitLighthouse.org.

1. Thomas More, *A Dialogue of Comfort,* in *The Complete Works of St. Thomas More,* ed. Louis L. Martz and Frank Manley (New Haven: Yale University Press, 1976) 12:155.

2. Rev. 7:17; 21:4.

3. Ps. 82:6; John 10:34.

CHAPTER 13

1. See the profile of Saint Germain (who was the "Wonderman of Europe") in *The Masters and Their Retreats,* by Mark L. Prophet and Elizabeth Clare Prophet.

CHAPTER 14

1. Asha is one of the six high deities of Zoroastrianism, attendants of Ahura Mazda. Asha represents personified righteousness.

2. Ps. 24:1.

3. I John 4:4.

4. Luke 15:7.

5. II Tim. 2:15.

CHAPTER 16

1. See Matt. 20:1–16.

2. John 10:30.

3. Rev. 19:10; 22:9.

CHAPTER 17

1. Ps. 91:10.

2. Luke 23:43.

3. Ps. 46:10.

4. Matt. 24:40.

5. See "The Initiation of the Ten," 2000 *PoW,* vol. 43, no. 7, February 13, 2000.

6. I Cor. 15:53.

7. In the 1920s jazz music and dance styles became popular, especially in the United States.

8. The Yom Kippur War had just erupted on the world scene on October 6, 1973. Egypt and Syria launched a surprise attack on Israel who then retaliated by crossing the Suez Canal to attack the Egyptian Third Army. The war escalated into a grave crisis between the superpowers, the United States and the Soviet Union, threatening to lead to a nuclear war. A compromise was swiftly worked out, however, resulting in a UN-monitored cease-fire on October 24, 1973.

9. Rev.12:1.

10. These rosaries are available at our online bookstore. The rosaries for the seven rays (one for each day of the week and Sunday evening) and the rosaries for the five secret rays (for weekday evenings) are on *Mother Mary's Scriptural Rosaries for the New Age*, 2 MP3 audios. For 15-minute scriptural rosaries, for children and adults, see *A Child's Rosary to Mother Mary*, 2 MP3 audios. Visit the bookstore at www.SummitLighthouse.org. These rosaries are also available for purchase as downloads or CDs at www.AscendedMasterLibrary.org.*

11. Phil. 2:5.

12. Luke 21:26.

13. Isa. 21:11.

14. Eph. 6:11.

CHAPTER 18

1. II Tim. 2:15.

2. The angel that Mighty Victory is speaking of is called the Angel de la Independencia. She is a golden, winged angel standing as a symbol of the victory of Mexico on a 50-ft. high stone column. The statue is situated in the center of the fourth traffic circle on the Paseo de la Reforma in Mexico City.

CHAPTER 19

1. On December 31, 1973, Gautama Buddha released the thoughtform for 1974. He said: "Out of the golden capsule, spherical in shape, is unfolded before my gaze the image of the face of Almighty God. And this thoughtform is placed in the heart of the earth, in the heart of the sun of even pressure. Thus it has been said that no man shall see the face of God and live [Exod. 33:20]. God says, 'No man shall see the face of God and live as man,' for to see that face, that Image Holy, is to be transformed in the likeness of God."

2. See Rev. 19:20; 20:2, 3.

3. See Ray-O-Light's dictation, "O Fearlessness, How I Love Thee," 1974 *PoW*, vol. 17, no. 3, January 20, 1974.

---

*Throughout these notes, AML is the abbreviation for the Ascended Master Library. www.AscendedMasterLibrary.org

4. Ps. 46:10.
5. Matt. 25:40.
6. Heb. 13:2.

CHAPTER 20

1. Matt. 18:6.
2. On April 26, 1975, Lucifer was found guilty of total rebellion against Almighty God and was sentenced to the second death by the unanimous vote of the Four and Twenty Elders at the Court of the Sacred Fire on the God Star, Sirius.

CHAPTER 21

This dictation by Mighty Victory is published as decree 22:02 in the decree book, *Prayers, Meditations and Dynamic Decrees for Personal and World Transformation,* available at the bookstore at SummitLighthouse.org.

1. See John 10:3.
2. Eph. 3:16, 17.

CHAPTER 22

1. The Dark Cycle began on April 23, 1969, and marked the beginning of a period of the intensification of mankind's returning individual and collective karma. In this period of transition from the Piscean to the Aquarian age, the Great Law required that the evolutions of earth deal directly with the momentums of personal and planetary karma set aside for centuries by the grace of God through Jesus Christ and other avatars. In the face of the same propensity for darkness prevalent before the Flood, when "the wickedness of man was great in the earth" and "every imagination of the thoughts of his heart was only evil continually" (Gen. 6:5), the Lords of Karma implemented this action in order to deter an even greater abuse of life's opportunity and to forestall that cataclysm which might be the ultimate consequence of the rising tide of world sin. The Dark Cycle concluded on April 22, 2002.
2. Mark 15:34; Matt. 27:46.
3. Matt. 22:12, 13.
4. Matt. 5:16.
5. Dan. 12:7; Rev. 12:14.

CHAPTER 23

1. Matt. 13:30.

CHAPTER 24

1. See song 556, "Victory, O Victory," sung to the melody of "Gaudeamus Igitur,"

published in the *Book of Hymns and Songs,* available at the bookstore at Summit-Lighthouse.org.

2. Ps. 2:4.

3. John 8:44.

4. "Keep Moving! Fearlessness Flame for Personal and Planetary Initiations in 1976" by Ray-O-Light, given December 28, 1975, is published in the 1982 *PoW,* book 1, vol. 25, no. 29, July 18, 1982, pp. 305–13.

CHAPTER 25

1. Prov. 4:7.

2. The Jupiter Effect refers to a theory put forward by scientists John Gribbin and Stephen Plagemann that a rare planetary alignment of nine planets lined up visibly in the sky and reaching its maximum on March 10, 1982, would cause a major slippage of the San Andreas Fault with the consequent destruction by earthquake of Los Angeles and other California cities.

3. May Day is the day of the celebration of Saint Germain's Ascension Day (1684) and his Coronation Day (1954) as Hierarch of the Aquarian Age.

4. The twelve hierarchies of the Sun surround the central altar of Alpha and Omega. They are cosmic beings and solar hierarchies who act as step-down transformers for the energies of God and are referred to by the names of the signs of the zodiac.

5. These *Pearls of Wisdom* by Sanat Kumara are published as the book *The Opening of the Seventh Seal: Sanat Kumara on the Path of the Ruby Ray* (The Summit Lighthouse), available at the bookstore at SummitLighthouse.org.

6. Matt. 24:27.

CHAPTER 26

1. John 1:1.

2. Before the dictation, the messenger read selections from an undocumented source on the life of Ludwig van Beethoven. On one occasion, Beethoven is reported to have said: "My kingdom is the air. Just like the wind, tones whirl around and so often eddy in my soul. I never wrote noisy music, for my instrumental works need an orchestra of about sixty good musicians and I am convinced that only such a number can bring out the quickly changing gradations in performance."

3. In her meditations on freedom before and after the conference, the messenger said that she understood why the friends of freedom did not rise on the planetary body. "I see clearly," she said. "It is the discouragement, depression and forces of confusion that are anti-freedom. As a conglomerate of energy and consciousness, they are condemnation. And this condemnation is in opposition to the release of the stupendous power of God on the twelve o'clock line by its hierarch, the Great Divine Director. So I decided to make a new vow to Almighty God to give my calls daily for the binding of the forces of condemnation on every friend of freedom on earth."

4. The "terrible crystal" is the purging light of the ruby ray contained in the sacred fire and the word of Sanat Kumara. The messenger described it as "the pure white fire, sometimes tinged with yellow, that bears the judgment of the LORD."

5. Heb. 4:12.

6. Luke 12:51.

CHAPTER 27

1. Heb. 11:1.

2. On July 2, 1981, during *An Inner Retreat*, Archangel Michael thrust his sword of blue flame "into the very heart of America—making it, therefore, congruent with the arch of Saint Louis," the city over which Archangel Chamuel and Archeia Charity maintain an etheric retreat. "Realize that it is a rallying point whereby love in the heart of the archangel of the first and the third ray converge by the power of God." See Archangel Michael, "I AM for the Union," 1981 *PoW,* vol. 24, no. 31, August 2, 1981, pp. 333–34.

3. Refers to the annual Independence Day parade with floats, choreography, and spirited dramatic readings by students from all over the world. The parade featured the second-place prize-winning float "The Caribbean," sponsored by the Sons and Daughters of Afra Study Groups from the Los Angeles area, who released "violet flame" (violet smoke) and clouds of "infinite energy" (violet balloons) to saturate the Caribbean. First prize was awarded to the Washington, D.C. Teaching Center for their presentation on the theme "I Claim the Mantle!" which included readings by Keepers of the Flame portraying George Washington, Abraham Lincoln, John Kennedy, and Ronald Reagan as well as a colorful depiction of the Goddess of Freedom, Portia, the mighty Blue Eagle, and the Flaming Sword.

4. Further teachings on twin flames, given at the *"Twin Flames in Love!"* seminars March 10–12, April 21–24, 1978, are available on *Twin Flames in Love,* and in 1978 *PoW,* vol. 21, nos. 34–47, pp. 177–246. See also Gautama Buddha, April 5, 1980, "Keeping the Light of the Guru-Chela Relationship and the Cosmic Integration of Twin Flames," 1980 *PoW,* vol. 23, no. 23, June 8, 1980, pp. 139–44.

5. On April 18, 1981, Gautama Buddha came for "the arcing of the flame of Shamballa to the Inner Retreat as the Western abode of the Buddhas and the bodhisattvas and the bodhisattvas-to-be who are the devotees of the Mother light." See 1981 *PoW,* book 1, vol. 24, no. 20, May 17, 1981, pp. 226, 227.

6. Refers to the transfer of the light of the ascension, the "forcefield of Luxor," to the heart of the messenger December 28, 1979. See Serapis Bey, "Start a Flame of Purity." Also refers to the final balancing of the karma of the messenger, announced by Saint Germain on November 5, 1980: "In the presence of that light of the one-hundred-percent balance of that karma, there is opportunity for the entire Spirit of the Great White Brotherhood to anchor through the messenger untold momentums of light and victory and freedom even while she then is able to bear a more than ordinary measure of your own personal karma—which she is so delighted

to do to see you accelerate on the Path that you, too, might attain your victory!" See Saint Germain, "A Victory Celebration: Almighty God Is the Winner!" 1980 *PoW,* vol. 23, no. 46, November 16, 1980, p. 304.

7. *indulgence:* in Roman Catholicism, plenary (full) or partial remission of temporal punishment due for sins whose guilt and eternal punishment have already been pardoned; usually granted in exchange for prayers and devotional acts. It was the abuse of indulgences in the late medieval period, when indulgences could be obtained by monetary contributions, that instigated the Protestant Reformation.

8. Saint Germain has said that he made "two million right decisions" during hundreds of thousands of years of service on behalf of earth and her evolutions before making his ascension in 1684.

9. Acts 2:1.

10. Refers to *The Class of the Archangels,* December 28, 1980–January 1, 1981, Camelot. See 1981 *Pearls of Wisdom,* book 1, vol. 24, nos. 4–15, pp. 43–186. During the class, Archangel Zadkiel announced: "Blessed hearts, this is a great moment! And this is why *The Class of the Archangels* was convoked: that we might release, through the etheric plane into the etheric bodies of our students, certain grids and forcefields and momentums of light that will be the foundation of the golden age" (vol. 24, no. 6, February 8, 1981, p. 70).

11. Refers to the *Freedom Class of 1961* (July 1–4)—the first Summit Lighthouse conference attended by the messenger Elizabeth Clare Prophet.

12. Refers to the dispensation announced by Kuan Yin July 3, 1981: "On this planetary body sufficient numbers of chelas of the ascended masters with considerable momentum of light in embodiment make it possible for the will of the lightbearers collectively . . . to override even the majority of the mass consciousness with its will to self-destruction and death. . . . The majority of light upon earth, not in numbers but in attainment, will be the determining factor in our judgments for the remainder of this decade." See 1981 *PoW,* vol. 24, no. 33, August 16, 1981, p. 354.

13. Ps. 24:1.

14. The name *Jeremiah* means literally "Yahweh hurls!" On July 3, 1981, during *An Inner Retreat,* the messenger presented "Jeremiah: Heartbeat of Freedom," the first in a series of lectures on the prophet Jeremiah, continued during the *Seminar of the World Teachers* (July 6–19, 1981). Lecture available from AML.

CHAPTER 28

1. Prior to this dictation, the messenger read Mark 14:1–25; John 13; Mark 14:26–72 on the Last Supper and Peter's denial of Christ. See also Matt. 26:31–35, 69–75; Luke 22:31–34, 54–62; John 18:15–18, 25–27.

2. *Watchers* and *Nephilim:* see 1983 *PoW,* vol. 26, no. 24, June 12, 1983, p. 207, n. 1.

3. Matt. 26:56; Mark 14:50.

4. In Alfred, Lord Tennyson's epic poem *Idylls of the King* (1885), King Arthur (an

incarnation of the ascended master El Morya) addresses his knights who have sworn their vow to quest the Grail. "'Ah, Galahad, Galahad,' said the King, 'for such / As thou art is the vision, not for these. / O my knights, / Your places being vacant at my side, / while ye follow wandering fires / Lost in the quagmire! Many of you, yea most, / Return no more.'" Despite his warning, the knights embark, and when only few return, Arthur again laments: "Was I too dark a prophet when I said / To those who went upon the Holy Quest, / That most of them would follow wandering fires, / lost to me and gone? / The King must guard / That which he rules, and / may not wander from the allotted field / Before his work be done. . ." Arthur's court, weakened by the absence of his knights, became divided, leading to the destruction of Camelot and the death of the king.

5. As taught by Mother Mary to the messenger Elizabeth Clare Prophet, the twelve lines of the cosmic clock correspond to the twelve solar hierarchies, with accompanying God-qualities. See Elizabeth Clare Prophet's *The Great White Brotherhood in the Culture, History, and Religion of America*, pp. 173–206; and *Predict Your Future: Understand the Cycles of the Cosmic Clock*; The Summit Lighthouse.

6. Isa. 14:12.

7. Mary, the Mother of Jesus and Queen of the Angels, is the divine complement (archeia) of Archangel Raphael. Together, they serve on the fifth (green) ray of truth. When Mary was chosen by God to incarnate on earth to give birth to the Christ, Archangel Raphael remained in the planes of Spirit, manifesting the balance of flow between heaven and earth, "as Above, so below." Archeia Mary tells of her experience with Raphael before the throne of Alpha and Omega in chapter 10 of *Vials of the Seven Last Plagues*, pp. 66–68, The Summit Lighthouse, paperback. See also Mark L. Prophet and Elizabeth Prophet, *Mary's Message for a New Day* (The Summit Lighthouse), pp. 33–46 (previously titled *My Soul Doth Magnify the Lord!*, pp. 25–39).

8. Mark 14:72.

9. Prior to the Allied victories in 1945 that brought World War II to a close, Prime Minister Winston Churchill, President Franklin Delano Roosevelt, and Premier Josef Stalin met at Yalta (February 4–11, 1945). The "Big Three" made far-reaching decisions concerning the postwar world. They approved plans for the creation of the United Nations and agreed to carve up Germany into four military zones to be occupied and controlled by the United States, Great Britain, the Soviet Union, and France. In exchange for Stalin's promise to enter the war against Japan, Churchill and Roosevelt agreed to place the Mongolian People's Republic under Soviet protection and cede to the Soviets the Kuril Islands, the southern half of Sakhalin Island, an occupation zone in Korea, and certain rights in Manchuria. Under the terms of the Yalta Pact, Churchill and Roosevelt ultimately gave the Soviets control of Manchuria, paved the way for the Chinese Communists' victory over Chiang Kai-shek, the Chinese Nationalist leader, and opened the door to Communist aggression in Korea. The decisions made at Yalta permitted the Soviet occupation of East Berlin and East Germany, and the creation of the Communist governments in the eastern European countries of Poland, Czechoslovakia, Yugoslavia, Hungary,

Romania, and Bulgaria. In short, Roosevelt and Churchill* entrusted the security of eighty million eastern Europeans and hundreds of millions of Chinese to the Soviet Union, resulting in the murder of millions of freedom-fighters in those countries. In his book *FDR: The Other Side of the Coin,* Hamilton Fish states that U.S. entry into World War II was initiated by Roosevelt during peace negotiations with Japan, when he circumvented Congress and issued a secret war ultimatum to Emperor Hirohito on November 26, 1941. It demanded that Japan immediately "withdraw all military, naval, air, and police forces from China and Indochina, to support no other government . . . in China except Chiang Kai-shek," and, in effect, abrogate Japan's pact with the Axis powers. On the morning of December 7, Japan responded to Roosevelt's threat by bombing the bulk of the U.S. fleet moored at Pearl Harbor, which resulted in the death of 2,280 U.S. military personnel, 68 civilians, and the destruction of 19 naval vessels and 188 aircraft. Fourteen hours before this attack, Roosevelt learned of the planned Japanese invasion but chose to remain silent.

10. The ascended masters teach that the seven rays of God are magnified corresponding to the seven days of the week: Saturday, the seventh (violet) ray of freedom; Sunday, the second (yellow) ray of wisdom; Monday, the third (pink) ray of love; Tuesday, the first (blue) ray of the will of God; Wednesday, the fifth (green) ray of truth; Thursday, the sixth (purple and gold) ray of peace; Friday, the fourth (white) ray of purity.

11. Matt. 27:15–26; Mark 15:6–15; Luke 23:13–25; John 18:39–19:16.

CHAPTER 29

1. Deut. 7:6; 14:2, 21; 26:19; 28:9; Isa. 62:12.

2. Rev. 20:14; *Corona Class Lessons,* by Jesus and Kuthumi (The Summit Lighthouse), pp. 193–99.

3. In preparation for the dictation, the messenger read Isaiah chapters 61 and 62 containing Isaiah's prophecy of the day of vengeance of our God and the restoration of Israel.

4. On May 8, 1983, Jesus gave a dictation on Ascension Hill at Camelot wherein he declared his Second Coming: "Thus I come in the Second Advent with clouds of glory, with hosts of the LORD, and with light. And that Second Advent is as the appearing of the sign of the descent of the entire chain of Christed One—of Sanat Kumara, Gautama Buddha, Lord Maitreya, and myself therefore embodying this Word in the messenger for a holy purpose. . . . I have come because it is the hour of the Second Advent . . . the coming of The LORD Our Righteousness within you!" See 1983 *PoW,* vol. 26, no. 43, October 23, 1983.

5. Matt. 6:5, 6.

6. Isa. 2:12; 13:6, 9, 13; 34:8; 61:3; 63:4; Jer. 46:10; Ezek. 30:3; Joel 1:15; 2:1, 31;

*Elizabeth Clare Prophet has explained that Roosevelt and Churchill had greatly differing views of postwar Europe, that Churchill privately opposed the Yalta agreement but supported it publicly so as to not endanger his alliance with America (Oct. 10, 1992).

Zeph. 1:7, 8, 14, 18; Zech. 14:1; Acts 2:20; I Thess. 5:2; II Pet. 3:10, 12; *Lost Teachings on Finding God Within,* by Mark L. Prophet and Elizabeth Clare Prophet (The Summit Lighthouse), pp. 101–18.

7. Ps. 139:7–10.

8. Phil. 3:14.

9. Jesus and Kuthumi, *Corona Class Lessons.*

10. Matt. 20:16; 22:14.

11. Matt. 7:13, 14.

12. Matt. 17:1–9; Mark 9:2–9; Luke 9:28–36; Elizabeth Clare Prophet, "Healing through the Transfiguration," in Jesus and Kuthumi, *Corona Class Lessons,* following p. 118.

CHAPTER 30

1. Referencing the fourth vision: the man with the measuring line: The Reverend C. I. Scofield's interpretation of Zechariah 2 quoted at the beginning of this and the following *Pearl* is as follows: "As in Zech. 1:8–11, the 'man' of verse 1 is 'the angel that talked with me' of verse 3. The measuring-line (or reed) is used by Ezekiel (Ezek. 40:3, 5) as a symbol of preparation for rebuilding the city and temple in the kingdom-age. Here also it has that meaning, as the context (vs. 4–13) shows. The subject of the vision is the restoration of nation and city. In no sense has this prophecy been fulfilled. The order is: (1) The LORD in glory in Jerusalem, v. 5 (cf. Matt. 24:29, 30); (2) the restoration of Israel, v. 6; (3) the judgment of Jehovah upon the nations, v. 8, 'after the glory' (Matt. 25:31, 32); (4) the full blessing of the earth in the kingdom, vs. 10–13" (*The Scofield Reference Bible,* p. 966, n. 3).

2. See Matt. 16:18.

CHAPTER 31

Before this dictation, the messenger read Matthew 21:1–7 and John 12:17–50.

1. Gen. 14:18; Ps. 110:4; Heb. 5:5–10; 6:20; 7. For further teaching on the subject of the Priesthood of Melchizedek, see:

- Elizabeth Clare Prophet, March 23, 1978, "The Mystery of the Priesthood of Melchizedek," on *The Second Coming of Christ II;* lecture available at Ascended Master Library (AML).

- Kuthumi, June 30, 1978, "Revolutionaries for the Coming Revolution: An Outer Order of the Priesthood of Melchizedek," on *"Find Your Way Back to Me";* at AML.

- Elizabeth Clare Prophet, January 24, 1982, "The Story of Our Father Abraham and of His Chela and of His Guru" and "The Apostle Paul on the Priesthood of Melchizedek," on *In the Heart of the Inner Retreat 1982;* at AML.

- The Beloved Messenger, February 15, 1986, "Christ the High Priest," 1986 *PoW,* book 1, vol. 29, no. 29, June 14, 1986, pp. 281–85.

- Archangel Zadkiel, May 25, 1986, "The Priesthood of the Order of Melchizedek," 1986 *PoW,* book 2, vol. 29, no. 57, November 9, 1986; on *The Healing Power of Angels,* Vancouver, B.C.; at AML.

- Saint Germain, May 28, 1986, "The Intercession of the Priesthood of Melchizedek," 1986 *PoW,* book 2, vol. 29, no. 58, November 10, 1986; dictation at AML.

- The Ascended Master Melchizedek, "To Sup with You in the Glory of Christ," and Elizabeth Clare Prophet, teachings on Melchizedek, "The Subtle Essence," June 15, 1986; at AML.

2. See Serapis Bey, December 28, 1985, "The Descent of the Mighty Blue Sphere," 1986 *PoW,* book 1, vol. 29, no. 15, April 13, 1986, pp. 121–32.

3. Gen. 3:24.

4. See Sanat Kumara, December 31, 1984, "The Turning Point of Life on Earth: A Dispensation of the Solar Logoi," 1985 *PoW,* book 1, vol. 28, no. 6, February 10, 1985, pp. 60–61. Also El Morya and Sanat Kumara, December 29, 1985, and January 26, 1986, 1986 *PoW,* book 1, vol. 29, nos. 17 and 24, April 27 and June 9, 1986, pp. 144–45, 219.

5. John 12:32.

6. Jer. 31:34.

CHAPTER 32

1. Wesak, May 13, 1987, marked the conclusion of the ten-year dispensation for the turning of the tide announced by Gautama Buddha in his May 3, 1977, Wesak address. See Gautama Buddha, "One Decade for the Turning of the Tide: The Great Central Sun Messengers, the Cosmic Christs, and the Buddhas Come Forth," 1978 *PoW,* vol. 21, no. 28, July 9, 1978, pp. 148–50.

2. Rev. 3:4, 5; 6:9–11; 7:9, 13, 14.

3. See n. 1 above.

4. I Cor. 9:27.

5. Matt. 23:27.

6. John 9:5. See Archeia Hope, January 2, 1987, "The Eternal Now Is My Hope," 1987 *PoW,* vol. 30, no. 4, January 25, 1987, p. 79.

7. I Pet. 3:4.

CHAPTER 33

1. On May 17, 1987, the U.S.S. *Stark,* a Navy frigate on routine patrol in the Persian Gulf, was hit by two Exocet missiles fired from either one or two Iraqi fighter jets. Thirty-seven U.S. sailors died in the attack.

2. See Archangel Jophiel, "The Hour of the Trumpet Judgments," 1987 *PoW,* vol. 30, no. 40, October 4, 1987, pp. 401–2.

3. John 4:35.
4. Rev. 8:1. See Saint Germain, "The Opening of the Seventh Seal," 1987 *PoW,* vol. 30, no. 37, September 13, 1987. In the lecture prior to Saint Germain's dictation, the messenger read and interpreted Revelation 8–11 on the opening of the seventh seal and the seven trumpet judgments. Lecture and dictation, delivered July 4, 1987, are available at the Ascended Master Library.
5. Matt. 3:10; Luke 3:9.
6. Deut. 14:2; Titus 2:13, 14; I Pet. 2:9.
7. Rom. 8:26, 27.

CHAPTER 34

1. Rev. 4:8; 15:4.
2. John 14:16, 26; 15:26; 16:7.
3. Eph. 5:14.
4. The gift of "a path of light": the light that is, and is the emanation of, the Christ consciousness.
5. John 5:25; 10:27, 28.

CHAPTER 35

1. *kal:* Hindi [Skt. *kala*], time; *desh:* Hindi [Skt. *desha*], place, space. See *Lost Teachings on Your Higher Self* (The Summit Lighthouse), pp. 3–40.
2. On December 25, 1986, Jesus announced that the God and Goddess Meru had placed themselves within golden-white spheres to be sustained over the Royal Teton Ranch as their presence with us (1986 *PoW,* book 2, vol. 29, no. 78, December 23, 1986, p. 682).
3. This refers to the seven Solar Logoi and the seven Holy Kumaras.
4. *starling:* a little star; *Oxford English Dictionary:* an inhabitant of a star.
5. Hindu tradition describes the Kumaras as the seven (sometimes four) mind-born sons of Brahma who forever retain their youthful purity and innocence and are called the "eternal youths" or "princes." Sanat Kumara [Skt. *sanat,* always, and *kumara,* youth] is said to be the most prominent of the Kumaras.
6. See Gautama Buddha, July 3, 1988, "Concerning Maitreya's Mystery School: The Line Is Drawn, the Standard Will Be Kept," 1988 *PoW,* book 2, vol. 31, no. 67, October 9, 1988.

CHAPTER 36

1. Gen. 2:9; 3:22, 24; Rev. 2:7; 22:2, 14.
2. In his dictation on August 8, 1988, El Morya announced that there would be no new dispensations for his chelas or for his world service from the Lords of Karma.

In short, he was "benched" until karma incurred by dispensations misappropriated or unappropriated by chelas and world servers might be sufficiently balanced. After a year-long intense worldwide effort to balance the karma, by the messengers and Keepers of the Flame together, El Morya, on August 8, 1989, made the announcement that he was "unbenched." El Morya said it was by the grace and intercession of Mother Mary and Kuan Yin as well as the extraordinary devotion of the messengers and the chelas.

3. The God and Goddess Meru, Manus of the sixth root race, are positioned at their retreat over Lake Titicaca in South America; and their spherical golden-white causal bodies are focused over the Royal Teton Ranch.

4. The Temple of the Sun is the etheric retreat of Helios and Vesta, located in the center of the physical sun. The Temple of the Sun is also the name of the retreat of the Goddess of Liberty located in the etheric plane over Manhattan (see *The Masters and Their Retreats*, by Mark L. Prophet and Elizabeth Clare Prophet, pp. 484–86).

5. *Archangel Michael's Rosary for Armageddon* includes prayers, decrees and hymns to the seven archangels and nine choirs of angels for the resolution of problems affecting your family, relationships, community and nation. Booklet and CD. For more information, visit the bookstore at SummitLighthouse.org or call customer service at 1-800-245-5445 or +1 406-848-9500.

6. *Victoria* is the feminine form of *Victor*. Both Mighty Victory and his twin flame are affirming here that they are the masculine and feminine forms of Victory. (*Victoria* is the Latin word for *victory*, which is derived from the Latin *victus*, pp. of *vincere* 'to conquer, win'.) The name of Mighty Victory's twin flame, Justina, was revealed in a dictation given by her on January 1, 1978.

7. For information about the Buddha of the Ruby Ray in the heart of the earth, see *The Masters and Their Retreats*, by Mark L. Prophet and Elizabeth Clare Prophet.

8. See 1988 *PoW*, book 2, vol. 31 no. 80, November 26, 1988, p. 633 n. 19; 1986 *PoW*, book 2, vol. 29, no. 78, December 23, 1986, pp. 681, 682.

CHAPTER 37

1. "Balance the Threefold Flame in Me!" decree 20.03; no. 6 on *Lanto, Lord of the Second Ray: Dynamic Decrees with Prayers and New Age Songs for Chelas of the Wisdom of God 1*.

2. For information about the rising tide of the astral plane, see 1989 *PoW*, vol. 32, no. 20, May 14, 1989, p. 226 n. 2.

3. Rev. 17:14. Rev. 19:11–16.

4. "Blessed is the man that endureth temptation: for when he is tried, he shall receive the crown of life, which the Lord hath promised to them that love him." James 1:12. See Rev. 2:10; 3:11; Mark L. Prophet, *Understanding Yourself*, pp. 81–82 (pocketbook ed.); Gautama Buddha, *Quietly Comes the Buddha*, pp. 85–86; Archangel Michael, 1985 *PoW*, book 1, vol. 28, no. 10, March 10, 1985, pp. 110–11; Serapis Bey and Saint Germain, 1982 *PoW*, book 2, vol. 25, no. 36, September 5, 1982,

pp. 343–44; no. 38, September 19, 1982, pp. 373–74; Mother Mary, 1973 *PoW,* vol. 16, no. 30, July 29, 1973, pp. 128–29.

5. Mal. 3:1.

6. Matt. 19:26; Mark 10:27; Luke 18:27.

7. See Elizabeth Clare Prophet, May 26, 1975, "The Eightfold Path and the Middle Way of Enlightenment," on the audio album *The Buddha and the Mother,* 1988 *PoW,* book 2, vol. 31, no. 63, September 25, 1988, p. 491; no. 64, October 1, 1988, pp. 494, 496 n. 3; 1983 *PoW,* vol. 26, no. 21, May 22, 1983, pp. 166–67.

8. Phil. 3:14.

9. Alpha's document was signed and sealed at 1 a.m. MST.

10. The *Only Mark* audio series contains the dictations of the ascended masters delivered through the messenger Mark L. Prophet, beginning with the final dictation given through him on February 18, 1973, and continuing back to 1958.

11. 1988 *PoW,* book 2, vol. 31, no. 77, November 13, 1988, p. 584; no. 78, November 19, 1988, p. 608; no. 80, November 26, 1988, p. 623.

CHAPTER 38

This dictation was by Mighty Victory and his twin flame, Justina.

1. In his dictation given June 27, 1992, Saint Joseph asked that we make the Call that night to be taken to the Royal Teton Retreat and from there angels would escort us to Yugoslavia (see 1992 *PoW,* book 2, vol. 35, no. 26, June 28, 1992, pp. 373–74). Prior to the dictation, the messenger and congregation had given Ashram rituals 4 and 5—Sacred Ritual for Soul Purification and Sacred Ritual for Transport and Holy Work. These two rituals assist the soul in performing world service while out of the body during the hours of rest. The rituals are published in *Ashram Notes,* by El Morya, pp. 37–42, 46–59, and *Ashram Rituals,* booklet, pp. 33–52. They are also available as the audio CD set D90028 at the bookstore at SummitLighthouse .org; and as separate rituals at AML.

2. On the day of Mighty Victory's dictation, June 28, 1992, two powerful earthquakes rocked southern California, killing one and injuring dozens of people. The first quake, at 4:58 a.m. (PDT), registered 7.4 on the Richter scale. Its epicenter was about 80 miles east of Los Angeles, and it was felt as far away as Denver. Following the quake there were more than 20 aftershocks, including one that measured 6.0 on the Richter scale. The second quake, about three hours later, at 8:07 a.m., was a magnitude of about 7.0 on the Richter scale and was centered in the San Bernardino Mountains, about 20 miles west of the first one. According to seismologist Kate Hutton, at the California Institute of Technology in Pasadena, scientists were considering whether the two earthquakes might portend an even larger shock on the San Andreas Fault itself. The first quake was 25 miles away and the second was 10 miles away from the fault. The most serious damage appeared to be concentrated in desert communities east of Los Angeles near the earthquake epicenter. Local

radio stations described the quakes as "gentle giants" because they did not cause major damage in heavily populated cities like Los Angeles, Las Vegas and Palm Springs. (Associated Press and Reuters)

3. On the day prior to Mighty Victory's dictation, June 27, 1992, Mount Spurr Volcano, which is 80 miles west of Anchorage, Alaska, erupted for the first time in 39 years. The eruption was large enough to throw steam and ash 5 miles into the atmosphere. (Associated Press and Reuters)

CHAPTER 39

Mighty Victory delivered this dictation representing the Cosmic Christ Consciousness of the Entire Spirit of the Great White Brotherhood.

1. Mighty Victory, with his twin flame, Justina, previously dictated on June 28, 1992, at *FREEDOM 1992: Joy in the Heart.* See chapter 38.

2. Mighty Victory's twin flame came forth in the 20th century. On January 1, 1978, at the *God Is Mother* New Year's class in Pasadena, California, beloved Justina dictated for the first time. In this landmark address, titled "The Forgiveness of Eve," she said: "Now I step forth, for Almighty God has weighed these several systems of worlds and the evolutions therein, and Almighty God has pronounced that certain evolutions of lightbearers do now contain within themselves enough consciousness of the victory of the feminine ray that I might stand forth and be with my Beloved . . . the focal point for the Father-Mother God in total awareness of the victory of evolutions in these systems. Beloved ones, the one whom you call Mighty Victory is indeed androgynous, as I am, as is Alpha, as is Omega. But as we come forth together, descending into lower and lower dimensions of awareness, we bring a greater complement of the spectrum of that cosmic polarity as a polarity of manifestation to those of lesser evolution. Therefore, though one may be sufficient in the whole, always twin flames are required for the transmutation of a cosmos." Justina's dictation is on *God Is Mother,* album II; dictation is available at AML.

3. Deut. 29:4; Isa. 6:9, 10; 29:10; Matt. 13:9–17; Mark 4:11, 12; John 12:37–40; Acts 28:24–28; Rom. 11:8, 10.

4. For *Pearls of Wisdom* on "souls will be lost," see 1986 *PoW,* book 2, vol. 29, no. 62, November 16, 1986, p. 546; 1989 *PoW,* vol. 32, no. 24, June 11, 1989, pp. 263–65; no. 32, August 6, 1989, pp. 470–71; 1990 *PoW,* vol. 33, no. 39, October 7, 1990, pp. 507–8; 1991 *PoW,* vol. 34, no. 1, January 6, 1991, p. 12; no. 11, March 17, 1991, p. 154; no. 49, October 16, 1991, p. 565; 1992 *PoW,* book 2, vol. 35, no. 34, p. 443; 1993 *PoW,* vol. 36, no. 8, February 21, 1993, p. 103; no. 35, August 29, 1993, pp. 505–6. See also 1991 *PoW,* vol. 34, no. 28, June 26, 1991, pp. 372–74; no. 43, September 8, 1991, pp. 503–7; 1992 *PoW,* book 2, vol. 35, no. 31, August 2, 1992, p. 416; 1994 *PoW,* vol. 37, no. 16, April 17, 1994, p. 160.

5. "What is worth postponing": see 1994 *PoW,* vol. 37, no. 30, July 24, 1994, pp. 354–56; no. 31, July 31, 1994, p. 370.

6. I Cor. 2:7.

7. Matt. 5:5.

8. Mighty Victory and Jesus Christ with their legions were co-sponsors of Summit University Summer Session 1994. In November 1993, beloved Jesus announced: "For Summit University Summer Session 1994, Mighty Victory, with his legions, will join me as co-sponsor for the most powerful release of illumination's flame in this century and a sustained momentum of victory for all lightbearers until April 23, 2002. . . . As for me, I come in the mantle and the armour of the Faithful and True and my legions attend me—and you. . . . Gather on the mountain with me and the armies of heaven, and together we shall work a work in our day that *none* shall turn back."

9. Rev. 19:11–21.

CHAPTER 40

1. For the novena to the Great Divine Director, see Saint Germain, "Divine Direction for the Path of Your Choosing," in 1975 *PoW*, vol. 18, no. 32, August 10, 1975, pp. 159–64, and decree 10.08, "The Great Divine Director," in *Prayers, Meditations and Dynamic Decrees for Personal and World Transfomation.*

2. Decree 50.05, "Beloved Cyclopea, Beholder of Perfection," is recorded at intermediate and advanced paces. See bookstore at www.SummitLighthouse.org.

3. I Kings 19:12.

4. Saint Germain released the violet flame dispensation in the early 1930s through the I AM Activity, which he founded through his messengers Guy and Edna Ballard. Both Ballards have now ascended and are known and loved as Godfre and Lotus, their ascended master names.

5. In a 1993 dictation, El Morya said: "The need of the hour is for careful spokesmen who may study the issues and study them well, who may also study the art and the craft of setting forth for public consumption those articles, those chapters, those books that may give an understanding of the pros and cons of the issues, of what is burdening the planetary body and what is burdening the bodies of the people. . . . You must see a vision and you must be able to impart that vision. . . .

   "What is needed is a spiritual army of lightbearers who recognize that they must study and burn the midnight oil and know the issues and be able to discuss them intelligently. . . . See yourselves in areas of specialization. One by one or in committee, you must take up one of the central issues of our time and you must become experts on that issue. . . . And then you must also wield the sword of the Spirit as experts as you give your dynamic decrees and make your calls. . . . Hermes Trismegistus . . . is the sponsor of my own path and the path of the messengers and all the Mercurians who bring forth the writings of the deep things of God, of public issues, setting forth that which comes forth from that diamond-shining mind of God for the edification of the root races." (El Morya, June 29, 1993, "The Victory of the Will of God: A Cause That Is Right," in 1993 *PoW*, vol. 36, no. 41, September 9, 1993, pp. 565, 566, 567, 569).

SUMMIT UNIVERSITY®

Summit University is a modern-day mystery school that teaches the science of the world's religions and the true spiritual foundation of all science. Students not only immerse themselves in a range of subjects in the fields of spirituality, religion, culture and science, but also experience self-transcendence through reflection, meditation and interactive learning.

In 1971, Mark L. Prophet and Elizabeth Clare Prophet founded Summit University in Santa Barbara, California, to provide in-depth courses of study on spiritual topics and to serve as a platform for the release of the original teachings of the ascended masters.

Ascended masters are the enlightened ones, the saints and adepts of East and West who have found liberation from the wheel of rebirth. Included in their ranks are the great spiritual lights of major world religions, such as Gautama Buddha, Jesus Christ, the Virgin Mary, Krishna, Zarathustra, Saint Francis and Bodhidharma.

In the mystery school environment provided by Summit University, the masters teach their students how to follow in their footsteps, make a profound difference in the world, and reunite with their divine source.

Summit University provides a variety of avenues for learning, including online courses and in-person seminars. Our online school offers courses at different levels, ranging from short extension courses to in-depth academic studies. Students can enroll in leadership studies, ministerial studies or general studies, or take individual courses for credit or audit. We also conduct seminars in multiple languages at our campus in Gardiner, Montana, and select locations around the world. As our university expands, we continue to add new courses and programs to our curriculum.

For up-to-date information, visit SummitUniversity.org or email us at info@SummitUniversity.org.

SUMMIT UNIVERSITY PROGRAMS

Try the following Summit University programs to acquire the tools you need to be victorious in all you do!

EXTENSION COURSE: **The Victory Way of Life. How to Conquer Adversity and Thrive! (RELS 0201)**

This captivating, self-directed Summit University extension course helps you welcome the cosmic being Mighty Victory and his legions of victory angels into your life and claim their buoyant, joyous consciousness of victory!

- Find out why *attitude* is a key to living a victorious life.
- Turn self-defeating habits into *victory* habits.
- Learn how to balance your threefold flame in your etheric, mental, emotional and physical bodies for *greater overall life balance.*
- Discover how to work with Victory's angels on the perplexing problems of drugs, crime, terrorism and education, and ride their *joyous wave of victory!*

http://summituniversity.org/OnlineVictoryCourse

SEMINAR: **Claim the Victory Way of Life!**

This practical three-day seminar, held at locations around the world, provides you with your own personalized blueprint for goal achievement—the Victory way. The seminar includes:

- Three life-changing lectures by Elizabeth Clare Prophet on the Victory Way of Life that unfold Mighty Victory's inner matrix for victory.
- Twelve detailed exercises that will crystallize your individual roadmap to victorious overcoming.
- Enlightening recorded dictations by several ascended masters on how to make the Victory Consciousness your very own.

http://summituniversity.org/VictorySeminar

For more program choices, visit SummitUniversity.org.

Keepers of the Flame Fraternity®

The Keepers of the Flame Fraternity is a spiritual order founded by the ascended master Saint Germain—a worldwide community of spiritual seekers dedicated to keeping the flame of life on earth.

This flame is a spiritual fire. It burns in the secret chamber of your heart. It is the flame of life—your own portion of Spirit, given to you when your soul was born out of the Infinite.

Long ago, before the dawn of recorded history, there was a time when none kept that flame. It was then that Sanat Kumara, the Ancient of Days, came to keep the flame on a dark star—as the first Keeper of the Flame. In each age since, there have been those who have also carried that torch: Gautama, Moses, Jesus, Krishna, Kuan Yin and Confucius, to name a few. Now the door is open for many to follow in their footsteps.

What does the Fraternity offer?

Monthly lessons (confidential to members only) provide profound insights and spiritual practices to tap into your cosmic consciousness and fulfill your life's purpose.

By joining the Fraternity, you can also become part of a global community of spiritual seekers who come together—in conferences, retreats, community forums, mentoring programs, online meetings, and more—to join the mission of Saint Germain to bring in a golden age of Aquarius.

Go to www.TSL.org/KOF-1free to explore this exciting opportunity.

Mark L. Prophet (1918–1973) and Elizabeth Clare Prophet (1939–2009), were visionary pioneers of modern spirituality and internationally renowned authors. Their books are published in more than 30 languages, and millions of copies have been sold online and in bookstores worldwide.

Together, they built a worldwide spiritual organization that is helping thousands to find their way out of human problems and reconnect to their inner divinity. They walked the path of spiritual adeptship, advancing through the universal initiations common to mystics of both East and West. They taught about this path and described their own experiences for the benefit of all who desire to make spiritual progress.

Mark and Elizabeth left an extensive library of spiritual teachings from the ascended masters and a thriving, worldwide community of people who study and practice these teachings.

SummitUniversity®
63 Summit Way, Gardiner, Montana 59030 USA
1-800-245-5445 / +1 406-848-9500

Se habla espanol.

SummitUniversity.org
info@SummitUniversity.org

SummitLighthouse.org
TSLinfo@TSL.org

CPSIA information can be obtained
at www.ICGtesting.com
Printed in the USA
FFOW02n0004100617
36453FF